Professional Communication

(For B. Pharm)

Professional Communication

(For B. Pharm)

Kumkum Bhardwaj
Prof. & Head
Dept. of English
I.T.S. Engineering College
Greater Noida, U.P. India

TECHSAR™
NEW DELHI

Published and Printed by

Techsar Pvt. Ltd.
4435-36/7, Ansari Road, Daryaganj
New Delhi-110 002 (India)
E-mail: tech_info@techsarworld.com
Website: www.techsarworld.com

ISBN: 978-81-89866-84-6

Reprint 2025

Preface

'A Textbook of Professional Communication' has been especially designed according to the syllabus of Professional Communication course (PH 116) for the first year B.Pharm students of UP Technical University. This purpose oriented and need based textbook focuses on communication in different contexts, teaching students how to communicate in a variety of situations. As a practical self-learning guide, the book provides a comprehensive coverage of all topics of the professional communication syllabus for B.Pharm students of UPTU. I believe that the approach adopted for presentation of material would quicken the pace of learning.

The book, which has been divided into five units, contains thirty three chapters and four appendices.

Unit 1 consists of English grammar and usage. **It contains sixteen chapters**, including parts of speech, structure of sentences, tenses, use of articles, use of prepositions, Subject –Verb Agreement, Active-Passive Voice and Direct-Indirect Speech. The essentials of grammar, covering all aspects that are difficult from the student's point of view have been included in this unit. In each chapter numerous examples have been given to facilitate understanding of the basic concepts of English grammar.

Unit II contains material on comprehension and composition. **Chapter 17** discusses the meaning of listening comprehension, listening vs. hearing, types and essential requirements for active listening. It also discusses barriers to effective listening and techniques to improve listening ability. **Chapter 18** deals with reading comprehension. It comprises scanning and skimming technique, reading speed, various methods of reading speedily, barriers to reading skills and necessary elements of good reading. **Chapter 19** concentrates on the art of comprehension including how to answer questions and multiple choice questions, explaining the italicized portions, summarizing a passage and assigning a suitable title or heading to the comprehension passage. **Chapter 20** deals with the requisites of good sentence and paragraph writing. It discusses structure, coherence, length, and emphasis in sentence writing and unity, coherence and emphasis in paragraph writing. **Chapter 21** describes the meaning and essentials of précis writing. It also describes the ways of abridging sentences. **Chapter 22** focuses on the essentials of a good letter and also elements, style, tone and layout of formal and informal letters. **Chapter 23** discusses importance, structure, types, and style of essay writing.

Unit III is devoted to various aspects of the voice. **Chapter 24** focuses on voice modulation. It includes speaking styles, paralinguistics and paralanguage, significance of voice in communication, pitch variation/tone, speaking speed, waviness, pause and accent neutralization. It also deals with stress/accent. It describes meaning and importance of stress, word stress, sentence stress, stress in compound words, and stress-shift. Besides, it concentrates on the significant role of eye contact for small and large groups etc.

Unit IV deals with presentation techniques. **Chapter 25** includes definition, components and importance, advantages and limitations of non-verbal communication. It also deals with various features of body language including facial expression, eye contact, gesture and posture and use of space, time and environment in non-verbal communication. **Chapter 26** focuses on tips for a successful presentation comprising preparing, and planning for presentation, audience analysis, guiding principles for the use of visual aids etc. **Chapter 27** describes meaning, significance, techniques, types and general rules for role playing, **Chapter 28** deals with meaning, types, general rules and evaluation of debates.

Unit V demonstrates the application of behavioural Science. **Chapter 29** concentrates on dimensions of personality types. **Chapter 30** discusses elements and kinds of decision making, decision making process, effective decision skills, improving creativity in decision making, individual and group decision making, distinction between individual and group decisions, common errors in decision making. **Chapter 31** includes definition and characteristics or nature of motivation, motivation process, types, various theories and importance of motivation. **Chapter 32** discusses definition, characteristics, components, sources, types, processes and functions of attitudes in influencing the behaviour of an individual. **Chapter 33** describes the thinking process, various types of concepts, problem solving, nature and characteristics of creative thinkers. It also describes the meaning of effective thinking, characteristics of effective thinkers and various thinking situations.

Each chapter in the book contains review exercises and provides guidelines with solved exercises (whenever required) for using the practice material as follows.

The book also has **five appendices** to make it completely learner-centric. **Appendix A** contains rules of punctuation and capitalisation. **Appendix B** describes idiomatic expressions with prepositions including some of the most important and common combinations of prepositions used in English. **Appendix C** describes distinction between similar expressions, which the students would find useful in performing their day-to-day language tasks. **Appendix D** deals with various types of common errors in English that are often made in the use of parts of speech, articles, quotations, pairs of words etc. **Appendix E** provides previous years question papers. It will help the students in preparing for the professional communication paper thoroughly.

The entire material included in the book is class-tested. The experience of the question papers and the students' feedback has been taken into account for giving it a final shape. My endeavour has been to give a good book to the teachers and students, which would fulfill a long felt need for a comprehensive textbook. I would welcome their suggestions for the continuous improvements in this book.

Kumkum Bhardwaj

Acknowledgements

In accomplishing this task, I would like to extend my sincere thanks to Dr. L.N. Paliwal, Director, I.T.S. Engineering College, Greater Noida, under whose patronage I was able to write this book. With great pleasure, I acknowledge the congenial environment shared by my colleagues and faculty members of I.T.S. Engineering College.

I would like to express my deep sense of gratitude to Dr. B.K. Gupta, Director (P&D), RKG Institute to Technology, Ghaziabad for his constant encouragement. My gratitude to Dr. A.K. Mathur (retired Reader & Head, NAS College, Meerut) goes more than mere written word.

My very special thanks are due to my husband Ram Mohan who has been a source of inspiration to me throughout my endeavour. My sons—Sumit, Harshit and Madhur share no less credit for providing me congenial atmosphere and keeping my morale high. Without their patience and understanding, I could not have continued. I dedicate this book to my family.

In the end, I would like to thank all, my parents, friends, colleagues and well-wishers who have shown sympathetic considerations to me in various ways.

Kumkum Bhardwaj

Contents

Communication

Why Communication is needed?

The ability to communicate is basic to our daily life. It is difficult to name a human activity in which communication does not play an important role. In fact, research indicates that 70% of our total waking time is usually spent in communicating in some form or the other form, whether it is talking to people in person or on the telephone to achieve some purpose, reading or writing letters, e-mails, reports, proposals or other correspondence. In society, we share our thoughts, feelings, emotions, reactions, etc. with individuals as well as groups at all levels – higher, lower, or equal. In formal organizations, people interact with their colleagues and subordinates to achieve their common objectives. The working and maintenance of these formal and informal relationships is possible only through communication, which provides for exchange of information and sharing of ideas.

Communication, thus, has become a necessary element in human relationships by providing the foundation for human interaction.

Meaning of Communication

The word 'Communication' derived from two Latin words, **'communicare'**, which means to impart or to share and **'communis'**, which means common or what is shared by all. Hence, the sense of 'sharing' is inherent in the very origin and nature of communication. This sharing could be of information, knowledge or thoughts.

The quote John Adain, **"Communication is the process by which meanings are exchanged between people through the use of a common set of symbols."**

The Oxford Dictionary defines communication as **"the action of conveying or exchanging information or idea."**

According to Shirley Taylor, **"Communication may be defined as giving, receiving or exchanging information, opinions, ideas by writing, speech or visual means so that the material communicated is completely understood by everyone concerned."**

It means that in communication what is more important, apart from sharing of information in a group, is that the other person must understand the message conveyed to him or her. An effective communication can be said to exist only when it gets the desired action or response. Poor communication leads to interpersonal conflicts. We need to make sure that our ideas and information are completely understood. There is no point in having a discussion or communicating a message if the other person is not able to derive any message out of it. For example, in a group, where one member speaks only German, and the other does not know German, the individual speaking German will not be understood. **Communication,** therefore, **must include both the transference and the understanding of meaning.**

Process of Communication

Communication is a process or a flow. The main parts of communication are:

- ➢ The communication source (The Sender)
- ➢ Encoding
- ➢ The Message
- ➢ The Channel
- ➢ Decoding
- ➢ The Receiver
- ➢ Feedback (Response)

In the process of communication there are two parties, a sender and a receiver. **The communication source (sender)** initiates a message by **encoding** a thought and sends it through a channel to convey meaning. **The channel** is the medium, or the language used—words, actions, signals or objects, through which the message travels. The receiver is the object to whom the message is directed. The receiver receives the message, **decodes** it and acts on it. The transmission of the receiver's response to the sender is called **feedback.** In the process, the sender may get either the positive or negative response from the receiver, but since he has got some feedback, the communication process is complete. However, the communication is effective only when the message has been understood by the receiver and the sender gets the desired response from the receiver. Therefore, there should be cooperation between the sender and the receiver.

Communication takes place in a well-defined set-up. This is called the **communication environment.** A classroom, for example, is the communication environment where a teacher delivers lectures to his students. The following diagram shows the relationship between the various components of communication.

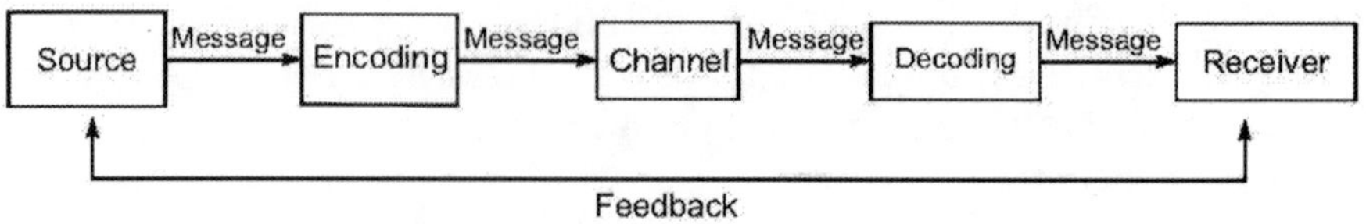

The Communication Process Module

Sources of distortion

In many cases the message fails to produce the desired response because of miscommunication and there is a **semantic gap** between the sender and the receiver. The problems occur when there are deviations in the process of communication. What the receiver understands from a sent message may not always be the same as what the sender intended to communicate. The failure occurs when:

- The sender is not clear about his objective.
- The sender uses inappropriate language or symbols to convey his ideas.
- The receiver is not able to understand and interpret the message properly.

Four attributes of the source and the receiver affect the encoded/decoded message

- Skill (vocabulary)
- Attitude (relationships, passive listening, lack of concentration, emotional responses etc.)
- Knowledge
- Social-Cultural Background

Successful communication depends on abilities pertaining to speaking, reading, listening and writing skills. These four skills may be further classified into two categories – receptive and productive. Listening and reading are called receptive skills, as we receive information. Speaking and writing are called productive skills, as we produce our thoughts and feelings while speaking to someone or writing something.

Our attitude influences our behaviour. We hold predisposed ideas on numerous topics / aspects, and our communication is affected by this attitude. Further, we cannot communicate what we do not know. Thus, the amount of knowledge the source holds about his or her subject will affect the message he or she seeks to transfer. Finally, just as our attitude influences our behaviour, so does our position in the social-cultural system in which we exist. Our culture, beliefs and values also influence us as a source of communication.

TYPES OF COMMUNICATION

Communication can be divided into two parts:

1. Verbal communication
2. Non-verbal communication

Verbal Communication

Verbal communication may be either written or oral. Language is the most commonly and effectively used medium of communication. According to Encyclopedia Britannica, language is a system of conventionally spoken and written symbols by means of which human beings, as members of a social group and participants in its culture, communicate.

Words are the main communication symbols. Every language selects some symbols for its selected sounds. For example, in English, the sound 'k' has the symbol of/ k /for it while the Hindi sound has the symbol/क/for it. These symbols form the alphabet of the language and join in different combinations to form meaningful words.

Verbal Communication can be further divided into two parts:

1. Written Communication

Advantages

- Can be kept as records
- Formal, objective and accurate
- More orderly
- Can be used for future reference
- Can be circulated

Disadvantages

- Can be misunderstood
- More costly in comparison to oral communication

Examples: Instructions, Memoranda, Letters, Hand Books, Pamphlets, Policy Statements

2. Oral Communication

- Interpersonal communication—instructions, speeches and meetings
- Through mechanical and electrical devices—telephones and loudspeakers
- Temporary in nature
- No permanent record of communication

Disadvantages

- Not always taken seriously by the receiver
- Words are often not clearly heard or understood
- Time consuming, especially in meetings and conferences

Non-verbal Communication

Non-verbal communication refers to all communication that occurs without the use of words. Communication need not necessarily be verbal in order to convey a message. A glance, a stare, a smile, a frown, a provocative body movement—all convey meaning. Non-verbal communication accounts for a larger part of the total message than do the words we send or receive. Scientific analysis says, through words we communicate 7%, through body movements 55% and through voice tone 38%.

Non-verbal communication includes:

1. **Body movements (Kinesics:** it includes facial expressions, eye contact, gestures, posture, physical appearance)
2. **Space** (**Proxemics:** the physical distance between the sender and the receiver)
3. **Time** (how we give importance to time)
4. **Pitch and tone (Paralanguage**: the intonations or emphasis we give to words)
5. **General environment**
6. **Colours**
7. **Sign language (Pictorial communication:** it includes pictures, graphs, signs, diagrams, charts etc.)

DIRECTIONS OF COMMUNICATION

Communication flows both formally and informally. Formal communication follows the official hierarchy and it flows through formal channels. This type of communication can flow in two directions- **vertical, lateral or diagonal.** Informal communication, usually known as **Diagonal or cross-wise**, flows in all directions. In the informal system, information flows along the well known **grapevine & rumours.**

1. Lateral/Horizontal Communication

Lateral or Horizontal communication occurs between people of the same status—sales staff, departmental heads, directors, managers etc. Lateral communication is often necessary to save time and facilitate coordination.

2. Vertical Communication

Vertical direction can be further divided into downward and upward direction.

a. Downward Communication

Communication that flows from one level in a group or organization to a lower level is Downward Communication.

- Managers communicating with subordinates.
- This pattern is used by group leaders and managers to assign goals, provide job instructions, point out problems that need attention and offer feedback about performance.
- Downward communication does not have to be oral or interpersonal.

b. Upward Communication

Upward Communication flows from a lower level in a group or organization to a higher level. It is used:

- ❖ To provide feedback to higher ups.
- ❖ To inform them of progress toward goals.
- ❖ To relay current problems.
- ❖ Superior – sub-ordinate discussions.

3. Diagonal/Cross-wise Communication

Diagonal or the cross-wise communication is free to move in any direction. This type of communication involves more than one department and there is often no line of authority.

- **Rumours**

(1) Rumours are always connected matters that we are greatly interested in, and never about matters that we are not interested in.

(2) Rumours are always over matters surrounded by uncertainty, doubt or ambiguity and involve conjecturing over what facts really are.

- **Grapevine**

(1) It is not controlled by management.

(2) It is perceived by most employees as being more reliable & believable than formal communication issued by top management.

(3) It is largely used to serve the self-interests of those people within it.

Communication, whether formal or informal, is all about understanding. Our aim should be to communicate a message successfully so that it is received without any misunderstanding.

TECHNICAL COMMUNICATION

Technical communication is that specific branch of communication, which transmits facts and information to a defined audience for a specific purpose. Technical writing enables business, corporations and public agencies to achieve their goals and maintain their operations. This type of writing explains the technical information to an audience that may or may not be technical.

Thus, we can say that technical writing engages a specific audience, uses plain and objective language, employs visual aids and is always purposeful. Examples of technical writing include business letters, memos, reports, instructions and manuals.

CHARACTERISTICS OF TECHNICAL WRITING

1. Clarity:

According to **Chinese philosopher Confucius, "In language, clarity is everything**." True to this dictum, technical writing is a precise and clean means of document writing and communication. As it is intended to convey specific information to a specific audience for a specific purpose, we should always be clear in technical writing. Clarity involves both clarity of expression as well as clarity of thought. It consists of a better understanding of the audience, words with clear meaning, phrases, clauses, sentences and well–organized paragraphs.

2. **Brevity:**

   Brevity is being brief but comprehensive in conveying the information. Brevity can be brought in writing by avoiding wordiness and repetition.

3. **Specific Audience / Audience Recognition:**

   Technical writing engages a specific audience. The workers who attend a meeting receive the memo that announces it. The consumers who program the VCR receive the manual that details the process. The executives who choose between two alternatives receive the feasibility report that explains them.

   Technical writing uses terminology, which the audience understands. One should always recognize one's audience in technical writing. Technical writing is always done according to the level of the audience. The ability to understand the level of the audience requires command on the language and visual and analytical skills.

3. **Objective Language:**

   For technical writing one should always use short, to-the -point words and paragraphs. Plain and objective language is a pre-requisite of technical writing. Because its purpose is to inform, instruct, or persuade a reader about a specific practical matter, technical writing focuses the reader's attention on the relevant facts. The reader should respond only to the subject. As far as possible, the words should not prompt the reader to add emotional, unusual, or unreasonable interpretations to the subject.

4. **Presentational Organization:**

   Technical writing is presentational. It involves the use of **highlighting techniques** (bullets, numbers, heading lists, diagrams etc.) to enable random reading. Such devices are used by technical writers in order to communicate effectively and to make their presentation apt for a quick glance for busy people.

5. **Visual Aids:**

   Technical writing communicates visually through graphs, tables, and drawings. Other types of writing like essays, novels, and poems seldom use there visual aids to communicate. Newspapers sometimes use visual aids in their analytical articles. But visual aids appear regularly in technical writing. Documents that explain experiments or projects almost always include tables or graphs. Manuals and sets of instructions rely heavily on drawings and photographs.

6. Accuracy:

In order to make a technical document accurate, emphatic and coherent, sound knowledge of the basic principles of grammar is essential. Generally, technical writing follows the same rules of punctuation as the traditional. There should be no errors anywhere in technical writing. Punctuation is as essential in technical writing as in literary works. Errors in spelling, grammar, punctuation, address, name, etc. gives the organization an unprofessional image.

ENGLISH AS AN INTERNATIONAL LANGUAGE

As English occupies an international status in today's world, it is the most common medium of technical writing. English is spoken in many countries, both as a native and as a second language. Although the United Nations and its various agencies have more than one language for transaction, English comes to be chosen as the preferred language of communication between the participating member-nations.

English is learned everywhere because a sound knowledge of English is a passport for better career, better pay, advanced knowledge, and for communication with the entire world. In this computer age, the use of English is bound to grow further. In his "Scientific English" Robert A. Day writes, "English is becoming the international language of business and of the computer. All scientists, wherever they are in the world and whatever their native language is, must acquire reasonable fluency in English".

Technical writing is scientific in nature. Scientists and scholars in all fields should learn to use English simply. Short, simple words in short, straight forward sentences, usually convey meaning more clearly. Professional English, therefore, must be simple, clear and direct. It should avoid, as far as possible, passive voice expressions and conditional sentences. The sentences in technical writing must be logical, effective and free from confusion and ambiguity.

PURPOSE

Technical writing has three basic purposes: to inform, to instruct, and to persuade.

Most technical writing **informs** to carry out proper functions in the workplace. People must supply or receive information constantly. They need to know the scheduled time for a meeting, explain the division's projected profits, the physical description of a new machine, the step in a process, or the results of an experiment.

Technical writing also **instructs**. It gives readers directions for using equipment and for performing duties. Someone must tell consumers how to use their new purchase, whether it is a television or a mobile phone.

Finally, technical writing **persuades** on the job, people must persuade others to do certain things.

SCOPE

The scope of technical communication is very wide and comprehensive. Technological knowledge, coupled with information technology, has changed the manner of communication in professional situations. There are a variety of interactive technologies for communication today, ranging from the traditional forms of communication such as letters, memos, and newsletters to fastest, result-oriented forms of communication such as e-mail, voice mail, video conferencing, and so on.

Widely recognized categories of technical communication are **external communication** and **internal communication**. External communication may include any communication that an organization does with people from other organizations. Internal communication includes any communication within the organization. Memorandums, different kind of reports and proposals, presentations, office instruction etc. are the examples of internal communication.

Technical communication depends on two basic forms of communication: oral and written. **Oral communication** is one in which speaking and listening skills are used. It provides immediate feedback, gives personal touch and better understanding. **Written communication** in which writing and reading skills are used is one. It is impersonal. It provides a permanent record and the paper can be used as legal document.

Thus, technical writing is important for all kinds of professionals, who are required to write technical reports, proposals, manuals, web-material, e-mails, letters, proposals, memos and so on.

THE ROLE OF DICTION AND STYLE IN THE CONTEXT OF WRITTEN TECHNICAL COMMUNICATION

Diction

The word 'diction' means 'words'. Words have meanings of mainly two types; **denotative** and **connotative**. The denotative meaning of a word is its literal dictionary meaning. These words are used in scientific writing. Connotative means the implication of another meaning, besides the primary meaning of a word. Connotative can be favourable or unfavourable, depending on the attitude of the speaker or writer. In English, grammatical meaning is determined by word order. For example, 'blue sky' and 'sky blue' mean different things. In 'blue sky', 'blue' modifies 'sky'; in 'sky blue', 'sky' modifies 'blue'. To write effective sentences, knowledge of how to chose the right word is necessary.

Style

'Style' means 'the choice and arrangement of words'. Style is the manner of doing and saying some thing. It is the way one expresses one's thoughts and feelings in words. A man's way of writing reflects his personality and his attitude to life. As a man thinks and feels, accordingly he writes. If his thoughts are clear, precise and simple, his style will be simple, effective and scientific. Therefore as **Emerson** says, **"A man's style is his mind's voice."**

The same facts can be expressed in different ways. Thus, style is that feature, which distinguishes one person's writing from another's. Several writers have made an attempt to define 'style'. According to **Jonathan Swift**, "**Style is proper words in proper places.**"

Style covers all the parts of a piece of writing. It determines:

- The choice of words and phrases
- Their arrangement
- Sentence structure—simple, complex, compound or mixed.
- Punctuation marks
- Length of sentences
- Arrangement and distribution of ideas in paragraphs or points
- The tone of the writer.

Style of writing can be formal or informal. One writing style might be appropriate for one purpose but it might not suit another. While the formal prose is acceptable for reports, a slightly informal style could be adopted when it comes to business correspondence. The choice of style depends upon the sender, the reader, the occasion and the content.

DIFFERENCE BETWEEN DICTION AND STYLE

Following are the differences between diction and style:

1. Style is the reflection of personality while diction is the expression of intellectual proficiency.
2. Style is more refined than diction.
3. Style is abstract while diction is concrete.
4. Good style needs much experience in writing and can be perfected by practice but good diction requires good knowledge of the language and can be mastered by learning.

STYLE OF TECHNICAL WRITING

In the context of written technical communication, diction plays an important role to shape the style. The style of technical writing is scientific, precise and clear. **Alan Warner highlights, " ------ for making reports, writing letters, composing essays and articles, the cleaner our English the better."**

English used in technical communication is plain English which could be understood with ease. Plain English refers to the writing and providing essential information in a way that gives the reader a good chance of understanding the document at first reading.

This means pitching the language and using appropriate structure at a level of sophistication that suits the readers. However, it does not always mean using simple words at the expense of the most accurate words or writing whole documents in kindergarten language.

As a consequence of growing interest in plain English, instruction manuals, government forms and documents, and many other technical material for public use have been greatly simplified. Medical labels, nutrition facts, etc., are presented in readable and easily understandable form. Corporates have begun to use the services of skilled technical literature writers for this purpose.

Following are the characteristics of plain English:

- Use simple, everyday words rather than fancy ones.
- Plan before you write.
- Prefer the shorter word to the longer one.
- Prefer verbs over nouns and adjectives.
- Prefer the specific word to the general.
- Use words your readers are likely to understand.
- Write short sentences with an average of no more than 20 words.
- Use active voice rather than the passive.
- Be a miser with compound and complex sentences and a spendthrift with simple sentences.
- Write short paragraphs conveying only one idea in a paragraph.
- Avoid paragraphs that exceed five typed lines for business letters and ten lines for longer compositions.
- Write with the ear. Do not write anything that you could not comfortably say.
- Write for the eye as well as the mind. Prepare an overall design, positioning understandable headings, sub-headings, and captions for each segment, showing the organization of the text. Make the whole document visually appealing.
- Use appropriate underlining, ink color that contrasts sharply with the paper, lists, boxes or panels, bold or other typefaces to emphasize points.
- Use 'white space' in margins, between sections, paragraphs, and lines to make the document look good.

SIGNIFICANCE OF TECHNICAL WRITING

Writing is the major means of communication within an organization. Upto 30% of work time of professionals is engaged in written communication. In the highly competitive environment today, success depends not only on one's professional knowledge and skills, but also on the ability to present that knowledge effectively. It makes professional relationship possible by encouraging people to achieve individual as well as organizational objectives.

In this age of globalization, where the professional world has become more diverse, competitive and result-oriented, the significance of technical writing has increased like never before. Revolution in information technology is having an immense impact on technical communication skills.

Knowledge of technical or professional skills will be useless if one does not have the ability to express that knowledge effectively. Thus, in the changed technological environment communication skills are as important as technical or professional skills.

TECHNICAL WRITING vs GENERAL WRITING

How are they similar?

- Both use examples, stories, statistics etc. to develop ideas.
- Both demand excellent grammar and punctuation – this give the writer credibility (grounds for being believed).
- Both use an introduction, body and conclusion to organize ideas.

How are they different?

All writing that is done without reference to any specialized technique and terminology is defined as a general writing. A personal letter, a social lecture & a speech delivered on the occasion of general importance can be taken as general writing. While professional and scientific documents, drafts, letters etc. fall under technical writing. In today's scenario, professional style of writing has an immense role to play in the overall understanding of the perspective of the situation.

The main objective of writing is to make the other person understand properly and closely so that he/she can derive a meaningful interpretation and act accordingly. This is possible only when we communicate in a way, which does not have different perceptions for different people about an aspect. For example, if the communication is simple but at the same time logical and data-based, it will be understood by different people in a similar way. So it becomes imperative for a sender to communicate professionally. This is how general writing is different from technical writing. While one deals primarily with feelings, emotions, opinion and persuasion, the other emphasizes the dispassionate, factual recording of scientific investigation.

Following aspects make technical writing different from general writing.

1. Technical writing is related to the professional world but general writing is related to the society.
2. General writing is largely an inborn or natural talent. While technical writing is properly planned. For example, technical writing is based on data collection, analysis of that data for arriving at a meaningful corrective action or recommendation. In the case of a layman's writing, instead of

data, emotions or perceptions of an individual play an important role. Therefore, the sender perceives an aspect and translates it in writing based on his/her environment and surroundings, way of thinking etc. and thus, lacks the logical approach of technical writing.

3. The style of technical writing is scientific, precise and clear, while the style of general writing may be literary, ornamental and elegant.
4. The purpose of technical writing is to instruct, to inform and to persuade, while the purpose of general writing is to amuse, to inspire and to educate the society.
5. Technical writing uses highlighting technique for random reading while general writing relies on a traditional linear (line-by-line) format.
6. General writing, like in essays, uses longer paragraphs, sentences and words, whereas technical writing uses short paragraphs, sentences and words to get straight to the point.
7. Technical writing communicates visually through graphs, tables, and drawings. Other types of writing like essays, novels, and poems seldom use visual aids to communicate. Newspapers sometimes use visual aids in their analytical articles. But visual aids appear regularly in technical writing. Documents that explain experiments or projects almost always include tables or graphs. Manuals and sets of instructions rely heavily on drawings and photographs.
8. The scope of technical writing is limited to conducting smooth business activities while general writing plays many roles in the world at large.

It may, thus, be summarized that technical writing is important for a clear understanding of a given situation so that a meaningful inference can be drawn and necessary action be executed in a more logical and scientific manner.

Syllabus

PROFESSIONAL COMMUNICATION-I

UNIT-I

English Grammer

Parts of speech, Articles, Preposition, Tenses. Active-Passive voice. Direct- Indirect speech. Verb. [12]

UNIT-II

Letter writing. Precis and Essay writing

Comprehension

Speed reading scanning & skimming [08]

UNIT-III

Working on accent neturalisation, pauses, stresses, non words, voice modulation, eye contact for small & large groups. [08]

UNIT-IV

Presentation techniques, - Tips.

Importance of non-verbal communication, debates, Role plays [06]

UNIT-V

Personality types

Decision making

Motivation

Attitude

Thinking [06]

BOOKS RECOMMENDED

1. Wren P.C and Martin., "High School Grammer and Composition". S. Chand & Co.
2. Robbins, S "Organizational Behaviour". Pearson Education.

Unit I

English Grammar and Usage

- Parts of Speech
  - Noun
  - Pronoun
  - Adjective
  - Verb
  - Adverb
  - Preposition
  - Conjunction
  - Interjection
- Articles
- Tenses
- Concord-Agreement of the Verb with its Subject
- Structure of Sentence
- Elements of a Series
- Active and Passive Voice
- Reported Speech-Direct and Indirect Narration

Parts of Speech

1
CHAPTER

The words that form sentences are categorised into classes according to the function that they perform. These classes of words are known as **Parts of Speech.** In English we have eight parts of speech: noun, pronoun, adjective, verb, adverb, preposition, conjunction and interjection.

DEFINITIONS

1. **Noun**: A noun is the name of a person, place or thing; such as: Nisha, girl, gold, kindness, crowd etc.
2. **Pronoun**: A pronoun is a word which stands for, or replaces a noun; such as: he, you, I, it, me, your, his, her, our, himself etc.
3. **Adjective:** An adjective is a word which qualifies (describes or determines) a noun or pronoun, such as:
   - An Indian scientist
   - a tall boy
   - the blue sky
   - some milk
   - much trouble
   - two huts
   - many birds
   - my book
   - his house etc.
4. **Verb**: A verb is a word which expresses action or being (a state); such as:
   - Ram went to the Laboratory. (Action)
   - He is sleeping. (State)
   - It is dark. (State)
   - The heat melts the snow. (Action)
   - He did me a great favour. (Action)

   Verbs are chief vehicles of our actions, thoughts and feelings. Without verbs there can be no real communication.

5. **Adverb**: An adverb is a word which qualifies a verb, an adjective or another adverb; such as:

   - Mohan runs fast. (qualifies the verb 'run')
   - Sir Jagdish Chandra Bose was a very great scientist. (qualifies the adjective 'great')
   - She sings very well. (qualifies the adverb 'well')
   - She is a very good student.

   Adverbs are generally formed by adding –ly to an adjective; such as:

Adjective	Adverb
slow	slowly
quick	quickly
regular	regularly

   Often the adjective and the adverb have the same form; such as:

Adjective	Adverb
early	early
fast	fast
late	late
little	little

6. **Preposition**: A preposition is a word which shows the relation of a noun or pronoun to some other word in the sentence; such as:

   - He lives in Delhi.
   - There is a small temple on the top of the mountain.
   - He travels by air.
   - He is fond of music.
   - We have not met for a week.
   - How far is Delhi from Pilani?
   - Between us there is no secret.

   Certain words are followed by particular prepositions. It is, therefore, necessary to familiarize yourself with the right use of prepositions after nouns, verbs, adjectives etc.

7. **Conjunction**: The conjunction is a word that joins words, clauses or sentences together as shown below.

   - Ram and Rattan are brothers.
   - He is intelligent but not careful.
   - As he was slow, he could not finish his work.
   - When I went to his place, he was not in.
   - Neither you nor Rishi is to blame.
   - He took medicine so that he may recover.

8. Interjection: The interjection is that part of the sentence which expresses some sudden feeling or emotions. Some examples are given below.

- Wow! We have won the game.
- Alas! He died so young.
- Hush! Even walls have ears.

Each **part of speech** explains not what the word *is*, but how the word *is used*. In fact, the same word can be a noun in one sentence and a verb or adjective in another.

REVIEW EXERCISE

Name the part of speech of each underlined word in the following sentences:

1. I got the book **from** my brother.
2. **Ouch!** That hurts.
3. I ate **an** apple.
4. **She** is a teacher.
5. She is **young.**
6. He is a **student.**
7. My brother gave me a book. I enjoyed reading **it.**
8. Students **write** papers in my classes.
9. **Although** students write papers in my classes, they take tests in other classes.
10. My Biology textbook was **expensive.**
11. Our mid-term exam is **on** Wednesday.
12. I passed **the** exam.
13. The exam was easy **so** I got a good grade.
14. I bought a dictionary **and** some paper.
15. I was **very** tired after the exam.
16. We study **in** the library.
17. My teacher talks **easily** but carefully about difficult ideas.
18. **Oh,** now I understand what you meant.
19. He does his homework **carefully.**
20. I go to college **because** I want a better job.

Answers

1. *preposition,*	2. *interjection*	3. *article*
4. *pronoun*	5. *adjective*	6. *noun*
7. *pronoun*	8. *verb*	9. *conjunction*
10. *adjective*	11. *preposition*	12. *article*
13. *conjunction*	14. *conjunction*	15. *adverb*
16. *preposition*	17. *adverb*	18. *interjection*
19. *adverb*	20. *conjunction*	

Noun

2

CHAPTER

A Noun is a word used as the name of a person, place or thing (anything that we can think of).

Kinds of Noun

1. **Common Noun:** A common noun is a noun referring to a person, place, or thing in a general sense. Common here means 'shared by all.'
   - The class is studying grammar.
   - The nearest town is 60 miles away.
   - She is a good girl.
2. **Proper Noun:** A proper noun represents the name of a specific person, place, or thing. Proper nouns are always written with a capital letter at the beginning.
   - Jawaharlal Nehru was the first prime minister of India.
   - India is a democratic country.
   - Hari is a good boy.
3. **Collective Noun:** A collective noun is the name of a number of persons or things taken together and considered as one unit, as;
   - The flock of geese spends most of its time in the pasture.
   - The police dispersed the crowd.
   - I saw a fleet of ships in the harbour.
4. **Abstract noun:** An abstract noun is a noun which names quality, action, virtue or state, which one cannot perceive through one's five physical senses.
   - We all love honesty.
   - Cleanliness is next to godliness.
   - I love to remember the happy days of childhood.

Abstract nouns are formed:

i. From Adjectives	Kind	Kindness

	Honest	Honesty
	Brave	Bravery
ii. **From Verbs**	Obey	Obedience
	Grow	Growth
iii. **From Common Nouns**	Child	Childhood
	Slave	Slavery

5. **Countable Noun:** A countable noun **is** a noun with both a singular and a plural form, and it names anything (or anyone) that one can count,e.g., book, pen, apple, boy, sister, doctor, horse.
   - We painted the table red and the chairs blue.
   - I bought two dozen oranges.
   - The book cost me five hundred rupees.
6. **Uncountable Noun:** An uncountable noun is a noun which does not have a plural form, and which refers to something that one could (or would) not usually count. An uncountable noun always takes a singular verb in a sentence,e.g., milk, oil, sugar, furniture, honesty.
   - Oxygen is essential to human life.
   - The furniture is heaped in the middle of the room.

Gender

Nouns are grammatically classified into four **genders**.

1. **Masculine Gender,** for all males: man, boy, lion.
2. **Feminine Gender,** for all females: woman, girl, lioness.
3. **Common Gender,** where the sex cannot be told from a form of the word. They can be either males or females: friend, cousin, parent, candidate, examiner, artist, singer.
4. **Neuter Gender,** for inanimate (without life) objects: book, chair, house.

Note: All nouns which stand for a group are Neuter, for example: army, class, crowd.

Number

Nouns can be singular, plural or collective.

1. **Singular nouns** denote only one thing or person, for example: book, boy, girl, woman.
2. **Plural nouns** denote more than one object/person, like: books, boys, girls, women.
3. **Collective nouns** denote a number of persons or things taken as a whole.

If the individual or things are thought of separately, it is called a **Noun of Multitude.** Some examples of collective nouns are class, army, crowd, parliament.

➢ ***Remember***

1. *Some nouns have the same form for the plural as for the singular:*
   - *sheep, deer, fish, series, species etc.*
2. *Some nouns are singular in form but plural in sense:*
   - *cattle, people, poultry, gentry, company, police, alphabet etc.*
3. *Some nouns are always used in the plural:*
   - *spectacles, thanks, trousers, savings, lodgings, scissors, compasses, people etc.*
4. *Some nouns though plural in form are used in the singular:*
   - *means, news, innings, scissors, spectacles, assets, tongs, wages, riches etc.*
5. *Some nouns have no plural:*
   - *information, advice, knowledge, furniture, progress etc.*

Case

1. **Nominative Case:** When a noun is used as the subject of a verb, it is said to be in the Nominative Case. To find the nominative, put 'who' or 'what' before the verb.
   - Hari threw the ball. ('Hari' is in the nominative case)
2. **Objective/ Accusative case:** When a noun is used as the object of a verb, it is said to be in the Objective Case. To find the objective, put 'whom' or 'what' before the verb and its subject.
   - Hari threw the ball. ('ball' is in the objective case)

   If a noun comes after a preposition it is also said to be in the objective case.
   - The pen is on the desk.

   ➢ ***Remember:***

   The nominative generally comes before the verb and the objective after the verb.
   - *The window was broken. (nominative)*
   - *He broke the window. (objective)*
3. **Possessive Case:** Possessive case is used to express ownership or possession.
   - I like to read Shakespeare's tragedies.
   - Ratan's business is flourishing.

A possessive case is also used to denote authorship, origin, kind etc.

- Shelley's poems
- A mother's love
- Hari's school
- A week's holiday

➢ ***Remember:***

a. The use of apostrophe with 's' denoting possessive case should be restricted to:

i. *Living things; as,*

- *the Director's secretary, the baker's shop, a boy's foot, a cat's tail*

ii. *Thing personified; as,*

- *Nature's law, India's heroes, fortune's favourite*

iii. *Certain dignified objects; as,*

- *At duty's call, the court's decree*

iv. *Space, time or weight; as,*

- *A day's journey, in a year's time, a foot's length, an hour's talk*

v. *A few familiar phrases; as,*

- *At his wit's end, at a stone's throw, for mercy's sake*

Except these the use of possessive case with other nouns sounds awkward. We must say;

- *The leg of the table is bent. (not, 'The table's leg)*
- *The attitude of the public seems uncertain. (not, 'The public's attitude')*

b. The apostrophe 's' is omitted;

i. *After plural ending in 's', we should never put the apostrophe with 's'.*

- *Horses' tail, boys' school, monkeys' chatter*

But after those plurals which do not end in 's', apostrophe should be used.

- *Men's club, women's dresses, children's books*

ii. *Where too many hissing sounds come together.*

- *For conscience' sake, for goodness' sake, for Jesus' sake*

iii. *The words his, hers, its, theirs, yours, ours, mine are possessive and they are not written with the possessive sign (').*

- *Yours faithfully, its colour*

c. The words; church, house, shop etc. are often omitted after possessive case.

- *I will dine at my uncle's.*
- *You can get good biscuits at Polson's.*

d. ***Avoid the use of double possessives.*** *We should say*

- *The wife of my uncle's secretary, (not, 'My uncle's secretary's wife')*

Nouns in Apposition

When one noun follows another to describe it, the noun which follows is said to be in 'apposition' to the noun which comes before it.

- Kapil, our captain, made fifty runs.
- George, my uncle, is a very humorous person.

REVIEW EXERCISES

Exercise 1

Fill in the blanks with suitable collective nouns.

1. A _________ of birds flew high in the sky.
2. They saw a _____ of lions at the zoo.
3. The farmer has a _____ of cattle on his farm.
4. He ate a _____ of grapes today.
5. Our friend shows us a _____ of stamps.
6. We saw a _____ of sheep on our way home.
7. Police have arrested a _____ of thieves.
8. She bought a _____ of bananas from the market.
9. The _____ of pupils are listening attentively to their teacher.
10. You can put the _____ of tools in that box.

Answers

1. *flock*	2. *troop*	3. *herd*
4. *bunch*	5. *collection*	6. *flock*
7. *gang*	8. *bunch*	9. *class*
10. *set*		

Exercise 2

Fill in the blanks with abstract nouns from the nouns in brackets.

1. I had a very happy ______ (child).
2. I forgot to renew my ______ (member) in the sailing club.
3. We formed a deep and lasting_________(friend)
4. He hopes to take over the _____ (leader) of the party.

5. There are lots of nice people in the _____ (neighbour).
6. In the _____ (king) of Thailand, the king commands the respect of every citizen.
7. She seems to be enjoying _____ (mother).
8. He had barely reached _____ (man) when he married.

Answers

1. *childhood*	2. *membership*	3. *friendship*
4. *leadership*	5. *neighbourhood*	6. *kingdom*
7. *motherhood*	8. *manhood*	

Exercise 3

a. Write each group of words using a possessive noun.

1. the pens of the doctors _________
2. the car of Dr. Agarwal _________
3. the dresses of the women _________
4. the basket of the Gates _________
5. the room of the teachers _______
6. the bubbles of the four fish _________
7. the house of Mr. Williams _________
8. the baton of the conductor _________
9. the cameras of the photographers _________
10. the ball of the children_________

Answers

1. *the doctors' pens*	2. *Dr. Agarwal's car*	3. *the women's dresses*
4. *Gates' basket*	5. *the teachers' room*	6. *the fish' bubbles*
7. *Mr. Williams' house*	8. *the conductor's baton*	

9. *the photographers' camera*
10. *the children's ball*

Exercise 4

Write each singular noun in plural form.

1. tooth _________
2. leaf _________
3. key _________
4. search _________
5. pencil _________
6. guess _________

7. berry ________
8. half ________
9. knife ________
10. colony ________

Answers

1. *teeth,* 2. *leaves,* 3. *keys,*
4. *searches,* 5. *pencils,* 6. *guesses,*
7. *berries* 8. *halves* 9. *knives*
10. *colonies*

Exercise 4

In each sentence, select the proper noun(s).

1. Is Hari coming to the dance?
   a. Hari
   b. dance
   c. Hari, dance
2. Hari invited Ram and Mohan to the zoo.
   a. Hari, Ram
   b. Hari, Ram, Mohan
   c. Hari, Ram, Mohan, Zoo
3. Carol and I went to the beach.
   a. Carol
   b. I
   c. Carol, I
4. Buffalo sponsored this free concert.
   a. Buffalo
   b. concert
   c. The city, concert
5. Ram doesn't like this location.
   a. location
   b. Ram
   c. like
6. Rose, Honey, and I went to see the new reptile house.
   a. Rose, Honey, I
   b. Rose, Honey, I, reptile house
   c. Rose, Honey
7. Lisa does not like certain bands.
   a. Lisa, bands

b. certain bands
c. Lisa

8. Professor Smith teaches John English.
   a. professors, semester, college
   b. Professor Smith, John, English
   c. John's, college, professors
9. Jane and her friends are going to the beach.
   a. Jane
   b. friends
   c. Jane, friends, beach
10. The car that was driven by Tanu was stolen last week.
   a. week
   b. car
   c. Tanu

Answers

1. *a*	2. *b*	3. *a*
4. *a*	5. *b*	6. *c*
7. *c*	8. *b*	9. *a*
10. *c*		

Exercise 5

Choose the correct word (countable/uncountable noun)

1. In my fridge I have some______________ (chicken/chickens)
2. On my desk there are a lot of ________(paper/papers)
3. An envelop is made of _______________(paper/papers)
4. The young woman had beautiful _________(hair/hairs)
5. The old man had only a few__________(hair/hairs)
6. In the room there is some_____________(furniture/furnitures)
7. The man carried some _____________(luggage/luggages)
8. In a factory there is a lot of ___________(equipment /equipments)
9. In this book there is a lot of _________(information/informations)
10. By taking __________many dangers can be avoided.(thought/thoughts)

Answers

1. *chicken*	2. *papers*	3. *paper*
4. *hair*	5. *hairs*	6. *furniture*
7. *luggage*	8. *equipment*	9. *information*
10. *thought*		

Pronoun

3 CHAPTER

A word that is used instead of a noun is called a pronoun.

Relative Pronouns

Relative Pronouns relate or refer to some noun or pronoun going before. The noun or pronoun to which a relative pronoun refers is called its **antecedent.**

Examples

- This is the boy who helped me.
- That is the book which I mentioned.

In the above sentences boy and book are antecedents of the relative pronouns who and which.

Important relative pronouns are *who, whom, what, that, which.*

Examples

- She is the girl whom Radhey met there.
- I do not know what he means. (Here the antecedent is not expressed)
- My watch which was lost has been found.
- He is the man that was wanted.

➢ ***Remember***

1. *Which is used only for things or animals.*
2. *Which and who are used both for the singular and the plural.*
   - *The boy who came here is my nephew.*
   - *The boys who came here are my students.*
   - *The book which you lent me is interesting.*
   - *The books which he lent me are interesting.*
3. *That is used both for persons and things.*
   - *My daughter that is in London sent me a letter.*
   - *This is the house that Ashoka built.*

4. *That is also used after superlatives.*
    - *Kalidasa is the greatest dramatist that India ever had.*
5. *Where the antecedent is both a person and a thing, that, not who or which, is used:*
    - *He talked of places and persons that interested him in India.*
6. *That follows the opening 'It is....'*
    - *It is the painting that Rama likes most.*

The relative pronoun should be placed as near its antecedent as possible:

- The wrestler who won the contest is the father of three children.

The meaning of the above sentence will be quite changed if the relative pronoun is placed away from its antecedent.

- The wrestler is the father of three children who won the contest.

The improper placing of relative pronoun may result in an absurd sentence such as the following:

- Mohan with his family lives in a rented house which consisted of his wife and four children.

Personal Pronouns

Personal pronouns stand for: the person speaking, the person spoken to and the person or the thing spoken of. They are accordingly classified as personal pronouns of

Pronouns as SUBJECTS	*Pronouns as OBJECTS*	*Pronouns that show POSSESSION*
I	Me	my (mine)
You	You	your (yours)
he, she, it	him, her, it	his, her (hers), it (its)
We	Us	our (ours)
They	Them	their (theirs)
Who	Whom	whose

➢ ***Remember:***

1. *Only the pronouns of the third person observe the distinction of gender. 'She' refers to the feminine gender. 'He' refers to the masculine gender. 'It' refers to things, animals, birds and a small child (when the sex is unknown or unimportant).*

EXAMPLES

- *Rajni is not only smart, she is also beautiful.*
- *Mohan is not only intelligent but he is also sincere.*
- *The Taj Mahal is beautiful, it draws a large number of visitors.*
- *Please go and get me the book, it is on the table.*
- *The child is crying, give it some milk.*

2. ***Order of Pronouns:***

When pronouns of the First Person, Second Person and Third Person occur together in a sentence, the order is as follows: Second Person, Third Person, First Person:

- *You, he and I will leave for Delhi tonight.*

But good manners require that the order be reversed if it is a question of confessing a fault or sharing a blame.

- *I, he and you are to blame.*

Distributive Pronouns

Distributive pronouns separate one person or thing from a given number of persons or things. *Each, every, either* and *neither* are distributive pronouns.

Each is used to denote everyone of a number of persons or things taken singly.

- Each of these children gets a prize.

Every is used to indicate each one of a group.

- I have read every book on that shelf.

Either means one or the other of the two.

- Either of these books will do.

Neither is the negative of either. It means not one nor the other of the two.

- He gave me two books, but neither is very interesting.

Indefinite Pronouns

Indefinite pronouns are those which refer to persons or things in a general way, but do not refer to any person or thing in particular. These are one, none (no-one), any, anyone, anything, everything, nothing, anybody, everybody, nobody, some, somebody, all, few, others etc.

➤ ***Remember***

1. *None is used both in the singular and the plural according to the sense.*
   - *None of them was present in the house.*
   - *Are they in the house? No, there are none.*
2. *Anybody, everybody, everyone, anyone and each are followed by the pronoun he or she according to the context. But when the gender is not clear, the masculine is used.*
   - *Everyone in the class (which consists of boys and girls) knows that he must do his work regularly.*
3. *Somebody, anybody, everybody etc. are used with a singular verb, though some of them have a plural sense.*
   - *Is everybody safe?*
   - *Everyone has come.*

Interrogative Pronouns

If the relative pronouns are used for asking questions, they are called interrogative pronouns.

- What do you want?
- Whose is this umbrella?

Pronouns-Antecedent Agreement

The word or phrase, which a pronoun refers back to or replaces, is called the antecedent. In other words, **Antecedent is a word or group of words for which a pronoun stands.**

Example

- She is a woman who seldom complains. ('Woman' is the antecedent of the pronoun 'who'.)
- Uncle Henry came for a brief visit, but he stayed all winter. ('Uncle Henry' is antecedent of the pronoun 'he')

As pronouns are words used in place of nouns, they agree in person, number, gender and case with the nouns for which they are used.

Some sentences are structured in such a way that pronouns are unclear; lacking clear or appropriate antecedents, such pronouns must be replaced by clear words and phrases. In addition, some pronouns are separated from their antecedents; in such cases, repetition of the antecedent provides necessary clarity. Otherwise it will create confusion.

1. **We should not use a pronoun to replace one among several possible antecedents.**

Example

- Ambiguous: Jane took Joan and her mother shopping.

  Whose mother did Jane take, Jane's or Joan's? The sentence should read:

  Acceptable: Jane took Joan and Joan's mother shopping. Or

  Jane took her mother and Joan shopping. Or

  Jane's mother went shopping with Jane and Joan.
- Ambiguous: When the president objected to Mr. Carter, he told him to mind his own business. (Who told whom?)

  Acceptable: When the president objected to Mr. Carter, Mr. Carter told him to mind his own business.

- Ambiguous:: Each damaged article is marked in such a way that it cannot be erased. (what does 'it' refer to? To the article or to the mark?)

  Acceptable: Each damaged article is marked in such a way that the mark cannot be erased.

2. The number of the pronoun should agree with the number of its antecedent.

a. If the antecedent is singular, its pronoun must be singular. If the antecedent is plural, the pronoun must be plural.

- Ambiguous: Taxes and insurance are necessary evils in any business, and it must be considered carefully in anticipating profits.

  Acceptable: Taxes and insurance are necessary evils in any business, and they must be considered carefully in anticipating profits.

b. When two or more singular nouns are joined by and (and refers to different persons or things), the pronoun used for them is in the plural.

- Mohan and Shyam are good boys.
- They are regular in their work.

c. When two or more singular nouns are joined by and but refer to one person or thing, the pronoun is in the singular:

- Ambiguous: The soldier and statesman were honored for his services.

  Acceptable: The soldier and statesman was honored for his services.

- Ambiguous: Bread and butter are a good diet.

  Acceptable: Bread and butter is a good diet.

d. A singular pronoun must be used with each, everybody anybody, somebody etc.

- Ambiguous: When the meeting began, everybody took their seats at the desk assigned to them.

  Acceptable: When the meeting began, everybody took his or her seat at the desk assigned to him or her.

  Or

  When the meeting began, all the members took their seats at the desks assigned to them.

- Ambiguous:Every dentist and physician in the city will ask to give some of their time to the children's clinic.

  Acceptable: Every dentist and physician in the city will ask to give some of his time to the children's clinic.

- Ambiguous: Everybody should make plans for their retirement.

Acceptable: Everybody should make plans for his/her retirement.

- Ambiguous: The aim of the commission is to stimulate the physical growth of the child and to improve their morale.

  Acceptable: The aim of the commission is to stimulate the physical growth of the children and to improve their morale.

e. When two nouns are joined by either...or..., neither...nor, the pronoun is in the singular.

- Either Jyoti or Rahim is to blame.

But in the case of difference of gender the pronoun is in the plural.

- Neither Mohan nor Mira have neglected their work.

In the case where one is singular and the other is plural, the pronoun agrees with the noun nearer to it.

- Neither the teacher nor the students have finished their work.

3. **A pronoun should refer to a definite antecedent.**

   A pronoun depends for meaning upon a noun or another pronoun. If there are two possible antecedents in a sentence & the pronoun does not refer to the right one, it will be known as 'faulty reference of pronoun'. The fault may be corrected by dropping the pronoun & repeating the noun or by using a synonym for the noun or by changing the construction of the sentences. In order to make pronoun antecedents clear and obvious, we should place pronouns as close to their antecedents as possible.

Example

- Ambiguous: When a student hands in a theme to the teacher, he is not always satisfied with it. (Who? Teacher or student?)

  Acceptable: A student is not always satisfied with a theme when he hands it in to the teacher.

- Ambiguous: The hive is constructed so that the bee may work all around each frame and so that it may be removed when full without disturbing the others. (Is the bee removed?)

  Acceptable: The hive is constructed so that the bee may work all around each frame and so that the latter, when full, may be removed without disturbing the other frames.

- Ambiguous: Jack told Carl that he was ungrateful. (Is 'he' Jack or Carl?)

  Acceptable: Jack said to Carl, "I am ungrateful."

  Or

  Acceptable: Jack confessed to Carl that he was ungrateful.

- Ambiguous: After Mrs. Henry scolded little Sylvia, she regretted her rudeness. (To whom do 'she' and 'her' refer?)

  Acceptable: After scolding little Sylvia, Mrs Henry regretted her own rudeness.

  Or

  Acceptable: After Mrs. Henry scolded her, little Sylvia regretted her rudeness.

4. **Avoid implied reference for a pronoun.**

   When the antecedent of pronoun is not expressed in the sentence, but is implied in some word or group of words, it creates confusion.

Example

- Ambiguous: We took the oranges out of the boxes, and threw them on to the floor.

  Acceptable: We took out the oranges, and threw the boxes on to the floor.

- Ambiguous: There are several inconsistencies in the new football rules, and the coaches say that these must be changed before they are adopted.

  Acceptable: There are several inconsistencies in the new football rules, and the coaches say that these inconsistencies must be changed before the revised code is adopted.

- Ambiguous: Girls, sitting at both sides of a table, wrap the magazine in thin paper & then put them in pasteboard cartons.

  Acceptable: Girls, sitting at both sides of a table, wrap the magazine in thin paper & then put the packages in pasteboard cartons.

- Ambiguous: If a person sees an advertisement for help and thinks it worth applying for, he must do so.

  Acceptable: If a person sees an advertisement for help & thinks the position worth applying for, he must do so.

5. **A pronoun cannot usually represent an entire thought or a group of words.**

   We should be especially careful to avoid a broad or vague 'this' or 'which' reference.

Example

- Ambiguous: Pat blamed the teacher for the unclear lesson, which was foolish. (What was foolish? Blaming the teacher? The lesson? The lesson's being unclear?)

Acceptable: Foolishly, Pat blamed the teacher for the unclear lesson.
Or
Pat was foolish to blame the teacher for the unclear lesson.
Or
Confused about the lesson, Pat was foolish to blame the teacher.

6. **Do not use a pronoun to refer to an unidentified or vague antecedent.**

Example

- Ambiguous:Kelly dropped out of school because they emphasized sports too much.
  (Who are they?)
  Acceptable: Kelly dropped out of school because the teachers emphasized sports too much.
  Or
  Kelly dropped out of school because the students emphasized sports too much.
- Ambiguous: It was a shame that it couldn't find the road leading home.
  Acceptable: It was a shame that the baby couldn't find the road leading home.
- Ambiguous: In India, they have many curious customs.
  Acceptable: In India there are many curious customs.
- Ambiguous: He was always friendly, which made everybody like him.
  Acceptable: His friendliness made everybody like him.
- Ambiguous: He completed his report in time, which pleased the directors.
  Acceptable: His completion of the report in time pleased the directors.
  Or
  By completing the report in time he pleased the directors.
  Or
  The Directors were pleased by his early completion of the report.
- Ambiguous: He once lost his money that he had invested in share market and this made him suspicious of all investments.
  Acceptable: He once lost his money that he had invested in share market and this experience made him suspicious of all investments.

7. **When a noun like firm, company etc. is the subject of a verb and the pronoun is plural, or vice versa, both should be singular or both plural.** The choice will depend on the meaning.

Example

- Ambiguous: Company has shown that they are interested in the welfare of their employees.

Acceptable: Company has shown that it is interested in the welfare of its employees.

8. The related pronoun should come, in most instances, immediately after its antecedent.

Example

- Ambiguous: There was a stir in the audience that suggested disapproval.
  Acceptable: A stir that suggested disapproval swept the audience.
- Ambiguous: He wrote three articles about his adventures in Spain, which were published in The Tribune.
  Acceptable: He published three articles in The Tribune about his adventures in Spain.
- Ambiguous: This is a portrait of Benjamin Harrison, who became President in 1889. He was the grandson of Williams Henry Harrison.
  Acceptable: This is a portrait of Benjamin Harrison, grandson of William Henry Harrison, who became President in 1889.

REVIEW EXERCISES

Exercise I

Replace the personal pronouns by possessive pronouns.

1. This book is__________ (you).
2. The ball is __________(I).
3. The blue car is__________ (we).
4. The ring is __________(she).
5. We met Paul and Jane last night. This house is________ (they).
6. The luggage is ________(he).
7. The pictures are __________(she).
8. In our garden is a bird. The nest is________ (it).
9. This cat is _________(we).
10. This was not my fault. It was__________ (you).

Answers

1. *yours*	2. *mine*	3. *ours*
4. *hers*	5. *theirs*	6. *his*
7. *hers*	8. *its*	9. *ours*
10. *yours*		

Exercise 2

Fill in the correct reflexive pronouns.

1. I did not want to believe it and then I saw the UFO__________.
2. The girl looked at __________in the mirror.
3. Freddy, you'll have to do your homework_________.
4. You don't need to help them. They can do it_________.
5. I introduced __________to my new neighbour.
6. Boys, can you make your beds_________?
7. She made ___________a pullover.
8. What happens when a fighting fish sees __________in the mirror?
9. The father decided to repair the car_____________.
10. We can move the table_____________.

Answers

1. *myself*	2. *herself*	3. *yourself*
4. *themselves*	5. *myself*	6. *yourselves*
7. *herself*	8. *itself*	9. *himself*
10. *ourselves.*		

Exercise 3

Choose the correct relative pronoun (who, which, whose).

1. This is the bank ___________was robbed yesterday.
2. A boy_________ sister is in my class was in the bank at that time.
3. The man __________robbed the bank had two pistols.
4. He wore a mask ____________made him look like Mickey Mouse.
5. He came with a friend __________waited outside in the car.
6. The woman__________ gave him the money was young.
7. The bag __________contained the money was yellow.
8. The people _________were in the bank were very frightened.
9. A man _________mobile was ringing did not know what to do.
10. A woman __________daughter was crying tried to calm her.
11. The car_________ the bank robbers escaped in was orange.
12. The robber _________mask was obviously too big didn't drive.
13. The man __________drove the car was nervous.
14. He didn't wait at the traffic lights____________ were red.
15. A police officer ____________car was parked at the next corner stopped and arrested them.

Answers

1. *which*	2. *whose*	3. *who*
4. *which*	5. *who*	6. *who*
7. *which*	8. *who*	9. *whose*
10. *whose*	11. *which*	12. *whose*
13. *who*	14. *which*	15. *whose*

Exercise 4

Write the correct form of pronoun in the following:

1. Despite her parents complaints, she decided to live by ____ in New York City. (her/herself)
2. If you happen to see your parents this weekend, give ____ my best regards. (him/her/them)
3. I can't understand ____ when she speaks German with ____ . (her, me/ him,me)
4. He should be ashamed of ____ .(himself/him)
5. Mary was worried about the children, so she convinced ____ husband not to accept the job abroad.(his/her)
6. We came across a friend of ____ at the mall yesterday. (ours/us)
7. I can't find ____ pencil. Can I use ____ , Mary? (my, yours/mine, your)
8. I cut ____ when I was peeling the potatoes. (me/myself)
9. This house is too expensive for ____ . We can't pay such a high rent.(us/we)
10. Each plan has ____ merits. (it/its)
11. He ____ said so. (herself/himself)
12. I do my work and they do ____ . (their/theirs)
13. Give it back to ____ . It's ____. (me/mine)
14. Despite ____ old age, he is very active.(his/its)
15. They enjoyed ____ a lot at the cocktail party. (theirselves/themselves)

Answers

1. *herself*	2. *them*	3. *her, me*
4. *himself*	5. *her*	6. *ours*
7. *my, yours*	8. *myself*	9. *us*
10. *its*	11. *himself*	12. *theirs*
13. *me, mine*	14. *his*	15. *themselves*

Exercise 5

Use the correct form of the interrogative pronoun in the following:

1. __________do you wish to see you?

2. __________shall I give this to?
3. To __________ did you give the key?
4. By _________ was the book written?
5. _______are you seeking?
6. _________of you have done this?
7. _________do you think I am?
8. _______came here yesterday?
9. _________have you decided to do?
10. ________is better, honour or riches?

Answers

1. *what/whom*	2. *who*	3. *whom*
4. *whom*	5. *what*	6. *which*
7. *what/who*	8. *who*	9. *what*
10. *which*		

Exercise 6

Write the correct form of pronoun in the following:

1. This is the teacher _________told me my son has been misbehaving in class.
2. My husband, _________I love, sent me flowers at work last night.
3. This is the girl __________ car hit that tree down last week.
4. Those were the boxes _______ were sent to you last month, but never made it here.
5. _________is going to take the dog for a walk?
6. ____________shall I fear, but the ones who hurt me?
7. I asked you __________ one of these shoes you think would go with my outfit.
8. _____________ house is it, anyway? Are we allowed to stay in here?
9. I have friends ________ love me so much, they threw a surprise birthday party for me last night.
10. That young man to ______________ we owe some thanks, saved our mom's life in that car accident.

Answers

1. *who*	2. *whom*	3. *whose*
4. *which*	5. *who*	6. *whom*
7. *which*	8. *whose*	9. *who*
10. *whom*		

Exercise 7

Choose the correct relative pronoun (who, whom, what, which, whose):

1. ____________ is the girl in the blue dress?
2. ____________ is the name of the team in red?
3. For ____________ did Shelia make these cookies.
4. ___________of the names did you choose for the puppy?
5. ____________ completed the assignment?
6. ___________ likes to play pinball at the arcade?
7. _________is the highest ranking official in the United States?
8. To _____________ should the check be made payable?
9. To _____________ did Mark lend his video game?
10. ___________of the cars is parked in the driveway?

Answers

1. *who* 2. *what* 3. *whom*
4. *which* 5. *who* 6. *who*
7. *who* 8. *whom* 9. *whom*
10. *which*

Exercise 8

Write the correct form of pronoun in the following:

1. Mira left ___________notebook in the bus. (her, his, yours)
2. The colorful picture of the flowers is __________ (yours, theirs, mine)
3. Hari strummed____________ guitar and invited everyone to sing. (his, her, their)
4. The computer quickly stores information on________ huge memory. (his, its, her)
5. These warm chocolate chip cookies melt in __________ mouth. (its, your, yours)
6. Is____________ seat belt always fastened? (your, mine, its)
7. The fluffy brown puppy is______________ (its, my, theirs)
8. _____________hand shot up when the teacher asked for volunteers. (theirs, her, mine)
9. I didn't get a cheeseburger, so I tasted ___________(mine, its, hers)
10. He sold______________car.(theirs, his, yours)

Answers

1. *her* 2. *mine* 3. *his*
4. *its* 5. *Yours* 6. *your*
7. *theirs* 8. *her* 9. *hers*
10. *his*

Adjective

4

CHAPTER

An adjective is a word used with a noun to tell something more about it.

Kinds of Adjectives

1. **Adjectives of Quality or Descriptive Adjectives :**
   They denote some quality or attribute. They describe a person or a thing, such as:
   - He is a good boy
   - Sita is a clever girl.
   - The ship sustained heavy damage.

   Adjectives of quality answer the question-'of what kind?'
2. **Adjectives of Quantity**

   These indicate how much a thing is meant, such as:
   - I ate some sugar.
   - We have had enough exercise.
   - There is a little water in the glass.

   Adjectives of quantity answer the question-'how much?'
3. **Adjectives of Number**

   They denote the number or order of the things, such as:
   - There are two books in my bag.
   - The third chapter of this book is very interesting.
   - My son is nine years old.

Adjectives of number answer the question-'how many?'
Adjectives of number are of three kinds:

a. **Definite Numeral Adjectives:** Denote an exact number
   - One, two, three, etc. - These are called **cardinals.**
   - First, second, third, etc. These are called **ordinals.**

b. **Indefinite Numeral Adjectives:** Do not denote an exact number.
   - I have called several times.
   - Some dreams are like reality.

c. **Distributive Numeral Adjectives**: Refer to each one of a number.

- Each girl must take her turn.
- Every man has his duties.

4. Demonstrative Adjectives

These show which or what thing is meant, such as:

- This boy is better than Hari.
- That boy is industrious.
- These mangoes are sour.

4. Interrogative Adjectives

They ask which or what thing is meant, such as:

- What noise is this?
- Which book is yours?

5. Distributive Adjectives

These show that persons or things are taken separately or in separate lots, such as:

- Each player must take his turn.
- Either pen will do.

6. Possessive Adjectives

My, our, her, his, their, its etc. when used before nouns are possessive adjectives.
my mother, our college

Comparison of Adjectives

Adjectives have three degrees of comparison.

a. **The Positive** expresses simple quality.
sweet, dark, heavy

b. **The Comparative** expresses a higher degree of the quality than denoted by the simple adjective.
sweeter, darker, heavier

c. **The Superlative** expresses the highest degree of the quality.
sweetest, darkest, heaviest

➢ ***Remember***

1. *The comparative degree is used when the comparison is between two things or persons. It is generally followed by than.*
   - *Honey is sweeter than milk.*
2. *But in the case of some Latin comparatives, 'to' instead of 'than' is used.*
   - *He is junior to me.*

Some other such words are: senior, inferior, superior, prior.

3. *The superlative degree is used when the comparison involves more than two persons or things.*
   - *Mohan is the tallest boy in the class.*
4. *But when selection is meant between two things, comparative is preceded by 'the' and followed by 'of'.*
   - *Mohan is the taller of the two.*
5. *When two qualities of same person are compared, the comparative is always formed by adding more.*
   - *He is more intelligent than industrious.*
6. *Avoid the use of double comparative.*
   - *Mohan is more taller than Hari. (wrong)*
7. *The superlative is usually preceded by 'the' and followed by 'of'.*
   - *He is the tallest of all the boys in the class.*
8. *The following adjectives, being superlative in meaning, do not admit comparison.*
   - *Ideal, extreme, excellent, unique, perfect, universal*
9. *The adjective is used before the noun.*
   - *I like the new book.*

The Correct Use of Some Adjectives

1. Some, any:

'Some' and 'any' are used to express quantity or degree. 'Some' is normally used in affirmative sentences; 'any' is used in negative or interrogative sentences.

- I will buy some books.
- He will not buy any books.
- Have you bought any books?

'Any' can be used after 'if' in affirmative sentences.

- If you need any money I will help you.

'Some' is used in questions which are really requests or offers or the questions which expect the answer 'yes'.

- Will you have some tea? (offer)
- Would you like some tea? Yes, please.

2. Each, every

'Each' and 'every' are similar in meaning, but 'every' is a stronger word than 'each'. 'every' means 'each without exception'.

➤ ***Remember***

1. *'Each' is used in speaking of two or more things; 'every' is used only in speaking of more than two.*

2. *'Each' directs attention to the individuals forming any group; 'every' for the total group.*
3. *'Each' is used only when the number in the group is limited and definite; 'every' when the number is indefinite.*
   - *Each one of these chairs is broken.*
   - *He came to see us every three days.*

3. Little, a little, the little

i. 'Little' means not much or hardly any. Thus the adjective 'little' has a negative meaning.
   - There is little hope of his recovery.
   - He showed little concern for his friend.
   - Vicky has made little progress and so he is not feeling very pleased.

ii. 'A little' means some though not much. 'A little' has a positive meaning.
   - He has a little knowledge of French.
   - Vicky has made a little progress and so he is feeling quite pleased.

iii. 'The little' means not much but all there is.
   - The little wheat they had was damaged by sea water.
   - The little knowledge of English that he has is likely to be very useful to him.

4. Few, a few, the few

i. 'Few' means not many or hardly any. Thus the adjective 'few' has a negative meaning.
   - Few persons can keep a secret.
   - There are few students in the class.

ii. 'A few' means some. 'A few' has a positive meaning and is opposed to none.
   - A few days' rest is all that is needed.
   - A few poems he has written are all of great excellence.

iii. 'The few' means not many, but all there are.
   - The few friends he has are all very intelligent.
   - Have you got the few oranges left?

REVIEW EXERCISES

Exercise I

Directions: Pick out all the adjectives in the following sentences and describe to which class each of them belongs:

1. Which pen do you prefer?
2. He is a man of few words.
3. He was absent last week.
4. Some dreams are like reality.
5. Hari won the second prize.
6. What time is it?
7. The way was long.
8. There should not be much talk.
9. He comes here every day.
10. A cross child is not liked.

Answers

1. *which-Interrogative Adjective*
2. *few-Indefinite Numeral Adjective*
3. *absent- Descriptive Adjective*
4. *Some-Indefinite Numeral Adjective*
5. *second- Definite Numeral Adjective*
6. *what- Interrogative Adjective*
7. *long-Adjective of quality*
8. *much-Adjective of quantity*
9. *every- Distributive Numeral Adjective*
10. *cross- Descriptive Adjective*

Exercise 2

Directions: Supply suitable adjectives:

1. He is as ________ as a horse.
2. Even ________students can understand this chapter.
3. I accepted the offer on __________conditions.
4. He is a very __________ man.
5. Mohan is an __________boy.
6. He gave her a ______________salary.
7. It has been ____________ of you to help us.
8. ______________men must be respected.
9. I have known her for a __________time.
10. He is too ________ to reach the painting.

Answers

1. *strong*　2. *dull*　3. *certain*
4. *rich*　5. *industrious*　6. *handsome*

7. *kind* 8. *honest* 9. *long*
10. *short*

Exercise 3

Complete each sentence by choosing the correct word.

1. There is so (many, much) smoke coming out of the chimney.
2. There are (plenty of, a large amount of) fish in the pond.
3. (A little, A few) minutes is all it takes for him to shave.
4. The postman put (a great deal of, a lot of) letters into the bag.
5. He threw (a little, some) nuts to the monkeys.
6. She uses only (a few, a little) cooking oil in her cooking.
7. My hens lay (a large amount of, several) eggs very day.
8. (A great deal of, A large number of) dust has collected on the desk.
9. We saw (a large amount of, many) cows grazing in the field.
10. The baker sells (a large amount of, a large number of) biscuits.

Answers

1. *much* 2. *plenty of* 3. *a few*
4. *a lot of* 5. *some* 6. *a little*
7. *several* 8. *a great deal of* 9. *many*
10. *a large amount of*

Exercise 4

Fill in the correct form of the words in brackets (comparative or superlative).

1. My house is (big) ________than yours.
2. This flower is (beautiful) _________than that one.
3. This is the (interesting)___________ book I have ever read.
4. Non-smokers usually live (long) __________than smokers.
5. Which is the (dangerous) ___________animal in the world?
6. A holiday by the sea is (good) ___________than a holiday in the mountains.
7. It is strange but often a coke is (expensive)__________ than a beer.
8. Who is the (rich)__________ woman on earth?
9. The weather this summer is even (bad) ___________than last summer.
10. He was the (clever) __________thief of all.

Answer

1. *bigger* 2. *more beautiful* 3. *most interesting*
4. *longer* 5. *most dangerous* 6. *better*

7. *more expensive* 8. *richest* 9. *worse*
10. *cleverest*

Exercise 5

Fill in the comparative and superlative forms of the objectives

1. happy, ____________, ____________
2. old, ____________, ____________
3. bad, ____________, ____________
4. dificult, ____________, ____________
5. large, ____________, ____________
6. good, ____________, ____________
7. little ____________, ____________
8. easy, ____________, ____________
9. much,____________,____________
10. in, ____________, ____________

answers

1. *happy, happier, happiest*
2. *old, older/elder, oldest/eldest*
3. *bad, worse, worst*
4. *difficult, more difficult, most difficult*
5. *large, larger, largest*
6. *good, better, best*
7. *little, less/lesser, least*
8. *easy, easier, easiest*
9. *much,more, most*
10. *in, inner, inmost/innermost*

Exercise 6

Insert 'a', 'some' or 'any', whichever is suitable

1. I am going to buy __________posters.
2. They didn't have __________ hair clasps.
3. There are not________ shops in this part of the town.
4. Have you got ________ brother or sister? No, I don't.
5. There are ________ beautiful leather jackets in the shop window.
6. I haven't got __________ stamps but my sister has got ________.
7. We need ________kilo of apples.
8. Have you got __________ water?

9. There's _______ newspaper on the table.
10. I can pay. I've got _________money.
11. Are there_________ letters for me this morning? No, there aren't.
12. We saw ________white bears in a zoo.
13. Do you know __________ good hotels in London?
14. Could you lend me _________ money?
15. How about_________ cup of coffee?

Answers

1. *some*	2. *any*	3. *any*
4. *any*	5. *some*	6. *any, some*
7. *a*	8. *any*	9. *a*
10. *some*	11. *any*	12. *some*
13. *some*	14. *some*	15. *a*

Exercise 7

Fill in the correct words in brackets (any, many, much, a few, a little, some).

1. How _________ books do you have on your shelf?
2. Would you like ________juice?
3. How ________ money do you have?
4. I only have ________ rupees.
5. I want to make orange juice. Have you got _________ oranges?
6. No, I don't have any. But I have________ apples, if you'd like to make apple juice instead.
7. There are __________ people trying to go to the U2 concert this weekend.
8. How many dollars did you bring for the trip? I just have _________dollars.
9. Radhika spent a lot of money on her car. Now she only has _________ money left to pay for her living expenses.
10. How _________ time do you have left before you have to go to school?

Answers

1. *many*	2. *some*	3. *much*
4. *a few*	5. *any*	6. *some*
7. *many*	8. *a few*	9.. *a little*
10. *much*		

Exercise 8

Fill in the correct words (any, anything, nothing, something, everything) in brackets.

1. I don't have _________ to do today.

2. Are there ________ dogs in the house?
3. I know ____________about it!
4. There is ___________I need to do tomorrow afternoon.
5. My friend doesn't know____________ about her Birthday Party!
6. Did you bring ____________you needed for the trip?
7. My friend's decisions have __________ to do with me.
8. If there is ___________you need you can call me, okay?
9. I think there is ______________ wrong with my computer. It is not working very well.
10. My mom asked me how I was and I said _______________ was fine.

Answers

1. *anything* 2. *any,* 3. *nothing*
4. *something* 5. *anything* 6. *everything*
7. *nothing* 8. *anything* 9. *something*
10. *everything*

Exercise 9

Fill in the correct words (some, any, a little, a few,) in brackets.

1. We need to buy __________ bread rolls if you want to make hotdogs for your lunch.
2. I need _________ money to go shopping.
3. I love coffee but I only take a _______ milk and two teaspoons of sugar in it.
4. I can't go right now because I still have a ________ orders to fill by 5 o'clock.
5. I've got _______salad sandwiches for my lunch today.
6. I haven't got ___________ tea. Can you go to the corner store and buy ________ more?
7. I need a ____________ help with my homework. Do you have time to help me?
8. Is there ___________ orange juice left in the fridge?
9. Do you think I could have a _______ more butter please?
10. Would you like ___________ cream in your coffee?

Answers

1. *some* 2. *some* 3. *little*
4. *few* 5. *some* 6. *any, some*
7. *little* 8. *any* 9. *little*
10. *some*

Exercise 10

Fill in the correct words (some, any, a little, a few,) in brackets.

1. I love Thailand. I've already been there a ________ times and I plan to go back this summer.
2. Since I started my new job, I've got very __________ time to do the things I enjoy.
3. Do you want ________ more potato chips?
4. Despite their marketing efforts, I only managed to sell a _____ CDs.
5. My boss has very ____________ tolerance for silly mistakes.
7. There are ________ grapes in the fridge.
7. We haven't got __________ bread, so I am going to buy ________.
8. When we were in London, we visited ____________ very interesting places.
9. I went out to buy__________ milk but they didn't have ________ in the shop.
11. If I had ________ sweets, I would give you _________.

Answers

1. *few*	2. *little*	3. *some*
4. *few*	5. *little*	6. *some*
7. *any, some*	8. *some*	9. *some, any*
10. *some, some*		

Verb

5

CHAPTER

A verb is a word that tells or asserts something about a person or thing. Verb comes from the Latin word 'verbum' that means 'word'. A verb may tell us:

i. What a person or thing does; as,
   - I go.
   - He laughs.
   - The bell rings.

ii. What is done to a person or thing; as,
   - The dog is kicked.
   - Hari is scolded.

iii. What a person or thing is; as,
   - He is a brave boy.
   - The glass is brittle.

Forms of Verb

The verbs may be grouped under two classes: the Principal Verb and the Auxiliary Verb.

I. The Principal Verb

The Principal verb is used in a sentence in order to signify the action or the state of a subject.

- Jack built a house.
- Sunil runs fast.

The Principal verb can further be divided into Transitive Verb and Intransitive Verb.

i. **A transitive verb** denotes an action which passes from the doer to another person or thing.

Examples

- Ram throws the ball.
- She loves her child.

ii. **An intransitive verb** denotes an action which does not go beyond the doer.

Examples

- Hari runs fast.
- Gopal comes here everyday.

2. The Auxiliary Verb

Auxiliary verbs or helping verbs or such as will, shall, may, might, can, could, must, ought to, should, would, used to, need etc. are used in conjunction with main verbs to express shades of time and mood. The combination of helping verbs with main verbs creates what are called verb phrases or verb strings. In the following sentence, "will have been" are helping or auxiliary verbs and "studying" is the main verb; the whole verb string is underlined:

- As of next August, I will have been studying chemistry for ten years.

Shall, will and forms of have, do and be combine with main verbs to indicate time and voice. As auxiliaries, the verbs be, have and do can change form to indicate changes in subject and time.

- I shall go now.
- He had won the election.
- They did write that novel together.
- I am going now.
- He was winning the election.
- They have been writing that novel for a long time.

The auxiliary verb is a helping verb. (Auxiliary means helping.)It helps the principal or main verb to form tenses, moods or voices.

Examples

- I have done the job.
- Ranjit will come tomorrow.

There are twelve Auxiliary verbs. These are listed below:

1.	To be (is, am, are, was, were, be, being, been)	7.	May (may, might)
2.	To have (have, has, having, had)	8.	Must
3.	To do (do, does, did)	9.	Ought

4.	Shall (shall, should)	10.	Need
5.	Will (will, would)	11.	Dare
6.	Can (can, could)	12.	Used

'To be', 'to do', and 'to have' are used as Principal verbs also. The verbs can, could, may, might, will, would, shall, should, must and ought are called modal verbs or modals.

Modals

Modal verbs are used before ordinary verbs and convey a range of judgements about the likelihood of events.

- You must run to catch the train.
- She might be there.
- You could get there by lunchtime if you hurry.
- You'll hit the roof.

To show a high degree of certainty about the likelihood of events, modal verbs of high modality are used. If we feel tentative about something, we use low modality.

High Modality	Medium Modality	Low Modality
must	will	may
ought to	should	might
has to	can	could
	need to	would

As well as modal verbs, modality can be expressed through choices of nouns, adjectives, and adverbs.

- **Modal Nouns:** possibility, probability, obligation, necessity, requirement
- **Modal Adjectives:** possible, probable, obligatory, necessary, required, determined
- **Modal Adverbs:** possibly, probably, perhaps, maybe, sometimes, always, definitely, never, certainly

Uses of 'Shall' and 'Will' and 'Should'

'Shall' is used to express the simple future for first person I and we, 'Will' is used in the simple future for all other persons. As,

- Shall we meet by the river?
- She will complain about bullying.

Using will in the first person would express determination on the part of the speaker; as,

- Oh! We will finish this project by tonight!

Using shall in second and third persons would indicate some kind of promise about the subject, as in,

- This shall be revealed to you in good time.

'Shall' is often used in formal situations (legal or legalistic documents, minutes to meetings, etc.) to express obligation, even with third person and second person constructions:

- The board of directors shall be responsible for payment to stockholders.
- The college president shall report financial shortfalls to the executive director each semester.

'Should' is usually replaced, nowadays, by *would*. It is still used, however, to mean 'ought to'; as,

- You really shouldn't do that.
- If you think that was amazing, you should have seen it last night.

'Should' is also used with the first person pronouns in expressions of liking and in tentative expressions of opinion such as

- I should prefer iced tea.
- I should imagine they'll vote Conservative.
- I should have thought so.

Uses of 'Do', Does' and 'Did'

In the simple present tense, 'do' will function as an auxiliary to express the negative and to ask questions. 'Does', however, is substituted for third person, singular subjects in the present tense. The past tense 'did' works with all persons, singular and plural.

- I don't study at night.
- She doesn't work here anymore.
- Do you attend this school?
- Does he work here?

These verbs also work as 'short answers', with the main verb omitted.

- Does she work here? No, she doesn't (~~work here~~).

With 'yes-no' questions, the form of 'do' goes in front of the subject and the main verb comes after the subject:

- Did your grandmother know Truman?
- Do wildflowers grow in your backyard?

Forms of 'do' are useful in expressing similarity and differences in conjunction with
'so' and 'neither'.

- My wife hates spinach and so does my son.
- My wife doesn't like spinach; neither do I.

'Do' is also helpful because it means you don't have to repeat the verb.

- Larry excelled in language studies; so did his brother.
- Raoul studies as hard as his sister does.

The so-called emphatic 'do' has many uses.

a. To add emphasis to an entire sentence

- He does like spinach. He really does!

b. To add emphasis to an imperative

- Do come in. (actually softens the command)

c. To add emphasis to a frequency adverb

- He never did understand his father.
- She always does manage to hurt her mother's feelings.

d. To contradict a negative statement

- You didn't do your homework, did you?
- Oh, but I did finish it.

e. To ask a clarifying question about a previous negative statement

- Ridwell didn't take the tools.
- Then who did take the tools?

f. To indicate a strong concession

- Although the Clintons denied any wrong doing, they did return some of the gifts.

In the absence of other modal auxiliaries, a form of 'do' is used in question and negative constructions known as the get passive:

- Did Rinaldo get selected by the committee?
- The audience didn't get riled up by the politician.

Uses of 'Have', 'Has' and 'Had'

Forms of the verb 'to have' are used to create tenses known as the present perfect and past perfect. The perfect tense indicates that something has happened in the past; the present perfect indicates that something happened and might be continuing to happen, the past perfect indicates that something happened prior to something else happening.

'To have' is also in combination with other modal verbs to express probability and possibility in the past.

a. As an affirmative statement, 'to have' can express how certain you are that something happened (when combined with an appropriate modal + have + a past participle):
   - Gagan must have left already.
   - Seema might have known about the gifts.
   - They may have voted already.

b. As a negative statement, a modal is combined with not + have + a past participle to express how certain you are that something did not happen:
   - Seema might not have known about the gifts.
   - I may not have been there at the time of the crime.

c. To ask about possibility or probability in the past, a modal is combined with the subject + have + past participle:
   - Could Seema have known about the gifts?

d. For short answers, a modal is combined with 'have':
   - "Did Seema know about this?" "I don't know. She may have."
   - "The evidence is pretty positive." "She must have."

'To have', sometimes combined with 'to get', is used to express a logical inference:

- It's been raining all week; the basement has to be flooded by now.
- He hit his head on the doorway. He has got to be over seven feet tall!

Have is often combined with an infinitive to form an auxiliary whose meaning is similar to 'must.'

- I have to have a car like that!
- She has to pay her own tuition at college.
- He has to have been the first student to try that.

Uses of 'Can' and 'Could'

i. The modal auxiliary 'can' is used

a. To express ability (in the sense of being able to do something or knowing how to do something):
   - He can speak Spanish but he can't write it very well.

b. To express permission (in the sense of being allowed or permitted to do something):
   - Can I talk to my friends in the library waiting room?

c. To express theoretical possibility:

- American automobile makers can make better cars if they think there's a profit in it.

ii. The modal auxiliary 'could' is used

a. To express an ability in the past:

- I could always beat you at tennis when we were kids.

b. To express past or future permission:

- Could I park my car in your backyard?

c. To express present possibility:

- We could always spend the afternoon just sitting around talking.

d. To express possibility or ability in contingent circumstances:

- If he studied harder, he could pass this course.

In expressing ability, 'can' and 'could' frequently also imply willingness:

- Can you help me with my homework?

'Can' versus 'May'

Whether the auxiliary verb 'can' can be used to express permission or not depends on the level of formality of situation; as,

- Can I leave the room now?
- I don't know if you can, but you may.

Uses of 'May' and 'Might'

When used in the context of granting or seeking permission, 'might' is the past tense of 'may'. 'Might' is considerably more tentative than 'may'.

- May I leave class early?
- If I've finished all my work and I'm really quiet, might I leave early?

In the context of expressing possibility, 'may' and 'might' are interchangeable present and future forms and might + have + past participle is the past form:

- She might be my advisor next semester.
- She may be my advisor next semester.
- She might have advised me not to take biology.

Uses of 'Will' and 'Would'

In certain contexts, 'will' and 'would' are virtually interchangeable, but there are differences. Notice that the contracted form 'll is very frequently used for will.

'Will' can be used to express willingness:

- I'll wash the dishes if you dry.
- We're going to the movies. Will you join us?

It can also express intention (especially in the first person):

- I'll do my exercises later on.

and prediction:

- Specific: The meeting will be over soon.
- Timeless: Humidity will ruin my hairdo.
- Habitual: The river will overflow its banks every spring.

'Would' can also be used to express willingness:

- Would you please take off your hat?

It can also express insistence (rather rare):

- Now you've ruined everything. You would act that way.

and characteristic activity:

- Customary: After work, he would walk to his home in West Hartford.
- Typical (casual): She would cause the whole family to be late, every time.

In a main clause, 'would' can express a hypothetical meaning:

- My cocker spaniel would weigh a ton if I let her eat what she wants.

Finally, 'would' can express a sense of probability:

- I hear a whistle. That would be the five o'clock train.

Uses of 'Used to'

The auxiliary verb construction 'used to' is used to express an action that took place in the past, perhaps customarily, but now that action no longer customarily takes place:

- We used to take long vacation trips with the whole family.
- Didn't you use to go jogging every morning before breakfast?
- It didn't use to be that way.

'Used to' can also be used to convey the sense of being accustomed to or familiar with something:

- The tire factory down the road really stinks, but we're used to it by now.
- I like these old sneakers; I'm used to them.

'Used to' is best reserved for colloquial usage; it has no place in formal or academic text.

Mood

Mood in verbs refers to one of three attitudes that a writer or speaker has to what is being written or spoken.

1. Indicative mood

The Indicative mood is used to make a statement or ask a question.

- They've got some work.
- What are you reading?

2. Imperative mood

The imperative mood is used when we're feeling authoritative and want to give a directive, strong suggestion, or order:

- Get your homework done before you watch television tonight.
- Please include cash payment with your order form.
- Get out of town!

Notice that there is no subject in these imperative sentences. The pronoun 'you', singular or plural, depending on context is the understood subject in imperative sentences.

3. Subjunctive mood

The subjunctive mood is used in dependent clauses that do the following:

i. Express a wish
ii. Begin with 'if' and express a condition that does not exist (is contrary to fact)
iii. Begin with 'as if' and 'as though' when such clauses describe a speculation or condition contrary to fact
iv. Begin with 'that' and express a demand, requirement, request, or suggestion.

- She wishes her boyfriend were here.
- If John were more aggressive, he'd be a better hockey player.
- We would have passed if we had studied harder.
- He acted as if he were guilty.
- I requested that he be present at the hearing.

The present tense of the subjunctive uses only the base form of the verb.

- He demanded that his students use two-inch margins.
- She suggested that we be on time tomorrow.

The past tense of the subjunctive has the same forms as the indicative except for the verb 'to be', which uses 'were' regardless of the number of the subject.

- If I were seven feet tall, I'd be a great basketball player.
- He wishes he were a better student.
- If you were rich, we wouldn't be in this mess.
- If they were faster, we could have won that race.

Verbal- Infinitives, Gerunds and Participles

Infinitives, gerunds and participles are called 'verbal.' Verbal is a verb form that functions in a sentence as a noun, an adjective, or an infinitive.

I. An infinitive

An infinitive is the 'to' form of a verb. For example:

- I like to play cards.
- Everybody wishes to enjoy life.

Remember

An infinitive is split when one or more words separate the 'to' and the verb. As;

- ***Below standard:*** *He was wrong to suddenly leave the country.*
  Correction: *He was wrong to leave the country suddenly.*
- ***Below standard:*** *I have tried to consciously stop worrying about it.*
  Correction: *I have consciously tried to stop worrying about it.*
- ***Below standard:*** *He wanted me to finally make an announcement.*
  Correction: *He finally wanted me to make an announcement.*

There is nothing ungrammatical about splitting an infinitive, but sometimes a split results in clumsiness or ambiguity in the sentence. Therefore, we should avoid placing a modifier between the 'to' and the verb form in an infinitive for the sake of clarity and right emphasis.

A gerund is a noun made by adding '–ing' to verb. For example,

- Selling is an art.
- Working is a pleasure.

➢ **Remember**

The gerund being a verb- noun, may be used as

i. *The subject of a verb:*

- *Seeing is believing.*

ii. *Object of a transitive verb*

- *Stop shouting.*
- *He likes reading poetry.*

iii. *complement of a verb*

- *Seeing is believing.*

A participle

Participle is a form of verb used as an adjective to modify a noun or a pronoun. It is made by adding '-ing' to a verb. For example,

- Working women lead an active life.
- Our living conditions need to be improved.

A participle, though it is derived from a verb, can never be used as an adverb and cannot make a statement about a subject.

➢ *Remember*

1. *A verb + -ing, like, reading, is not always a participle. It is a **participle** only when it is used as an adjective. When it is used as a noun, it is a **gerund.** For example,*
   - *Reading is beneficial. (Here the word 'reading' is used as a noun, therefore it is a gerund.)*
   - *The boy, reading the paper, is my senior. (Here the word 'reading' is used as an adjective, therefore it is a participle.)*
   - *There was a sound of marching feet. (Here the word 'marching' is used as an adjective, therefore it is a participle.)*
2. *A participle should clearly refer to the noun. A single participle is generally placed just before the noun that it modifies. For example,*
   - *The foaming water poured from the broken pipe.*
3. *A participle phrase usually follows the noun. For example,*
   - *The boy carrying the banner rode in a wagon drawn by four horses.*
4. *A participle, which does not modify a definite noun or pronoun, is called **a dangling** or **hanging participle**. A dangling construction is the result of carelessness in writing or thinking. We can eliminate a dangling construction by (1) shifting the modifier so that it would clearly refer to the word it modifies or (2) expanding the dangling phrase into a subordinate clause.*
   - ***Dangling construction:** The boy watched the approaching officer, whistling to keep up his courage.*

     ***Correction:** The boy, whistling to keep up his courage, watched the approaching officer.*

- ***Dangling construction:*** *The man left the office feeling satisfied.*

  Correction: The man, feeling satisfied, left the office.

- ***Dangling construction:*** *Being built on solid rock, the engineers knew that the building would not settle.*

  Correction: *The engineers knew that the building, being built on solid rock, would not settle.*

REVIEW EXERCISES

Exercise 1

Name the verb (transitive/ intransitive) in the following sentences:

1. Birds fly in the air.
2. The dog sleeps on the rug.
3. Time changes all things.
4. The sun shines brightly.
5. An old man stood by the gate.
6. You speak too softly.
7. I wrote a letter to my friend.
8. He could not spare the time.
9. She looked down from her balcony.
10. Your pencil lies on the table.

Answers

1. *fly-Intransitive Verb*
2. *sleeps-Intransitive Verb*
3. *changes-Transitive Verb*
4. *shines- Intransitive Verb*
5. *stood- Intransitive Verb*
6. *speak- Intransitive Verb*
7. *wrote -Transitive Verb*
8. *could (not)spare- Transitive Verb*
9. *looked- Intransitive Verb*
10. *lies- Intransitive Verb*

Exercise 2

Chose the correct alternative to fill in the blanks.

1. I ________(used, used is, used to, was used, am used) live there when I was a boy.

2. You __________(should, would, ought) be punctual.
3. Yesterday we __________(have, had) to get up early.
4. __________(Shall, Will, Would) I assist you?
5. You ____________(ought, should, must) to pay your debts.
6. He was afraid that if he asked you again you____________ (can, may, might) refuse.
7. I don't think I____________ (shall, should, can) be able to go.
8. You ______________(couldn't wait, didn't need to wait, needn't have waited) for me, I could have found the way.
9. If you ______________(should, would, shall, will) see him, convey him my regards.
10. ____________(Shall, Might, Could) you show me the way to the station.

Answers

1. *used to*
2. *should*
3. *had*
4. *shall*
5. *ought*
6. *might*
7. *shall*
8. *needn't have waited*
9. *should*
10. *could*

Exercise 3

Chose the correct alternative to fill in the blanks.

1. I ____________ (has, have, had, should have) go to see the doctor last week because I was very ill.
2. I could ___________ (has, have, had, should have) bought that car but I didn't have enough money to pay for the petrol.
3. I ___________(have been to, have to, had to) go now because I am already late for my class.
4. I ________ (might be, may be, could be, can be)able to come to your party if I have the time.
5. Do you_________ (has to, have to, had to) clean the house every day or every week?
6. I __________ (could, would, can, may) speak French without a problem now because I have had many lessons.
7. They____________ (will not, do not, shall not) have to do their homework today because it is a holiday at the school.
8. I __________(could, should, might, ought,) to help you with your shopping because you have a lot of bags.
9. When __________ (will, shall, would , should) you be able to come and see us in our new house?
10. I may __________ (have to, had to) go to Paris next week because there is a very big exhibition there.

Answers

1. *had to*	2. *have*	3. *have to*
4. *may be*	5. *have to*	6. *can*
7. *do not*	8. *ought*	9. *will*
10. *have to*		

Exercise 4

Fill in the blanks with the appropriate auxiliaries or modals.

1. I __________ go to see the doctor last week because I was very ill.
2. I could__________ bought that car but I didn't have enough money to pay for the petrol.
3. I __________ go now because I am already late for my class.
4. I may __________ able to come to your party if I have the time.
5. Do you __________ clean the house every day or every week?
6. I __________ speak French without a problem now because I have had many lessons.
7. They don't __________ do their homework today because it is a holiday at the school.
8. I __________ help you with your shopping because you have a lot of bags.
9. When will you be __________ come and see us in our new house?
10. I may __________ go to Paris next week because there is a very big exhibition there.

Answers

1. *had to*	2. *have*	3. *have to*
4. *be*	5. *have to*	6. *can*
7. *have to*	8. *ought to*	9. *able to*
10. *have to*		

Exercise 5

Fill in the blanks with the words in brackets as gerund.

1. My friend is ______ playing basket ball. (good)
2. She ______ bullying. (complain)
3. They are __________ losing the match. (afraid)
4. She doesn't __________ working on the computer. (feel)
5. We are ______ to going out at the weekend. (look forward)
6. Seema ______ living on a small island. (dream)
7. Hari __________being late. (apologize)

8. Do you __________ staying in a foreign country. (agree)
9. The girl ______ going out with her friend. (insist)
10. Andrew ______ climbing trees this afternoon. (think)

Answers

1. *good+at*
2. *complains+about*
3. *afraid+of*
4. *feel +like*
5. *looking forward+ to*
6. *dreams+of*
7. *apologized +for*
8. *agree+with*
9. *insisted+on*
10. *thinks+ of*

Exercise 6

Fill in the blanks with words in brackets as gerund or infinitive

1. We decided ____________ a new car.(buy)
2. They've got some work __________ (do)
3. Vivek gave up __________ (smoke)
4. He would like _________ an aeroplane. (fly)
5. I enjoy _________ picture postcards.(write)
6. Do you know what _________ if there is a fire in the shop? (do)
7. Avoid __________ silly mistakes.(make)
8. My parents wanted me _________ home at 11 o'clock. (be)

Answers

1. *to buy*
2. *to do*
3. *smoking*
4. *to fly*
5. *writing*
6. *to do*
7. *making*
8. *to be*

Exercise 7

Fill in the blanks with the suitable auxiliary verbs.

1. The flight ________ delayed because of bad weather.
2. _________ you do much sightseeing when you were on vacation in Madrid?
3. They ________ leaving for the airport when I last saw them.
4. I __________ forgotten to set my alarm clock, so I ____________ late for my train.
5. ___________ it raining when you left for office this afternoon?
6. The employees ________ informed last night that their company was going into receivership.
7. The police located the artwork which ______________ been stolen from the gallery.

8. The fire _________ caused by an electrical problem.
9. She was surprised that he knew her name. She _________ never met him before.
10. How many times _________ your travel documents checked before you boarded the airplane?

Answers

1. *was*
2. *did*
3. *were*
4. *had, was*
5. *Was*
6. *were*
7. *had*
8. *was*
9. *had*
10. *were*

Exercise 8

Chose the correct form of verb.

1. Have you _________ your ticket for the film on Friday yet? (getting, get, got)
2. I have _________numerous plants in my garden this year. (grow, grows, grown)
3. Hari and Radha _________for the coast on Monday morning. (leaves, leaving, left)
4. Can you _________the mirror on that wall, please? (place, put)
5. The bridesmaids _________beautiful red coloured dresses at the wedding last Saturday.
6. Radhika _________ her son to his judo practice. She should be back shortly. (take, took)
7. R.K. Narayan _________a number of memorable novels and stories set in India. (write, wrote, written)
8. Seema's husband is a driver. He _________a taxi for a living. (driving, drives, drive)
9. After looking at a variety of coloured allets, John finally _________ the colour for her family room walls. (choose, chose, choosen)
10. He has to _________four new tyres for his car. He wants higher quality tyres so they will last longer. (buy, buying, bought)

Answers

1. got
2. grown
3. left
4. put
5. wore
6. took
7. wrote
8. drives
9. chose
10. buy

Exercise 9

Chose the correct form of verb.

1. You seem to be having trouble there. ________ I help you?

   a. would b. will c. shall

2. I don't have enough money to buy lunch. ________ you lend me a couple of dollars?

   a. may b. could c. shall

3. That ice is dangerously thin now. You ________ go ice-skating today.

   a. mustn't b. might not c. would mind not to

4. It's way past my bedtime and I'm really tired. I ________ go to bed.

   a. should b. ought c. could

5. He ________ have committed this crime. He wasn't even in the city that night.

   a. might b. shouldn't c. couldn't

6. John is over two hours late already. He ________ missed the bus again.

   a. should have b. must have c. will have

7. I'm really quite lost. ________ showing me how to get out of here?

   a. Would you mind b. Would you be c. Must you be

8. That bus is usually on time. It ________ to be here any time now.

   a. might b. has c. ought

9. I read about your plane's near disaster. You ________ terrified!

   a. might have been b. must have been c. shall have been

10. It's the law. They ________ have a blood test before they get married.

    a. might b. could c. have to

11. Professor Villa, we've finished our work for today. ________ we leave now, please?

    a. May b. Can c. Must

12. Yesterday I ________ finish my Geography project.

    a. have to b. had to c. must

13. She will ________ wait in line like everyone else.

    a. has to b. must c. have to

14. Bicyclists ________ remember to signal when they turn.

    a. May b. Can c. Must

15. Angela, you __________ leave your clothes all over the floor like this.

    a. must not   b. could not   c. will not

Answers

1. *c*   2. *b*   3. *a*
4. *a*   5. *c*   6. *b*
7. *a*   8. *c*   9. *b*
10. *c*   11. *a*   12. *b*
13. *c*   14. *c*   15. *a*

Exercise 10

Chose the verb or verb string that best completes the sentence.

1. It is very important that all employees _______________ in their proper uniforms before 6:30 a.m.

   A. are dressed   B. will be dressed   C. be dressed

2. I wish my brother _________ here.

   A. were   B. was

3. The coach insisted that Fabio _______ the center position, even though he's much too short for that position..

   A. plays   B. play

4. He moved that the meeting _______________.

   A. was adjourned   B. be adjourned

5. My mother would know what to do. Oh, would that she _______ here with us now!

   A. were   B. was

6. If only the boy _______ a little more responsible in his choice.

   A. was   B. were

7. If Mrs. Gupta ________ ill that night, the family would not have gone to Ford Theatre.

   A. were   B. had been

8. Her employees treated Mrs. Greenblatt as though she _______ a queen.

   A. was   B. were

9. If his parents _____________ more careful in his upbringing, Holden Caulfield would have been quite different.

   A. had been   B. were

10. I wish I _________ better today.

    A. feel   B. felt

Answers

1. *C*	2. *A*	3. *B*
4. *B*	5. *A*	6. *B*
7. *B*	8. *B*	9. *A*
10. *B*		

Exercise 11

Write the phrases in brackets in their correct form into the gaps.

1. Yesterday I ______________ (can/to watch) a film, today I can't.
2. Last week we______________ (can/to go) swimming, this week we can't.
3. If you try hard, you___________ (can/to pass)your examination.
4. May be the Smiths ________________ a new house next year. (can/to build)
5. When I was five, I ____________ (not, can, to swim)
6. He was so busy, he __________ a letter to me. (not/can/to write)
7. For three weeks I ____________ to him on the phone. (not/can/to speak)
8. Dennis _____________ the trumpet after four months. (can/to play)
9. Next year we ______________ a new car. (can/to look for)

Answers

1. could watch	2. could go	3. can pass
4. will be able to build	5. could not swim	6. could not write
7. could not speak	8. could play	9. will be able to look for

Adverb

6 CHAPTER

An adverb is a word that adds information to a verb, an adjective or an adverb.

Kinds of Adverbs

The principle kinds of adverb are:

1. **Adverbs of Time**

   Some adverbs of time are soon, early, late, then, ago, before, since, presently, immediately, already, never, hence.

Examples

- She came early.
- He is late.
- Please come soon.
- The train has already left.
- Ravi came to see me immediately after his arrival.
- I shall never forget it.

2. **Adverbs of Place**

   Some adverbs of place are here, there, everywhere, somewhere, anywhere, above, below, under, in, out, far, near, off, away, hither, thither, thence, within, without.

Examples

- Gopal lives there.
- I searched for him everywhere.
- He has gone out.
- How far can you walk?
- His house is near the school.
- He is away from home now.

3. **Adverbs of Manner**

   Adverbs of manner include nearly all those adverbs which are formed from adjectives and after end in –ly.

Examples

- He works hard.
- Face your problems boldly.
- She walks slowly.
- He has done his job well.

4. **Adverbs of Degree/Quantity**

   Some adverbs of quantity are much, very, exactly, almost, hardly, rather, too, all, altogether, partly, somewhat, quite, scarcely, utterly, wholly, pretty, about, nearly so.

Examples

- I do not think much of it.
- You are partly responsible for this.
- The milk is too hot to drink.
- I could hardly listen to him.
- I felt rather tired at the end of the day.
- It is almost dark.

5. **Adverbs of Reason/Consequence**

Examples

- He therefore gave up studies.
- It is late, so I must go.
- She is deaf. Hence she could not hear you.
- It was late, so I went home.

6. **Adverbs of Number**

   Some adverbs of number are once, twice, thrice, first, secondly, thirdly.

Examples

- He came here once a week.
- I have warned you twice.
- He first asked my name.

Comparison of Adverbs

Many adverbs admit of comparison like adjectives and have three degrees of comparison,

• **Positive**	• **Comparative**	• **Superlative**
Fast	faster	fastest
Slow	slower	slowest

Adverbs of more than one syllable generally form their comparative and superlative degrees by the addition of *-er* and *-est*:

soon	sooner	soonest
fine	finer	finest

Adverbs of more than one syllable generally form their comparative and superlative degrees by the addition of *more* or *most*.

slowly	more slowly	most slowly
loudly	more loudly	most loudly

Some adverbs are irregular in comparative degree

bad	worse	worst
little	less	least

Position of Adverbs

1. The position of the adverb affects the meaning of the sentence.

Examples

- I only spoke to him. (spoke to him but did not do anything else)
- I spoke only to him. (to none else)

2. Adverbs are generally placed close to the words they qualify. They are generally placed:

Examples

i. Before adjectives or other adverbs
   - Delhi is too hot in June.
   - This is good enough.

➢ *Remember: 'enough' comes after the adjective.*

ii. After intransitive verbs
   - We laughed heartily.
   - He ran fast.

iii. After the object of a transitive verb:
   - The girl cut her finger badly.
   - He lifted the weight easily.

iv. Between the principal verb and the auxiliary, or between two auxiliaries.

- He has already agreed.
- They have always been consulted.

v. When an adverb qualifies a whole sentence or is used for emphasis, it is generally placed at the beginning of the sentence.

- Luckily he was away from the scene of the accident.
- Never was a man so badly treated.

➤ ***Remember***

Avoid the use of double adverbs: for example;

- He came in slowly slowly.

REVIEW EXERCISES

Exercise 1

Write the correct adverb:

1. slow____________
2. perfect__________
3. terrible__________
4. hard__________
5. good___________
6. heavy ___________
7. fast__________
8. quiet____________
9. fantastic_____________
10. great____________

Answers

1. *slowly*	2. *perfectly*	3. *terribly*
4. *hardly*	5. *well*	6. *heavily*
7. *fast*	8. *quietly*	9. *fantastically*
10. *greatly*		

Exercise 2

Rewrite the sentence with the adverb (in brackets) in its correct position.

1. I play tennis on Sundays. (often)

2. Have you been to London? (ever)
3. Peter doesn't get up before seven. (usually)
4. Our friends must write a test. (also)
5. I was joking. (only)
6. The weather is bad in November. (always)
7. Did you enjoy the flight? (both)
8. I have met him before. (never)
9. Meera watches TV. (hardly)
10. He plays on the computer. (always)
11. He listens to the radio. (often)
12. They read a book. (sometimes)
13. Priya gets angry. (never)
14. Tarun is very friendly. (usually)
15. I take sugar in my coffee. (sometimes)
16. Ramon is hungry. (often)
17. My grandmother goes for a walk in the evening. (always)
18. The boy helps his father in the kitchen. (usually)
19. They watch TV in the afternoon. (never)
20. Chetan smokes after dinner. (seldom)

Answers

1. *I <u>often</u> play tennis on Sundays.*
2. *Have you <u>ever</u> been to London?*
3. *Peter doesn't <u>usually</u> get up before seven.*
4. *Our friends must <u>also</u> write a test.*
5. *I was <u>only</u> joking.*
6. *The weather is <u>always</u> bad in November.*
7. *Did you <u>both</u> enjoy the flight?*
8. *I have <u>never</u> met him before.*
9. *Meera <u>hardly</u> watches TV.*
10. *He <u>always</u> plays on the computer.*
11. *He <u>often</u> listens to the radio.*
12. *They <u>sometimes</u> read a book.*
13. *Priya <u>never</u> gets angry.*
14. *Tarun is <u>usually</u> very friendly.*
15. *I <u>sometimes</u> take sugar in my coffee.*
16. *Ramon is <u>often</u> hungry.*
17. *My grandmother <u>always</u> goes for a walk in the evening.*
18. *The boy <u>usually</u> helps his father in the kitchen.*

19. *They <u>never</u> watch TV in the afternoon.*
20. *Chetan <u>seldom</u> smokes after dinner.*

Exercise 3

Fill in the blanks with words in brackets as adjective or adverb.

1. He __________ reads the book. (quick)
2. Madhuri is a __________ girl. (pretty)
3. The class is __________ loud today. (terrible)
4. Manoj is a __________ singer. (good)
5. You can __________ open this tin. (easy)
6. It's a __________ day today. (terrible)
7. She sings the song __________. (good)
8. He is a __________ driver. (careful)
9. He __________ drives the car (careful).
10. The dog barks __________ . (loud)
11. Shyam works __________ . (slow)

Answers

1. *He <u>quickly</u> reads the book.*
2. *Madhuri is a <u>pretty</u> girl.*
3. *The class is <u>terribly</u> loud today.*
4. *Manoj is a <u>good</u> singer.*
5. *You can <u>easily</u> open this tin.*
6. *It's a <u>terrible</u> day today. (terrible)*
7. *She sings the song <u>well</u>.*
8. *He is a <u>careful</u> driver.*
9. *He <u>carefully</u> drives the car.*
10. *The dog barks <u>loudly</u>.*
11. *Shyam works <u>slowly</u>.*

Exercise 4

Find the adjective in the first sentence and fill the gap with the adverb.

1. Joanne is happy. She smiles__________.
2. The boy is loud. He shouts__________.
3. Her English is fluent. She speaks English__________.
4. Our mum was angry. She spoke to us__________.
5. My neighbour is a careless driver. He drives__________.
6. The painter is awful. He paints__________.

7. Jim is a wonderful piano player. He plays the piano__________.
8. This girl is very quiet. She often sneaks out of the house____________.
9. She is a good dancer. She dances really__________.
10. This exercise is simple. You__________have to put one word in each space.

Answers

1. *happily*
2. *loudly*
3. *fluently*
4. *angrily*
5. *carelessly*
6. *awfully*
7. *wonderfully*
8. *quietly*
9. *well*
10. *simply*

Exercise 5

Fill in the correct adverb form (comparative or superlative) of the adjectives in brackets.

1. I speak English ____________ now than last year (fluent)
2. She greeted me ____________ of all. (polite)
3. She smiled _______________ than before. (happy)
4. This girl dances _______________ of all. (graceful)
5. Could you write ______________ ? (clear)
6. Planes can fly _______________ than birds. (high)
7. He had an accident last year. Now, he drives ____________ than before. (careful)
8. Jim can run ___________ than John. (faster)
9. Our team played _____________ of all. (worst)
10. He worked ____________ than ever before. (harder)

Answers

1. *more fluently*
2. *most politely*
3. *more happily*
4. *most gracefully*
5. *more clearly*
6. *higher*
7. *more carefully*
8. *faster*
9. *worst*
10. *harder*

Prepositions

7

CHAPTER

A preposition may be defined as a connecting word depicting the relation of a noun or a noun substitute to some other word in the sentence.

Kinds of Prepositions

Prepositions are of five kinds:

1. **Simple Prepositions:**
   - at, by, of, for, in, on, off, out, till, to, up, with, through, etc.

1. **Compound Prepositions:**
   - about, across, against, before, beside, into, until, within, etc.

2. **Double Prepositions:**
   - from among, from beneath, from under, out of, etc.

3. **Participle Prepositions:**
   - accepting, considering, during, regarding, notwithstanding, etc.

4. **Phrase Prepositions:**
   - along with, according to, away from, because of, in place of, in spite of, etc.

Position of the Preposition

A preposition is generally placed before a noun or a pronoun it governs.

Examples

- She died of fever.
- I went up the hill.
- Agra is famous for the Taj Mahal

➢ ***Remember:***

A preposition is placed at the end of a sentence if:

1. A preposition governs a relative pronoun.

Examples

- *This is the girl who (whom) I was speaking of.*
- *Here is the book which you were looking for.*

The relative pronoun 'that' cannot take a proposition before it.

Examples

- *Here is the pen that you asked for.*
- *The boy spoiled the paper that I was writing on.*

A preposition is placed at the end of a sentence when relative pronoun is understood.

Examples

- *That is the boy I was speaking about.*
- *That is the house Mohan lives in.*

2. *If a preposition governs an interrogative pronoun or adverb.*

Examples

- *What are you looking at?*
- *Where are you going to?*

When the preposition is used with the infinitive placed at the end.

- *The knife is to cut with.*
- *Do you have a chair to sit in?*

Some Chief Relations Indicated by Prepositions

1. **'after'** and **'in'**
   When we speak of space of time, 'after' refers to the past; 'in' refers to the future.

Examples

- Anil came back after a week.
- Anil will come back in a week.

Both mean 'at the close of.'

2. **'in'** and **'within'**

   'In' means at the end of a given period of time; 'within' means before the end of the given period.

Examples

- My father will return in a month. (at the end of one month)
- My father will return within a month. (before the end of one month)

3. **'in'** and **'into'**

'In' denotes rest or motion inside anything; 'into' denotes motion or movement towards the inside of anything.

Examples

- The boy is in the garden. (rest inside)
- The boy is walking in the garden. (act of moving inside)
- The boy walked into the garden. (movement towards inside)

> ***Remember:***
>
> Be careful to write the two words 'in' and 'to' separately when the sense is separate.

Examples

- *He took her into the room. (towards inside the room)*
- *The snake crawled into its hole. (towards inside the hole)*
- *He took her in to dinner. (inside the house for dinner)*

4. **'at'** and **'in'**:

a. 'at' and 'in' are used while speaking of things which are in at rest or fixed at rest.

Examples

- He is at the top of the class.
- The students are sitting at their desks.
- He is lying in his bed.

b. In speaking of places, 'at' is used for a smaller place, and in for a bigger place.

Examples

- I live at Vaishali in Ghaziabad.
- Ram lives in Gurgaon.
- My uncle lives in Delhi.
- I was waiting for her at a shop in Green Park.

c. In speaking of time, we use 'at' for a point of time and 'in' for a period of time.

At five, at dawn, at sunset, at midnight, in the morning in May, in 2007

Example

- The train will arrive at seven o'clock in the evening.

➢ ***Remember***

1. *Regarding the phrases of time, 'morning', afternoon', and 'evening' are preceded by the preposition 'in', whereas 'dawn', 'daybreak', 'noon', 'midday' and 'midnight' are preceded by the preposition 'at'.*
2. *When these time phrases are qualified by 'last' or 'next' they are not preceded by any preposition.*

Examples

- *I shall read this book in the evening.*
- *I shall see you at night.*
- *The sun is hottest at midday.*
- *I met him last evening.*
- *I shall meet him next Sunday.*

5. **'on'** and **'upon':**

'on' shows rest, 'upon' shows movement.

Examples

- He sat on a bench.
- The cat jumped upon the table.

6. **'by'** and **'with':**

When something has been done by a person with the help of an instrument, a tool or weapon, we use 'by' for the agent or the doer of the action and 'with' for the instrument.

Examples

- The lion was killed by the hunter with a gun.
- The letter has been written by me with a pen.
- You cannot kill two birds with one stone.

7. **'between'** and **'among'**

'between' refers to two persons or things; 'among' refers to more than two.

Examples

- Distribute these sweets between John and Jack.
- He divided his property between his two sons.

- Distribute these sweets among the students of the class.
- The five robbers divided money among themselves.

8. **'till'** and **'to'**

'till' is used for time; 'to' is used for place.

Examples

- I slept till eight o' clock.
- He walked to the end of the road.

9. **'since',** and **'for'**

We use 'since' with a specific date or time. We use 'for' when we measure time (seconds, minutes, hours, days, months, years). 'For' refers to a period of time, not to a point of time, and should not be replaced by 'since' or 'from'.

Examples

- I have been living in this house since 1990.
- He's worked here since 2000.
- She's been sitting in the waiting room since half past two.
- I have not seen him since he left school.
- I have been ill for ten days.
- He held his breath for seven minutes.

10. **'beside'** and **'besides'**

'beside' means by the side of; 'besides' means in addition to.

Examples

- The child walked beside his mother.
- Besides being fined, he was beaten by the teacher.

11. **'on', 'over'** and **'above'**

'On' denotes contact with the surface on which something is lying. 'Above' denotes a higher position but does not imply contact or covering. 'Over' means a higher position as well as contact or directly above.

Examples

- This book is lying on the table.
- This house rises above all the houses in the city.
- At noon, the sun is over us.

12. 'ago' and **'before'**

'Ago' refers to the past time and 'before' denotes precedence between two events.

Examples

- He was married five years ago.
- He was married five years before his coming to Agra.

➢ ***Remember***

Examples

1. *It is wrong to place any preposition after 'order', 'reach', attack', 'resist', 'pick', 'pervade', 'request', 'proceed', 'succeed', 'inform', 'obey', 'resemble', 'assist', 'violate', 'combat', 'benefit', 'afford', 'accompany' etc. when these verbs are used in the active voice.*
    - *They have ordered two computers.*
    - *He reached Mumbai at 2 o' clock.*
    - *He attacked him brutally.*
    - *They have violated all social norms.*

Prepositions in Common Use

1. Prepositions of Time

At	used for fixed time	at 3.30, at sunrise, at noon, at sunset, at dawn.
	used for festivals coming at a fixed time every year	at Diwali, at Holi, at Christmas.
On	Used for a day or date	On Sunday, on Monday, on his birthday, on Christmas day, on 15th August
	Used for the part of a certain day/date	On Sunday morning, on the morning of the 15th August.
In	Used for a period of time	In the morning, in the evening, in March, in summer
During	Used for a known period of time	During my holidays, during the winter, during 2007, during the war, during his young age
By	Used for a certain time, at that time or before it, usually before it or up to that time	by 4 p.m., by evening
For	Used with a period of time	For twelve days, for six months, for two years, forever
Since	Used with a point of time	Since morning, since six o'clock

2. Prepositions of Place

In	Used with a country, a large city, a square, a street, a corner, a room, a forest, a field, or any enclosed space	In America, in Delhi, in a room, in a corner, in a forest
At	Used with a small village, an address, a certain point	At Hapur, at 24, at Vaishali, at my new address, at bus stop, at home, at work

3. Prepositions of Travel and Movement

By	We travel	By bus, by car, by train, by plane
On	We walk	On foot, (He comes to school on foot.)
	We ride	On horseback, on cycle, on bike
From....to	We travel	From our starting point to our destination.

Words followed by appropriate prepositions

Preposition must suit not only the sense intended by the writer, but also the idiom imposed by custom. Thus, in speaking of a death as caused by a disease, we say,

- He died of fever.

  But in speaking of death as caused by something else, we say,

- He died from a blow.

  Similarly, we agree 'with' a person but agree 'to' a proposal.

- I agree with you. (agree with somebody)
- I agree to your proposal. (agree to something)

➢ ***Remember***

1. *We agree to a proposal, with a person, on a price, in principle.*
2. *We argue about a matter, with a person, for or against a proposition.*
3. *We compare to show likenesses, with to show differences (sometimes similarities).*
4. *We correspond to a thing, with a person.*
5. *We differ from an unlike thing, with a person.*
6. *We live at an address, in a house or city, on a street, with other people.*

Prepositions with Nouns, Adjectives, and Verbs

Prepositions are sometimes so firmly joined to other words that they have practically become one word. This occurs in three categories: nouns, adjectives, and verbs.

1. Nouns and Prepositions		
approval of	fondness for	need for
awareness of	grasp of	participation in
belief in	hatred of	reason for
concern for	hope for	respect for
confusion about	interest in	success in
desire for	love of	understanding of

2. Adjectives and Prepositions		
afraid of	fond of	proud of
angry at	happy about	similar to
aware of	interested in	sorry for
capable of	jealous of	sure of
careless about	made of	tired of
familiar with	married to	worried about

3. Verbs and Prepositions		
apologize for	give up	prepare for
ask about	grow up	study for
ask for	look for	talk about
belong to	look forward to	think about
bring up	look up	trust in
care for	make up	work for
find out	pay for	worry about

Phrasal Verb

A combination of verb and preposition is called a **phrasal verb**. The word that is joined to the verb is then called a **particle**.

Examples

- The children were sitting around, doing nothing.
- The witness finally broke down on the stand.
- Our boss called off the meeting.
- She looked up her old boyfriend.

Unnecessary Prepositions

In everyday speech, we fall into some bad habits, using prepositions where they are not necessary. It would be a good idea to eliminate these words altogether, but we must be especially careful not to use them in formal, academic prose.

Examples

- She met ~~up with~~ the new coach in the hallway.

- The book fell off ~~of~~ the desk.
- He threw the book out ~~of~~ the window.
- She wouldn't let the cat inside ~~of~~ the house. [or use "in"]
- Where did they go ~~to~~?
- Put the lamp ~~in~~ back of the couch. [use "behind" instead]
- Where is your college ~~at~~?

REVIEW EXERCISES

Exercise 1

Complete the following sentences with the correct preposition: **at, in,** or **on.**

1. Will you wait for me _____ the bus stop?
2. Jane is _____ her bedroom.
3. Daria's books are lying _____ the floor.
4. The girls didn't want to spend a long time _____ the carnival.
5. I let the cat sit _____ my lap, but then suddenly it jumped _____ my face!
6. Do you live _____ the city or _____ the country side?
7. Sunil arrived _____ the school building just in time.
8. The rancher built a fence to keep his cows _____ the pasture.
9. Kabir and Sahil are out practicing _____ the football field.
10. From afar, Heathcliff could see a light _____ the window.
11. The old house had so much grime _____ the windows that Bradley could hardly see inside.
12. The shepherd boy grazed his flock _____ the grassy hillside.
13. The audience threw tomatoes _____ the terrible comedian.
14. Wrestling isn't real; those guys _____ the ring are just pretending.
15. Anil works _____ the field of network administration, while Madhur works _____ web design.
16. The car stalled and got stuck _____ the street.
17. Andrew lives _____ Third Street.
18. If he doesn't make any money on his book, he'll be out _____ the street.
19. I'll use my cellular phone when I'm _____ the bus, but never while I'm _____ the car.
20. Passengers are not allowed to use electronic devices _____ airplanes during takeoff and landing.

Answers

1. *at* 2. *in* 3. *on*
4. *at* 5. *in, at* 6. *in, at*

7. *at*	8. *in*	9. *at*
10. *in*	11. *on*	12. *in*
13. *at*	14. *in*	15. *in, at*
16. *in*	17. *on*	18. *on*
19. *in* 20. *on*		

Exercise 2

Complete the following sentences with the correct preposition: to, toward, on, onto, in, or into. Some sentences may have more than one possible correct answer.

1. Anil has returned ______ his home town.
2. The dog jumped ______ the lake.
3. Are the boys still swimming ______ the pool?
4. The boy fell ______ the floor.
5. The plane landed ______ the runway.
6. We drove ______ the river for an hour, but turned north before we reached it.
7. The kids climbed ______ the monkey bars.
8. Judy got ______ her friend's car.
9. The baby spilled his cereal ______ the floor.
10. We cried to the man on the ladder, "Hang ______!"
11. I just called ______ say I love you.
12. Mahesh and Neeraj moved the table ______ the dining room.
13. Anil left your keys ______ the table.
14. Dr. Gupta apologized for interrupting us, and told us to carry ______ with our discussion.
15. I'd like ______ ask you a question.
16. Hari drove Mike ______ the airport.
17. The girl almost fell ______ the river.
18. The waitress noticed that there was no more Diet Pepsi ______ Arun's glass.
19. Lee and Sarah took the bus that was heading ______ the university.
20. Mary jumped ______ the stage and danced.

Answers

1. *to*	2. *in/into*	3. *in*
4. *on/onto*	5. *on*	6. *toward*
7. *on/onto*	8. *in/into*	9. *on*
10. *on*	11. *to*	12. *into*

13. *on* 14. *on* 15. *to*
16. *to* 17. *in/into* 18. *in*
19. *toward* 20. *on/onto*

Exercise 3

Complete the following sentences with the correct prepositions.

1. Agra is famous ________ Taj.
2. My son is afraid ________ the dark.
3. Maria is married ________ my cousin.
4. The second hotel was different________ the first.
5. I graduated from college ______2002.
6. I like to go to bed ________ midnight on Saturdays.
7. He migrated to Britain five years ________.
8. The artist had been painting ________ two decades before he sold his first painting.
9. In Europe autumn begins ________ September.
10. We always eat a roast dinner ________Christmas day.

Answers

1. *for* 2. *of* 3. *to*
4. *from* 5. *in* 6. *at*
7. *ago* 8. *for* 9. *in*
10. *on*

Exercise 4

Complete the following sentences with the correct prepositions.

1. I've been studying Italian ________I was five years old.
2. The chairman of the board has been employed in the finance industry ________1984.
3. I had a crash yesterday afternoon. Fortunately I didn't do too much damage _____ my car.
4. I wouldn't want his shift. He has to wake up ______3 am everyday.
5. I don't know what time they'll be back this evening. It all depends ________ the road conditions today.
6. I have to go________ a check-up next week.
7. I called in to make an appointment and I can see the doctor ______ 3 pm.
8. I'm meeting an old friend for lunch ________ noon.
9. I haven't seen her ________ a long time.
10. What are you doing ________ Christmas Day?

Answers

1. *since* 2. *since* 3. *to*
4. *at* 5. *on* 6. *for*
7. *at* 8. *at* 9. *for*
10. *on*

Exercise 5

Complete the following sentences with the correct prepositions.

1. I'm tired ________ waiting for you.
2. I haven't smoked __________ ages.
3. The police car chased the robbers _______ the streets.
4. You can look the word ____________ in a dictionary.
5. She had problems __________ reading the instructions.
6. I'm looking________ my key. Has anyone found it?
7. The song was written __________ Madonna.
8. I can't come to the party. Don't wait_________ me.

Answers

1. *of* 2. *for* 3. *through*
4. *up* 5. *in* 6. *for*
7. *by* 8. *for*

Exercise 6

For each question, choose the single best answer.

1. My best friend lives ______ Akbar Road.
   a. in
   b. on
   c. at
2. I'll be ready to leave ____ about twenty minutes.
   a. in
   b. on
   c. at
3. Since he met his new girlfriend, John never seems to be ______ home.
   a. on
   b. in
   c. at

4. The child responded to his mother's demands ______ throwing a tantrum.
   a. with
   b. by
   c. from
5. I think she spent the entire afternoon ______ the phone.
   a. on
   b. in
   c. at
6. I will wait ______ 6:30, but then I'll go home.
   a. from
   b. until
   c. at
7. The police caught the thief _____ the corner of Cascade and Plum Streets.
   a. from
   b. in
   c. at
8. My fingers were injured so my sister had to write the note _____ me.
   a. for
   b. with
   c. to
9. I am not interested _____ buying a new car now.
   a. to
   b. for
   c. in
10. What are the main ingredients ______ this casserole?
    a. about
    b. of
    c. to
11. My best friend, John, is named ______ his great-grandfather.
    a. after
    b. to
    c. about
12. Grandpa stayed up ______ two in the morning.
    a. for
    b. since
    c. until
13. My parents have been married ______ forty-nine years.
    a. since
    b. for
    c. unti

14. He usually travels to Philadelphia _______ train.
    a. by
    b. at
    c. with
15. You frequently see this kind of violence ____ television.
    a. with
    b. in
    c. on
16. I told Mom we'd be home _______ an hour or so.
    a. to
    b. in
    c. at
17. I was visiting my best friend _____ the hospital.
    a. of
    b. in
    c. at
18. The professor _______ South Africa amazed the American students with her stories.
    a. from
    b. of
    c. in
19. I'll see you ____ home when I get there.
    a. by
    b. in
    c. at
20. It's been snowing ________ Christmas morning.
    a. since
    b. for
    c. until

Answers

1. *b*	2. *a*	3. *c*
4. *b*	5. *a*	6. *b*
7. *c*	8. *a*	9. *c*
10. *b*	11. *a*	12. *c*
13. *b*	14. *a*	15. *c*
16. *b*	17. *c*	18. *a*
19. *c*	20. *a*	

Conjunctions

8

CHAPTER

A conjunction or connective is a word used to connect words, phrases, and clauses.

- John and Mary went to the store <u>and</u> the library.
- Vipul read the book <u>or</u> the magazine.
- The horse ate the straw <u>but</u> the cow ate the hay.

Kinds of Conjunction

Conjunctions are mainly divided into the following classes: Co-coordinating and Subordinating conjunctions. In addition, there are correlative and compound conjunctions.

1. Coordinating conjunctions

A coordinating conjunction connects words, phrases and clauses that are of the same type: (nouns, verbs, independent clauses, dependent clauses, phrases). These are and, as, but, for, nor, or, yet, so, otherwise, as well as etc.

Examples

- John <u>and</u> Mary went to the store.
- Vipul smiled <u>and</u> laughed at the joke.
- He is poor <u>but</u> he is honest.
- Steve ran out of the store <u>and</u> into the street.

Kinds of Coordinating Conjunctions

Coordinative conjunctions are of four kinds: Cumulative, Alternative, Adversative, Illustrative.

i. Cumulative Conjunction

Cumulative conjunctions add one statement or fact to another. They are not only....but also, and, both and, also, too, as well as, now, not less than etc.

Examples

- He is not only rich but also honest.
- He is both a singer and dancer.
- The one received a prize and the other was promoted.
- Mira as well as Ria is guilty.

ii. Alternative Conjunction

Alternative conjunctions express a choice between one statement and another. They are either…or, neither…nor, else, otherwise, or. Either Ram or Shyam is guilty.

Examples

- I have neither a pen nor a paper.
- Run fast else you will miss the bus.
- Work hard (or/else/otherwise) you will fail.

iii. Adversative Conjunction

Adversative conjunctions express contrast between two statements. They are however, whereas, while, only, still, yet, but, nevertheless.

Examples

- He worked hard, still he failed.
- He was angry, but he kept quiet.
- Go where you like, only do not stay here.
- He is a rich man, while/whereas his father was very poor.

iv. Illustrative Conjunction

By these conjunctions one statement is inferred or proved from another. They are: then, for, therefore, so.

Examples

- He is honest, therefore he is respected.
- It is time to go, let us start then.
- He was innocent, so he was pardoned.
- He will die some day, for all men are mortal.

2. Subordinate Conjunction

A subordinating conjunction joins a dependent clause with an independent clause to form a complex sentence. These are after, although, because, before, how, if, until, when, as, since, then, though, if, that, whether, while etc.

Examples

- He left the game before it was over.
- He was put into jail as he had committed a theft.
- When I went to her place, she was not in.
- He knew that he would win a prize.
- I shall not attend his party unless he invites me.
- After she had learned to drive, Alice felt more independent.
- If the paperwork arrives on time, your cheque will be mailed on Tuesday.

Kinds of Subordinating Conjunctions

Subordinate conjunctions may be further classified according to the purpose which they serve. These conjunctions denote:

i. **Time**
then, before, after, as, while, so long, as long, till, since, until

ii. **Cause or Reason**
since, because, for, as

iii. **Purpose**
that, lest

iv. **Effect or Result**
that

i. **Condition**
if, unless, provided, that, as if, whether or not

ii. **Place**
where, whence, whither

iii. **Manner or Extent**
as, far as, according as

iv. **Comparison**
as-as, no less than, as much as, than

ix. **Concession or Contrast**
though, although, yet, however, notwithstanding

3. Correlative Conjunctions

Correlative Conjunctions are always used in pairs to join two concepts together into one thought. The most common correlative conjunctions are both...and, either...or, neither...nor, not only...but also, so...as, and whether...or.

Examples

- <u>Both</u> my grandfather <u>and</u> my father worked in the steel plant.
- <u>Either</u> the cow <u>or</u> the horse won first prize at the fair.
- I am trying to decide <u>whether</u> to go to medical school <u>or</u> to go to law school.
- The explosion destroyed <u>not only</u> the school <u>but also</u> the neighbouring bus stop.
- She wants <u>not only</u> money <u>but also</u> fame.
- Neither the car nor the truck would start on the cold morning.
- It is <u>both</u> good <u>and</u> cheap.

4. Compound Conjunctions

There are also compound conjunctions, each consisting of a combination of words. Some of them are: in order that, provided that, as soon as, though, even if, on condition that.

Examples

- He took medicine <u>so that</u> he might recover.
- <u>As soon as</u> I reached the station, the train left.
- I agree to these terms <u>provided that</u> you will put your signature.

Position of Corrective Conjunctions

The position of corrective conjunction in the sentence is very important. Careless use of such conjunctions as 'and', 'as', 'but', & 'while' conceals the exact relationship of meaning that one intends to convey.

1. **Do not use the conjunction 'as' in sentences where it could imply either time or cause.**
    - Faulty: As the river rose to flood stage, many people fled to higher ground.
      Revised: When the river rose to flood stage, many people fled to higher ground. (Time intended)
      Revised: Because the river rose to flood stage, many people fled to higher ground. (Cause intended)
2. **Do not use the conjunction 'as' in the sentence of 'whether' or 'that'.**
    - Faulty: I don't know as I want to go tomorrow.
      Revised: I don't know whether/that I want to go tomorrow.
3. **Use the conjunction 'but' to connect contrasted sentences.**

- Faulty: He was so healthy in college, and today he is in poor physical condition.
  Revised: He was so healthy in college, but today he is in poor physical condition.

4. Do not use the preposition 'like' as a substitute for the conjunctions 'as if' or 'as though' in formal writing.

- Faulty: He looks like he were exhausted.
  Revised: He looks as if/as though he were exhausted.(formal)
  He looks like he is exhausted. (Informal)

5. Do not use the conjunction 'while' in the sense of 'and' 'but'.

- Faulty: John is a doctor, while Ray is an engineer.
  Revised: John is a doctor and Ray is an engineer.
- Faulty: Monday was a good day, while Tuesday was warmer.
  Revised: Monday was a good day, but Tuesday was warmer.

6. Do not use the conjunction 'while' in cases where time or concession is intended.

- Faulty: While I was working at night in the library, I saw John often.
  Revised: When I was working at night in the library, I saw John often. (Time intended)
  Although I was working at night in the library, I saw John often. (Concession intended)

7. Unless it is essential, place the formal connectives such as, however, therefore, nevertheless, etc. within the sentence rather than at the beginning.

- Faulty: Therefore, the committee decided to postpone the meeting.
  Revised: The committee, therefore, decided to postpone the meeting.
- Faulty: However, we realized that the case was hopeless.
  Revised: We, however, realized that the case was hopeless.

REVIEW EXERCISES

Exercise I

In the following sentences replace any connectives that are used weakly or inaccurately:

1. She decided to take route 8 to New York, as she had taken it once before.
2. Defeated in 1964, Richard Nixon did not know, as he ever wanted to run for office again.
3. My parents bought a new house and they still like the old one.

4. While it was very cold, I continued to study.
5. I won a national merit scholarship but I was very proud.
6. I don't know if I could paint, as I have never tried.
7. I really don't feel like I should take the risk of going out in this weather-not with the cold I have.
8. She was dead tired, but she lay down to rest.
9. As the furnace broke down, the superintendent closed the office.
10. Please let us know if the goods arrived safely.
11. This paper is white, while the other is grey.
12. The examiner then makes enquiries of the financial condition of the firm.
13. These trips are written up fully by the monthly magazine bulletin.
14. I argued with him for a long time and I could not bring him to my point of view.
15. The dog is always to be found in the kitchen and in the garden.
16. He came, he saw and he conquered.
17. The house is very old and is well preserved.
18. Most children like milk or cookies.
19. What you say but what you do are two different things.
20. Neither the car or the truck would start on the cold morning.
21. Not only did he lose his keys, but he lost his wallet.
22. Ganesh had to begun his thesis over again while his computer crashed.
23. As it is raining, we have an umbrella.
24. Although he ran the race in his fastest time, but he still lost.
25. Although there was no way he could write the letter, he wrote it anyway.

Answers

1. *She decided to take route 8 to New York because she had taken it once before.*
2. *Defeated in 1964, Richard Nixon did not know whether/that he ever wanted to run for office again.*
3. *My parents bought a new house but they still like the old one.*
4. *Although it was very cold, I continued to study.*
5. *I won a national merit scholarship and I was very proud.*
6. *I don't know if I could paint because I have never tried.*
7. *I really don't feel as if I should take the risk of going out in this weather, not with the cold I have.*
8. *She was dead tired and she lay down to rest.*
9. *Because the furnace broke down, the superintendent closed the office. (Time intended) When the furnace broke down, the superintendent closed the office. (Cause intended)*
10. *Please let us know whether the goods arrived safely.*
11. *This paper is white, and/where as the other is grey.*

12. *The examiner then makes enquiries about/regarding the financial condition of the firm.*
13. *These trips are written up fully in the monthly magazine bulletin.*
14. *I argued with him for a long time but I could not bring him to my point of view.*
15. *The dog is always to be found in the kitchen or in the garden.*
16. *He came, he saw, he conquered.*
17. *The house is very old but is well preserved.*
18. *Most children like milk and cookies.*
19. *What you say and what you do are two different things.*
20. *Neither the car nor the truck would start on the cold morning.*
21. *Not only did he lose his keys, but also his wallet.*
22. *Ganesh had to begun his thesis over again when his computer crashed.*
23. *Because it is raining, we have an umbrella.*
24. *Although he ran the race in his fastest time, he still lost.*
25. *While there was no way he could write the letter, he wrote it anyway.*

Exercise 2

Fill in the blanks with suitable conjunctions:

1. We will visit Australia __________ New Zealand during our next visit.
2. My teeth were hurting __________ I made an appointment to go the dentist.
3. Have you seen __________ heard the latest musical by Lalit Mohan?
4. I wanted to go to the rock concert __________ all the tickets were already sold out.
5. I wanted to eat Sushi for dinner __________ I went to a Japanese restaurant.
6. I wanted to eat fish for lunch ________ the fish and chip shop had closed for the day.
7. I am going to do my homework __________ take a shower when I get home from school.
8. My father wanted to watch a soccer match on television ________ my mother was already watching another program.
9. My brother wanted to buy a novel ________ I went to the book store after I finished work.
10. I wanted to visit my grandmother last week ________ she had an accident and had to be taken to hospital.

Answers:

1. *and*	2. *so*	3. *or*
4. *but*	5. *so*	6. *but*
7. *and*	8. *but*	9. *so*
10. *but*		

Interjections

9

CHAPTER

Interjections are words or phrases used to exclaim or protest or command like Oh!, Um or Ah! They sometimes stand by themselves, but are often contained within a larger structure.

- Wow! I won the lottery!
- Oh, I don't know about that.
- Ouch, that hurt!
- Oh no, I forgot that the exam was today.
- Hey! Put that down!
- I heard one guy say to another guy, "He has a new car, eh?"
- I don't know about you but, good lord, I think taxes are too high!

When interjections are inserted into a sentence, they have no grammatical connection to the sentence. Interjections of mild emotions are set off from the rest of the sentence with a comma. If the interjection is more forceful, however, it is followed with an exclamatory mark (!). Interjections have no real grammatical value and are rarely used in formal or academic writing.

The table below shows some interjections with examples.

interjection	*meaning*	*example*
ah	expressing pleasure	"Ah, that feels good."
	expressing realization	"Ah, now I understand."
	expressing resignation	"Ah well, it can't be helped."
	expressing surprise	"Ah! I've won!"
alas	expressing grief or pity	"Alas, she's dead now."
dear	expressing pity	"Oh dear! Does it hurt?"
	expressing surprise	"Dear me! That's a surprise!"
eh	asking for repetition	"It's hot today." "Eh?" "I said it's hot today."
	expressing enquiry	"What do you think of that, eh?"
	expressing surprise	"Eh! Really?"
	inviting agreement	"Let's go, eh?"
er	expressing hesitation	"Lima is the capital of...er...Peru."

hello, hullo	expressing greeting	"Hello John. How are you today?"
	expressing surprise	"Hello! My car's gone!"
hey	calling attention	"Hey! look at that!"
	expressing surprise, joy etc.	"Hey! What a good idea!"
hi	expressing greeting	"Hi! What's new?"
hmm	expressing hesitation, doubt or disagreement	"Hmm. I'm not so sure."
oh, o	expressing surprise	"Oh! You're here!"
	expressing pain	"Oh! I've got a toothache."
	expressing pleading	"Oh, please say 'yes'!"
Ouch, ah	expressing pain	"Ouch! That hurts!"
uh	expressing hesitation	"Uh...I don't know the answer to that."
uh-huh	expressing agreement	"Shall we go?" "Uh-huh."
um, umm	expressing hesitation	"85 divided by 5 is...um...17."
well	expressing surprise	"Well I never!"
	introducing a remark	"Well, what did he say?"

REVIEW EXERCISES

Exercise 1

Underline the interjection in each sentence.

1. Brrr! The theater is as cold as ice!
2. Aha! There are some empty seats!
3. Ouch! Someone stepped on my toe!
4. Well, I suppose I should have studied more!
5. I wish that giggling would stop. Shhh!
6. Say, who told you about the party?
7. Hooray! We won the championship!
8. Help! I can't hold on any longer!
9. Hey! Leave my friend alone!
10. Wow! I never thought she's going out with him!

Answers

1. Brrr 2. Aha 3. ouch 4. well 5. shhh 6. say 7. hooray 8. help 9. hey 10. wow

Exercise 2

Use an appropriate interjection of your own for each of the emotions listed.

1. grief ____________________
2. joy ____________________
3. confusion ____________________
4. astonishment____________________

5. severe pain___________
6. silence_____________
7. attention______________
8. remark_____________
9. relief___________
10. greeting__________

Answers

1. *alas*	2. *Wow/ Hooray/Yahoo*	3. *hmm/uh*
4. *oh/o*	5. *ouch/oh/ah*	6. *shh*
7. *hey*	8. *well*	9. *aha*
10. *hi*		

Exercise 3

Rewrite each sentence below. Begin with the interjection in parentheses. Add the correct punctuation after each interjection and at the end of each sentence.

1. They're announcing the winners (Shh)
2. I guess I'll have to make a speech (Well)
3. That wasn't so bad after all (Phew)
4. I don't know if I can stand it any longer (Help)
5. Are you busy? (Say)
6. Sit still (Oh)
7. You shouldn't have done that (No)
8. Either you quit doing that or I will leave (Stop)

Answers

1. *They're announcing the winners. Shh!*
2. *Well, I guess I'll have to make a speech!*
3. *Phew, That wasn't so bad after all!*
4. *Help, I don't know if I can stand it any longer!*
5. *Say, are you busy?*
6. *Oh, sit still!*
7. *No, you shouldn't have done that.*
8. *Stop! Either you quit doing that or I will leave!*

Exercise 4

1. Which of the following interjections is not an expression of surprise or wonder?

   a. Gee! b. Gosh! c. Boo!

2. You are vegetarian and you are offered a dish of raw meat. What do you think?
   a. Ugh! b. Hurrah! c. Yippee!
3. Somebody has just stepped on your toe. Which interjection would best fit the situation?
   a. Yoo-hoo! b. Ouch! c. Eh!
4. You are most likely to hear or use the interjection boo ___.
   a. at a theatrical performance
   b. while listening to a political speech
   c. on both of the above mentioned occasions
5. ___, Mary! Come here! I want to talk to you.
   a. Oops b. Mmm c. Hey
6. 'Ta' is synonymous of ___.
   a. take it easy b. thank you c. tra-la-la
7. Your children are making a lot of noise and you want to hear the news on the radio. How do you urge silence?
   a. Shh! b. Tut-tut. c. Ow!
8. ___! The spinach soup is out of this world!
   a. Mmm b. Yuk c. Uh
9. A: I scored 660 points at the TOEFL test!
   B: ___! That's amazing!
   a. Wow b. Aha c. Woe
10. Which is the odd man out? (Which word fits in a different group?)
    a. hey b. yoo-hoo c. oops
11. The interjection 'Woe!' is a synonym of ___.
    a. Alas! b. Bother! c. Really!

Answers

1. *a* 2. *a* 3. *b*
4. *b* 5. *c* 6. *c*
7. *a* 8. *a* 9. *a*
10. *c* 11. *a*

Articles 10

CHAPTER

The words 'a', 'an', and 'the' are known as articles. The articles are not a separate part of speech, they are a form of adjectives, called **demonstrative adjectives**. 'A' and 'an' are called the indefinite articles because they do not refer to any particular person or thing. 'The' is called the definite article because it is used to refer to a particular or definite person or thing. 'A' and 'an' are used only with singular nouns. 'The' can be used with both singular and plural nouns. As a general rule, an article is used before a countable singular noun.

Examples

- I saw a boy in the park. (any boy)
- The boy was eating an orange. (The boy= particular boy, an orange=any orange)
- The boys were playing in the park.

Uses of 'A'

'A' is used:

➢ **a** + singular noun beginning with a consonant; as: a cat, a book, a girl, a pen, a baby etc.

➢ **a** + singular noun beginning with a consonant sound; as: a unit, a university, a united, a universal, a European (for here, 'u' is pronounced as 'yoo' not as an open vowel 'u'), a one rupee note, a one eyed man (for here, 'o' is pronounced as 'w' and not as an open vowel) etc.

➢ The article 'a' is mainly used in the following cases:

1. In the sense of one:

   - I bought a dozen mangoes.
   - A stitch in time saves nine.
   - Twelve inches make a foot.

2. In the sense of some, any or a single:
    - I have a great regard for him.
    - He did not speak a word in the meeting.
    - There is not a man here who will not support you.
3. in the sense of the same:
    - Birds of a feather flock together.
4. In the sense of a certain:
    - One evening a student came to my house.
    - Today I saw a beggar in the street.
5. In the sense of every
    - He gets a salary of Rs. 10,000 a month.
    - Rice costs 30 Rs. a kilo.
    - I earn Rs. 500 a week.
6. To represent the whole class:
    - A cow is a useful animal.
    - An ass is a beast of burden.
    - A child cries when he is hungry.
7. Before a proper noun to make it a common noun:
    - He is a Milton. (an inspired poet)
    - He is a second Newton. (a great scientist)
    - Here comes a Daniel. (a wise and upright judge)
8. Before a proper noun to imply that the person is a stranger to the speaker:
    - A Mr. Gupta is waiting for you. (A man called Mr. Gupta)
    - A Dr. Sinha called when you were away.
    - A Miss Meeta rang an hour ago. (a girl called Meeta)
9. In exclamation (before a singular countable noun)
    - What a lovely sight!
    - What a beautiful dress!
10. In certain phrases:
    - A bad cold
    - As a rule
    - A severe pain
11. With most when the superlative is used in the sense of 'very' or 'very much'.
    - This is a most beautiful painting.
    - This is a most fantastic story.

Uses of 'An'

'An' is simply a variant of 'a'. It is used:

- an + singular noun beginning with a vowel:
    - an elephant
    - an inkpot
    - an uncle
- an + singular noun beginning with a vowel sound:
    - an hour
    - an honest man
    - an heir (for here, word is beginning with a silent or aspirared 'h')
- an + abbreviations beginning with a vowel sound:
    - an SDO
    - an MLA
    - an MP
    - an MA

Uses of 'The'

- 'The' definite article is used before singular and plural nouns when the noun is particular or specific.
- **Remember:**

'The' signals that the noun is definite. It refers to a particular member of a group. Compare the indefinite and definite articles in the following examples:

	Indefinite (a or an)	Definite (the)
Singular	**a** dog (any dog)	**the** dog (that specific dog)
	an apple (any apple)	**the** apple (that specific apple)
Plural	**some** dogs (any dogs)	**the** dogs (those specific dogs)
	some apples (any apples)	**the** apples (those specific apples)

- 'The' article 'the' is mainly used in the following cases:

1. When we speak of things which are unique in themselves.
    - Singular nouns : The sun, the moon, the earth, the sea, the sky
    - Plural Nouns : The Himalayas, the scriptures

- Remember: 'God' does not take an article before it.

2. When we speak of a particular person or thing:
    - Call the boy (who is) waiting outside.
    - The girl who stood first was given a prize.

3. When a singular countable noun is mentioned at first, we use 'a/an'. When we refer again to the noun already mentioned we use 'the'
   - I saw a saint. The saint came to me.
   - I gave money to the saint.
4. When a particular person or thing is meant
   - I dislike the fellow.
   - The students are playing in the park.
   - The book you mentioned is out of print.
   - I have invited the Guptas to tea.
5. When a singular noun is used to represent the whole class of things to which it belongs
   - The camel is the ship of the desert.
   - The dog is a faithful animal.
   - The lion is the king of beasts.

     ➢ Remember:

     1. A whole class of things can be indicated in three ways:
        - A cow is a useful animal.
        - The cow is a useful animal.
        - Cows are useful animals.

All the three sentences mean the same thing.

2. 'Man', 'woman' used in the general sense to denote the whole class never take an article.
   - Man is mortal.
   - Woman is man's mate.

6. Before an adjective to make it a noun in the plural. In this case it refers only to human beings.
   - The rich should help the poor. (Rich people. Poor people)
   - The literate are generally polite. (literate people)
   - The educated should teach the illiterates. (educated people, uneducated people)
7. Before an adjective in the superlative degree
   - The best painting will get a prize.
   - He is the greatest man of the world.
   - The darkest cloud has a silver lining.
8. Before comparative adjective to denote selection of the two
   - This is the more beautiful of the two dresses.
   - Radhika is the more intelligent of the two sisters.

9. Before an adjective to indicate an abstract idea
    - He is a lover of the good and the beautiful.
10. As an adverb with comparatives
    - The more you earn the more you spend.
    - The higher you go the cooler it is.
11. When an adjective functions as noun to denote nationality, party or community
    - The English
    - The French
    - The Indian
    - The Congress
12. Before a noun with special emphasis
    - He is the hero of the day.
    - This is just the book I want.
13. Before the names of oceans, seas, bays, gulfs, rivers, canals
    - The Arabian Sea
    - The Ganga
    - The Bay of Bengal
    - The Panama Canal
14. Before the names of directions
    - The north
    - The south
    - The east
    - The west
15. Before a range of mountains or a group of islands
    - The Himalayas
    - The Alps
    - The Andamans
    - The West Indies
    - The British Isles

        ➢ Remember: Single mountain or island do not take an article. We say Mount Abu, Mount Everest, Ceylon, Ireland, Sicily
16. Before a descriptive geographical name
    - The Punjab
    - The Uttar Pradesh
    - The United Kingdom

17. Before the name of a newspaper, magazine, or a well-known book
    - The Tribune
    - The Times of India
    - The Bible
    - The Gita
        - ➢ Remember: If the title of the book is the name of a person or if the author's name is given in genitive, no article is used; as Oliver Twist, Emma, Homer's Illiod, Balmiki's Ramayana
18. Before the name of a ship or an aeroplane
    - The Titanic
    - The Jaladurga
    - The Kanishka
19. Before the name of a public building
    - The Parliament House
    - The Town Hall
    - The Cinema
    - The Circus

Omission of Articles

The article is omitted:

1. Before a proper noun
    - Shakespeare was a great dramatist.
    - Delhi is the capital of India.
2. Before a common noun used in the universal sense
    - Man is mortal.
    - Boys like to play with balls.
3. Before an abstract noun
    - Honesty is the best policy.
    - Wisdom is better than wealth.
4. Before material noun
    - Iron and steel are used to make machines.
    - Gold is a precious metal.
5. Before a common noun used as a nominative of address
    - Come here boy.
    - Go outside child.
    - Students, why are you making noise?

6. Before the nouns such as school, hospital, church, temple, etc. when these words express their primary meaning.
   - He has gone to school. (to learn)
   - I go to temple every day.
   - She is still in bed.

But if these nouns are referred to as places of meeting or for other than primary purpose 'the' is used.

   - My mother went to the school to meet the principal.
   - I am going to the hospital to see my uncle.

7. Before the noun indicating seasons or festivals
   - We are going there at Holi.
   - Spring is the best time for shopping.
8. Before the names of meals as breakfast, lunch, tea, dinner, etc.
   - He invited me to dinner.

   But we say

   - I enjoyed the dinner you gave me.

   Because it has been made specific by the use of the clause 'you gave me'.
9. When countable nouns come in pairs
   - They are brother and sister.
   - Both husband and wife agreed with me.
10. When the noun is preceded by a demonstrative or distributive adjective like each, every, either, neither, this, that, some, any, other or number
    - Every man supported me.
    - There are forty boys in each class.
11. When the noun is used with possessive adjective like my, our, your, his, her, their, before etc.
    - This is my pen.
    - Where is your book?
    - Here is his shirt.

Repetition of the Article

1. a. I have a red and white shirt. (one shirt, partly red partly white)
   b. I have a red and a white shirt. (two shirts, one red and the other white)
2. a. The horse and tonga is at the door. (one horse attached to tonga)
   b. The horse and the tonga are at the door. (two horses one for riding and the other attached to tonga)
2. a. The poet and teacher was honoured. (one person)
   b. The poet and the teacher were honoured. (two persons)

3. a. He is a better writer than speaker. (one person who has both skills)
   b. He is a better writer than a speaker. (a comparison between two persons one writer and the other speaker)

Position of the articles

1. The article comes before its noun:
   - a boy, a girl, a cow
2. When a noun is qualified by an adjective the article is placed before the adjective
   - A young man, a clever girl, a good boy, a blue shirt, etc.
3. When the adjective is modified by an adverb, the article is placed before the adverb
   - This is a very good boy.
   - This is an extremely difficult work.
4. When a noun is qualified by 'such' or 'what' the article is placed after 'such' or 'what'
   - He is such a nice guy.
   - What a fine pen!
5. When the adjective is modified by too, how, so, the article is placed before the noun
   - How nice a boy.
   - So good a book.

   'The' follows all, half, both, double
   - He promised to get me half a dozen oranges.
   - Both the girls got the prize.
6. 'A' is used after many, quite, such
   - I have never seen such a wonderful movie.
   - He gave me quite a surprise.

REVIEW EXERCISES

Exercise I

Fill in the blanks with the appropriate article, '**a**', '**an**', or '**the**', or leave the space blank if no article is needed.

1. I want ____ apple from that basket.

2. _____ church on the corner is progressive.
3. Miss Lin speaks _____ Chinese.
4. I borrowed _____ pencil from your pile of pencils and pens.
5. One of the students said, "_____ professor is late today."
6. Vivek likes to play _____ volleyball.
7. I bought _____ umbrella to go out in the rain.
8. My daughter is learning to play _____ violin at her school.
9. Please give me _____ cake that is on the counter.
10. I lived on _____ Main Street when I first came to town.
11. Albany is the capital of _____ New York State.
12. My husband's family speaks _____ Polish.
13. _____ apple a day keeps the doctor away.
14. _____ ink in my pen is red.
15. Our neighbors have _____ cat and _____ dog.

Answers

1. *an*
2. *The*
3. *no article needed*
4. *a*
5. *the*
6. *no article needed*
7. *an*
8. *the*
9. *the*
10. *no article needed*
11. *no article needed*
12. *no article needed*
13. *An*
14. *The*
15. *a, a*

Exercise 2

Fill in the blanks with the appropriate articles:

1. __________new book-shop has been opened near our school.
2. __________Battle of Panipat is __________famous event in history.
3. __________earth moves round __________sun.
4. Oranges are sold by __________dozen.
5. We have __________understanding on this issue.
6. Kalidas is __________Shakespeare of India.
7. He hopes to return by __________4 o'clock flight.
8. Excuse me, I have__________urgent piece of work.
9. He is __________man I was speaking about.
10. Cow is __________useful animal.

Answers

1. *a*
2. *the, a*
3. *the, the*
4. *the*
5. *an*
6. *the*
7. *the*
8. *an*
9. *the*
10. *a*

Exercise 3

Fill in the blanks with the appropriate articles:

1. Copper is _________useful metal.
2. I first met him________year ago.
3. He is not____honourable man.
4. He returned after_____hour.
5. Milk is sold by________litre.
6. The children found ________egg in the nest.
7. Rustam is ______young Parsee.
8. _______lion is ________king of beasts.
9. I bought ____dog, _______ox, and_______horse.
10. _______rich should help_______poor.

Answers

1. *a*	2. *a*	3. *an*
4. *an*	5. *the*	6. *an*
7. *a*	8. *The, the*	9. *a, an, a*
10. *The, the*		

Exercise 4

Insert articles where necessary:

1. Neil Armstrong was first man to walk on moon.
2. It was proudest moment of my life.
3. Only best quality is sold by us.
4. He neglects attending church though church is only a few yards from his residence.
5. My favourite flower is rose.
6. Brave soldier lost arm in battle.
7. I like to live in open air.
8. Have you told him about accident?
9. River was spanned by iron bridge.
10. Doctor says it is hopeless case.

Answers

1. *Neil Armstrong was <u>the</u> first man to walk on the moon.*
2. *It was <u>the</u> proudest moment of my life.*
3. *Only <u>the</u> best quality is sold by us.*

4. *He neglects attending church though* _the_ *church is only a few yards from his residence.*
5. *My favourite flower is* _the_ *rose.*
6. *The Brave soldier lost* _an_ *arm in* _the_ *battle.*
7. *I like to live in* _the_ *open air.*
8. *Have you told him about* _the_ *accident?*
9. _The_ *river was spanned by* _an_ *iron bridge.*
10. *Doctor says it is* _a_ *hopeless case.*

Exercise 5

Fill in the blanks with the appropriate article.

1. There is ______ new English book on the desk.
2. She's reading ______ old comic.
3. They've got ______ idea.
4. He is drinking ______ cup of coffee.
5. The girl is ______ pilot.
6. Leipzig has got ______ airport.
7. This is ______ expensive bike.
8. Look! There's ______ bird flying.
9. My father is ______ honest person.
10. My friend likes to be ______astronaut.

Answers

1. *a*	2. *an*	3. *an*
4. *a*	5. *a*	6. *an*
7. *an*	8. *a*	9. *an*
10. *an*		

Exercise 6

Fill up the blanks with suitable articles:

1. Many ________ flower is born to blush unseen.
2. Yesterday ______ European was run over by ________lorry.
3. ________few miles from Srinagar ________river leaves ________ valley and enters ________dark gorge.
4. Honest men speak ________truth.
5. Copper is ________useful metal.
6. French defeated ________ Germans.
7. He is _____honour to his profession.

8. We started late in _____afternoon.
9. Only ________ best quality is sold by us.
10. Set back the clock; it is ________hour fast.

Answers

1. a	2. a, a	3. A, the, the, the
4. the	5. a	6. the
7. an	8. the	9. the
10. an		

Exercise 7

Fill in the blanks with the appropriate article if one is needed:

Though you can make ___1___ decision on purely economic grounds, buying ____2____ computer is often more like joining____3______religious cult. Buy ____4_____ Apple, for example, and almost by default you join Apple chairman Steve Jobs in his crusade against IBM. Every machine has its "users' groups" and ___5___ band of loyal enthusiasts who tout its merits. That makes it all ____6_____ more difficult for ____7_____ uninitiated to decide what machine to buy. Students have _____8_____ huge advantage, however. The computer companies are so eager for students' business (it builds "brand loyalty") that many offer huge discounts.

In the past six months, IBM, Apple, and others have brought out new computers, and ________9____fierce competition has forced prices down. Also, time is on your side: next year at this time you'll have even more choice and more computing power and features for ________10_____ same price. On _______11______other hand, this will probably be true for many years. So for those who need or want _________12_____computer now, it's ______13_____ great time to buy one.

Answers

1. *the*	2. *a*	3. *a*
4. *an*	5. *a*	6. *the*
7. *the*	8. *a*	9. *the*
10. *the*	11. *the*	12. *a*
13. *a*		

Exercise 8

Write the following paragraphs, inserting **'a'**, **'an'**, or **'the'** where needed.

Most people have fewer hours to give to time-consuming activities of clubs than they used to have, but most people in small town belong to club or two. One of clubs is likely to be social and benevolent organization, such as Rotary or Elks.

Business people are likely to belong, also to either Kiwanis Club or Lions. Such business people's organizations may meet as often as once a week in one of private dining rooms of town's leading hotel for lunch. They have good lunch, hear good program, and continue their fundraising program for worthy organization, such as local hospital.

Answer

Most working people have fewer hours to give to time-consuming activities of clubs than they used to have, but most people in ***a*** *small town belong to* ***a*** *club or two. One of* ***the*** *clubs is likely to be* ***a*** *social and benevolent organization, such as* ***the*** *Rotary or Elks. Business people are likely to belong, also to either* ***the*** *Kiwanis Club or* ***the*** *Lions. Such business people's organizations may meet as often as once a week in one of* ***the*** *private dining rooms of* ***the*** *town's leading hotel for lunch. They have* **a** *good lunch, hear* ***a*** *good program, and continue their fundraising program for* ***a*** *worthy organization, such as* ***a*** *local hospital.*

Tenses

11

CHAPTER

Tense denotes time. This is the form taken by a verb to show the time of the action and its completeness or incompleteness. There are three main divisions of time: past, present and future. Therefore, there are three main tenses in English.

1. **The Present Tense:** A verb that refers to present time is said to be in the Present Tense.
2. **The Past Tense:** A verb that refers to past time is said to be in the Past Tense.
3. **The Future Tense:** A verb that refers to future time is said to be in the Future Tense.

Examples

- I love my friends. (Present)
- I loved my friends. (Past)
- I will always love my friends. (Future)
- I play football today. (Present)
- I played football yesterday. (Past)
- I will play football tomorrow. (Future)

Each of these three tenses has four forms which denote various shades of meaning.

i. **Indefinite or Simple**: It simply states an action without indicating anything about its completeness or incompleteness.

• I write.	Present Indefinite
• I wrote.	Past Indefinite
• I shall write.	Future Indefinite

ii. **Imperfect or Continuous**: It indicates that the action is in progress (continuing) and is not yet complete.

• I am writing.	Present Continuous
• I was writing	Past Continuous
• I shall be writing.	Future Continuous

iii. Perfect: It indicates that the action has been completed or perfected.

- I have written. Present Perfect
- I had written. Past Perfect
- I shall have written. Future Perfect

iv. Perfect Continuous: It shows that the action which began sometime before is still continuing.

- I have been writing. Present Perfect Continuous
- I had been writing Past Perfect Continuous
- I shall have been writing. Future Perfect Continuous

All these sentences are in the active voice. Thus there are twelve forms of tenses in the active voice. But there are only eight in the passive voice.

Tense Table (verb 'go')

Tense	*Simple*	*Continuous*	*perfect*	*Perfect Continuous*
Present	go goes	am going is going are going	has gone have gone	has been going have been going
Past	went	was going were going	had gone	had been going
Future	will go shall go	will be going shall be going	will have gone shall have gone	will have been going shall have been going

REVIEW EXERCISE

Exercise I

Give the tenses of the verbs in the following sentences:

1. I wish you good morning.
2. We saw a movie last night.
3. Your suggestions have been totally rejected.
4. I shall see you tomorrow.
5. It's five o'clock, they will have arrived by now.
6. When the play ended we went home.
7. The girl is looking outside.
8. I was sleeping when you came to see me.
9. I shall have been writing a letter.
10. He has been suffering from fever since last Sunday.
11. Why do you often get late?
12. The child is no longer crying.
13. We shall be playing the match tomorrow.

14. I shall have finished this task by the end of this week.
15. He did not invite us to the party.

Answers

1. *Present Indefinite*
2. *Past Indefinite*
3. *Present Perfect*
4. *Future Indefinite*
5. *Future Perfect*
6. *Past Perfect*
7. *Present Continuous*
8. *Past Continuous*
9. *Future Perfect Continuous*
10. *Present Perfect Continuous*
11. *Present Indefinite*
12. *Present Continuous*
13. *Future Continuous*
14. *Future Perfect*
15. *Past Indefinite*

Exercise 2

Give the tenses of the verbs in the following sentences:

1. Hari is asking a question.
2. He helped his father last Sunday.
3. Seema lives with her mother.
4. He has written an e-mail.
5. There will be some rain in the north.
6. I did not see him yesterday.
7. Are you going to watch the new film?
8. I do not want to go there.
9. The cat is sitting on the wall.
10. Seema and her friend have just arrived in Mumbai.

Answers

1. *Present Continuous*
2. *Past Indefinite*
3. *Present Indefinite*
4. *Present Perfect*
5. *Future Indefinite*

6. *Past Indefinite*
7. *Future Continuous*
8. *Present Indefinite.*
9. *Present Continuous*
10. *Present Perfect*

Exercise 3

Give the tenses of the verbs in the following sentences:

1. They are riding a bike.
2. She looked at a picture.
3. We often take photos.
4. I have just had a cup of tea.
5. Alice will learn French next year.
6. Yesterday Shyam didn't listen to music.
7. She is going to tidy up the room.
8. Vibhu always sends text messages.
9. Karen is making breakfast now.
10. Have you ever been to Africa?

Answer

1. *Present Continuous*
2. *Past Indefinite*
3. *Present Indefinite*
4. *Present Perfect*
5. *Future Indefinite*
6. *Past Indefinite*
7. *Future Continuous*
8. *Present Indefinite*
9. *Present Continuous*
10. *Present Perfect*

USE OF THE TENSES

1. PRESENT TENSE

I. Present Indefinite or Simple

Examples		*Usage*
• He laughs.	Affirmative Sentence	Singular Noun+1st form of the verb+s/es

• We laugh.	Affirmative Sentence	Plural Noun+ 1st form of the verb
• He does not laugh.	Negative Sentence	Singular Noun+does not+1st form of the verb
• They do not laugh.	Negative Sentence	Plural Noun+do not+1st form of the verb
• Do they laugh?	Interrogative Sentence	Do/does+subject+1st form of the verb

➢ ***Remember:***

Simple present tense is used to express:

a. *General truth or permanent facts.*
   - *Two and two make four.*
   - *The earth moves round the sun.*

b. *An event taking place at the present moment.*
   - *He studies in B.Pharm.*
   - *I live in New Delhi.*
   - *There goes the vendor.*

c. *Daily routine, a habit or a custom.*
   - *She goes for a walk everyday.*
   - *They always speak the truth.*
   - *Why do you often get late?*

d. *An action, which must happen in the near future.*
   - *Her wedding comes off next week.*
   - *Hari goes to England next month.*

e. *To read or write a subordinate clause, when main clause refers to future.*
   - *If you work hard, you will pass.*
   - *We will wait here until he comes.*

f. *To quote someone.*
   - *Keats says, "A thing of beauty is a joy for ever."*

g. *Exclamation.*
   - *How well he plays flute!*
   - *Here comes the bird!*

ii. Present Continuous

Examples		*Usage*
• He is laughing. • We are laughing. • I am laughing.	Affirmative Sentence	Subject+be(is/am/are)+1st form of the verb+ing
• I am not laughing • She is not laughing. • They are not laughing.	Negative Sentence	Subject+be(is/am/are)+not+1st form of the verb+ing
• Are they laughing?	Interrogative Sentence	be(is/am/are)+Subject+ +1st form of the verb+ing

➢ ***Remember:*** *The present continuous tense is used to denote:*

a. An action, which is going on at the time of speaking.

- *I am reading a story now.*
- *We are waiting for a bus at the moment.*

b. An action which is likely to happen in the near future.

- *We are holding a meeting tomorrow.*
- *We are not going out tonight.*

iii. Present Perfect

Examples		*Usage*
• He has laughed. • We have laughed. • I have laughed.	Affirmative Sentence	Subject+has/have+3rd form of the verb
• He has not laughed. • They have not laughed.	Negative Sentence	Subject+has/have+not+3rd form of the verb
• Have they laughed? • Has he laughed?	Interrogative Sentence	Has/have +Subject+3rd form of the verb

➢ ***Remember:*** *The Present Perfect Tense is used to express:*

a. An action which has just been completed.

- *She has returned from Calcutta.*
- *I have solved two exercises so far.*
- *Have you finished your work?*

b. An action having taken place in the past and continuing in the present.

- *We have known him for three years.*
- *We have lived here for five years.*

iv. Present Perfect Continuous

Examples		*Usage*
• He has been laughing for ten minutes.	Affirmative Sentence	Subject+has/have been+1st form of the verb+ing
• He has not been laughing since 5 pm.	Negative Sentence	Subject+has/have+not+been1st form of the verb+ing
• Have they been laughing for five minutes? • Has he been laughing since 5 pm?	Interrogative Sentence	Has/have +Subject+been1st form of the verb+ing for/since

➢ ***Remember:*** *The Present Perfect Continuous Tense is used to express*

a. An action which began in the past but is still going on.

- *She has been reading a book since morning.*
- *I have been suffering from fever for two days.*

b. *An action which began in the past and has just been completed, but whose result is still in the present.*

- *My shoes are dirty because I have been washing my car.*
- *I have been cleaning my room since morning and I am very much tired now.*

REVIEW EXERCISES

Exercise 1

Fill in the blanks with the correct forms of the verb (Present Tense) given in brackets:

1. My uncle __________(stay) with us for last three weeks.
2. I usually__________ (sit) in the first row of the class.
3. It was cloudy in the morning but the sun__________(shine) now.
4. He __________ (live) in a village. City life may not suit him.
5. Deepa _____ never _________ by train. (travel)
6. Why _______ she_________?(cry)
7. Rahul __________ this book for the last two days. He ____not _________ yet. (finish)
8. Deepak __________ (come) here on holiday every year since 2002.
9. How long__________ (you wait) here?
10. It __________ (rain) for over 2 hours.
11. My brother_________ (fly) kites every Sunday.
12. The train_________ not ______ yet. (arrive)
13. Since when________ you______ for me? (wait)
14. My dog_________ (not eat) properly. I must take him to the vet.
15. I ___________ two questions so far. (solve)

Answers

1. *My uncle has been staying with us for last three weeks.*
2. *I usually sit in the first row of the class.*
3. *It was cloudy in the morning but the sun is shining now.*
4. *He has been living in a village. City life may not suit him.*
5. *Deepa has never travelled by train.*
6. *Why is she crying?*
7. *Rahul has been reading this book for the last two days. He has not finished it yet.*
8. *Deepak has been coming here on holiday every year since 2002.*

9. *How long have you been waiting here?*
10. *It is raining for over 2 hours.*
11. *My brother flies kites every Sunday.*
12. *The train has not arrived yet.*
13. *Since when have you been waiting for me?*
14. *My dog does not eat properly. I must take him to the vets.*
15. *I have solved two questions so far.*

Exercise 2

Fill in the blanks with the correct forms of the verbs given in brackets:

1. The scene at the lake ____(a)_____(be) very pleasant in the morning. Some boys____(b)________(swim)in the cool, fresh water. Little children _____(c)______(come) with their parents. They______(d)______(play)on the green grass at the moment. Those who ______(e)_______(complete) their morning exercises ________(f)_______(relax) before going home.

2. Drug addiction ____(a)______(become)a serious problem and the reasons for it ________(b)________(be) not difficult to find. The home environment ______(c)_____(be) a major contributory factor. Modern life ______(d)_____(become) very hectic. When both the parents ______(e)________(work) hard, they____(f)____(not find) spare time for their children. Lonely youngsters________(g)_____(try) to experiment with drugs. The parents realize the fact only when they __ (h)_________(become) drug addicts.

Answers

1. *(a) has become (b) are swimming (c) have come (d) are playing (e) have completed (f) are relaxing*
2. *(a) has become (b) are (c) is (d) has become (e) are working (f) do not find(g) try (h)have become*

2. PAST TENSE

i. Past Indefinite or Simple

Examples		*Usage*
• He walked. • We walked.	Affirmative Sentence	Subject+2nd form of the verb
• He did not walk.	Negative Sentence	Subject+did not+1st form of the verb
• Did they walk?	Interrogative Sentence	Did+subject+1st form of the verb

➤ ***Remember:***

The Past Indefinite Tense is used:

a. *When past showing time (yesterday, ago, last etc.) is given in the sentence.*

- *Hari came to my office yesterday.*
- *She went to the cinema last night.*
- *Last year I took my exams.*

b. *To express a past action or event.*

- *I saw many animals in the zoo.*
- *Graham Bell invented the telephone.*
- *I got married in 1992.*

c. *To express a habit or custom in the past.*

- *My grandfather drank tea every day.*
- *Gandhiji always spoke the truth.*

d. *To express an action going on at the time stated.*

- *She was watching the television when I went to her house.*
- *Yesterday when I went to see my friend, I found her door locked.*
- *When I was a child we always went to the seaside on bank holidays.*

e. *In clauses with if, as though, it's time, wish, would rather, if only*

- *If only I knew her response.(I do not know)*
- *I wish I were/was a bird.(I cannot be)*
- *Suppose we spent the next weekend at Goa? (we are not going to)*

ii. Past Continuous Tense

Examples		*Usage*
• He was walking. • We were walking.	Affirmative Sentence	Subject+was/were+1st form of the verb+ing
• You were not walking.	Negative Sentence	Subject+was/were+not+1st form of the verb+ing
• Was I walking?	Interrogative Sentence	Was+subject+1st form of the verb +ing

➢ ***Remember:***

The past continuous tense is used to express::

a. *An activity which was in progress at some point of time in the past.*

- *They were working all day yesterday.*
- *The baby was sleeping in the room.*
- *He was not writing in his notebook.*

b. *This tense is often used together with the simple past tense to show that one activity was is progress while another took place.*

- *I was driving to work when I crashed my car.*

- *My sister was studying for her exams when I entered her room.*
- *When the telephone rang she was cooking.*

iii. Past Perfect Tense

Examples		*Usage*
• He had walked. • We had walked.	Affirmative Sentence	Subject+had+3rd form of the verb
• He had not walked.	Negative Sentence	Subject+had not+3rd form of the verb
• Had they walked?	Interrogative Sentence	Had+subject+3rd form of the verb

➢ ***Remember:***

The Past Perfect Tense is used to denote:

a. *An action which had been completed before another action had begun.*
   - *The train had left before I reached the station.*
   - *The film had started by the time we got to the cinema.*
   - *I went to bed after I had switched off the television.*

b. *An unfulfilled wish in the past.*
   - *I wish I had accepted the letter.*
   - *We wish we had heeded our parents' advise.*

c. *An unfulfilled condition in the past.*
   - *If you had worked hard, you would have passed.*
   - *If I had gone to university, I would have studied computers.*
   - *If I had known you wanted the book I would have given it.*

d. *to denote an action which contains the words 'already', 'before', 'till', 'since', etc.*
   - *I had not read this book before.*
   - *He had already heard the news.*
   - *We waited till it got dark.*

iii. Past Perfect Continuous Tense

Examples		*Usage*
• He had been walking for one hour.	Affirmative Sentence	Subject+had +been+1st form of the verb+ing
• I had not been walking since morning.	Negative Sentence	Subject+had+not+been+1st form of the verb+ing
• Had they been walking for half an hour.	Interrogative Sentence	Had+subject+been=1st form of the verb +ing

➢ ***Remember:***

The past perfect continuous tense is used to denote an action that had been going on for some time before action took place in the past.

- *He had been working here for two years.*
- *She had been studying for her examinations.*

REVIEW EXERCISES

Exercise 1

Fill in the blank with the correct form of the verbs given in the brackets (use past tense)

1. We ______ (have) the car for five years when we sold it.
2. I _________ (need) to know what ________ (happen) to my car.
3. By the time we got there, he ______ (leave).
4. He ___________ (not write) in his diary.
5. I quickly _________ (take) my lunch and ____ (go) out.
6. My mother _______ (sleep) while I _________ (listen) to music.
7. He ________ (make) necessary corrections in his answers before he________ (hand over) the answer scripts to the invigilator.
8. After I _________ (do) my homework I watched the television.
9. When I came round in the hospital I realized I________ (crush) the car.
10. While they________ (dance) we_______ (sing).
11. At 10 a.m., all the members _______ (arrive).
12. We went for a walk after the rain_______ (stop).
13. Did you_______ (buy) this book yesterday?
14. They_________ (rehearse) the play since 1:30 p.m. when I ________ (join) them.
15. Last summer we __________ (travel) a lot.

Answers

1. *had had*
2. *needed, had happened*
3. *had left*
4. *was not* writing
5. took, went
6. slept, listened
7. had made, handed over
8. had done
9. had crushed
10. danced, sang
11. had arrived
12. had stopped
13. buy
14. had been rehearsing, joined
15. travelled

Exercise 2

Read the following paragraphs and fill in the blanks with the correct form of the verbs given in the brackets (use past tense)

1. Last week it______ (a) ______ (rain) for two days in Mumbai. Many houses ___ (b) ______ (collapse) while several others ____ (c) _____ (damage) badly. Water____ (d) _______ (enter) the houses. There ______ (e) ____ (be) knee deep water on the roads. Many trees ______ (f) ____ (uproot) and the rain _____ (g) _____ (destroy) the crops completely.
2. Soon after Gandhiji's death Nehru _______ (a)______(find) himself in a great dilemma. Gandhi ___ (b)______ (be) a source of great strength for him. He ___ (c)_____ (use) to guide him at every step. In his address to the nation Nehru _____ (d) _____ (say) that the light ___ (e) _____(go) out of the life of the Indian people. Nobody______ (f)______(expect) that he ______(g)___(leave) his countrymen so soon. Nehru ____ (h)____(advise) the people to live upto his expectations.

Answers

1. *(a) rained (b) collapsed (c)were damaged badly (d)entered (e)was (f) were uprooted(g) destroyed.*
2. *(a) found (b) was (c)used (d) said (e) had gone (f) expected (g) would leave (h) advised*

3. FUTURE TENSE

i. Future Indefinite or Simple

Examples		*Usage*
• He will write.	Affirmative Sentence	***He, she, it, they, you***
• We shall write.		Subject+will+1st form of the verb
		I, we: Subject+shall+1st form of the verb
• He will not write.	Negative Sentence	Subject+will/shall+not+1st form of the verb
• Will they write?	Interrogative Sentence	Will/shall+subject+1st form of the verb

➢ ***Remember:***

The Future Indefinite Tense is used to express:

a. *A future action or event*
    - *He will reach here at 6 p.m.*
    - *We shall not go for picnic in case of rain.*
    - *He will speak to us about it.*

b. The principal clause of a conditional sentence.

- *If you work hard, you will pass the examination.*
- *If you hire a taxi, you will catch the train.*
- *If ever you go to China,you will see some queer things there.*

ii. Future Continuous

Examples		*Usage*
• She will be writing.	Affirmative Sentence	Subject+will/shall+be+1st form of the verb+ing
• I shall not be writing.	Negative Sentence	Subject+will/shall+not+be+1st form of the verb+ing
• Will they be writing?	Interrogative Sentence	Will/shall+Subject+be +1st form of the verb+ing

➢ ***Remember:***

The Future Continuous Tense is used to denote:

a. An action that will be going on at some time in the future.

- *We shall be playing the match tomorrow.*
- *What will you be doing this time tomorrow?*

b. polite way of asking about plan.

- *Will you be using your car tomorrow?*
- *Will you be requiring anything else?*

iii. Future Perfect Tense

Examples		*Usage*
• He will have written.	Affirmative Sentence	Subject+wiil+have+3rd form of the verb
• He will not have written.	Negative Sentence	Subject+wiil+not+have+3rd form of the verb
• Will they have written?	Interrogative Sentence	will+have+ Subject +have+3rd form of the verb

➢ ***Remember:***

The Future Perfect Tense is used to express:

a. A past action in progress now that will complete at a given time in future.

- *I shall have finished the work before morning.*
- *In another year or so, you will have forgotten all about him.*

b. Possibility /assumption

- *It's 5 o'clock, they will have arrived by now.*

iv. Future Perfect Continuous

Examples		*Usage*
• She will have been writing for half an hour.	Affirmative Sentence	Subject+will/shall+have+been+1st form of the verb+ing
• I shall not have been writing since 4:30 p.m..	Negative Sentence	Subject+will/shall+not+have+been +1st form of the verb+ing
• Will they have been writing since morning?	Interrogative Sentence	Will/shall+Subject+have+been +1st form of the verb+ing

➢ ***Remember:***

The Future Perfect Continuous Tense is used to express an action that will have been going on at or before some point of time in future.

- *By the time you return we shall have been working for four hours.*
- *We shall have been solving the sums since morning.*

REVIEW EXERCISES

Exercise 1

Fill in the verbs in the correct tenses into the gaps:

1. ________ any one object if I turn the heating down?
2. I ________come to the conclusion that nowadays nobody cares about anything.
3. No matter what happens next I________ help you.
4. They ________for 3 hours when the storm suddenly broke.
5. I assumed you ________ paying for the repairs until the end of last year.
6. ________ get tired of answering the same questions every day?
7. She ________working on that manuscript for 2 years now.
8. I ________there once a long time ago and haven't been back since.
9. She ________trying to pass her driving test but fails every time.
10. I ________ complete silence now while I try this experiment.

Answers

1. *does*	2. *have*	3. *will*
4. *had been running*	5. *had been*	6. *do you ever*
7. *has been*	8. *went*	9. *keeps*
10. *want*		

Exercise 2

Fill in the blanks with the correct form of the verbs given in the brackets (use future tense)

1. They ________(board) the train by this time tomorrow.

2. If you work hard you will ________.(succeed)
3. My cousin (to exercise) ____________ for 2 years next week in preparation for a role in a movie.
4. Where ________ you ________so many dolls? (keep)
5. This time tomorrow, I _________(take) my last examination.
6. By 2020, I ________(teach) for thirty years.
7. I __________ (meet) the President tomorrow.
8. I wonder what I ____________(do) this time next year.
9. We ____not________(go) for picnic in case of rain.
10. He ___________(miss) the train unless he hurries.
11. At the end of his career, Kabir (to entertain) ____________ audiences for many many years.
12. She______________(sleep) since evening.
13. By the time you return we _____________(work) for four hours.
14. When _________your vacation __________?(begin)
15. Akhil ___________(be) here soon.
16. __________(be) we _________________(wait) for you since morning?
17. You _____________hockey then. (play)
18. If I lose my job now I __________(take)a long holiday and apply for a new job later.
19. By the time the movie will stop, it ___________(rain) outside for 4 hours at least.
20. if the demand increases prices__________(rise)

Answers

1. *would have boarded*
2. *succeed*
3. *will have been exercising*
4. *will, keep*
5. *shall be taking*
6. *shall have taught*
7. *shall be meeting*
8. *shall be doing*
9. *shall not go*
10. *will miss*
11. *will have been entertaining*
12. *will have been sleeping*
13. *shall have been working*
14. *will, begin*
15. *will be*
16. *will, have been waiting*
17. *will be playing*
18. *will take*
19. *will have been raining*
20. *will rise*

Exercise 3

Fill in the blanks with the correct form of the verbs given in the brackets:

1. She ________ (has been/have been) working on that manuscript for 2 years now.

2. ___________ (do, does, did)any one object if I turn the heating down?
3. I ___________(has, had, have, have been) come to the conclusion that nowadays nobody cares about anything.
4. No matter what happens next, I (will, shall, would be, must be) ___________ help you.
5. They __________ (have been, had been, will have been) running for 3 hours when the storm suddenly broke.
6. I assumed you _________(had been, have been) paying for the repairs until the end of last year.
7. ______(Do , will , would) you ever get tired of answering the same questions every day?
8. Many people ___________(have, has, had) tried but no-one has succeeded so far.
9. By the end of this year I realize I ___________(shall have been, shall be, will be, shall be) have been writing tests for three years now.
10. Do you mind _________ (open, opened, opening, opens) the door as I find it very hot in here?
11. honestly think that the time ___________ (have, has, had) come when we should celebrate our success.

Answers

1. *Has been*
2. *does*
3. *have*
4. *will*
5. *had been*
6. *had been*
7. *Do you*
8. *have*
9. *shall have been*
10. *opening*
11. *has*

Exercise 4

Fill in the blank with the appropriate form of the verbs given in the brackets.

1. I am ___________a letter. (write)
2. Ulysse was ___________by the music of the sirens. (enchant)
3. I shall have __________my job by evening. (finish)
4. He has been ___________through a bleak period. (pass)
5. We ________resuming the match on Monday. (be)
6. No sooner did he arrive than he started _________orders to every one around. (issue)
7. They went to Japan. _________they? (do)
8. The president proposed that the meeting ___________to an earlier date. (advance)
9. You may ________if you wish to. (go)
10. The director might have ________home already. (go)

Answers

1. *writing* 2. *enchanted* 3. *finished*
4. *passing* 5. *will be* 6. *issuing*
7. *didn't* 8. *shall be advanced* 9. *go*
10. *gone.*

Exercise 5

Choose the correct answer.

1. If people were a little more tolerant ....

i. our world would have been a better place.
ii. our world would be a better place.
iii. our world will be a better place.

2. If my father had locked his car properly ...

i. his car would never have been stolen.
ii. his car will not be stolen.
iii. his car would not be stolen.

3. If the ozone layer peels off a little more we ...

i. ran a much higher risk of attracting skin cancer.
ii. would run a much higher risk of attracting skin cancer.
iii. will run a much higher risk of attracting skin cancer.

4. I would never feel comfortable on a plane if ...

i. I know it's the pilot's maiden trip.
ii. I knew it's the pilot's maiden trip.
iii. I would know it's the pilot's maiden trip.

5. A dog will never bite you if ...

i. you will look it straight in the eyes, I'm told.
ii. you look it straight in the eyes, I'm told.
iii. you looked it straight in the eyes, I'm told.

6. The first thing I will do is drive to Spain if ...

i. I would get my driving license.
ii. I got my driving license.
iii. I get my driving license.

7. If John hadn't responded in such an aggressive manner he ...

i. would never have a black eye.
ii. Won't have a black eye.
iii. would never have had a black eye.

Answers

1. *(ii.) our world would be a better place.*
2. *(i.) his car would never have been stolen.*
3. *(iii.) will run a much higher risk of attracting skin cancer.*
4. *(ii) I knew it's the pilot's maiden trip.*
5. *(ii) you look it straight in the eyes, I'm told.*
6. *(iii) I get my driving license.*
7. *(iii) would never have had a black eye.*

Exercise 6

Fill in the verbs in the correct tenses into the gaps:

1. The weather ______ nice at the weekend. (to be)
2. We ________TV when it started to rain. (to watch)
3. I wanted to visit you yesterday, but you _________ at home. (not/to be)
4. Look! It________, so we can't ____________to the beach. (to rain) (to go)
5. There are a lot of clouds. It _________soon. (to rain)
6. The sun ___________in the East. (to rise)
7. Since 1993 they ________their son every year. (to visit)
8. While the doctor _________Mr Jones, his son ________in the waiting room. (to examine) (to wait)
9. If I study, I _________the exams. (to pass)
10. I __________to the cinema yesterday. (to go)

Answers

1. *will be*	2. *were watching*	3. *were not.*
4. *is raining , go to*	5. *is going to rain*	6. *rises*
7. *have been visiting*	8. *was examining , was waiting*	
9. *will pass*	10. *went*	

Exercise 7

Fill in the verbs in the correct tenses into the gaps:

1. He dare not ________this office again. (enter)
2. We need not have ____________to Mumbai at all. (go)
3. You ought to ________the dentist very soon. (see)
4. Jim had _________ for London before I _________. (leave) (arrive)
5. If only you had told me the truth, I would not _________there.(go)
6. If I am not mistaken, you _____that book a year ago. (borrow)
7. What do you _________in the evening.(do)

8. Gopal ________in this office for the last two years. Everyone here ________him. (work) (like)
9. We have to get up early tomorrow; our train ________at six o' clock. (leave)
10. When I________ the station, the train________.(reach) (leave)

Answers

1. *enter*
2. *gone*
3. *see*
4. *left, arrived*
5. *have gone*
6. *borrowed*
7. *do*
8. *has been working, likes*
9. *will leave*
10. *reached, had left*

Exercise 8

Fill in the verbs in the correct tenses into the gaps:

1. Peter ________12 next week. (to be)
2. My friend ________to music every evening. (to listen)
3. They ________their car. It looks new again. (to clean)
4. Listen! Mrs Jones ________the piano. (to play)
5. He ________his arm two weeks ago. (to break)
6. They ________a test now. (to write)
7. We ________a film tomorrow evening, but we haven't got the tickets yet. (to watch)
8. It's time you ________for the station.(leave)
9. ________you mind if I ________a cigar. (be) (smoke)
10. We ________English for five years now. (study)

Answers

1. *will be*
2. *listens*
3. *have cleaned*
4. *is playing*
5. *broke*
6. *are writing*
7. *are going to watch*
8. *should leave*
9. *will, smoke*
10. *have been studying*

Exercise 9

Fill in the past tense or past participle of given verb:

1. A better day for a drive could not have been ________(chose)
2. He has ________his best days. (see)
3. The young boy was ________by a mad dog. (bite)
4. He ________to talk nonsense. (begin)

5. I think he should have ____________ and told us. (write)
6. He _______ us good bye. (bid)
7. His voice______ as he spoke. (shake)
8. He had ___________his speech before we arrived. (begin)
9. It has ________the test of time. (stand)
10. Suddenly the wind________.(arise)

Answers

1. *chosen*	2. *seen*	3. *bitten*
4. *began*	5. *written*	6. *bade*
7. *shook*	8. *began*	9. *stood*
10. *arose*		

Exercise 10

Fill in the verbs in the correct tenses into the gaps:

1. Many people __________ but no one has succeeded so far.(try)
2. That programme is so boring that it's like __________paint dry.(watch)
3. By the end of this year, I realize, I _____________ tests for three years now.(write)
4. Do you mind __________the door as I find it very hot in here? (open)
5. I honestly think that the time ____________ when we should celebrate our success.(come)
6. How anyone __________ to live in those conditions in the 18th century is difficult to imagine.(manage)
7. Have you ever __________ of this writer before?(hear)
8. That stupid dog _______ (be) always ___________all day long.(bark)
9. They were eating dinner when the lights _________out.(go)
10. No one ___________ your story when you tell them.(believe)

Answers

1. *have tried*	2. *watching*	3. *shall have been writing*
4. *opening*	5. *has come*	6. *managed*
7. *heard*	8. *is, barking*	9. *went*
10. *will believe*		

Exercise 11

Fill in the verbs in the correct tenses into the gaps:

1. Everybody ___ by the terrible news yesterday.

   a. shocked　　　b. was shocked

2. Dr. Sharma___ at the university since 1989.

   a. has been teaching b. has been taught

3. Not much ___ about the accident since that time.

   a. has said b. has been said

4. A new book ___ by that company next year.

   a. will publish b. will be published

5. He ___ the girl's name now.

   a. remembers b. is remembered

6. The secretary ___ to her new boss yesterday.

   a. introduced b. was introduced

7. Our plan ___ by the members of the committee.

   a. is being considered b. is considered

8. He ___ responsible for the accident.

   a. was holding b. was held

9. A prize ___ to whoever solves this equation.

   a. will be giving b. will be given

10. When the manager arrived, the problem ___ .

   a. had already been solved b. had already solved

Answers

1. *b* 2. *a* 3. *b*
4. *b* 5. *a* 6. *b*
7. *a* 8. *b* 9. *b*
10. *a*

Exercise 12

Fill in the verbs in the correct tenses into the gaps:

1. She failed most of her exams, and now she wishes she ___________ harder.

   a. works b. worked
   c. would work d. had worked

2. I have to get the bus to work every day. I wish I ___________ a car.

   a. have got b. had
   c. would have d. had had

3. The weather's terrible today. I wish it ___________ a bit warmer.

   a. have got b. had been
   c. would have d. had had

4. It really annoys me that you never do anything around the house! I wish you __________ from time to time.

   a. wash up
   b. washed up
   c. would wash up
   d. had washed up

5. I missed my English class yesterday because I went to the doctor's. I wish I __________ it.

   a. Don't miss
   b. Didn't miss
   c. Wouldn't miss
   d. Hadn't missed

6. The last bus always seems to leave early. I wish the driver __________ until the right time before leaving.

   a. waits
   b. waited
   c. would wait
   d. had wait

7. My sister will have to cancel her party next week. She wishes she __________ cancel it, but she's broken her leg.

   a. Does not have to
   b. would not have to
   c. did not have to
   d. would not have had to

8. We went to a new restaurant for lunch and I've been feeling sick all afternoon. I wish we __________ there.

   a. go
   b. did not go
   c. would not go
   d. had not gone

9. The two brothers are always fighting. Their mother wishes they __________.

   a. don't
   b. won't
   c. would not
   d. had not

10. I gave that man in the pub my phone number. I wish I __________.

   a. won't
   b. didn't
   c. wouldn't
   d. hadn't

Answers

1. *d*
2. *b*
3. *b*
4. *c*
5. *d*
6. *c*
7. *c*
8. *d*
9. *c*
10. *d*

Concord : Agreement of the Verb with its Subject

12 CHAPTER

A verb must agree with its subject in number or person. Such agreement is called concord. There are certain rules to make the verb agree with its subject:

1. **In English, number concord only affects present tense verbs plus the past tense of 'be'.**
   - I walk.
   - He walks.
   - He was.
   - They were.
2. **Usually singular subjects take singular verbs and plural subjects take plural verb.**
   - They run fast.
   - He runs fast. etc.
3. **Two or more singular subjects joined by <u>and</u> take a plural verb.**
   - Fog, smoke and heavy rain cancel scheduled flight.
   - Are your father and mother at home?

   But if the mind suggests one idea or refers to the same person or thing, the verb is singular.
   - The novelist and poet is dead.
   - Bread and butter is my favourite food.
   - The horse and carriage is at the door.
   - Honour and glory is his reward.
   - Slow and steady wins the race.
   - Time and tide waits for none.
4. **Words connected to a singular subject by 'with', 'together with', 'along with', 'in addition to', 'as well as' etc. (are parenthetical) do not affect the number of the verb.**
   - The student, along with his guardian, is waiting outside the director's room.

- The manager, along with his team, has arrived.
- Justice, as well as mercy, allows it.
- He, as well as you, is mistaken.
- The ship, with its crew, was lost.

5. **Singular subjects separated by 'or', 'nor', 'neither...nor', or 'either...or' take a singular verb.**
   - Either the television or the newspaper is a good source for news.
   - Our happiness or our sorrow is due to our own action.
   - Neither the driver nor the cleaner feels sleepy.

   Plural subjects separated by 'or', 'nor', 'neither...nor', or 'either...or' take a pverb.
   - Neither the teachers nor the parents are to blame.

   When two noun phrases are joined by 'or 'nor', 'neither...nor', or 'either...or' and one has a plural subject, the verb must be plural, and the plural subject should be placed nearest the verb.
   - Neither the chairman nor the directors are present.
   - Neither the inspector nor the officers were able to help us.

   When the subjects joined by 'or', 'nor', 'neither...nor', or 'either...or' are of different persons, the verb agrees with the nearer.
   - Either he or I am mistaken.
   - Either you or he is mistaken.
   - Neither my friend nor I am mistaken.

6. **Phrases separating the subject and verb do not influence the number of the subject. A subject following the verb still agrees in number with the verb.**
   - Here come mother and father now.
   - Here comes mother now.
   - Do the watchman and son cycle to work together?

7. **Context determines the number of collective nouns. For example; team, audience, family, group.**

   When the collective nouns act as individuals the verb is plural.
   - The team are discussing next year's schedule.
   - The audience were taking turns to give donations to the trust.
   - The committee are divided on one minor point.
   - The staff vote on every issue.

   When a collective noun acts as a single unit the verb is singular.
   - The team wins every game it plays.

- The audience was cheering the band.
- The committee has issued its report.
- The staff is adequate.

8. **Plural words and phrases count as singular if they are used as names, titles, and quotations etc.**

   When a plural noun denoting distance, weight, height or amount of money is illustrated as a single unit, it takes a singular verb.

   - Ten km. is a long walk.
   - Fourteen minutes is allowed to each speaker.
   - Hundred rupees is a lot of money for a poor fellow.
   - The government is doing well.

   Phrases like 'a lot of', 'many a', great deal of', 'some of', 'most of', 'plenty of', are singular when they refer to quantity and are plural when they refer to number.

   - A lot of money is needed.
   - A lot of books have been purchased.

9. **Two nouns qualified by 'each', 'every' or 'even though' connected by 'and' require a singular verb.**

   - Every boy and every girl was given a packet of sweets.

10. **'Pains' and 'means' take either the singular or the plural verb, but the construction must be consistent. (Not varying/ singular)**

    - Great pains have been taken.
    - Much pains has been taken.

    In the sense of 'income', the word 'means' always takes a plural verb.

    - My means are ample/sufficient.

11. **Words, plural in form and singular in meaning, take a singular verb.**

    - The news is true.
    - Linguistics is the study of language.
    - The wages is meagre in this factory.

12. **When 'number' is preceded by 'the', it takes a singular verb and when by 'a', plural verb.**

    - The number of crimes in Delhi is increasing.
    - A number of meetings were held to discuss the issue.
    - The number of people who reported for work this morning is small.
    - A number of books are missing from the library.

13. 'It' always takes a singular verb, irrespective of whether the subject is plural or singular.

- It is the people who matter in a democracy.
- It is the fundamental principle that matters.

14. In sentences beginning with 'there', the number of the verb is determined by the true subject, which generally follows the verb.

- There are various methods of collecting data.
- There is no need for typing this report.

15. 'A pair of' when applied to things where the two components are always thought together ('scissors', shears', 'shoes', 'gloves', 'trousers',) takes a singular verb.

- A pair of trousers is hanging on the peg.
- A pair of scissors is kept in the drawer.
- A pair of spectacles is lying on the table.

But if we omit the words 'a pair of' and only use the plural words, then, it must take a plural verb.

- The scissors are very sharp.
- His shoes are very expensive.

16. Certain nouns are used in singular so they take singular verb.

- The scenery of Kashmir attracts the tourists.
- The furniture of my drawing room is old fashioned.
- No information has been received so far.

REVIEW EXERCISES

Exercise 1

Choose the correct form of the verb (is, are, am, was, were, has, have) that agrees with the subject.

1. The price of this jeans ________reasonable.
2. The books borrowed from the library _________on my desk.
3. The boy who won the two medals_________ a friend of mine.
4. Bread and butter _________our daily food.
5. The famous singer and composer ________arrived.
6. Collecting matchboxes __________one of his favourite pastimes.
7. The quality of the candies__________ poor.
8. Neither his father nor his mother __________come.
9. Neither parent _________fond of playing mahjong.
10. None of my friends__________ there.

Answers

1. *is*	2. *are*	3. *is*
4. *is*	5. *has*	6. *is*
7. *was/is*	8. *has*	9. *is*
10. *was/is*		

Exercise 2

Choose the correct form of the verb (is, are, has, have) that agrees with the subject.

1. Many a student ______made the same mistake.
2. Gold, as well as platinum, ______ recently risen in price.
3. The boss, as well as his colleagues, _________ been robbed by the robber.
4. Ten tons_________ a heavy load.
5. Fifty miles ______ a long distance.
6. Thirty years _________ a long time.
7. One of the books __________been missing.
8. The poor_____ suffering.
9. You should decide which one of the three choices A, B, or C _______best suited to the question.
10. One of the most intelligent students ______John.

Answers

1. *has*	2. *has*	3. *has*
4. *is*	5. *is*	6. *is*
7. *has*	8. *are*	9. *is*
10. *is*		

Exercise 3

Write the correct form of the verb that agrees with the subject:

1. She and her friends _________ at the fair.(be)
2. The book or the pen ________ in the drawer.(be)
3. The boy or his friends________ every day. (run)
4. His friends or the boy _____ every day. (run)
5. The President, accompanied by his wife ___ travelling to India. (be)
6. All the books, including yours, _______in that box. (be)
7. The committee_______ how to proceed. (decide)
8. The woman with her children _______down the street. (walk)
9. The people who listen to that music—few. (be)
10. Either _____ correct. (be)

Answers

1. are	2. is	3. run
4. runs	5. is	6. are
7. decides	8. walks	9. are
10. is		

Exercise 4

Choose the correct form of the verb that agrees with the subject:

1. Annie and her brothers (is, are) at school.
2. Either my mother or my father (is, are) coming to the meeting.
3. The dog or the cats (is, are) outside.
4. Either my shoes or your coat (is, are) always on the floor.
5. George and Tamara (doesn't, don't) want to see that movie.
6. Benito (doesn't, don't) know the answer.
7. One of my sisters (is, are) going on a trip to France.
8. The man with all the birds (live, lives) on my street.
9. The movie, including all the previews, (take, takes) about two hours to watch.
10. The players, as well as the captain, (want, wants) to win.
11. Either answer (is, are) acceptable.
12. Every one of those books (is, are) fiction.
13. Nobody (know, knows) the trouble I've seen.
14. (Is, Are) the news on at five or six?
15. Mathematics (is, are) John's favorite subject, while Civics (is, are) Andrea's favorite subject.
16. Eight dollars (is, are) the price of a movie these days.
17. (Is, Are) the tweezers in this drawer?
18. Your pants (is, are) at the cleaner's.
19. There (was, were) fifteen candies in that bag. Now there (is, are) only one left!
20. The committee (debates, debate) these questions carefully.
21. The committee (leads, lead) very different lives in private.
22. The Prime Minister, together with his wife, (greets, greet) the press cordially.
23. All of the CDs, even the scratched one, (is, are) in this case.

Answers

1. *are*	2. *is*	3. *are*
4. *is*	5. *don't*	6. *doesn't*

7. *is* 8. *lives* 9. *takes*
10. *want* 11. *is* 12. *is*
13. *knows* 14. *is* 15. *is, is*
16. *is* 17. *are* 18. *are*
19. *were, is* 20. *debates* 21. *lead*
22. *greets* 23. *are*

Exercise 5

Choose the correct form of the verb that agrees with the subject.

1. Some of the voters ________ still angry. (is/are)
2. A large percentage of the older population ________ voting against her. (is/are)
3. Two-fifths of the troops________ lost in the battle. (was/were)
4. Two-fifths of the vineyard________ destroyed by fire. (was/were)
5. Forty percent of the students ________in favor of changing the policy. (is/are)
6. Forty percent of the student body ________ in favour of changing the policy. (is/are)
7. Two and two ________ four. (is/are)
8. Four times four divided by two________ eight. (is/are)
9. The department members, but not the chair, ________ decided not to teach on Valentine's Day. (has/have)
10. It is not the faculty members but the president who ________ this issue. (decide/decides)
11. It was the speaker, not his ideas, that ________provoked the students to riot. (has/have)
12. My assets ________wiped out in the depression. (was/were)
13. The average worker's earnings ________gone up dramatically. (has/have)
14. Our thanks ________to the workers who supported the union. (go/goes)
15. My glasses ________on the bed. (was/were)
16. My pants ________ torn. (was/were)
17. A pair of plaid trousers ________ in the closet. (is/are)
18. There ________ two reasons [plural subject] for this. (is/are)
19. There ________ no reason for this. (is/are)
20. Here ________ two apples. (is/are)
21. Either my father or my brothers ________going to sell the house. (is/are)

22. Neither my brothers nor my father ____going to sell the house. (is/are)
23. ________ either my brothers or my father responsible? (is/are)
24. ______either my father or my brothers responsible? (is/are)
25. Everyone ________finished his or her homework. (has/have)
26. Everyone_______ done his or her homework. (has/have)
27. Somebody ________left her purse. (has/have)
28. None of you __________ responsibility for this incident? (claim/claims)

Answers

1. *are*	2. *is*	3. *were*
4. *was*	5. *are*	6. *is*
7. *is*	8. *is*	9. *have*
10. *decides*	11. *has*	12. *were*
13. *have*	14. *go*	15. *were*
16. *were*	17. *is*	18. *are*
19. *is*	20. *are*	21. *are*
22. *is*	23. *are*	24. *is*
25. *has*	26. *has*	27. *has*
28. *claims*		

Exercise 6

Select one answer from the choices provided after each sentence. The word you choose should fit the blank in the sentence.

1. Either the physicians in this hospital or the chief administrator ____ going to have to make a decision.

   a. is
   b. are

2. ______ my boss or my sisters in the union going to win this grievance?

   a. Is
   b. Are

3. Some of the votes __________ to have been miscounted.

   a. seem
   b. seems

4. The tornadoes that tear through this county every spring _____ more than just a nuisance.

   a. are
   b. is

5. Everyone selected to serve on this jury _____ to be willing to give up a lot of time.

   a. have

   b. has

6. He seems to forget that there __________ things to be done before he can graduate.

   are

   is

7. There _______ to be some people left in that town after yesterday's flood.

   have

   has

8. Some of the grain __________ to be contaminated.

   appear

   appears

9. Three-quarters of the students __________ against the tuition hike.

   a. is

   b. are

10. Three-quarters of the student body __________ against the tuition hike.

    a. is

    b. are

11. A high percentage of the population _________ voting for the new school.

    a. is

    b. are

12. A high percentage of the people _________ voting for the new school.

    a. was

    b. were

13. Kara Wolters, together with her teammates, _________ a formidable opponent on the basketball court.

    a. present

    b. presents

Answers

1. is	2. is	3. seem
4. are	5. has	6. are
7. have	8. appears	9. are
10. is	11. is	12. were
13. presents		

Structure of Sentence

13

CHAPTER

The construction of clear, correct and well-balanced sentences is essential to all successful writing. In order to compose a good sentence, the most important thing is to master the art of arranging words, phrases and clauses in their most effective setting.

1. SENTENCE

A sentence is a group of words that expresses a complete thought. It begins with a capital letter and ends with a period or a question mark.

Every sentence has two essential parts:

i. **Subject:** The word(s) denoting the person or thing about which we say something is called the subject of the sentence.

ii. **Predicate:** The word(s) which denote what we say about the subject is called the predicate of the sentence.

- The boy (*Subject*) is standing near the bank. (*Predicate*)
- Nature (*Subject*) is the best teacher. (*Predicate*)

Thus the most elementary form of a sentence is noun-Verb. For example;

- Flower (*Subject (Noun)*) grows. (*Predicate (Verb)*)

2. SENTENCE CLASSIFICATION ACCORDING TO FUNCTION

There are four kinds of sentences:

i. **Declarative sentences:** Sentences, which only make a statement whether in the affirmative or negative, are called Declarative sentences.

- It's lunch time.
- We are going to the game on Friday.
- My parents keep telling me that I should make good grades so I can get a job or go to college.
- He is intelligent.

ii. **Imperative sentences:** Sentences, which contain command, request or wish are called Imperative sentences.

- Wash the car.
- Clean up your room.
- Please donate to the community charity fund.
- Bring me a cup of coffee please.

iii. **Interrogative sentences:** Sentences which inquire about something are called Interrogative sentences.

- What is your name?
- What time does the movie start?
- How many people from your graduating class went to college?
- What are they serving in the cafeteria today?

iv. **Exclamatory sentences:** Sentences, which express some feeling or reaction of the mind in connection with the assertion made, are called Exclamatory sentences.

- What a lovely sight it is!
- Hurrah! I have finished the task.
- What a beautiful night!
- Have a nice day!

3. PHRASE

A combination of words that makes sense, but does not contain a finite verb, is called a phrase.

- A girl with a huge bag came this morning.
- The boy along with his mother is standing outside the office.

4. CLAUSE:

A combination of words containing a finite verb but actually a part of larger sentence is called a clause.

- This is the boy who stood first in the class.

The clauses are of two types:

i. **Independent clause:** A clause which gives its meaning independently is called an independent or main clause. It contains a subject and verb and is complete in itself in both context and meaning.

Simple sentences consist of just one main clause:

- Finally, we arrived.
- We knew each other well.

- Have you got the time?
- I spoke to her mother.
- The door opened.

Compound sentences consist of two or more main clauses – clauses of equal weight, joined together by 'for', 'or' 'and', 'but', 'yet', 'nor', 'so' etc. This relationship is called coordination.

- My mother is not at home but the keys are here so I'm not locked out.
- It is late, so she is not going.
- I like reading and I love Shakespeare.

ii. **Dependent clause:**

A clause which cannot give its meaning fully by itself without the help of another clause is a dependent clause. A dependent clause is always a subordinate clause.

- If you work hard, you will get excellent grades.
- He burns easily if he doesn't use sun cream.
- Where is the cup of tea that you promised to make?
- Everything she buys is really expensive.
- The class I taught last year did quite well.

5. KINDS OF SUBORDINATE CLAUSES:

There are three kinds of subordinate clauses: the noun clause, the adjective clause and the adverb clause.

In a complex sentence, the noun clause acts as a noun, the adjective clause acts as an adjective, and the adverb clause acts as an adverb.

a. Functions of the Noun Clause

The noun clause functions as

i. **Subject to a verb :**

- That he is intelligent is accepted by all.
- Whom the God loves dies young.

ii. **Object to a verb, a participle or an infinitive :**

- He got what he wanted.
- I am desirous of knowing what your views are.
- I wish to say that your conduct has been admirable.

iii. **Object to preposition :**

- Your success in life will depend on how you conduct yourself.
- You will be rewarded or punished for what you do.

iv. Complement to a verb:

- The truth is that he is not guilty.
- They made him what he wanted to be.

v. In opposition to a noun or pronoun:

- The news that he has arrived is true.
- It is clear that he is clever.

b. Functions of the Adjective Clause

An adjective clause does the work of an adjective in relation to some noun or pronoun in some other clause. It is always introduced by a Relative pronoun or a Relative verb.

- He who works hard will succeed.
- Gopal has read all the books which are there in his library.
- Govind is the boy whom I love.
- They went into the house which had just been built.
- I have found the book which I lost yesterday.

c. Function of the Adverb Clause

An adverb clause does the work of an adverb. It may show:

i. Time (answering the question 'when?'):

- Speak to me before you leave.
- As we entered the station, the train came in.

ii. Place (answering the question 'where?'):

- We met where he wanted.
- Wherever you go, you will be respected.

iii. Cause (answering the question 'why?'):

- He was punished because he was guilty.
- As it was hot, he sat down under a tree.

iv. Manner (answering the question 'how?'):

- He acted as he was told.
- He shouted as if he were mad.

v. Condition (stating the circumstances):

- If you work hard, you will succeed.
- I shall open the window, provided no one objects.

vi. Purpose (answering the question 'why?' or 'what for?'):

- Study in order that you may learn.
- He came to me so that we might work together.

vii. Contrast:

- Even if he opposes us, we must try.
- Though he is poor, he is honest.

viii. Comparison (answering the question 'how much?'):

- Rani is as clever as Sita.
- She is more intelligent than her brother.

ix. Result (stating the effect):

- He was so timid that everybody bullied him.
- It was so cold that many perished.

6. TYPES OF SENTENCES:

A sentence can be an independent clause, or can be formed by combining clauses, usually with the addition of a linking word or phrase. A clause is a grammatical structure in which several components of meaning are brought together to form a message. The verb is the essential element of any clause.

i. Simple sentences: A simple sentence has a single independent clause. It requires a subject and a verb.

- Mohan plays cricket.
- I write a letter.
- I like English.
- Anil is eating his favourite fruit.
- The good old man having suffered so long, at last died yesterday.

ii. Compound sentence:

Compound sentences consist of two or more independent clauses i.e., each is capable of standing on its own and conveying a message. Each has equal status and provides equally important information. These clauses may be linked with connective words or phrases such as: 'and', 'but', 'or', 'yet', 'so', 'and so', 'and then', 'either...or', 'neither...nor', 'not only...but also'.

• He came	Independent clause
and dined with me.	Independent clause
• She ran to school	Independent clause
and threw her bag down in the corridor.	Independent clause
• Karl went on camp	Independent clause
but the others stayed at home.	Independent clause
• You could ring her at the office	Independent clause
or try her on her cell phone.	Independent clause
• Ram studies during the day	Independent clause
and he plays in the evening.	Independent clause

iii. Complex sentence

A complex sentence consists of one independent clause with one or two subordinate clauses. The independent clause can function as a complete sentence. The subordinate clause also contains a subject and a verb but cannot function as an independent sentence. These subordinate clauses are linked with the independent clause by subordinate conjunctions like 'while', 'because', 'since', 'although', etc.

➢ **Remember:**

1. *A complex sentence is useful when one wants to combine several shorter sentences into one.*
2. *In complex sentences coordinate conjunctions are used to link equally important ideas only.*

• They smiled	Independent clause
as if they meant it.	Dependent clause
• The plant died	Independent clause
because it wasn't watered.	Dependent clause
• If the container has a hole in it	Dependent clause
the raspberries will leak all over the bench.	Independent clause
• We surveyed the damage	Independent clause
as the wind subsided.	Dependent clause
• He said	Dependent clause
that he was going to Delhi.	Independent clause

iv. Compound-complex sentences

Compound-complex sentences contain a combination of independent and dependent clauses.

• The girls walked out of the shop	Independent clause
and laughed loudly	Independent clause
('they' has been omitted due to ellipsis)	
as they headed for the car.	Dependent clause
• An elderly man was admitted to hospital	Independent clause
after suffering a heart attack	Dependent clause
and falling down the stairs.	Dependent clause

7. REQUISITES OF A GOOD SENTENCE:

Following are the three basic requisites of a good sentence:

i. Clarity
ii. Consistency
iii. Economy

i. Clarity:

All sentences should clearly state the writer's thoughts without any possibility of ambiguity. One important aid to achieve clarity is **correct punctuation**. Another aid to clarity is **clear pronoun reference.** For clarity each pronoun should not be too far away from the noun it refers to. Also there should be **correct word order,** that is, the related elements in a sentence should be kept close together.

ii. Consistency:

All sentences follow some pattern. One sentence pattern which may cause trouble is the **parallel construction.** As we know the connectives are used to express the logical relationship between the sentences. Sometimes the same thoughts are expressed in sentences, but sometimes we have changed thoughts. Parts of a sentence that express same thoughts, should be parallel (the same) in grammatical form. A noun may be balanced with another noun, a phrase with another phrase, or a clause with another clause. Parallel constructions must be logically connected by the coordinating conjunctions and, but, or, etc.

There should be **subject-verb agreement** in number and person and **pronoun-antecedent agreement** in gender, number or person.

iii. Economy:

Economy of words means one's ability to write precisely and effectively. The writer should **avoid long-winded sentences**. Useless repetition of words should be avoided and the principle of reduction should be applied. It means reducing a sentence to a clause, a clause to a phrase, a phrase to a word, whenever and wherever possible.

REVIEW EXERCISES

Exercise I

Complete the following sentences by using suitable word or phrase in the space given:

1. A group of words is a __________
2. A group of words with a subject and a verb is __________
3. what are the two types of clauses __________ and__________
4. Which clause expresses a complete thought __________
5. select the complete sentences:
    a. The man, having read the paper, decided to leave.
    b. The man having read the paper.
    c. Having read the paper, the man decided to leave.
    d. The man decided to leave since he had read the paper.
6. Which two sentences are not punctuated correctly?
    a. After studying the situation, he decided not to get involved.

b. He decided not to get involved, after studying the situation.
c. He decided not to get involved after studying the situation.

7. Which of the following are punctuated correctly?
   a. Anne enjoyed her high school reunion, she hadn't seen her old friends in over ten years.
   b. Anne enjoyed her high school reunion; she hadn't seen her old friends in over ten years.
   c. Anne enjoyed her high school reunion. She hadn't seen her old friends in over ten years.
   d. Anne enjoyed her high school reunion she hadn't seen her old friends in over ten years.
8. select the correct sentences:
   i. a. When he mowed the yard, the dogs ran away.
   b. He mowed the yard, the dogs ran away.
   ii. a. The pen is on the table it's next to the phone.
   b. The pen is on the table; it's next to the phone.
   iii. a. The girl in front of me accidentally unplugged the computer. I lost everything I had typed.
   b. The girl in front of me accidentally unplugged the computer, I lost everything I had typed.
9. Locate the error in each of the following sentences
   a. I used to go the library whenever my wife is at work.
   b. The kids always clean the kitchen, my wife straightens up the den, and I worked in the yard.
   c. When Peggy was a pup, she was so uncoordinated that she often falls down.
10. Join the following sentences with suitable conjunctions:
   a. He threw the Frisbee, __________ I caught it.
   b. I ran after the cat, __________ I couldn't catch it.
   c. He filled up her food bowl, __________ she wouldn't eat.
   d. They wanted to go walking without me, _________ I gave them my saddest look.
   e. I scratched my ear, ________ there was a bug in it

Answers

1. *phrase* 2. *clause*
3. *main/independent clause, subordinate clause*
4. *main/independent clause*

5. *a, c, d*
6. *a, c*
7. *b, c*
8. *i. a, ii. b, iii. a*
9. *a. ....my wife was.....b. ....I work in the yard*
   c. ....she often fell down.
10. *a. and, b. but, c. yet, d. so, e. for*

Exercise 2

Rewrite the following sentences after removing awkward constructions:

1. You are either late or I am early.
2. Jim not only has been outstanding in athletics, but also in his studies.
3. He was both intelligent as well as courteous.
4. The questionnaire asks for this information: number of employees; what is our union status; and how much do we pay.
5. To see a play is more interesting than reading it.
6. Being punctual is more profitable than to be late.
7. She likes to sew and cooking.
8. Sam is tall, with blue eyes, and has a congenial manner.
9. She likes to listen to music and reading the latest novels.
10. He spent his time studying Spanish, working at the convenience store, and he jogged every afternoon.

Answers

1. *Either you are late or I am early.*
2. *Jim has been outstanding not only in athletics, but also in his studies.*
3. *He was both intelligent and courteous. /He was intelligent as well as courteous.*
4. *The questionnaire asks for this information: number of employees, union affiliation and pay scale.*
5. *Seeing a play is more interesting than reading it.*
6. *Being punctual is more profitable than being late.*
7. *She likes sewing and cooking.*
8. *Sam is tall, blue eyed and congenial.*
9. *She likes listening to music and reading the latest novels.*
10. *He spent his time studying Spanish, working at the convenience store, and jogging every afternoon.*

Exercise 3

Rewrite the following sentences after framing them properly:

1. He barely kicked that ball twenty yards.
2. I only gave him three dollars.

3. I almost listened to the whole album.
4. Elizabeth came over while I was playing the piano with a piece of pound cake.
5. I tried calling to tell you about that TV show five times.
6. Although very spicy, he managed to finish the sandwich.
7. The young girl was walking the dog in a long skirt.
8. The dog was chasing the boy with the spiked collar.
9. Big dog almost ran around the yard twenty times.
10. He nearly ate a whole box of chocolates.

Answers

1. *He kicked that ball barely twenty yards.*
2. *I gave him only three dollars.*
3. *I listened to almost the whole album.*
4. *While I was playing the piano Elizabeth came over with a piece of pound cake.*
5. *I tried calling you five times to tell you about that TV show.*
6. *Although the sandwich was very spicy, he managed to finish it.*
7. *The young girl in a long skirt was walking the dog.*
8. *The dog with the spiked collar was chasing the boy.*
9. *Big Dog ran around the yard almost twenty times.*
10. *He ate nearly a whole box of chocolates.*

Exercise 4

In the following sentences replace any connectives that are used weakly or inaccurately:

1. My parents bought a new house and they still like the old one.
2. While it was very cold, I continued to study.
3. I won a national merit scholarship but I was very proud.
4. I don't know if I could paint, as I have never tried.
5. As the furnace broke down, the superintendent closed the office.
6. This paper is white, while the other is grey.
7. The examiner then makes enquiries of the financial condition of the firm.
8. These trips are written up fully by the monthly magazine bulletin.
9. I argued with him for a long time and I could not bring him to my point of view.
10. The house is very old and is well preserved.

Answers

1. *My parents bought a new house but they still like the old one.*

2. *Although it was very cold, I continued to study.*
3. *I won a national merit scholarship and I was very proud.*
4. *I don't know if I could paint, because I have never tried.*
5. *Because the furnace broke down, the superintendent closed the office. (Time intended) When the furnace broke down, the superintendent closed the office. (Cause intended)*
6. *This paper is white, and/whereas the other is grey.*
7. *The examiner then makes enquiries about/regarding the financial condition of the firm.*
8. *These trips are written up fully in the monthly magazine bulletin.*
9. *I argued with him for a long time but I could not bring him to my point of view.*
10. *The house is very old but is well preserved.*

Exercise 5

Improve the construction of the following sentences:

1. Everybody should make plans for their retirement.
2. When the meeting began, everybody took their seats at the desk assigned to them.
3. When she put the cat on the table, it collapsed.
4. When I loaded the new program on the computer, it crashed.
5. I told him, and he believed it, that the market was closed.
6. He was a jolly old fellow and he loves to eat.
7. We completed our registration forms and attended several lectures; also tests in English and Mathematics were taken.
8. The thief ran away, with a long knife in the hand.
9. The man gave orders in the brown suit.
10. My bag containing a pen, a diary and two notebooks were lost yesterday.

Answers

1. *Everybody should make plans for his/her retirement.*
2. *When the meeting began, everybody took his or her seat at the desk assigned to him or her.*
3. *When she put the cat on the table, the table collapsed.*
4. *When I loaded the new program on the computer, the computer crashed.*
5. *I told him that the market was closed, and he believed it.*
6. *He was a jolly old fellow and he loved to eat.*
7. *We completed our registration forms and attended several lectures; also took tests in English and Mathematics.*
8. *The thief with a long knife in the hand ran away.*

9. *The man in the brown suit gave orders.*
10. *My bag containing a pen, a diary and two notebooks was lost yesterday.*

Exercise 6

Tick the correct of the two choices:

1. If I lose my job now I ...
   a. would start a business of my own.
   b. will take a long holiday and apply for a new job later.
2. If he calls me 'lazy' again I ...
   a. won't ever help him again if he's in trouble.
   b. go and tell his parents.
3. She won't ever speak to me again if ...
   a. I let her down now.
   b. I would let her down now.
4. If the demand increases prices ...
   a. rise.
   b. will rise.
5. Our dog will start licking you if ...
   a. you pat him on the back.
   b. you will give it a cuddle.
6. Don't be offended. If Jane is annoyed she ...
   a. will start yelling at people.
   b. starts yelling at people.
7. If he doesn't answer the phone this time I ...
   a. won't call again.
   b. don't call again.
8. If you wait a minute...
   a. I'll come with you.
   b. I'll let you come.

Answers

1. b	*2. a*	*3. a*
4. b	*5. a*	*6. b*
7. a	*8. a*	

Elements of a Series

14

CHAPTER

The literary meaning of word 'series' is **"a set of things in a logical sequence**." Or **putting ideas in a more logical sequence".** In the context of language, 'a series' is a sequence of sentences or clauses, which imply some logical order in terms of grammatical correctness.

The Elements of a series are sentences, sentence fragments, clauses, marks of punctuation and the order of these. We should be sure that all items in a series are in logical order as well as in parallel form.

Logical order means

1. Using a natural and chronological sequence for the events you want to relate. And related parts of a sentence are not unnecessarily separated by other elements.
2. Logical order may sometimes refer to climatic order – that is building up ideas in increasing order of importance. In a series of words and phrases, which vary considerably in relative importance, the elements should be arranged with the weakest first and the strongest last.

For example

- Un emphatic: His life was tragic and brief.
  Emphatic: His life was brief and tragic.
- Un emphatic: He was a skillful politician, a distinguished lawyer, and an eminent jurist.
- Emphatic: He was an eminent jurist, a distinguished lawyer, and a skillful politician.

3. We should use effective repetition of key words or phrases and ideas to achieve emphasis.

For example

- It is true you may fool all the people some of the time; you can even fool some of the people all the time; but you can't fool all the people all the time.

- There is no mistake; there has been no mistake and there will be no mistake.

4. The shorter elements before a longer are kept in a series: As a general rule the shorter number of a series should precede the longer number.

For example

- Un emphatic: The book is beautifully illustrated in colours and interesting.
  Emphatic: The book is interesting and is beautifully illustrated in colours.

5. Negative statement kept before a contrasted affirmative statement makes a more emphatic sentence.

For example

- Incorrect: He failed because he was overconfident, not because he was over trained.
- Correct: He failed not because he was over trained but because he was overconfident.
- Incorrect: His actions were guided by a desire for power, not by love of humanity.
- Correct: His actions were guided not by love of humanity but by a desire for power,

6. Passive voice should not be used when active voice can be used more naturally and definitely.

Exercises

Rewrite the following sentences by arranging ideas in a more logical order.

1. He moved away from the city because he was ill, his rent was high, and he wanted to let his dog run.
2. She inherited a million dollars, a house and some jewellery.
3. The play closed after the first week and received terrible reviews.
4. The earthquake caused 100 deaths and toppled several of the buildings in the area.
5. As the car wound up the narrow road we found the trees becoming more scattered as we reared the top of the mountain.
6. The school itself will be benefited by this change, as well as the students.
7. The fire was put out before any serious damage was done by the fireman.
8. He accepted the position because he felt it was his duty not because he wanted the money.
9. The boys were arrested by the police carrying the banner.

Answers

1. *He moved away from the city because he wanted to let his dog run, his rent was high, and he was ill.*
2. *She inherited some jewellery, a house and a million dollars.*
3. *The play received terrible reviews and closed after the first week.*
4. *The earthquake toppled several of the buildings in the area and caused 100 deaths.*
5. *As the car wound up the narrow road and reared the top of the mountain, we found the trees becoming more scattered.*
6. *The school itself, as well as the students, will be benefited by this change.*
7. *The fire was put out by the fireman (or the fireman put out the fire) before any serious damage was done.*
8. *He accepted the position not because he wanted the money but because he felt it was his duty.*
9. *The boys, carrying the banner, were arrested by the police.*

Active and Passive Voice

15

CHAPTER

There are two ways of expressing an action by using a transitive verb. A transitive verb may be used in two voices; active voice and passive voice. The active voice is that form of the verb, which shows that the subject is the doer of the action.

- Mohan is writing a letter.

The passive voice is that form of the verb, which shows that something is done to the subject.

- The letter is being written by Mohan.

TRANSFORMATION FROM THE ACTIVE VOICE TO THE PASSIVE VOICE

1. When a verb is changed from the active into the passive voice, the object of the active voice becomes the subject and vice versa.

Subject		**Object**
I	is changed into	me
We	is changed into	us
You	remains as	you
He	is changed into	him
She	is changed into	her
It	remains as	it
They	is changed into	them

2. Change the verb into Past Participle (III form). Put proper form of the verb 'to be' before it according to the tense of the main verb in active voice and the number (singular/plural) of the new subject.
3. Tense of the verb is not changed. Only its form is changed.
4. By is used with the doer of action when it helps to complete sense.

➢ **Remember**

Such indefinite and vague subjects as 'someone', 'somebody', 'everybody', 'they', 'people' etc. are dropped. For example:

- *Someone has broken this toy. (active)*

- *This toy has been broken. (passive)*
- *People always admire this book. (active)*
- *This book is always admired. (passive)*

5. When a verb in the active voice takes two objects, a direct one and an indirect one, either of them may be used as the subject in the passive voice. For example:
   - Sita gave me a book. *(active)*
   - I was given a book by Sita. *(passive)*

     OR
   - A book was given to me by Sita. *(passive)*
6. Prepositions must not be left out with verbs requiring them.
   - She must look after the girl. *(active)*
   - The girl must be looked after. *(passive)*

The Forms of a Verb in Different Tenses in Active Voice

Form	*Present Tense*	*Past Tense*	*Future Tense*
Indefinite	I study English	I studied English	I shall study English
Continuous	I am studying English	I was studying English	I shall be studying English
Perfect	I have studied English	I had studied English	I shall have studied English
Perfect Continuous	I have been studying English	I had been studying English	I shall have been studying English

The Forms of a Verb in Different Tenses in Passive Voice

Form	*Present Tense*	*Past Tense*	*Future Tense*
Indefinite	English is studied by me.	English was studied by me.	English will be studied by me.
Continuous	English is being studied by me.	English was being studied by me.	–
Perfect	English has been studied by me.	English had been studied by me.	English will have been studied by me.
Perfect Continuous	–	–	–

The Forms of a Verb in Simple Present Tense
OR
Present Indefinite Tense

Active Voice	*Passive Voice*
Form of the Verb: *First Form + s/es*	*is/am/are + Third Form* *(according to subject)*
Mr. Gupta teaches me.	I am taught by Mr. Gupta.
She admires the hero.	The hero is admired by her.

Harish sells computers.	Computers are sold by Harish.
They like you.	You are liked by them.
We admire him.	He is admired by us.
I seldom keep him waiting.	He is seldom kept waiting by me.
She manages the hotel.	The hotel is managed by her.
They do not grow rice.	Rice is not grown by them.
Does he know you?	Are you known to him?
Do they speak English?	Is English spoken by them?
What do you want?	What is wanted by you?
Why do you tell a lie?	Why is a lie told by you?
Whom do you want?	Who is wanted by you?
Who teaches you English?	By whom are you taught English? Or By whom is English taught by you?

The Forms of a Verb in Simple Past Tense
OR
Past Indefinite Tense

Active Voice	*Passive Voice*
Form of the Verb: *Second Form*	***was/were + Third Form***
He threw the ball.	The ball was thrown by him.
The man cut down the tree.	The tree was cut down by the man.
He kept us waiting.	We were kept waiting by him.
They did not proclaim him leader.	He was not proclaimed leader by them.
The stone did not hit me on the head.	I was not hit on the head by the stone.
What did he speak to you?	What was spoken to you by him?
Which movie did you see last night?	Which movie was seen by you last night?
Did she run a great risk?	Was a great risk run by her?
Did they win the match?	Was the match won by them?
Did the mother punish the child?	Was the child punished by the mother?
Who wrote this book?	By whom was this book written?
Why did your brother write such a letter?	Why was such a letter written by your brother?
Where did you buy it?	Where was it bought by you?

The Forms of a Verb in Simple Future Tense
OR
Future Indefinite Tense

Active Voice	*Passive Voice*
Form of the Verb: *will/shall + First Form*	***will/shall + be + Third Form***
He will fly a kite.	A kite will be flown by him.
I will run a race.	A race will be run by me.
They will not beat me.	I shall not be beaten by them.
The teacher will scold the students.	The students will be scolded by the teacher.

Everybody will blame us.	We shall be blamed by everybody.
My mother will look after you.	You will be looked after by my mother.
I shall not speak a word to you.	Not a word will be spoken to you by me.
Shall I ever forget those happy days?	Will those happy days be ever forgotten by me?
When will she give up her studies?	When will her studies be given up by her?
Where will she keep her books?	Where will her books be kept by her?

The Forms of a Verb in Present Continuous Tense

Active Voice	*Passive Voice*
Form of the Verb: ***is/am/are + Present Participle*** ***(First Form of Verb + ing)***	***is/am/are + being + Past Participle*** ***(Third Form of Verb)***
Tapesh is building a house.	A house is being built by Tapesh.
He is running a race.	A race is being run by him.
I am painting a picture.	A picture is being painted by me.
They are flying kites.	Kites are being flown by them.
He is not running a race.	A race is not being run by him.
I am not watering the plants.	The plants are not being watered by me.
He is not driving a motor car.	A motor car is not being driven by him.
Is she singing a song?	Is a song being sung by her?
Are you writing a letter?	Is a letter being written by you?
What is she doing?	What is being done by her?
Why are you helping him?	Why is he being helped by you?

The Forms of a Verb in Past Continuous Tense

Active Voice	*Passive Voice*
Form of the Verb: ***Was/were + Present Participle*** ***(First Form of Verb + ing)***	***was + being + Past Participle*** ***(Third Form of Verb)***
I was writing a letter.	A letter was being written by me.
She was washing her clothes.	Her clothes were being washed by her.
We were playing a game.	A game was being played by me.
I was not laughing at my sister.	Was my sister not being laughed at by me.
Was he knocking at the door?	Was the door being knocked by him?
Was he reading a book?	Was a book being read by him?
What was she doing?	What was being done by her?
Why were you wasting my time?	Why was my time being wasted by you?

The Forms of a Verb in Present Perfect Tense

Active Voice	*Passive Voice*
Form of the Verb: ***Has/have + Past Participle***	***Has/have+been+ Past Participle***
I have completed the work.	The work has been completed by me.
They have built the house.	The house has been built by them.

We have locked our rooms.	Our rooms have been locked by us.
I have not invited all the friends.	All the friends have not been invited by me.
Has she stolen your book?	Has your book been stolen by her?
Has he invited you?	Have you been invited by him?
Have you written letters?	Have letters been written by you?
Why have you missed the lecture?	Why has the lecture been missed by you?

The Forms of a Verb in Past Perfect Tense

Active Voice	*Passive Voice*
Form of the Verb: ***Had + Past Participle***	***Had + been + Past Participle***
I had completed the work.	The work had been completed by me.
He had already seen the film.	The film had already been seen by him.
She had already missed the bus.	The bus had already been missed by her.
She had never read this book before.	This book had never been read by her before.
Had they seen us before?	Had we been seen by them before?
Why had he sold his house?	Why had his house been sold by him?
Why had he killed the wolf?	Why had the wolf been killed by him?

The Forms of a Verb in Future Perfect Tense

Active Voice	*Passive Voice*
Form of the Verb: ***will/shall+have+III form***	***Will/shall+have+been+III form***
The peon will have rung the bell.	The bell will have been rung by the peon.
He will have posted the letter.	The letter will have been posted by him.
I shall have finished the work in a fortnight.	The work will have been finished by me in a fortnight.
You will have won a prize by then.	The prize will have been won by you by then.
They will not have done this work.	This work will not have been done by them.
They will have purchased all the books by 2 p.m.	All the books will have been purchased by them by 2 p.m.

Change of Voice in Interrogative Sentences Which Begin With a Modal Auxiliary

Active Voice	*Passive Voice*
May I take this book?	May this book be taken by me?
May I have your bike for five minutes?	May your bike be had by me for five minutes?
Can we send our scooter by train?	Can our scooter be sent by train?
Will you help me?	Shall I be helped by you?
Must I reveal the secret?	Must the secret be revealed by me?
Should I take exercise daily?	Should exercise be taken by me daily?
Why should I read this paper?	Why should this paper be read by me?
How could I help you?	How could you be helped by me?

Change of Voice in Imperative Sentences
Or
Sentences of Command/Order/Request/ Advice

Active Voice	*Passive Voice*
Do it.	Let it be done.
Let him sell the book.	Let the book be sold by him.
Work hard.	You are advised to work hard.
Switch off the lights.	Let the lights be switched off.
Please help me.	You are requested to help me.
Kindly go through this book.	You are requested to go through this book.
Shut the windows.	You are ordered to shut the windows.

Miscellaneous

Active Voice	*Passive Voice*
She can read this book.	This book can be read by her.
We should obey our parents.	Our parents should be obeyed by us.
We ought to respect our teachers.	Our teachers ought to be respected by us.
One should keep one's promises.	Promises should be kept.
You will have to do it.	It will have to be done by you.
Sit down.	Be seated.
She knows me.	I am known to her.
People say that apples are good for health.	It is said that apples are good for health. Or, Apples are said to be good for health.
It is time to do this work.	It is time for this work to be done.
A stick is to walk with.	A stick is to be walked with.
They spoke to him.	He was spoken to by them.
Someone was knocking at the door.	The door was being knocked at (by someone).
The rose smells sweet.	The rose is sweet when (it is) smelt.
The book is printing.	The book is being printed.
My hair needs cutting.	My hair needs to be cut.
One cannot help it.	It cannot be helped.
They say that virtue is its own reward.	It is said that virtue is its own reward.
May I go out?	Am I allowed to go out?
God helps those who help themselves.	Those who are helped by themselves are helped by God.

REVIEW EXERCISES

Exercise 1

Rewrite the following sentences in passive voice:

1. The supervisor will review the report before he sends it to the manager.
2. We found errors in the article, but we have corrected them.
3. I have attached the current status report with some improvements.

4. Follow the recommended guidelines for replacing equipment.
5. The students welcomed the teacher.
6. Pooja will present her research at the conference.
7. Scientists have conducted experiments to test the hypothesis.
8. I have damaged your bicycle.
9. She slammed on the brakes as the car sped downhill.
10. The committee is considering action on the bill.

Answers

1. *The report will be reviewed by the supervisor before it is sent to the manager.*
2. *Errors were found in the article by us, but steps have been taken to correct them.*
3. *The current status report with some improvements has been attached by me.*
4. *The recommended guidelines for replacing equipment should be followed.*
5. *The teacher was welcomed by the students.*
6. *Research will be presented by Pooja at the conference.*
7. *Experiments have been conducted (by scientists) to test the hypothesis.*
8. *Your bicycle has been damaged by me.*
9. *The brakes were slammed on by her as the car sped downhill.*
10. *Action on the bill is being considered by the committee.*

Exercise 2

Put the following sentences in passive voice:

1. Someone gave me a book.
2. He showed the visitors his new building.
3. We must look into this matter.
4. You must work for success.
5. Somebody gave her a box of chocolates for her birthday.
6. They will look after you well.
7. He finished his work by eight o'clock.
8. We ate up all the biscuits yesterday.
9. You must not throw away empty bottles.
10. You must iron this dress for tonight.

Answers

1. *I was given a book.*
2. *The visitors were shown his new building (by him.)*
3. *This matter must be looked into by us.*

4. *Success must be worked for by you.*
5. *She was given a box of chocolates for her birthday.*
6. *You will be well looked after.*
7. *His work was finished by eight o'clock.*
8. *All the biscuits were eaten up by us yesterday.*
9. *Empty bottles must not be thrown away by you.*
10. *This dress must be ironed by you for tonight.*

Exercise 3

Rewrite the following sentences in passive voice:

1. Most of the class is reading a book.
2. The researchers will publish their results in the next issue of the journal.
3. We made mistakes.
4. The monkey bit the man.
5. The candidate believes that government must place a ceiling on the budget.
6. My sister broke my parents' favourite lamp.
7. A panel of famous fiction writers chose the winning novel.
8. Automobile accidents killed four motorists over the Memorial Day weekend.
9. The publishers never sent the book on glaciers to the bookstore.
10. The veteran pitcher threw a ball traveling at incredible speed.

Answers

1. *A book is being read by most of the class.*
2. *The results will be published by the researchers in the next issue of the journal.*
3. *Mistakes were made by us.*
4. *The man was bitten by the monkey.*
5. *It is believed by the candidate that a ceiling must be placed by the government on the budget.*
6. *My parents' favourite lamp was broken by my sister.*
7. *The winning novel was chosen by a panel of famous fiction writers.*
8. *Four motorists were killed by automobile accidents over the Memorial Day weekend.*
9. *The book on glaciers was never sent to the bookstore by the publishers.*
10. *A ball traveling at incredible speed was thrown by the veteran pitcher.*

Exercise 4

Rewrite the following sentences in passive voice:

1. We insist on punctuality in this office.

2. They make Fords in Cologne.
3. They make shoes in that factory.
4. Susan is cooking dinner.
5. Shakespeare wrote 'Hamlet.'
6. They were painting the house when I arrived.
7. He has written a novel.
8. I will finish it tomorrow.
9. They are going to build a new factory in Agra.
10. I don't think I can do it.

Answers

1. *Punctuality is insisted on in this office.*
2. *Fords are made by them in Cologne.*
3. *Shoes are made by them in that factory.*
4. *Dinner is being cooked by Susan.*
5. *'Hamlet' was written by Shakespeare.*
6. *The house was being painted by them when I arrived.*
7. *A novel has been written by him.*
8. *I will be finished tomorrow.*
9. *A new factory is going to be built in Agra.*
10. *I don't think it can be done by me.*

Exercise 5

Rewrite the following sentences in passive voice:

1. The impatient server cleared the dishes from the table.
2. Some of the performances amazed us.
3. Every employee should insist on adequate medical benefits.
4. Three committee members made a motion to table the matter.
5. The grocery clerk wrote a note on the brown paper bag.
6. You must tidy up this room.
7. They gave up the search after three hours.
8. No one brought up that question at the meeting.
9. We had to put off our visit until later.
10. His bank manager turned down his request for a loan.

Answers

1. *The dishes were cleared from the table by the impatient server.*
2. *We were amazed by some of the performances.*
3. *Adequate medical benefits should be insisted on by every employee.*

4. *A motion was made to table the matter by three committee members.*
5. *A note was written on the brown paper bag by the grocery clerk.*
6. *This room must be tidied up by you.*
7. *The search was given up by them after three hours.*
8. *That question was not brought up at the meeting.*
9. *Our visit had to be put off until later.*
10. *His request for a loan was turned down by his bank manager.*

Exercise 6

Put the following sentences in passive voice:

1. Someone has cheated me.
2. How can we bring about the desired results?
3. Did not they promise you a rise in salary at the beginning of the year?
4. What did they pay you for doing the job?
5. Someone should tell him never to do that again.
6. Why did they not offer him the job?
7. He asked me to meet you here at eleven o' clock.
8. We shall offer a high salary to a really suitable applicant.
9. The crowd gave the president a great reception.
10. We shall send you the machines as soon as they are available.

Answers

1. *I have been cheated.*
2. *How can the desired results be brought about by us?*
3. *Were you not promised a rise in salary by them at the beginning of the year?*
4. *What were you paid by them for doing the job?*
5. *He should be told never to do that again.*
6. *Why was he not offered the job by them.*
7. *I was asked by him to meet you here at eleven o' clock.*
8. *A high salary will be offered by us to a really suitable applicant.*
9. *The president got a great reception by the crowd.*
10. *The machines will be sent to you as soon as they are available.*

Exercise 7

Put the following sentences in passive voice:

1. People must not leave bicycles in the driveway.
2. They built that skyscraper in 1934.
3. The students will finish the course by July.
4. They are repairing the streets this month.

5. They make these tools of plastic.
6. They have finished the new product design.
7. They were cooking dinner when I arrived.
8. Did the plan interest you?
9. They had finished the preparations by the time the guests arrived.
10. You should take care when working with electrical equipment.

Answers

1. *Bicycles must not be left in the driveway.*
2. *The skyscraper was built in 1934.*
3. *The course will be finished by July.*
4. *The streets are being repaired this month.*
5. *These tools are made of plastic.*
6. *The new product design has been finished.*
7. *Dinner was being cooked when I arrived.*
8. *Were you interested in the plan?*
9. *The preparations had been finished by the time the guests arrived.*
10. *Care should be taken while working with electrical equipment.*

Exercise 8

Rewrite the following sentences in active voice:

1. The refreshments are going to be prepared by Karen.
2. Four motorists were killed by automobile accidents over the memorial day weekend.
3. The book on glaciers was never sent to the bookstore by the publishers.
4. A ball travelling at incredible speed was thrown by the veteran pitcher.
5. The dishes were cleared from the table by the impatient server.
6. English sheepdogs are bred and raised by the kennel on 3rd Avenue.
7. We were amazed by some of the performances.
8. Adequate medical benefits should be insisted on by every employee.
9. A motion was made to table the matter by three committee members.
10. A note was written on the brown paper bag by the grocery clerk.

Answers

1. *Karen is going to prepare the refreshments.*
2. *Automobile accidents killed four motorists over the memorial day weekend.*
3. *The publishers never sent the book on glaciers to the bookstore.*
4. *The veteran pitcher threw a ball travelling at incredible speed.*

5. *The impatient server cleared the dishes from the table.*
6. *The kennel on 3rd Avenue breeds and raises English sheepdogs.*
7. *Some of the performances amazed us.*
8. *Every employee should insist on adequate medical benefits.*
9. *Three committee members made a motion to table the matter.*
10. *The grocery clerk wrote a note on the brown paper bag.*

Reported Speech Direct-Indirect Narration

16

CHAPTER

We often have to give information about what people say or think. There are two ways of relating what someone has said; direct and indirect.

1. Direct Speech or Direct Narration

Quoting exactly what someone has said is called direct speech. Here what a person says appears within inverted commas ("....") without any change.

- She said, "I don't like horror movies."
- The actress said, "After this scene, I will need a rest."
- She said, "Today's lesson is on presentations."
- "I am going to the cinema", he said.
- Gita said to him, "I am not well today."
- I said to him, "What are you doing?"
- He said to me, "Please help me."
- I said to the shopkeeper, "Please give me a packet of biscuits."

Direct speech is mainly used in conversation in books, quotations, and plays.

2. Indirect Speech or Indirect Narration

An indirect speech gives the same meaning without using the speaker's exact words. Indirect speech does not use inverted commas to convey what the person said.

- She said that she didn't like horror movies.
- The actress said that after this scene, she would need a rest.
- She said that today's lesson was on presentations.
- He said he was going to the cinema.
- Gita told him that she was not well that day.
- I asked him what he was doing.
- He requested me to help him.
- I asked the shopkeeper to give me a packet of biscuits.

➢ ***Remember:***

1. ***In direct speech,*** *the verb which generally comes before the inverted commas is called the* ***Reporting Verb.*** *In the above mentioned examples 'says' and 'said' are the Reported Verbs.*
2. *The part within the inverted commas is called the* ***Reported Speech.***
3. *The first word of the reported speech begins with a capital letter.*
4. ***In indirect speech*** *no commas or inverted commas are used.*
5. *The reported speech is introduced by some conjunction; that, if, what, why etc.*
6. *The tense of reported verb is never changed.*
7. *The marks of punctuation (sign of interrogation or exclamation) other than full-stop are removed.*
8. *The reported speech is changed into assertive sentences.*
9. *Indirect speech is usually introduced by a verb in the past tense. So the verbs in direct speech have to be changed into a corresponding past tense.*
10. *In reported speech the word 'that' is often used; as,*
    - *He told me that he lived in Delhi.*

    However, 'that' is optional.
    - *He told me he lived in Delhi.*

    'That' is never used in questions, instead we often use 'if'.
    - *He asked me if I would come to the party.*

CONVERSION FROM DIRECT TO INDIRECT SPEECH

A. The Change of Tenses

Rule 1: If the Reporting Verb is in the present tense or future tense, the tense of the verb in the Reported Speech is not changed.

Direct	Indirect
• He says, "Hari writes a letter."	He says that Hari writes a letter.
• He says, "Hari wrote a letter."	He says that Hari wrote a letter.
• He says, "Hari will write a letter."	He says that Hari will write a letter.
• He will say, "Hari is writing a letter."	He will say that Hari is writing a letter.
• He will say, "Hari was writing a letter."	He will say that Hari was writing a letter.
• He will say, "Hari will be writing a letter."	He will say that Hari will be writing a letter.

Rule 2: If the Reporting Verb is in the past tense, the tense of the verb in the Reported Speech is changed according to the corresponding past tense as mentioned below.

Direct Speech		Indirect Speech
1. **Present Indefinite**	is changed into	**Past Indefinite**
• *I write*		• *I wrote*
2. **Present Continuous**	is changed into	**Past Continuous**
• *I am writing*		• *I was writing*
3. **Present Perfect**	is changed into	**Past Perfect**
• *I have written*		• *I had written*
4. **Present Perfect Continuous**	is changed into	**Past Perfect Continuous**
• *I have been writing*		• *I had been writing*
5. **Past Indefinite**	is changed into	**Past Perfect**
• *I wrote*		• *I had written*
6. **Past Continuous**	is changed into	**Past Perfect Continuous**
• *I was writing*		• *I had been writing*
7. **Past Perfect**	Remains unchanged	
• *I had written*		• *I had written*
8. **Past Perfect Continuous**	Remains unchanged	
• *I had been writing*		• *I had been writing*
9. **Future Indefinite**	is changed into	**Conditional**
• *I will write*		• *I would write*
10. **Future Continuous**	is changed into	**Conditional Continuous**
• *I will be writing*		• *I would be writing*
11. **Future Perfect**	is changed into	**Conditional Continuous**
• *I shall have been writing*		• *I would have been writing*
12. **Future Perfect Continuous**		**Conditional Perfect Continuous**
• *I shall have been writing*	is changed into	• *I would have been writing*

Corresponding Past Forms Verb

Verbs	*Past Forms*	*Verbs*	*Past Forms*
is, am	Was	go/goes	went
Are	Were	did	had gone
Will	Would	went	had gone
Shall	should/would	write	wrote
Can	Could	wrote	had written
May	Might	Was/were	had been
Must	must/had to	had	had had
has, have	had	has had/have had	had had

Exceptional Rules

Rule 1. If the reported speech expresses universal truth or habitual fact, the verb in it does not change.

Direct	Indirect
• The teacher said, "The earth revolves around the earth."	The teacher said that the earth revolves round the earth.

• She said, "Raj is a meritorious boy."	She said that Raj is a meritorious boy.
• I said, "God is everywhere."	I said that God is everywhere.
• He said, "Two and two make four."	He said that two and two make four.

Rule 2. If the reported speech describes a past historical fact, the Past Indefinite Tense remains unchanged.

Direct	Indirect
• She said, "I worked in Agra for five years."	She said that she worked in Agra for five years.
• He said, "Shivam was absent when the teacher came.	He said that Shivam was absent when the teacher came.
• The teacher said, "Columbus discovered America in 1442."	The teacher said that Columbus discovered America in 1442.
• He says, "When the cat is away the mice play."	He says that when the cat is away the mice play.

Rule 3. If the reported speech states two actions that took place at the same time, the Past Indefinite or Continuous Tense does not change.

Direct	Indirect
• I said, "Anil was reading a book while Kamal was playing cricket."	I said that Anil was reading a book while Kamal was playing cricket.
• He said, "The students were absent when the teacher entered the classroom."	He said that the students were absent when the teacher entered the class room.

Rule 4: If the reported speech expresses some hypothetical condition, the Past Indefinite Tense does not change.

Direct	Indirect
• I said, "If I were the president I would build a new building."	I said that if I were the president I would build a new building.
• He said to me, "if you were present there you would be very happy"	He told me that if I were present there I would be very happy.

B. The Change of Pronouns

Rule 1: Pronouns of the First Person (I/we) in the Reported Speech are changed into the Person of the Subject of the Reporting Verb as mentioned below:

	I	*My*	*Me*		*We*	*Our*	*Us*
I said	I	My	me	We said	we	our	Us
You said	You	your	you	You said	you	your	You

He said	He	His	him
They said	they	their	them
She said	She	her	her

Examples

Direct	Indirect
• I said, "I am writing a letter to my friend."	I said that I was writing a letter to my friend.
• You said, "I am writing a letter to my friend."	You said that you were writing a letter to your friend.
• He said, "I am writing a letter to my friend."	He said that he was writing a letter to his friend.
• She said, "I am writing a letter to my friend."	She said that she was writing a letter to her friend.
• We said, "We were writing a letter to our friend."	We said that we were writing a letter to our friend.

Rule 2: Pronouns of the Second Person (you) in the Reported Speech are changed into the Person of the Object of the Reporting Verb, i.e., the person to whom the speech reported is addressed as mentioned below:

	You (Subject)	*Your*	*You (Object)*
I said to him	He	his	him
He said to you	You	your	you
You said to me	I	my	me
You said to her	She	her	her
I said to them	They	their	them
He said to us	We	our	us

Examples

Direct	Indirect
• I said to him, "You are a good boy."	I told him that he was a good boy.
• He said to me, "You are honest."	He told me that I am honest.
• I said to you, "You may go."	I told you that you might go.
• I said to them, "you all are going to Delhi."	I told them that they all were going to Delhi.
• You said to her, "you are a good girl."	You told her that she was a good girl.

➢ ***Remember:***

1. *'We' remains unchanged when it denotes mankind generally or the speaker together with the person spoken to one of the two being expressed by a pronoun of the first person.*

Direct	***Indirect***
• *He said, "We must all die."*	*He said that we must all die.*
• *I said to him, "We are late."*	*I told him that we were late.*

2. *Pronouns of the third person in the reported speech are not changed.*

Direct	***Indirect***
• *He said, "He may go."*	*He said that he might go.*

C. The Other Changes

Rule 1: The words expressing nearness in time and place are generally placed into words expressing distance.

Direct *Words Expressing Nearness*		*Indirect* *Words Expressing Distance*
Now	is changed into	Then
This	is changed into	That
These	is changed into	those
Here	is changed into	There
Thus	is changed into	So
Ago	is changed into	Before
Hither	is changed into	Thither
Hence	is changed into	Thence
Today	is changed into	That day
Tonight	is changed into	That night
Tomorrow	is changed into	The next day
Yesterday	is changed into	The previous day/The day before
Last night	is changed into	The previous night/The night before
Next week	is changed into	The following week
Last week	is changed into	The previous week
The day before yesterday	is changed into	The day before previous day
The day after tomorrow	is changed into	The day after the next day
Come	is changed into	Go
Just	is changed into	Then

Examples

Direct	**Indirect**
• He said, "I am too weak to work now."	He said that he was too weak to work then.
• He said, "I want this book."	He said that he wanted that book.

• He said, "I will come here."	He said that he would go there.
• He said to me, "I shall see you tomorrow."	He told me that he would see me the next day.
• He said, "I saw this boy long ago.	He said that I saw that boy long before.
• He said, "I went to New York last week."	He said that he had gone to New York the week before.

➢ ***Remember:***

When the words showing nearness like 'this', 'here', 'before', etc. in Direct Speech refer to the objects present at the time of reporting, they remain unchanged.

Direct	***Indirect***
• *He said, "I will do it now or never."*	*He said that he would do it now or never.*
• *She said to me, "I shall not come to school today."*	*She told me that she will not come to school today. (The speech is reported that very day.)*
• *He said to me, "I shall wait for you here tomorrow."*	*He told me that he would wait for me here the next day. (The speech is reported at the same spot.)*

CONVERSION OF ASSERTIVE SENTENCES

Rules:

1. The Reported Verb 'said' is changed into 'told', 'replied', informed', 'remarked', or 'answered'.
2. If the reporting is not followed by an object, it is not changed.
3. Inverted commas ("....") are removed and the conjunction 'that' is used to connect the Reported Speech with Principle Clause.
4. Do not use the preposition 'to' after 'tell' or 'told'.

Examples

Direct	**Indirect**
• He said to them, "I shall write now."	He told them that he would write then.
• He said to us, "The car has come and we shall start soon."	He told us that the car had come and we should start soon.
• He said, "I am going to school everyday."	He said that he was going to school everyday.
• The teacher said to us, "the lecture will be delivered tomorrow."	The teacher told us that the lecture would be delivered the next day.

• He said to me, "I have finished my lunch."	He told me that he had finished his lunch.
• They said to us, "We live in Paris."	They told us that they lived in Paris.
• He replied, "I am going to find a new job."	He replied that he was going to find a new job.
• I said to her, "I shall give you a call."	I told her that I would give her a call.
• Anil said to me, "I am so happy today."	Anil told me that he was so happy that day.
• The president said, "I need a vacation."	The president said that he needed a vacation.
• He said, "I can go to school every day."	He said that he could go to school every day.
• He said, "I may go to school every day."	He said that he might go to school every day.
• He said, "I must go now."	He said that he had to go then.
• He said to me, "You needn't go."	He told me that I did not have to go.

CONVERSION OF INTERROGATIVE SENTENCES

Rules:

1. Change the Reporting Verb 'said' or 'told' into 'asked', 'inquired' or 'demanded'.
2. When the question is introduced by an interrogative word such as 'what', 'who', 'which', 'whom', whose', why', 'when', 'how' etc., the same word is used to introduce the indirect speech.
3. If the question begins with 'is', 'are', 'do', 'can', 'have', 'will' etc., that is if it requires 'yes' or 'no' for an answer, the Reporting Verb is followed by 'whether' or 'if'.
4. We change the question form into the assertive form by putting the nominative before the verb.
5. The mark of interrogation (?) is replaced by a full stop (.).
6. The conjunction 'that' is not used.

Examples

Direct	Indirect
• He said to me, "What are you doing?"	He asked me what I was doing.
• I said to him, "Do you write a letter to your parents?"	I asked him if he wrote a letter to his parents.
• He said to you, "What is your name?"	He asked you what your name was.

Direct	Indirect
• She said to me, "Can you spare some time for me?"	She asked me whether I could spare some time for her.
• I said to him, "Why did you strike me?"	I asked him (or I demanded of him) why he had struck me.
• The father said to the son, "Where are you going?"	The father enquired of the son where he was going.
• I said to her, "Do you go to school everyday?"	I asked her if she went to school everyday.
• I said to her, "Where do you go to school?"	I asked her where she went to school.
• My friend said, "How are you?"	My friend asked how I was.
• My friend said, "Whom did you call?"	My friend asked whom I had called.
• The teacher asked, "Where is Venus?"	The teacher asked where Venus is.
• You said to them, "Will you listen to such a man?"	You asked them whether they would listen to such a man.

CONVERSION OF IMPERATIVE SENTENCES

Rules:

1. In reporting command or request, the indirect speech is introduced by some verb expressing command or request. Such as 'order', 'advise', 'request', 'threaten', 'beg', 'propose', 'forbid', 'urge' etc.
2. Imperative mood is changed into infinitive mood by putting 'to' before the verb.
3. In the sentences of negative imperative, the auxiliary 'do' is not used and 'to' is placed after 'not'.
4. No conjunction is to be used to introduce the reported speech.
5. Sentences beginning with 'let':
    - When 'let' expresses a proposal, the Reporting Verb is changed into 'proposed' or 'suggested' and 'let' is replaced by 'should'.
    - If 'let' denotes permission, it is changed into 'to let' or some phrase as 'might be allowed'.
    - When 'let' expresses a condition or supposition, it is changed into 'might'.

Examples

Direct	Indirect
• The officer said to his servant, "Go away at once."	The officer ordered his servant to go away at once.
• The servant said to his master, "Pardon me, Sir."	The servant begged his master to pardon him.

• I said to my son, "Work steadily."	I advised my son to work steadily.
• You said to him, "I shall beat you."	You threatened to beat him.
• My friend said to me, "Please take your book."	My friend requested me to take my book.
• "Come quickly", he shouted, "and help me."	He shouted to them to come quickly and help him.
• Mother said, "Children do not leave the door open."	Mother forbade the children to leave the door open.
• He said to me, "Kindly help me."	He beseeched me to help him.
• The teacher said to the students, "Do not waste your time, as the examination is near."	The teacher advised the students not to waste their time as the examination was near.
• I said to my friends, "Let us go to the library."	I proposed to my friends that we should go to the library.
• The principal said to the peon, "Let the students come in."	The principal ordered the peon that the students might be allowed to come in. OR The principal ordered the peon to let the students come in.
• The boy said to his master, "Let me go home now."	The boy requested his master to let him go home then.

CONVERSION OF EXCLAMATORY SENTENCES

Rules:

1. In reporting exclamations and wishes, the indirect speech is introduced by some verb expressing exclamation or wish as 'pray', 'exclaim', 'cry', bless', 'wish', 'applaud', 'confess', 'bid' etc.
2. Use 'that' to introduce Reported Speech.
3. Replace the sign of exclamation (!) by a full stop (.).
4. In indirect speech, we say 'wished good morning', 'wished good evening', 'wished good afternoon'; but we say 'bade good bye', 'bade farewell', 'bade good night' etc.

Examples

Direct	Indirect
• He said to me, "May God pardon you!"	He prayed that God might pardon me.
• The teacher said, "May you succeed, my dear!"	The teacher wished that her student might succeed.
• She said, "Good bye friends!	She bade good bye to her friends.
• The prophet said to me, "May you be happy!"	The prophet blessed me with happiness.

• He said, Alas! I am wrong."	He exclaimed with grief that he was wrong.
• We said, "What a beautiful scene!"	We exclaimed with joy that it was a very beautiful scene.
• The little boy said, "O that I were a king!"	The little boy wished that he were a king.
• I said, "Congratulations!"	I congratulated him.
• He said, "Good Morning!"	He wished me good morning.
• I said to my friend, "Hello! Where are you going?"	I greeted my friend and asked him where he was going.

Some basic reporting verbs

• **accuse**

to accuse someone of doing something

"It was you who ate my chocolate, Elvira, wasn't it?"

He accused Elvira of eating his chocolate.

admit

to admit doing something

to admit that...

"OK, it was me. I ate your chocolate"

Elvira admitted eating the chocolate.

Elvira admitted that she had eaten the chocolate.

advise

to advise someone to do something

"Well, if I were you I'd start saving for my retirement."

He advised me to start saving for my retirement

agree

to agree that...

"Yes, you're right, it's a terrible problem."

She agreed that it was a terrible problem.

announce

to announce that...

"I'm afraid I've got some bad news. The company's closing."

The manager announced that the company was closing.

apologize

to apologize (to someone) for doing something

"I'm sorry I didn't get to the meeting."

He apologized for not going to the meeting.

ask

to ask someone to do something

"It's very hot in here. Would you mind opening the window?"

She asked him to open the window.

blame

to blame someone for doing something

"We lost the match because you didn't save that penalty."

He blamed the goalkeeper for losing the match.

complain

to complain about something

"The electrician said he was coming at ten o'clock so I took time off work and waited in all morning...."

She complained about the electrician.

congratulate

to congratulate someone on doing something

"Well done! I knew you'd pass your driving test this time."

She congratulated him on passing his driving test.

deny

to deny doing something

to deny that...

"It most certainly wasn't me that left the front door open."

He denied leaving the front door open.

He denied that he had left the front door open.

explain

to explain why...

to explain that...

"Sorry I'm late. The traffic was bad and then I couldn't find a parking space."

He explained why he was late.

He explained that he was late because of bad traffic.

forget

to forget to do something

"Oh no, I haven't got any money. I didn't go to the bank."

He forgot to go to the bank.

invite

to invite someone to do something

"Would you like to come to our house for dinner on Friday?

He invited them to come to his house for dinner on Friday.

offer

to offer to do something for someone

"Those bags must be heavy, John. Shall I take one?"
She offered to carry a bag for John.

promise

to promise to do something

"Yes, honest, I'll be there on time. I won't be late."
He promised not to be late.

refuse

to refuse to do something

"Well I'm not washing up. I did it last time."
He refused to do the washing up as he had done it the last time as well.

remind

to remind someone to do something

"Remember you have to go to the bank. You forgot yesterday."
She reminded me to go to the bank.

suggest

to suggest that someone should do something

to suggest that someone do something

"Why don't you go to the dentist if your tooth hurts?"
She suggested that he should go to the dentist.
She suggested that he went to the dentist.

threaten

to threaten to do something

"If you're late again we'll start without you."
They threatened to start without him the next time if he was late again.

warn

to warn someone about something

to warn someone (not) to do something

"Don't drive too quickly. The streets are very icy."
He warned him to drive carefully as the streets were icy.
He warned him against driving too quickly.

REVIEW EXERCISES

Exercise 1

Change the following sentences from direct to indirect:

1. I said, "She is busy".
2. I said, "I am working now".
3. I said, "She was here this morning".
4. I said "She was studying all yesterday."
5. I said, "She has worked here for 5 years."
6. I said, "She will work here from July."
7. I said, "We'll be living here for 6 months."
8. I said, "She can play the piano well."
9. The teacher said: "I want you to do your best, boys."

Answers

1. *I said she was busy.*
2. *I said I was working then*
3. *I said she was there that morning. OR*
   I said she had been there that morning.
4. *I said she was studying all through the previous day. OR*
   I said she had been studying all through the previous day.
5. *I said she had worked there for 5 years.*
6. *I said she would work there from July.*
7. *I said we would be living there for 6 months.*
8. *I said she could play the piano well.*
9. *The teacher told the boys he wanted them to do their best.*

Exercise 2

Change the following sentences from direct to indirect

1. "Do you like fish, Mary?", she asked.
2. He said, "I've failed my exam".
3. "I went to market this morning", she said.
4. "Don't lose the money!", she said to her son.
5. She said, "I didn't have my eyes tested yesterday".
6. "When did you see me?", he asked her.
7. The teacher told one of his pupils, "You'll come to harm if you don't work."
8. "Don't clean it yourselves!" mother said to the children.
9. The boy said, "I couldn't come because of my father's illness".
10. "Don't drive so fast", Susan shouted to John.

Answers

1. *He asked Mary if she liked fish.*

2. *He said he had failed his exam.*
3. *She said she had gone to market that morning.*
4. *She told her son not to lose the money.*
5. *She said she hadn't had her eyes tested the day before.*
6. *He asked her when she had seen him.*
7. *The teacher told one of his pupils he would come to harm if he didn't work.*
8. *Mother told the children not to clean it themselves.*
9. *The boy said he had not been able to come because of his father's illness.*
10. *Susan shouted to John not to drive so fast.*

Exercise 3

Change the following sentences from direct to indirect

1. "I got up early this morning", he said.
2. She said to me, "Don't worry about it".
3. "Do you have to leave so early?", he asked her.
4. "Have you had a good sleep", he asked her.
5. "What are you going to do tomorrow?", she asked me.
6. He said, "I didn't notice the speed limit".
7. "We'll get some tickets tomorrow", they told me.
8. "I'm leaving", the sailor said.
9. "They were here last week", Mrs. Benson told her husband.

Answers

1. *He said he had got up early that morning*
2. *She told me not to worry about it.*
3. *He asked her if she had to leave so early.*
4. *He asked her if she had had a good sleep.*
5. *She asked me what I was going to do the next day.*
6. *He said he had not noticed the speed limit.*
7. *They told me they would get some tickets the next day.*
8. *The sailor said he was leaving.*
9. *Mrs. Benson told her husband they had been there the week before.*

Exercise 4

Change the following sentences from direct to indirect:

1. "He always feels very cold", mother told the doctor.
2. "The children went to bed early today", father said.
3. "You look smart in these clothes", she told her daughter.
4. "Get out of my pub", the landlord said to the drunkard.

5. The children asked: "Shall we have to bring our books tomorrow?"
6. He asked the secretary: "How do you feel when the manager asks you to have dinner with him?"
7. He asked her, "Can you spare me a minute?"
8. He said, "I do not know how long it will take me."
9. I asked mother, "How much did this book cost?"
10. I asked him, "Did anybody see you?"

Answers

1. *Mother told the doctor he always felt very cold.*
2. *Father said the children had gone to bed early that day.*
3. *She told her daughter she looked smart in those clothes.*
4. *The landlord told the drunkard to get out of his pub.*
5. *The children asked if they would have to bring their books the following day.*
6. *He asked the secretary how she felt when the manager asked her to have dinner with him.*
7. *He asked her if she could spare him a minute.*
8. *He said he didn't know how long it would take him.*
9. *I asked mother how much that book had cost.*
10. *I asked him if anybody had seen him.*

Exercise 5

Change the following sentences from direct to indirect:

1. Mother said: "Susan, don't leave the door open!"
2. Mrs Brown asked Madhuri: "When did the Guptas sell their house?"
3. David asked his father: "Are you going to London tomorrow?"
4. She said, "I don't think we shall be late if we hurry".
5. "I'm not very well today", Susan said.
6. "You must send for the doctor at once", Mrs Johnson told her husband.
7. "You can go now, if you like", the teacher said to the boys.
8. "I think I'll have a holiday on Monday", the manager said.
9. "I've finished my work", the workman said.
10. "My wife is cooking the dinner", Mr Dickens said.

Answers

1. *Mother told Susan not to leave the door open.*
2. *Mrs Brown asked Madhuri when the Guptas had sold their house.*
3. *David asked his father if he was going to London the following day.*

4. *She said she didn't think they would be late if they hurried.*
5. *Susan said she was not very well that day.*
6. *Mrs Johnson told her husband he had to send for the doctor at once.*
7. *The teacher told the boys they could go if they liked.*
8. *The manager said he thought he would have a holiday on Monday.*
9. *The workman said he had finished his work.*
10. *Mr Dickens said his wife was cooking the dinner.*

Exercise 6

Change the following sentences from direct to indirect:

1. "We'll stay here until Tuesday", he said.
2. "I think it's going to rain", Tom said.
3. "Was Mr Gyan's operation successful?" he asked
4. "I can do this exercise", he said.
5. "I forgot to ask her name," he said.
6. "I've already had lunch," he said.
7. "I'll retire soon," he said.
8. "What did you have for breakfast?" she asked Teena.
9. "I'm inquiring about a certain patient," Mr Sinha said.
10. Tom said, "I saw you in town but you did not see me".

Answers

1. *He said they would stay there until Tuesday.*
2. *Tom said he thought it was going to rain.*
3. *He asked if Mr Gyan's operation had been successful.*
4. *He said he could do that exercise.*
5. *He said he had forgotten to ask her name.*
6. *He said he had already had lunch.*
7. *He said he would retire soon.*
8. *She asked Teena what he had had for breakfast.*
9. *Mr Sinha said he was inquiring about a certain patient.*
10. *Tom said he had seen us in town but we had not seen him.*

Exercise 7

Change the following sentences from indirect to direct:

1. She asked him how old he was.
2. She told me that she had been ill.
3. He asked his brother when he had arrived.

4. She said that she had been waiting there for half an hour.
5. She told me to tidy up the garden.
6. He asked the accused if he always caught the 8 o'clock train.
7. He told Mr Gupta that he had lived there since 1990.
8. He told the policeman that he had bought his car in 2000.
9. He let me know that he might be back late this evening.
10. I asked her where she was going so late at night.

Answers

1. *She asked him, "How old are you?"*
2. *She told me, "I was ill "/ She told me, "I have been ill ".*
3. *He asked his brother, "When did you arrive?"*
4. *She said, "I have been waiting here for half an hour".*
5. *She told me, "Tidy up the garden!"*
6. *He asked the accused, "Do you always catch the 8 o'clock train?"*
7. *He told Mr Gupta, "I have lived here since 1990".*
8. *He told the policeman, "I bought my car in 2000".*
9. *He said to me, "I may be back late tonight."*
10. *I said to her, "Where are you going so late at night?"*

Exercise 8

Change the following sentences from indirect to direct:

1. I asked him whether he often watched television.
2. I asked them if they were having a good time.
3. You asked him whether he had broken that vase the previous day.
4. He asked his wife if she was ready to leave.
5. You asked if John had understood the message.
6. He asked me why I had gone there.
7. He asked her why she had forgotten to write the letter.
8. The mother asked her daughter whether she needed any help.
9. I asked her what she was doing.
10. I wanted to know what the matter was.

Answers

1. *I said to him, "Do you often watch television?"*
2. *I said to them, "Are they having a good time?*
3. *You said to him, "Did you break that vase yesterday?*
4. *He said to his wife, "Are you ready to leave?"*
5. *You said, "Has John understood the message?"*

6. *He said to me, "Why have you come here?"*
7. *He said to her, "Why did you forget to write the letter."*
8. *The mother said to her daughter, "Do you need any help?"*
9. *I said to her, "What are you doing?"*
10. *I said, "What is the matter?"*

Exercise 9

Finish the sentences using reported speech.

1. Hari: "I clean the black shoes."
2. Manu: "Are you reading that book now?"
3. Rahul: "Who gave you the book yesterday?"
4. Ram: "Are you leaving next Friday?"
5. Dinesh: "Do you think it will rain tomorrow?"
6. Ganesh: "Where do you play football today?"
7. Neena: "Why didn't you go to New York last summer?"
8. Babloo: "Must I do the homework this week?'
9. Leena: "Did Max fly to London two weeks ago?"

Answers

1. *Hari told me that he cleaned the black shoes.*
2. *Manu asked me if I was reading that book at that time.*
3. *Rahul asked me who had given me the book the day before.*
4. *Ram asked me if I was leaving the following Friday.*
5. *Dinesh asked me if I thought it would rain the day after.*
6. *Ganesh asked me where I played football that day.*
7. *Neena asked me why I hadn't gone to New York the summer before.*
8. *Babloo asked me if he had to do the homework that week.*
9. *Leena asked me if Max had flown to London two weeks before.*

Exercise 10

Change the following sentences from direct to indirect:

1. He said, "I am going to France next week."
2. She said, "They haven't spoken to their parents for six years."
3. He said, "Seema doesn't want to go out with me."
4. She said, "You'll have to be here at 3 o'clock this afternoon."
5. I said, "I moved into my flat three years ago."
6. He said, "If I hear anything I'll phone you."
7. She said to them, "You can move into the flat as soon as you want."

8. He said, "You must bring me the money tomorrow."
9. She said to us, "I often go to the cinema."
10. She said to him, "I'm going to do it now if you'll let me."

Answers

1. *He said that he was going to France the following week.*
2. *She said that they had not spoken to their parents for six years.*
3. *He said that Seema did not want to go out with him.*
4. *She told me that I would have to be there at 3o'clock that afternoon.*
5. *I said that I had moved into my flat three years earlier.*
6. *He told me that if he heard anything he would phone me.*
7. *She told them that they could move into the flat as soon as they wanted.*
8. *He told us that we had to bring him the money the next day.*
9. *She told us that she often went to the cinema.*
10. *She told him that she was going to do it then if he would let her.*

Exericise 11

Change the following sentences from direct to indirect:

1. He said, "I'll teach English."
2. He said, "I can go to school every day."
3. He said, "I may go to school every day."
4. He said, "I might go to school every day."
5. He said, "I must go to school every day."
6. He said, "I have to go to school every day."
7. He said, "I should go to school every day."
8. He said, "I ought to go to school every day."
9. He said, "I must have a computer."
10. He asked, "Do you want to come with me?"

Answers

1. *He said (that) he would teach English.*
2. *He said (that) he could go to school every day.*
3. *He said (that) he might go to school every day.*
4. *He said (that) he might go to school every day.*
5. *He said (that) he had to go to school every day.*
6. *He said (that) he had to go to school every day.*
7. *He said (that) he should go to school every day.*
8. *He said (that) he ought to go to school every day.*
9. *He said (that) he had to have a computer.*
10. *He asked me if I wanted to come with him.*

Unit II

Comprehension and Composition

- Listening Comprehension Skills
- Reading Comprehension Skills
- The Art of Comprehension
- Paragraph Writing
- Precis Writing
- Letter Writing
- Essay Writing

Listening Comprehension Skills

17

CHAPTER

INTRODUCTION

As we all know linguistic skill consists of speaking and writing for sending messages, listening and reading for receiving them. Listening is a vital component of the entire process. The effectiveness of communication is determined by the extent to which listening and comprehension take place in the course of an interaction.

WHAT IS LISTENING COMPREHENSION?

Listening comprehension means an ability to understand the message, communicated orally. It is a four stage self-generated activity:

First stage : reception of the sound waves through the ears.
Second Stage: Interpretation of the sound received.
Third stage : Evaluation of the interpretation.
Fourth Stage: Reaction to the message.

Thus, Listening is a process of receiving, interpreting and reacting to the messages received from the communication sender.

LISTENING vs. HEARING

All hearing is not listening. Listening is making sense out of what we hear.

- **Listening** is voluntary. **Hearing** is an involuntary physical act, merely picking up sound vibrations. It is a physiological process in which the sound waves strike the eardrums.
- **Listening** requires concise efforts whereas **hearing** happens automatically.
- **Listening** is an active process whereas **hearing** is a passive process.
- **Listening** is a two-way interactive process engaging both the speaker and the listener. **Hearing** is a one-way process in which listener plays a passive part.

TYPES OF LISTENING

1. Passive Listening

The physical presence but mental absence of the listener can be defined as passive listening. When we hear one's speech rather indifferently, it is passive listening. In passive listening there is no invasion on the thought process which could probably change the trend of thinking or strengthen the preconceived ideas of the receiver. Passive listening makes a poor impression on the speaker.

This kind of listening is commonly found in classroom situations.

2. Marginal Listening

In marginal listening superficial listening takes place. When too much information is provided by the speaker, it leads to an information over load and listening tends to get hampered. In marginal listening the individual listens only at a superficial level and does not try to go beyond a brief understanding of the topics discussed.

The debates in the parliament and legislature give rise to the situation of marginal listening.

3. Projective Listening

In projective listening the receiver tries to view the contents of the presentation within his own frame of reference.

The arguments in the law courts are examples of projective listening.

4. Sensitive Listening

In sensitive listening the receiver is able to understand the viewpoint of the speaker in exactly similar terms as were intended by him. Sensitive listening can also be referred to as emphatic listening. Part of the emphasis in sensitive listening lies on the ability of the receiver to match his perceptions with those of the sender.

The doctor's conversation with the patient is an example of sensitive listening.

5. Active Listening

This is the most important type of listening. Active listening is an expression of one's genuine interest in what the speaker is saying. It requires paying attention, interpreting and remembering sound stimuli. In active listening, not only words, but also the tone, the facial expressions and the body movements contribute to communication.

When combined with sensitive listening, active listening creates the sense of confidence and trust in both parties.

Passive vs. Active listening

Effective listening is active rather than passive. In passive listening, we are much like a tape recorder. We absorb the information given. But active listening requires us to get inside the speaker so that we can understand the communication from his or her point of view.

FOUR ESSENTIAL REQUIREMENTS FOR ACTIVE LISTENING

1. Intensity

The active listener concentrates intensely on what the speaker is saying and tunes out the thousands of miscellaneous thoughts that create distractions.

2. Empathy

Empathy demands both knowledge of the speaker and flexibility of the listener. The listener should try to understand what the speaker wants to communicate.

3. Acceptance

An active listener demonstrates acceptance. He or she listens objectively without judging content.

4. A willingness to take responsibility for completeness

The listener dares, whatever is necessary, to get the full intended meaning from the speaker's communication.

Active listening requires immense involvement in the conversation, even when the listener's lips are sealed.

BARRIERS TO EFFECTIVE LISTENING

1. Physical barriers

- Noise
- Physical discomfort
- Physical distractions
- Distance

2. Psychological barriers

- Emotional disturbance
- Anxiety
- Lack of interest
- Wrong perception of the message

3. Linguistic barrier

- Improper message decoding
- Ambiguous language
- Jargon
- Listener's inadequate knowledge of the language

4. Cultural barrier

- Cultural differences
- Different values
- Different social norms

TECHNIQUES TO IMPROVE LISTENING ABILITY

1. We can improve listening comprehension by paying attention.
2. By making eye contact.
3. By showing interest in the speaker and speech.
4. The listener should respond non-verbally by exhibiting affirmative nods and appropriate facial expressions to encourage the speaker.
5. The listening comprehension requires concentration. We should avoid distracting actions and gestures.
6. The listening comprehension presupposes a coordination between the ear and the brain. Open your mind and practice accepting new information.
7. Paraphrases (restating what the speaker has said in our own words) help in developing effective active listening skills.
8. We should give the speaker adequate time to speak by all means. We should not jump to conclusions.

REVIEW EXERCISES

1. What do you mean by listening comprehension skill? What are the essential requirements for active listening?
2. Write a note on the importance of listening.
3. What are the barriers to listening comprehension? How can these barriers be overcome?
4. How can we develop effective listening skill?
5. What is the importance of concentration in listening?
6. Write short notes on:

   (a) Types of listening

   (b) Active and passive listening

   (c) Listening and hearing

Reading Comprehension Skills

18 CHAPTER

WHAT IS READING COMPREHENSION?

The act of reading is essentially a process of thinking. **Good reading means understanding through reading**. An eye passing over the written matter without the brain comprehending its sense is not reading. Reading comprehension is a two-fold process. It requires understanding of what is being presented and reproducing it as comprehended.

The comprehension process involves

- Speedy reading
- Quick understanding
- Precise reproduction

READING SPEEDS

According to **Edward Fry**, an educational psychologist, there are three reading speeds:

- **Study reading speed**

It is used for reading material which deals with difficult arguments, ideas etc. This type of reading aims at total comprehension and retention of what has been read.

- **Average reading speed**

It is faster than study reading. It is used for everyday reading of newspapers, magazines, novels etc.

- **Skimming reading speed**

This is the fastest reading speed. Its objective is only to get a rough idea of what the passage is about.

Following table shows the grading of three speeds of reading:

Speed	*Poor Reader*	*Good Reader*
1. Study reading	90-125 WPM* 80-90% Comprehension	200-300 WPM 80-90% Comprehension

2. Average reading	150-180 WPM 70% Comprehension	250-500 WPM 70% Comprehension
3. Skimming reading	Cannot skim	800 WPM 50% Comprehension

➢ * WPM means words per minute

BARRIERS TO READING COMPREHENSION

There are some factors which make it difficult to read with speed without missing the meaning:

1. Poorly equipped mind

The reader's ignorance of the symbols used, or his unfamiliarity with the subject, can affect his comprehending of the matter read. We can read more rapidly and profitably the things already known to us.

2. Prejudices and biased approach

Our prejudices, beliefs, biases, individuality might not be in harmony with the writer's viewpoint. In such a condition the comprehension will be imperfect.

3. Regression

Some readers suffer from a habit of looking back too much so as to hamper their progress. They move their eyes again and again to what has already been read. This visual wandering and regression makes them slow readers.

4. Vocalisation

Sometimes reading is made slow due to reader's habit to read aloud. Knowingly or unknowingly, he reads aloud to himself.

Some mechanical factors can also hamper reading comprehension. Among these we can mention such problems as **insufficient light, bad printing, loose binding, uncomfortable posture, presence of disturbing external elements like noisy environment or people staring at the reader.**

NECESSARY ELEMENTS OF GOOD READING

There are at least four tricks that can help us in overcoming the barriers of reading comprehension:

1. Command over the language

The reader should have a command over the language (word symbols). If his knowledge of the word symbols is inadequate, his understanding of written material will not be proper.

2. Reading much

One should read a lot of books, magazines, newspapers etc. so that one's mind should feel obliged to work faster in order to profit from it.

3. Unbiased and unprejudiced approach

The reader should keep his mind free from all bias or prejudice, then only will he be able to read a passage sincerely and grasp its meaning.

4. Concentration

Concentration is the key to all methods of reading faster and understanding more. The reader must be alert and attentive before he starts reading something.

5. Effective eye reading

Effective reading involves reading with fast eye movements. Eye reading makes reading fast, efficient and result oriented. It requires accurate visual perception of words and phrases, faster eye fixation and complete elimination of vocalization.

6. Underlining

To go on underlining the important parts is useful. It saves much time when a revision is made.

7. Looking for the key sentence

Instead of staying at every word, one should try to grasp the central idea in a paragraph.

8. Guessing

The reader should try to guess the meaning of the unfamiliar words with a reference to the context.

9. Prediction techniques

Prediction is a rapid reading skill. It involves the use of index, headings, subheadings, nonverbal context and linguistic clues to guess the information that a text contains.

VARIOUS METHODS OF READING SPEEDILY

F. P. Robinson, an educational psychologist, in his book 'Effective Study' devised a system of study called SQ3R. SQ3R suggests five types of reading styles for business purposes:

1. Labelling
2. Sampling
3. Studying
4. Skimming
5. Scanning

1. Labelling

Labelling helps the reader to remember the context of a document, when he intends not to go in detail on facts. In labelling, the reader surveys the title, section headings, special print, illustrations, graphs and tables. Then he builds up an idea of what the text as a whole is about.

2. Sampling

Sampling implies to have an outline picture of the whole. In sampling the reader reads preface, contents, introduction and conclusion and then he decides whether the book is worth reading in detail.

3. Studying

Studying is essentially a process of thinking. It requires repeated reading and taking notes of the essential points of the discourse.

4. Skimming

Skimming means looking at a text or chapter quickly in order to have a general/rough idea of the content. It can be described as a kind of superficial reading, skipping some parts. Skimming method is used to complete a lot of reading in a short period. In this reading the reader does not fix his eye on each and every word. He lets it move from one word to some other, jumping over a word or two.

Skimming reading is considered the most valuable reading tool of the busy office assistants as well as middle executives.

5. Scanning

Scanning means looking at a text to find some particular information. It is like making our eye see all but stay nowhere. The scanning method of reading means reading quickly in order to grasp the meaning. We examine the whole thing but not too curiously.

Skimming and Scanning methods are the popularly employed methods of reading comprehension. We skim through a report to have a rough idea of what it says but we scan a page of the telephone directory to find a particular number or name.

IMPORTANCE OF SKIMMING AND SCANNING METHODS

- The researchers show that when we read faster, our comprehension increases. The word-to-word reader generally fails to grasp the meaning of sentences or paragraphs.
- Skimming and scanning methods of reading save time. For example, we skim through a report to have a rough idea of what it says but we scan a page of telephone directory to find a particular name or number.

HOW CAN WE TEST OUR SKILL IN READING COMPREHENSION?

- By noting the time taken by our reading of a passage. The capacity to read 800 words per minute is supposed to be good.
- By preparing a précis of the passage read and to answer the questions based on it.

REVIEW EXERCISES

1. What is reading comprehension? What are the necessary elements of good reading?
2. What factors impede reading comprehension? How can these barriers to reading comprehension be overcome?
3. What are the various methods of reading speedily? How can we test our skill in reading comprehension?
4. Write a note on the importance of skimming and scanning methods.

The Art of Comprehension

19
CHAPTER

DEFINITION

Comprehension means the power of understanding. Hence, a comprehension passage aims at testing the student's knowledge and understanding of a given passage. This purpose of comprehension is achieved chiefly by setting suitable questions/exercises on a given passage, which the student is required to answer as accurately as he can in his own words. The exercises may vary in form and presentation, but all of them are designed to test the student's ability to understand and use the English language. The continuous practice of comprehension enables the student to express himself in a clear, correct and coherent manner.

HOW TO ANSWER QUESTIONS

Questions based on a particular passage are meant, as mentioned above, to test the student's comprehension and the power of expression. In this regard the student should always keep in mind the following points:

- In a comprehension question he is faced with objective queries on the passage, which he should try to appraise accurately. As he is not supposed to invent anything, he is not required to be original or knowledgeable in his answer. His main job is to get a good grasp of the passage and to answer the objective questions placed before him clearly, all the time keeping in mind the fact that answers to the questions asked are there in the passage itself.
- Before attempting to answer the question, he should read the passage carefully so as to get a good general idea of the passage.
- Read the passage twice or thrice in order to master the details and particular shades of meaning of different words, phrases and expressions.
- When you are able to understand what the passage is about, find out exactly that portion, which contains the answer to the question.
- Frame your answer on the basis of underlined portions using your own words.
- The answer should be neither too long nor too short. Avoid unnecessary and irrelevant details.

- In answering the questions, you should not add any new ideas of your own, unless you are asked to do so or to comment on some phrases or expressions.
- As comprehension is a test of English language, your language should be simple and correct.

HOW TO ANSWER MULTIPLE-CHOICE QUESTIONS

In the multiple-choice questions you are normally required to select the correct answer from three or more given choices. These questions often appear ridiculously easy, but appearances can be deceptive. While one or two of the choices may be way off the mark and obviously wrong, the others will probably have a very subtle difference in meaning to separate the correct choice from the wrong ones. That is why it is necessary to analyze the answers with a certain degree of concentration, and to carefully relate them to the question before making a final choice.

HOW TO EXPLAIN THE ITALICIZED PORTIONS

The explanation of the italicized portions of a passage does not require the mere substitution of easier words for difficult ones. Its chief aim is to make the portions in italics clearer. For this purpose, the following points should be remembered:

- Explain the italicized portions in your own simple and correct English, without being unnecessarily lengthy and superfluous.
- Explanation should contain the original ideas, and should be brief and to the point.
- Allusions and figures of speech should be made quite clear in easy language.
- Idioms and proverbs should be fully explained in simple and direct English.
- If the portion in italics is very difficult, it can be clarified by suitable examples.

HOW TO SUMMARIZE THE PASSAGE

A summary aims at saying in brief what has been said at great length. Thus, summary is an abridged statement or a shortened form of a passage. While summarizing a passage, the following points may prove useful:

- Read the original passage at least twice, think about it and try to understand its leading idea.
- You should enquire into the full meaning of metaphors and other figures of speech.
- Now draft a summary in the telegraphic form to include the main ideas.

- Compare your outlines with the original, noting carefully that you have neither omitted anything of cardinal importance nor included anything irrelevant or superfluous.
- Connect this outline summary into one continuous composition by adding the minimum words necessary for the purpose.
- Finally, read your summary carefully to make sure that it gives, in brief, the full impression of the original passage.

HOW TO SELECT A SUITABLE HEADING

Sometimes you are required to assign a suitable title or heading to the comprehension passage. For this purpose, try to find a word or phrase or a very short sentence that may sum up the main subject of the passage. In this connection, the following suggestions should be kept in mind:

- Read the opening and the concluding sentences of the passage very carefully. Very often the title is supplied by the 'topic sentence' of the passage, which is generally found at the beginning or at the end.
- If the first or the last sentence does not give the central idea, then you should select the heading from the passage as a whole.
- Try to pick some striking but relevant word or phrase from the original passage, and use it as the title.
- All the important words in your heading should begin with capital letters.

SOLVED EXERCISES

Comprehension-I

Without the knowledge of grammar, it is impossible for you to write correctly; and, it is by mere accident if you speak correctly; and, pray, bear in mind, that all well-informed persons judge of a man's mind (until they have other means of judging) by his writing or speaking. The labour necessary to acquire this knowledge is indeed not trifling; grammar is not like arithmetic, a science consisting of several distinct departments, some of which may be dispensed with; it is a whole, and the whole must be learnt, or no part is learnt. *The subject is abstruse,* it demands much reflection and much patience, but, when once the task is performed, it is performed for life, and in everyday of that life it will be found to be, in a greater or less degree, a source of pleasure or of profit, or both together. And what is the labour? *It consists of no bodily exertion;* it exposes the student to no cold, no hunger, no suffering of any sort. The study need subtract from the hours of no business, nor, indeed from the hours of necessary exercise; the hours usually spent on the tea and coffee shops and in the mere gossip which accompany them; *those wasted hours, of only one year, employed in the study of English grammar, would make you a correct speaker and writer for the rest of your life.*

You want no school, no room to study in, no expenses, and no troublesome circumstances, of any sort. I learnt grammar when I was a private soldier on the pay of six pence a day. The edge of my berth, that of the guard bed, was my seat to study in, my knapsack was my bookcase; a bit of board lying on my lap was my writing table; and the task did not demand anything like a year of my life. I had no money to purchase candle or oil, in winter time it was rarely that I could get any evening light but that of the fire, and only my turn even of that. And if I, under such circumstances, and without parents or friends to advise or encourage me, *accomplished this undertaking,* what excuse can there be for any youth, however poor, however pressed with business or however circumstances as to room or other conveniences?

QUESTIONS FOR COMPREHENSION

1. Read the above passage carefully and answer briefly the following questions set on it:
   (i) Why is the knowledge of grammar essential?
   (ii) How should grammar be learnt?
   (iii) What does the study of grammar demand?
   (iv) How did the author learn grammar? What is his opinion about learning grammar?
2. Explain the portions in italics.
3. Suggest a suitable title for the passage.
4. Write a précis of the above passage.

Answers

(i) The knowledge of grammar is essential for good speaking and writing by which one's mind is judged.

(ii) Grammar must be learnt as a whole. No part of it should be ignored.

(iii) The study of grammar requires no physical hardship, no special room or expenses. If a person spends his leisure time in studying grammar, he can master it in one year.

(iv) The author learnt grammar in less than a year. As a private soldier earning six pence a day he sat on his bed and studied. Unable to afford candle or oil, he read in winter by firelight. He, therefore, says that if he could learn grammar and with no outside encouragement, then any youth, however poor or busy, can do the same.

2. Explanations.
   (i) *The subject is abstruse*: To learn grammar as a whole is a difficult task.
   (ii) *It consists of no bodily exertion:* The study of grammar does not put the student to any physical hardship.

(iii) *Those wasted hours.... the rest of your life:* One can learn grammar in a year by spending only one's spare time in its study.

(iv) *Accomplished this undertaking:* Learnt grammar

3. A suitable title for the passage may be "Grammar for Life"
4. Summary

Knowledge of grammar is essential for correct speaking and writing. It must be learnt as a whole, and this demands much thought and patience. But, once acquired, it can give a lifetime's pleasure and profit. Its study requires no physical hardship, no special room or expenses. It demands only the utilization of one's leisure time. The author learnt it thus in about a year. Anybody, however poor or busy, can learn and master it in a short period, as did the author, by studying it only in his spare time.

Comprehension-2

There is no surer method of becoming good, may be great also, than an early familiarity with the lives of great and good men. So far as my experience goes, there is no kind of sermon so effective as the example of a great man. Here we see the thing done before us- actually done- *a thing of which we were not even dreaming; and the voice speaks to us with a potency as of many waters:* 'Go thou and do likewise.' Why not? No doubt, not every man is a hero and heroic opportunities are not given everyday, but if you cannot do the same thing, you may do something like it; even though you are not planted on as high or large a stage, you can still show as much manhood, and manifest as much *virtuous persistency* on a small scale. Every man may profit by the example of truly great men, if he is bent on *making the most of himself and his circumstances.*

QUESTIONS FOR COMPREHENSION

1. Answer briefly the following questions:

   (i) What is the surest method of becoming great and good?

   (ii) Why is the example of a great man better than any kind of sermon?

   (iii) How can a man profit by the example of great men?

2. Give a suitable heading to the above passage.
3. Summarize the above passage.
4. Explain the italicized portions.

Answers

(i) The surest method of becoming great and good is to read the biographies of great and good men.

(ii) Preaching by action is more effective than preaching by words. We imitate another's conduct and deeds more readily than we follow his advice. The noble example set by a great man inspires us to follow him more effectively than his preaching.

(iii) A man can profit by the example of great men if he firmly resolves to make the best use of his inherent qualities as well as of his external circumstances.

2. Heading

A suitable heading for the passage may be "The Influence of Great Men"

3. Summary

The surest method of becoming great and good is to read the biographies of great and good men. The example of a great man is far more inspiring than any kind of preaching. Every man is not a hero. Nor has he many chances of displaying his heroic qualities. But yet, he can show as much courage and constancy of purpose in his own sphere of work as a great hero does in his own, only if he makes up his mind to make the best use of his qualities and circumstances.

4. Explanations

(i) *A thing of which ....potency as of many waters:* The examples of truly great men effectively inspire us to follow their good and noble deeds.

(ii) *Virtuous persistency:* The good quality being persistent and constant.

(iii) *Making the most of himself and his circumstances:* Using his qualities and circumstances to the greatest advantage.

COMPREHENSION-3

Does economic progress clash with real progress. By economic progress, I mean *material advancement* without limit, and by real progress we mean moral progress, which again is the same thing as progress of the *material element* in us. The subject may, therefore, be stated thus: Does not moral progress increase in the same proportion as material progress? I know that this is a *wider proposition* than the one before us. But I venture to think that we always mean the larger one even when we lay down the smaller. For we know enough of science to realize that there is no such thing as perfect rest or repose in the *visible universe* of ours. If, therefore, material progress does not clash with moral progress, it must necessarily advance the latter.

-Mahatma Gandhi

QUESTIONS FOR COMPREHENSION

1. Answer the following questions:

(i) What does the passage speak about?

(ii) What does Mahatma Gandhi mean by economic progress and real progress?

(iii) What, according to Gandhiji, is the relationship between material progress and moral progress?

2. Explain the italicized words and phrases in the above passage.
3. Assign a suitable title to the passage.
4. Summarize the above passage.

Answers

1. (i) The passage speaks about the relationship between economic progress and real progress.

   (ii) By economic progress Mahatma Gandhi means material prosperity and by real progress he means moral progress. The former implies the rapid growth of wealth whereas the latter refers to the high standard of morality.

   (iii) According to Mahatma Gandhi, economic advancement and moral progress are opposed to each other. But he also holds that if material prosperity does not come into direct conflict with moral progress, it will certainly help and advance the latter.

2. Explanations

   (i) *material advancement:* Improvement in bodily comforts which is believed to follow the rapid growth of wealth.

   (ii) *material element:* moral and spiritual values

   (iii) *wider proposition:* a statement or question of greater extent

   (iv) *visible universe:* the material, concrete world before us

3. Title

   A suitable title for the passage may be "Economic versus Moral Progress".

4. Summary

   Gandhiji speaks about the relationship between economic progress and real progress. Economic progress means material prosperity, while real progress refers to moral progress. These two are opposed to each other. But, if material advancement does not clash with moral and spiritual progress, it will certainly promote the latter.

COMPREHENSION-4

Men have never succeeded in keeping free from war in the past nor are they likely to do so in the future so long as they are organized in separate national states, each of which controls its own army, navy and air force and each of which is, therefore, able to plunge the world into war whenever the individual who happens to control the government believes, however wrongly, that he can obtain an advantage for himself and his country by so doing. Only some form of world government, which controls all the world's armed forces and against which no single nation or group of nations could wage war, since they would not have the wherewithal to do so, can finally save the world from war.

Secondly, science, by accelerating man's speed of movement, has made the world into a single whole. Hence, any war which breaks out anywhere will destroy the whole of civilization and not merely some part of it, the part affected by the war, as has been the case in the past. That is why the new powers conferred upon men by science increasingly demand a world government, if they are not to result in man's destruction.

QUESTIONS FOR COMPREHENSION

1. According to the writer, wars are unavoidable because
   (a) The governments think they stand to gain some benefits out of these.
   (b) A dictator rightly thinks that wars are the only way he can prosper himself and help his country prosper.
   (c) Some nations possess vast military power and want to dominate others.
   (d) The world community is divided in national states and supposed national gains.
2. The need for a world government is all the more urgent in the modern age, because
   (a) Science has speeded up man's movements.
   (b) The nations are sick of so many wars and want peace.
   (c) Science, with its vast potential, will destroy the whole world in the absence of such a government.
   (d) A modern war, as in the past, would destroy the whole civilization.
3. Which one of the following statement is *not true*?
   (a) Wars generally take place due to selfishness and narrow nationalism.
   (b) In the past a war tended to destroy the whole civilization.
   (c) In case of a world government in control of the armed forces, no single nation will have the resources to start a war.
   (d) The choice before humanity is either a world government or total destruction.
4. The statement "since they would not have the wherewithal to do so" at the end of the first paragraph, means
   (a) They would not have any reason to do so.
   (b) They would have no control over the army, navy and air force.

(c) They would have no encouragement to do so.
(d) They would not possess the resources to do so.

5. Which *one* of the following would be the most suitable title for the passage?

(a) The need of a world government.
(b) Wars are unavoidable.
(c) Science and Civilization.
(d) Science and the modern world.

Answers

1. a	2. c	3. b
4. b	5. a	

COMPREHENSION-5

Since its birth in the middle of the 19th century, the women's rights movement has taken root and spread throughout the world. In many countries women have fought for the right to vote, the right to work, the right to be educated to the limit of their capacities, the right to own and dispose off property and equal rights within marriage. The cause has penetrated world governments via the United Nations which in 1946 set up a special commission to study the worldwide status of women and make recommendations to be the Social and Economic Council on ways of improving it. UNESCO too assessed the advancement of women by seeking to involve them in educational and cultural programmes.

In addition, a multitude of women's organizations exist in individual countries to further, at national and international levels, the eradication of remaining areas of discrimination. Through their affiliation with international feminist bodies they are in touch with women's activities and achievements in all parts of the world.

However, with half the world's population still illiterate, there is a great disparity in what has been and is still to be achieved. At one end of the scale, women's rights' workers are still pressing for elementary education; at the other for the removal of early protective legislation, which is now felt to be discriminatory because it denied women certain freedoms, for example, the right to work at night if they so choose. Nevertheless, despite the fact that the women's movement has progressed unevenly and with varying degree of success in different places, women in general are emerging from *chatteldom* and taking their place beside men as free and equal citizens.

QUESTIONS FOR COMPREHENSION

1. What is the aim of the women's rights' movement?
2. How far has this movement succeeded in achieving its aim?

3. How is the movement being sustained?
4. Why are the women's rights' workers pressing for removal of protective legislation?
5. Why is the progress of the feminist movement uneven and has affected its success?

Answers

1. The women's rights' movement aims at fighting for the basic rights of women, that is to vote, to work, to be educated, to own and dispose off property and for equal rights within marriage.
2. This movement has achieved partial success as many women across the world have not yet been able to acquire these rights.
3. This movement is being sustained at the global level with the help of world organizations like international feminist bodies, UNESCO and the Social and Economic Council and at the national level by various women's organizations.
4. They are doing so because protective legislation is discriminatory and denies women certain freedoms.
5. The progress of feminist movement is uneven because a large section of women are still illiterate and unaware of their rights.

COMPREHENSION-6

Truth is not the monopoly of science, and the values that derive from truth were known before the scientific revolution. Nevertheless, I shall base my derivation of these values on the practice of science. My reason is twofold. This procedure shows most clearly how we form an ethic by acting it. And it shows how practical these values are, if we are willing to use them.

It is commonly said that science is ethically neutral because its discoveries can be used for good or ill. This statement confuses two meanings of the science: the process of discovery and what is discovered at the end of it. Of course, what is discovered is neutral, whether it is Newton's Law or a semiconductor, or the Theory of Evolution. But the long and dedicated activity of the men who made these discoveries was not neutral; it was firmly directed and strictly judged. In practicing science, we accept from the outset an end, which is laid down on us. The end of the science is to discover what is true about the world. The activity of the science is directed to seek the truth, and is judged by that criterion. We can practice science only when we value the truth.

Truth is an individual value which dictates the conduct of science with regard to his work. It becomes the source of social values only when the society accepts the assumption that no belief will survive if it conflicts with what is true. This is an unspoken assumption, which the society of scientists makes as a body. They agree that the discovery of truth is an end in itself, not only for each scientist but for the culture of science. It follows that a whole nexus of social values can be deducted from the single injunction that the culture of science has a common duty to seek the truth.

Of course this assumes that the truth has not been found (and indeed that is not there to be found once and for all like a lost umbrella). A society which believes that the truth needs no more seeking is authoritarian. By contrast, the society of scientists must be organized to evolve step-by-step in the discovery of truth. Therefore, every individual scientist must value originality of mind and independence of character and the culture as a whole must safeguard them by placing a value or dissent. A dissent, in turn, must be protected by justice and freedom – freedom of thought, of speech and writing, of movement and assembly. We must not take these for granted as if they are self-evident and natural values in any society. Plato did not offer freedom of speech and writing in his Republic, and he didn't offer justice to those who demanded them, but exile. Freedom is valued in a culture that wants to encourage dissent and to stimulate originality and independence. It belongs to the society which is open to change, and which esteems the agent of change - the individual, above its own peace of mind.

QUESTIONS FOR COMPREHENSION

1. Why does the author base his derivation of the value from truth, on the practice of science?
2. What are the author's views on the common saying that science is ethically neutral?
3. What is the end of science?
4. How does the author establish a linkage between 'an individual value' and 'social value'?
5. Why should the right to dissent be protected in any society?

Answers

1. The author bases his derivation of the values from truth, on the practice of science because only science shows how an ethic is formed by enacting it and also on the practicality of these values, if they are used.
2. The author distinguishes between the procedure of science and its end and points out that it is the end and not the procedure which is ethically neutral.
3. Discovery of the truth about the world is the sole end of science.
4. The scientist's concern to discover the truth is an 'individual value' but when the society at large accepts and promotes the discovery of truth, then it becomes a 'social value'.
5. The right to dissent exhibits freedom and encourages originality and independence. A society which values individual freedom and encourages change would, therefore, protect the right to dissent, as it is the causative agent.

COMPREHENSION-7

Recent archaeological evidence indicates that European man is far older than was previously thought. And the evidence is breaking down a line of thinking called the *diffusion theory*. This theory suggests that civilization as we know it originated in the Middle East and then slowly diffused throughout the world, including Europe. It is a theory that has been generally accepted for years. An example of this change in thinking can be provided on the Island of Malta, where stand some ruined stone temples of unknown origin. Although scientists and archaeologists were quite certain that they were built before the ancient Greeks and Romans, the general opinion was that the time gap between these temples and the age of the ancient Greeks and Romans was not great.

Now through a miraculous new process of establishing the dates of civilizations, called radiocarbon dating, we can be certain that these temples were in fact under constructed before 3000 BC, that is, before the pyramids of Egypt. In fact, it has now become certain that many of the great tombs that are dotted around Europe were built around 4000 BC and are quite the oldest buildings in existence. So the diffusion theory is being replaced by a revolution in historical thinking, which suggests that the creation of civilized objects such as stone buildings and metallurgy was not passed on to Europe by superior beings from the East, but in fact occurred spontaneously in different parts of world.

QUESTIONS FOR COMPREHENSION

I. Answer as directed:

1. According to the older theories of civilization it was believed that (circle as many statements as are correct):
   (a) civilization started in the Middle East
   (b) civilization started in many different parts of the world at around the same time
   (c) the stone temples on the Island of Malta were created long before the age of the ancient Greeks and Romans
   (d) the great stone tombs of Europe were of more recent origin than the pyramids of Egypt
   (e) European man was much older than was previously thought
2. The older belief has been challenged by (circle one):
   (a) the diffusion theory
   (b) the existence of stone temples on the Island of Malta
   (c) an unacceptable historical revolution
   (d) a new process of dating civilization

3. The author expresses his views (circle one):
   (a) in a matter of fact style
   (b) in a manner full of excitement and delight
   (c) as if he would have preferred to accept the older belief
   (d) as if he was addressing a learned audience who opposed his views
4. The passage contains the following points. Put them in the order in which they occur in the passage.
   (a) an example of change in thinking
   (b) statement about the older theory
   (c) statement about the change in thinking and the process of establishing it
   (d) indication of change in belief

II. Answer the following questions briefly:

1. What does recent archaeological evidence indicate?
2. What does the diffusion theory suggest?
3. What were scientists and archaeologists quite sure about?
4. What is the process by which we can establish the dates of civilization?
5. What does the theory which has replaced the diffusion theory suggest?

Answers

I 1. (a), (c)
  2. (d)
  3. (d)
  4. (b), (a), (c), (d)

II 1. Recent archaeological evidence indicates that the European man is far older than what he was previously considered to be.
  2. The diffusion theory suggests that civilization originated in the Middle East and slowly spread throughout the world.
  3. Scientists and archaeologists were quite certain that some ruined stone temples of Malta were built before the age of ancient Greeks and Romans.
  4. We can establish the dates of civilization by a new process called radiocarbon dating.
  5. This theory suggests that the creation of civilized objects occurred spontaneously in different parts of the world.

UNSOLVED EXERCISES

Comprehension- I

It is physically impossible for a well-educated, intellectual or brave man to make money the chief object of his thoughts, just as it is for him to make his dinner the principal object of them. All healthy people like their dinners, but their dinner is not the main object of their lives. So all healthy- minded people who like making money ought to enjoy the process of making it; is something better than money. A good soldier, for instance, mainly wishes to do his fighting well. He is glad for his pay- very properly so, and justly *grumbles* when you keep him ten years without it- still, his main notion of life is to win a battle, not to be paid for winning them. So of clergyman. The clergyman's object is essentially to baptize and preach, not to be paid for preaching. So of doctors. They like fee no doubt- ought to like it; if they are brave and well-educated, the entire object of their lives is not fee. They, on the whole, desire to cure the sick; and if they are good doctors, and the choice were fairly put to them, would rather cure their patient and lose their fee than kill him and get it. And so with all the other brave and rightly trained men; *their work first, their fee second-* very important always, but still second.

QUESTIONS FOR COMPREHENSION

1. Answer the following questions in your own words:
   (i) Is money-making the principal object of the lives of brave, intellectual and well-educated people?
   (ii) What does a good soldier actually wish in life?
   (iii) What is the real aim of the life of clergyman?
   (iv) What does a good doctor essentially desire?
2. Explain the italicized parts.
3. Suggest an apt heading for the passage.
4. Write a précis of the passage.

COMPREHENSION-9

The Ramayana is the most popularly read book in India, and by far a large number of people read and recite it with devotion, but few appreciate one aspect of its greatness, that it places before us some ***high ideals of human conduct*** which ennoble the man and his surroundings and which must be followed at all costs. King Dashrath preferred death to ***going back on his words;*** Ram renounced his Kingdom to embrace the hardships of forest life; and Bharat reduced himself to a faithful custodian worshipper of his brother's footprints. Other characters in this holy book ***stand second to none*** in their sacrifice for the society. We give a loud thinking to our faith in socialism, but little do we care to follow the socialism actually practiced in this great ***epic.***

ANSWER THE FOLLOWING QUESTIONS

1. Which aspect of Ramayana's greatness is not fully appreciated?
2. What do you learn from King Dashrath, Ram and Bharat?

3. What is the guiding ideal of most of the characters in the Ramayana? What is its importance in modern India?
4. Explain the portions in italics.
5. Supply a suitable heading to the passage.

COMPREHENSION-10

Read carefully the following passage and answer in your own words as far as possible:

The town of Deadwood in South Dakota became famous in the nineteenth century when gold was discovered there. Gold attracted many fortune hunters, good and bad. Heroes like 'Deadwood Dick' the stagecoach driver have since become as familiar as Robinson Crusoe. The town itself acquired an extraordinary reputation and came to be known as the place where 'the coward never started and the weak died on the way'.

Bad men come and go, but the biggest villain in Deadwood has always been one thing: fire. The little town is built on the steep sides of a deep valley. If a fire breaks out, this valley acts like a chimney and sucks the flames up to the houses. In 1879 fire destroyed the town completely. When it was rebuilt, special water barrels were fitted into every roof.

In our own times, a great fire threatened the town yet again. It all began when some wastepaper alighted at the foot of the tree. The wind roared through the forest carrying the flames almost to the edge of the town. Fire brigades arrived from all parts of the country to save Deadwood.

Meanwhile, women and children prepared to leave the town. They seized as many of their belongings as they could and cars piled high with clothing packed the streets. The wind changed direction and it seemed as though no car would be able to leave; then it changed again and a long line of cars moved quickly out of the town.

As if this fire was not enough, the panic-stricken inhabitants heard that another fire had broken out twenty miles away near a town called Nemo. If these two fires joined, they would get quite out of control. Firemen desperately fought the flames for twenty-four hours and in the end aeroplanes were used as well. The planes began 'bombing' the fire with water and so prevented the two fires from joining forces. The big fire began to lose the battle and people who had left came back home. They found a blackened valley, but their houses were still standing. Deadwood had been saved from its worst enemy just in time.

QUESTIONS FOR COMPREHENSION

1. Choose the best answer in each exercise: a, b, c or d.

(i) Many people have heard of Deadwood because

a. it became famous when gold was discovered there.
b. of the big fires.
c. Robinson Crusoe lived there.
d. it is built on the steep sides of a deep valley.

(ii) The big fire that occurred recently was particularly dangerous because

a. of the wind.
b. the people didn't manage to get out of the town.
c. there was danger it would join up with another big fire.
d. firemen couldn't put it out.

(iii) 'Deadwood Dick', who lived many years... is very famous.

a. ago b. since
c. before d. away

(iv) As far as Deadwood is concerned, there is no enemy......... fire.

a. worst than b. bad as
c. worse than d. worse as

(v) familiar means :

a. of the family b. famous
c. well-known d. interesting

(vi) Panic-stricken inhabitants means:

a. terrible places b. terrible residents
c. frightened neighbours d. dying villagers

2. Sentence Structure

Rewrite this sentence:

By 'bombing' the fire with water the planes prevented the two fires from joining forces.

The planes began....

Summary and Composition

1. Suppose you had been present when the fire broke out in Deadwood. Describe what you saw up to the time the people began to return.
2. Write a composition of about 250 words on the following:
'Fire: man's best friend and worst enemy.'

COMPREHENSION-11

Read carefully the following passage and answer in your own words as far as possible:

The third week in August marked the beginning of the end of the long, dry winter; the days were getting hotter. We looked up at the afternoon clouds, and wished it would rain, to damp down the earth and wash out the old tracks and leave today's fresh. But it would not rain until October. The rhinos knew they were being hunted, and they kept moving big distances; on the hard, dry earth it was often impossible to pick up their tracks.

Then Thomson sprained his ankle, and 20 year old Richard Peek had to do the 'darting' – whether Thomson paid much attention to fortune-tellers, but he told Richard that if he took any risk he would kick him all the way back home, sprained ankle or no.

"Yes, Ron," Richard said. "O.K." He was delighted that he was going to do the 'darting'. So the next day Richard led the hunt. After three kilometres, Richard paused to confer with his "Shikari" (game scout). Moments later, we saw the animal. He was out in the open, on a long, low hill that ran down the river. We were very lucky; the wind was right, the cover was right, the river sand had muffled our footsteps. Richard was getting his first rhino handed to him on a platter.

When he got within forty metres, the beast stood there still, oblivious, a perfect target. Richard raised the dart gun and squeezed the trigger. The gun went click. A complete dud! The rhino heard the click and turned, ears forward, horn up. Richard's hands were visibly shaking as he rammed in a second dart and squeezed off another shot. The gun went click again.

The beast spun round with a snort and started towards Richard's cover. Richard was cursing and fumbling with a new cartridge. The rhino turned and lumbered away. I thought, there he goes, when suddenly he stopped and lay down. He lay down. Somebody up there really liked Richard. He raised the gun and fired. There was a crack and the dart flew true and smacked into the rhino's side.

Suddenly five adult rhinos came charging at us in the river bed. We ran, leaping for the trees. The nearest tree to me was like a telephone pole, but I ran up it with no trouble at all as a rhino thundered past underneath, hooking and snorting. The five beasts went charging up the riverbank together, great grey legs pounding and tail curled up over their backs, quite invincible looking. And then they were gone.

I slid down my tree and I was shaking with laughter and nerves. We were all laughing. It must have been a record. Rhinos don't go in herds like that. Richard came up grinning but shaking all over. "I thought the fortune-teller was going to be right," he said.

We returned to the stockade at two o'clock with Richard's first rhino. Thomson was very pleased. He stood on top of the stockade on his good leg, supervising Richard in the pen.

Richard was doing a good job down there. He had done a good job all day. The beast had been unconscious for nearly five hours, and was due to come round soon – Richard did not have much time. He had already earmarked the beast, and was preparing to give him an injection of nalorphine, the antidote, to the sleep-inducing drug of the dart!

The knots were loosened, Richard pressed the syringe plunger and the nalorphine went in. The labourers were still sitting on the beast. Richard opened his mouth to order the knots untied when Thomsom shouted, "Have you given him his penicillin?"

"No," young Richard said, shocked at himself for forgetting to give the penicillin before the nalorphine. This was the only mistake he had made all day. "Fasten the knots," he shouted, and then hastily grabbed another syringe and the penicillin bottle. As he stuck the needle into the beast's breast, it did not even twitch. It was fast of warning. The knots had not been tightened properly, and the great legs thrashed free. Thomson screamed, "Watch out!"

Richard leaped for the fence ....

(i) Suggest what the fortune-teller had said about Richard Peek to Ron Thomson.

(ii) Why did Richard think that the fortune-teller was going to be right?

(iii) What sort of a job do you think 'darting' is?

(iv) What was the only mistake made by Richard that day?

(v) Bearing in mind what the soothsayer must have said and the mistake made by Ricahrd, complete the last paragraph starting, "Richard leaped for the fence............

COMPREHENSION-12

Read the following passage and then answer the questions below:

The buffalo deserves his reputation as one of the most dangerous of big game animals. For ages past he has been hunted by the natives in Africa for his well-beloved meat and his tough hide, which can be worked into solid shields. With the white man's arrival in the Dark Continent he has been hunted for his big horns, a much-desired trophy. Naturally, the beast, which had been indifferent and unsuspecting at the beginning, has become cautious, vigilant and aggressive. It has learned to attack swiftly and unexpectedly, and with a strength that is almost elemental. It has acquired a perfect genius for utilizing the advantages which a difficult country affords it, and the sportsman often does not discover it till the last moment – until it is almost too late. Nevertheless, all these qualities, I am sure, have been gained by sad experiences with those upright walking, two-legged creatures who have always been antagonistic to all wildlife.

When the buffalo is in a bad humour – that is, when his temper is irritable and undependable – he may attack without the least provocation. Of course, there are various reasons for his ill humour, and some may not be known to me. However, an old, irritating wound, an internal complaint, and the interruption of his noon siesta are three of the most common reasons for his ugly disposition. He is dangerous in yet another way. Of all African animals the buffalo is the one which has a hereditary instinct, when wounded, pursued, or bedevilled by man, he leaves his tracks, lies in ambush and charge from the flank or rear at closest quarters. Many an unsuspecting hunter has lot his life through this method of attack, which has become known among big-game hunters as the 'buffalo hook'. Unlike the lion, which is usually satisfied with giving his victim a knockout blow or bite, the buffalo, when he has once come up with man, will not leave while there is a vestige of life remaining in the enemy.

EXERCISE

(a) For each of the questions (i) to (v) which follow select the best of the four choices given.

(i) Which of the following repeats most accurately the assertion contained in the first sentence?

(A) The buffalo is certainly the most dangerous of big animals.
(B) The buffalo is rightly considered to be one of the most dangerous of big game animals.
(C) Buffaloes are without question very dangerous animals.
(D) It is well known that buffaloes are one of the most dangerous of big game animals.

(ii) From what the writer says towards the middle of the passage it is clear that the aggressiveness of the buffalo is

(A) an instinctive tendency.
(B) a result of interference by hunters.
(C) a myth.
(D) something it has learned from human beings.

(iii) The reason why a sportsman often does not discover an attacking buffalo till the last minute is that

(A) it charges at a great speed.
(B) it is clever at stalking its quarry.
(C) it attacks with a strength that is almost elemental.
(D) it is cautious and vigilant.

(iv) From the latter part of the first paragraph we gather that the writer has

(A) a great fear of buffaloes.
(B) no sympathy for animals or for human beings.
(C) a great love and understanding of wild life.
(D) too much consideration for wild animals.

(v) From the last sentence we learn that buffaloes

(A) are less dangerous than lions.
(B) are not content until they kill their victims outright.

(C) are very easily satisfied.
(D) are much more powerful than lions.

(b) Answer the following questions in your own words as far as possible:

(i) How do the motives for hunting buffaloes of the African and the white man differ?
(ii) What do the elephant and the buffalo have in common?
(iii) Explain the meaning of the sentence: 'He may attack without provocation'.
(iv) What is meant by the term "the buffalo hook".
(v) In what respect does the buffalo differ from the lion?

(c) Five words or phrases from the passage are given below.
Give a word or phrase which is opposite to that given in passage.

(i) dangerous
(ii) aggressive
(iii) antagonistic
(iv) hereditary instinct
(v) pursued

COMPREHENSION-13

Read the following passage carefully and then answer the questions

To encourage a scout's activities there is a comprehensive system of badges. Boys love a token of achievement and these badges can be won for almost any kind of proficiency that a scout can attain. There is an element of absurdity in plastering oneself with insignia; but it is more absurd to the adult than to the juvenile mind. The advantages of the appeal to a boy are great enough to outweigh the disadvantages, and we must remember that scouting is a boy's game.

Another criticism of the movement has been that the uniform and the salute encourage a militaristic tendency. This is an empty charge, and it is counteracted by criticism from other quarters that scouts lack the discipline and smartness which the brigades inculcate with their greater stress on drill and their stricter standards of bearing.

There is the fact that it may be a cause of hardship to the poorest. It is also conspicuous and a trifle bizarre, with the result that some boys in the self-conscious stage are shy of it. This probably militates against the membership to some extent among other boys. On the other hand, it is neat and lends the tidiness of uniformity; and moreover it is, with the exception of the rather clumsy hat, a most sensible and serviceable dress.

The movement has also to meet the accusation of being irreligious. It is true that it is a secular organization, but it does not fail to emphasize the necessity of religion and to encourage worship. It must be remembered that it is a worldwide movement and under its shade is place for boys of every creed and sect, and even for those who subscribe to none. It is possible for any denominational group to form the troops within the movement, and among the members to inculcate the religious tenets to which it adheres and in that sense the churches can use the movement for their own religious needs. It is equally possible for a secular organization such as a school, factory or a club to form a troop, and it may or may not emphasize the religious element. Even if a troop is under no denominational aegis, it is part of the doctrine of scouting that religion in the broadest sense shall be a part of the scout's life and practice. It is a criticism from another direction that there is too much religion in the movement. The fact is that there is the widest latitude within which individual troops may operate, and the criticisms from opposing sides cancel out effectively.

(a) For each of the questions (i) to (v) which follow select the best of the four choices given.

(i) 'Plastering oneself with insignia' – by this the writer means

(A) wearing a great many badges of distinction.
(B) covering oneself with insignificant things.
(C) trying to show off.
(D) covering the insignia with plaster.

(ii) Older boys may be unwilling to join scouts because

(A) they feel rather shy to dress themselves in the fantastic uniforms.
(B) they do not like the clumsy hat.
(C) the movement militates against their conscience.
(D) they are sensible and serviceable to others.

(iii) Which of the following in the fourth paragraph is the counter – criticism to the accusation that the movement is irreligious?

(A) it is a secular organization.
(B) it is possible for any denominational group to form its troop within the movement.
(C) Churches can use the movement for their own religious needs.
(D) there is too much religion in the movement.

(iv) The passage contains one criticism against scouting to which no reply is given. It is that

(A) scouting is a boy's game (para 1)
(B) it encourages a militaristic tendency (para 2)
(C) it is a cause of hardship to the poorest to provide themselves with the uniforms (para 3)
(D) it may or may not emphasise the religious element (para 4)

(v) 'Criticism from the opposing sides cancel out effectively' with the result that

(A) there is neither any support for nor any opposition to the movement.
(B) the movement remains unaffected.
(C) the pros and cons regarding the movement cancel out each other.
(D) the opposing sides become frustrated.

(b) Answer the following questions in your own words as far as possible

(i) Why are older boys not so keen on scouting?
(ii) What are the three main arguments used to criticize the scout uniform?
(iii) What does the author concede when he writes, "There is an element of absurdity in plastering oneself with insignia." What does he say in defence of this criticism?

(c) For each of the following words taken from the passage give a word having the same or similar meaning.

(i) juvenile (ii) inculcate (iii) bizarre
(iv) tenets (v) latitude

COMPREHENSION-14

Read the following passage carefully and then answer questions.

As I stepped out of the train I felt unusually solitary, since I was the only passenger to alight. I was accustomed to arriving in the summer, when holiday-makers throng coastal resorts and this was my first visit when the season was over. My destination was a little village eight miles distant by the road, but only four if you took the cliff path over the moor. This I always did, unless it was raining; and I left my luggage at the bus office beside the railway station, to be sent for me on the next bus, so that I could enjoy my walk unhampered by suitcase.

It took me only a few minutes to come to the foot of the cliff path. Half way up I paused to enjoy the sight of the purple hills stretching away to my right and to my left the open sea. When I reached the top I had left all signs of habitation behind me. The moorland turf was springy under my feet, the air was like wine and I felt rejuvenated and intoxicated with it. Glancing seaward a minute or two later, I was surprised to notice that the sky was already aflame with the sunset. The air grew perceptibly cooler and I began to look forward to the delectable hot meal I should have when I reached the inn. It seemed to be getting dark amazingly quickly. I did not think that I had walked unduly slowly and I was at a loss to account for the exceptionally early end of daylight, until I recollected that on previous visits I had walked in high summer and now it was October and the nights were drawing in.

All at once it was night. The track was grassy and even in daylight showed up hardly at all against the moor, so it was difficult to keep on it now. If only I had been a smoker with matches always at hand, or if my torch had been in my pocket instead of in the suitcase, I could have walked with more assurance. As it was, I was terrified of hurtling over the edge of the cliff to the rocks below. When I did stray, however, it was towards the hills. I felt my feet squelching and sticking in something soggy. There was no bog to my knowledge near the track, so I must have wandered a long way off my course. I extricated myself with difficulty and very cautiously edged myself towards the sound of the sea. Then I bumped into a little clump of trees that suddenly loomed up in front of me. This was providential rest and shelter until the moon rose. I climbed up the nearest trunk and managed to find a tolerably comfortable fork in which to sit. The waiting seemed interminable and was relieved only by my attempts to identify the little strings and noises of animal life that I could hear. I grew colder and colder and managed to sleep only in uneasy, fitful starts, waking when my position got cramped. At last, when the moon came up I discovered that I was not more than fifty yards from the track and I was soon on my way again.

1. For each of the questions (i) to (v) which follow select the best of the four choices given.

(i) The writer felt unusually solitary because

a. he was feeling very lonely without his family.
b. he was missing the company of other holiday makers.
c. his destination was a little village eight miles away.
d. the bus was not there to meet him.

(ii) I left all signs of habitation behind me. This means that he

a. came to a place where there were very few houses.
b. was in front of a large collection of cottages.
c. had come very far from places where people lived.
d. had just passed a remote village.

(iii) It became darker sooner than the writer expected because

a. the nights are shorter in autumn than in summer.
b. the nights are longer in October than in the middle of summer.
c. the train arrived later than usual.
d. he had walked unduly slowly.

(iv) The reason why the writer found it difficult to keep to the path was a combination of two factors. They were

a. the darkness and the narrowness of the path.
b. poor visibility and the grass covering the track.
c. the darkness and his unduly slow pace.
d. poor visibility and the dew on the grass.

(v) When he settled himself in the fork of the tree, the writer

a. had a sound sleep.
b. was disturbed by the noises of animal life.
c. he was too afraid to sleep.
d. he tried to sleep but without much success.

2. Answer the following questions using your own words as far as possible:

(i) Explain why the writer was the only person to alight from the train.
(ii) Describe briefly how he felt when he reached the top of the cliff.
(iii) Give two reasons why the writer had to halt on his way to the village.
(iv) In a paragraph of under sixty words suggest what happened when the writer finally reached the inn.

3. For each of the words given below select a word from the passage having the same meaning.

(i) alone (ii) carried (iii) noticeably
(iv) confidence (v) endless

COMPREHENSION-15

Read the following passage carefully and then answer questions, which follow:

The impact of television on society is a matter of discussion for both psychologists as well as sociologists. Regarded as the magic box or idiots' lantern, its effects are now subject of scientific investigation, although the sociologists need more than one decade of widespread viewing before they can draw permanent conclusions.

It appears that television is changing our leisure habits. One-third of the regular viewers have ceased to go to the cinema, and 15 per cent admit that they have given up reading. On the other hand, many more people are visiting picture galleries, show jumping, soccer matches, Wimbledon Tennis Championship and other events popularized by television. Gardening as a leading hobby has remained unaffected, but conversation in the home has declined.

Before these effects can be labelled as desirable or undesirable, they need closer examination. Is it bad to abandon the cinema? Perhaps, but one might as well watch inferior American films at home than in cinema. Is it bad to abandon reading? Perhaps, but only if one assumes that the viewer was formerly reading Dickens rather than the 'Daily gossip'. Is it bad to abandon conversation? Perhaps, but some think we all talk too much. We can perhaps see an advantage in the change in conversational habits, the friendship, which can develop between total strangers over discussion of a compelling television programme.

But the social implications go beyond the field of leisure. The message of television is largely expressed in middle or lower middle class terms. The odd play or documentary will give glimpses of other worlds but the general background is fairly constant. Learning new social attitudes from the screen may by an advantage or a retrogression. Some think retrograde, the romantic notion of sex continually accentuated, though thinking back over the art forms of the centuries, one wonders whether this is so very new.

1. For each of the questions (i) to (v) which follow select the best of the four choices given.

(i) In the first paragraph the author

a. ridicules television by calling it a magic box or idiots' lantern.
b. regards those who watch television as mentally retarded people who need the help of psychologists.
c. show that the sociologists are very lazy for they need more than a decade to draw conclusions.
d. points out that it is now possible to investigate scientifically the effects of television on society.

(ii) 'Conversation in the home has declined.' It has declined because

a. conversation as an art is no longer practiced or enjoyed.
b. the time usually spent in conversation is now spent in viewing television.
c. people have started visiting Wimbledon Tennis Championship, soccer matches and other events popularized by television.
d. people have given up reading books, and have nothing to talk of as a result.

(iii) 'The message of television is largely expressed in middle or lower middle class terms.' This sentence in the fourth paragraph suggests that

a. television is not suitable for the upper and the working classes.
b. the language of the middle and lower class, which is different from that of others is being used by producers of TV programs.
c. the programs presented on television are meant for all, but their contents are specially meant to appeal to the middle classes.
d. television is used to send messages to the middle classes.

(iv) The fourth paragraph introduces a new thought. It is that TV

a. has created a social problem by fostering romantic notions of sex.
b. has kept alive the art of the centuries.
c. opened up new vistas of knowledge for all.
d. has taught new social attitudes to the middle classes which may or may not do them good.

(v) The writer has used certain words and phrases about the need for caution before we draw conclusions about the adverse effects of TV on society. He feels that the effects could be known.

a. only after the psychologists and sociologists express their views.
b. through 'widespread viewing'.
c. by closer examination of its effects on society.
d. after studying the 'social implications' of viewing television.

2. Answer the following questions using your own words as far as possible.

(i) Explain why the writer feels that it is necessary to examine the effects of the changes in leisure habits closely before labelling them desirable or undesirable.

(ii) Name two beneficial effects of television mentioned in the passage.

(iii) What adverse effects of television are revealed in the passage?

(iv) Explain the meaning of the words: *will give glimpses of other words.*

3. Give words or phrases similar in meaning to the following words taken from the passage.

(i) ceased (ii) abandon (iii) conversational
(iv) compelling (v) retrogressive

COMPREHENSION-16

From a distance the funfair looked like a fairy-tale city. Huge wheels revolved slowly; a giant screen covered with coloured lamps flashed on and off; and the brilliantly lit fountains glistened like rainbows against the night sky. It seemed a world, which contained only the pleasant things in life and it invited us to step out of the dark and enter.

When we did so, we were greeted with laughter and music. Everywhere people were travelling at high speeds; being lifted up into the sky and dropped; driving small cars and bumping into each other; shooting at targets; throwing balls at bottles, or simply standing and staring. We were not quite sure where to begin, but on seeing a stand marked 'The Ghost Train', we went towards it eagerly. When we had bought our tickets and taken our seats we were immediately carried towards a closed door. For a dreadful moment we thought we would crash into it but it slid open and we were completely in the dark. We could not understand why so many people were screaming. In a moment we realized why. A light went on in front of us and a big gorilla grinned hideously at us. The train went straight towards it and at the very last moment turned away: only just in time! We barely had the chance to recover, when a skeleton appeared. It screamed, extended a bony arm and made us scream as well. A little ahead a cackling witch was lying in wait for us. The train went towards every monstrous creature that lurked in the dark, always turning away just before it was too late.

We were relieved when a door opened and we found ourselves in the open air again. But to our amazement the train did not stop. It reentered the haunted house! This time we heard strange noises and louder screams than before. Invisible hands came out of the dark and brushed through our hair or across our faces. Doors opened and closed before our eyes and monsters reached out for us. We held on tightly and shut our eyes when we saw yet another closed door ahead. This time we were sure we would hit into it. All of a sudden it opened and brought us back to a happier world of people, lights and laughter.

MULTIPLE CHOICE QUESTIONS

Choose the best answer in each exercise : *a , b , c or d*

1. **They went to the funfair because**
   a. they wanted to travel on the Ghost Train.
   b. it had looked so attractive.
   c. they were quite near it.
   d. someone invited them to go in.
2. **Each time they approached a closed door**
   a. They expected it to open.
   b. They expected a monster to appear.
   c. They expected to crash into it.
   d. They expected to come into the open air.
3. **Where did the witch.... in wait for them?**
   a. lie b. lay
   c. laid d. lain
4. **They thought they would hit into a door. They were sure.... it**
   a. for b. to
   c. of d. in
5. **grinned means :**
   a. screamed b. laughed
   c. smiled d. cackled
6. **barely means**
   a. almost b. hardly
   c. only d. justly

Summary and Composition

1. Give an account of what happened to the people in the Ghost Train from the moment they were carried into the haunted house to the end of their ride.
2. Describe a funfair or carnival in your country.

Paragraph Writing

20 CHAPTER

INTRODUCTION

As we know, language is the art by which man expresses his thoughts, feelings and experiences, in order to share them with his fellow human beings. All three processes – thinking, speaking and writing - require the use of words arranged in a particular order so as to be understood by others.

Writing is more important than speaking when we want to select the right words to express a particular idea accurately. Writing composition is one of the means by which we can express ourselves adequately in any subject Mastering the skill of writing will help you later in life when you have to write notes, memoranda, reports, minutes of meeting, or letters etc. The basic unit of any writing, be it a composition, an essay, an article, or a short story, is the paragraph.

DEFINITION

A paragraph is a group of sentences which deals with one topic or idea. The paragraph, as defined by the **Concise Oxford Dictionary**, is a distinct unit in prose writing, marked by an indentation of the first line. Generally a paragraph may consist of 2-10 sentences.

In examination, in "Paragraph writing" or "the Expansion of Ideas" the examiner usually sets a sentence, a proverb or an old wise saying and asks the candidate to expand it into a paragraph of about 100-150 words.

Expansion means the amplification and explanation of the given topic, idea or proverb in a paragraph of the required length. As you know, the English language uses only 3 types of sentences. They are simple, complex and compound. Any paragraph may contain a combination of all the three types. Besides, a paragraph concentrates on a particular idea. A good paragraph clarifies the meaning of this idea or topic, elaborates it and examines it critically.

Good expansion depends on two factors:

- Power of thinking
- The ability to construct a paragraph

Keep in mind that the secret of clear writing is clear thinking. **Thinking** provides the matter as well as the manner in which an idea has to be expanded, while the **skill of constructing a paragraph** will give a suitable form to the amplification. Don't express your words in a roundabout way.

THE BASIC REQUIREMENTS OF A PARAGRAPH

The three basic requirements of a paragraph are unity, coherence and emphasis.

1. Unity

Just as each sentence deals with one thought, each paragraph must deal with one topic or idea. A paragraph is usually built around **a topic sentence** - a sentence, which states the main theme of a paragraph. This sentence usually occurs at the beginning of the paragraph. But there is no mandatory rule for this. It usually depends upon the order in which the writer has chosen to write the paragraph. Thus, unity in a paragraph means that every sentence in the paragraph must be closely connected with the main topic. To contribute to the unity of a paragraph, the entire paragraph should be developed in an orderly and logical manner.

2. Coherence

Coherence means consistency or uniformity. In a paragraph, all the sentences should be related to each other. When every sentence is linked to the one that went before, it provides coherence to the paragraph. Following are four devices which help to bring coherence:

i. **Pronouns:** A pronoun is used as a substitute for noun. It maintains a continuity of thought.
ii. **Connectives:** Connectives show the relationship between the new sentence and the preceding sentence. Some of these connectives are 'and', 'but', 'if', 'or', firstly', 'secondly', etc.
iii. **Synonyms:** Synonyms are substitutes for words already used and have similar meanings.
iv. **Repetition of key words:** The repetition of some key words not only makes the paragraph coherent but also emphasizes the author's point of view.

3. Emphasis

Emphasis means force or prominence. It means making important points stand out in the paragraph. Following devices help to give proper emphasis to significant ideas in a paragraph:

i. **Balance:** Balance means to make various parts of the sentence parallel to one another. It is used to give equal importance to two or more ideas or statements.

ii. **Emphatic Position:** This device is used to give emphasis to the most important idea in the paragraph.

iii. **Space:** It means to give more space to the main idea.

iv. **Repetition:** Emphasis may be achieved either by repeating some key words or synonyms of words.

v. **Contrast:** This device states the negative side of an issue, to emphasize the writer's positive point of view.

VARIOUS METHODS TO DEVELOP A PARAGRAPH

The method, by which a topic may be developed, varies according to the nature of the topic and its purpose. Correct interpretation and full understanding of the given idea or proverb is the first requisite of paragraph writing. However, there are various techniques or orders used to develop a paragraph.

1. Deductive Order

Deductive order is the most popular order used by the writers. In this order the topic sentence occurs in the beginning of the paragraph. The author moves from the general statement to particular details.

2. Inductive Order

In inductive order, the topic sentence usually comes at the end of the paragraph. In this order, the author moves from particular statements to the general statement. He gives details, arguments or illustrations, which finally lead to the conclusion.

3. Expository Order

In expository writing, the topic sentence is usually the first sentence. In this order the writer tries to interpret and discuss the same idea in several ways. It is used to explain how to perform an operation or how to operate a machine.

4. Time Order/Chronological Order

This order is the natural order of narration, in which one event leads to another. This order is preferred in historical narration when the matter refers to some developments in terms of time.

5. Enumeration/Linear Order

This order is also used in narration but with visible markers like, 'firstly', 'secondly', 'thirdly'....'finally' etc.

6. Spatial Order/Space Order

This order is useful in making area-wise arrangement of the matter.

Sometimes these ways of developing paragraphs are used in their pure forms and sometimes in combinations. It depends entirely on the intelligence and common sense of the author.

HOW TO WRITE A PARAGRAPH - PRACTICAL HINTS

- A paragraph must have a topic sentence. It is generally the first sentence, because it opens the subject to be dealt within the paragraph.
- All ideas should be connected with the leading idea and arranged according to their importance and order.
- Advantages are discussed in a paragraph. Give reasons for supplying the advantages.
- Linking verbs or transitive verbs (adverb that is followed by an object) help the writer to move smoothly from one idea to another.
- It should be impersonal and impartial. As far as possible avoid subjective approach.
- Bring originality in your writing. Begin your composition in the most natural and striking way possible.
- Keep strictly within the prescribed word limit. It is usually 100-150 words in paragraph writing.
- Mention only those points that are strictly relevant to the subject.
- Use simple but forceful language. Stick to the main topic.
- Write briefly, simply and to the point.
- Check your grammar and punctuation. Mistakes in grammar, spellings, punctuations, idioms etc. should be avoided.
- If a sentence given for expansion is:
  - *A metaphor or a simile-* explain its full meaning in plain language and give reasons to prove or disprove it.
  - *A conclusion-* should trace the steps by which conclusion has been arrived at.

OBJECTIVES OF PARAGRAPH WRITING

1. The personality of a writer is reflected in his style of writing.
2. It helps develop the habit of independent thinking and analyzing a quotation.

EXAMPLES

Exercise I: All that glitters is not gold

Shakespeare in his famous comedy 'The Merchant of Venice' says, "The World is still deceived with ornaments", which means that seeing is not always believing. Appearances are mostly deceptive. Things are not what they seem. Glittering appearances hide the foulness of wickedness within. Shining ornaments may allure an inexperienced person but the goldsmith at once finds out the reality. The artificial flowers may tempt the onlooker for some time but they soon lose their charm, as they have no life and fragrance. As in the physical world so in the world of morals there are appearances which belie the inward reality. Therefore, one should not be misguided by the face value of the things. Sometimes the people are deceived by fine dress. Wicked men use fine words to conceal their thoughts. Evil minded people throw dust in the eyes of others by showing kind behaviour and good manners. One should be attentive and careful in life and should not be beguiled by false appearances. A person, who has concern for us outwardly, may be our enemy in reality. A careful observation, a clear understanding and a vast experience of life will enable us to distinguish the chaff from the grain.

Exercise 2: Money is a good servant, but a bad master

It is everybody's duty to earn money as it is an essential commodity in the present day life. A man can obtain all the necessary comforts and amenities of life. Money is a great blessing if properly handled, and if one misuses it, it is like inviting troubles for oneself. Money gives man courage, confidence and social prestige. With money one can do constructive and nation building work. It can be utilized for providing comforts to the people in general and ameliorating the lot of down-trodden in particular. But there is the other side of the picture too. The love of Mammon is the cause of all evils in the world. "Prosperity doth best discover vice", says Francis Bacon, the father of English essayists. Excessive love of money is avarice. Lust of wealth degrades human character. A man, blinded by his wealth, becomes addicted to certain evils. Money makes him commit thefts, black marketing, gambling, even murders. Love of money for its own sake is a curse. A man who simply has a pile of treasure at home is no better than the proverbial miser-king Midas. It makes him cruel, mean, selfish and dishonest. So money is like a sharp-edged knife, which if used by a surgeon can cut to heal or if used by a thief, can cut to kill.

Exercise 3: A stitch in time saves nine

Timely action is a very important thing in life. We know well that the time gone part never comes back. Postponing an action is like defeating its very purpose. In the history of the world many ills would not have been happened, had timely action been taken at the outset. In daily life also, there are enough examples which prove that we must do things at the right moment. If we do not care for little ailments right at the time they being, very often they grow into serious disasters, which are difficult to control. A little cough, if neglected, might develop into diseases like asthma or tuberculosis. But very few people realize its significance. In Greek mythology, time has been presented as a man with a bald head having hair on the forehead only and walking with swift steps. If one wants to catch him, he has to take him by the forelock or else his hand will slip on his bald head. If one wants to do something in life, he has to make proper use of available time. What is required is the general alertness of mind. Once a deed is done, it cannot be undone; therefore nothing should be done rashly or impulsively.

Exercise 4: Where there is a will, there is a way

A man can do and attain any and everything in the world, if he has the will, perseverance, courage and endurance. He can scale down the heights of mountains, soar into space and can also delve deep into the womb of earth. He can convert waste land into green land and make the world a fairy land. He can cut roads through mountains and high passes make his own way. Mahatma Gandhi, Shivaji, Napolean, Lincoln, Mother Teresa and others emerged successful and left their imprints on the world. Physical or mental infirmities can never be obstacles in the way of a determined person. If a man has all the facilities and resources to achieve success but is weak willed, he can achieve nothing in his life. So it is rightly said that if a person has a strong will power and is determined to do something, a way of doing it will certainly be found.

Exercise 5: Sweet are the uses of adversity

"Sweet are the uses of adversity", writes William Shakespeare in his famous comedy "As You Like It". Adversity means troubles, misfortunes, harsh conditions or difficulties. Our life is a blend of joys and sorrows. Normally man loves a life of ease and comfort and dreads pain and adversity. But sorrows and suffering are the inevitable lot of human beings. However, adversity has its own uses. Behind every tragedy is hidden the message of hope. In time of trouble a man's strength of character is really tested. If he faces adverse circumstances coolly and remains unperturbed, it shows the inner calm and composure of his being. Adversity is, thus, a kind of educative training that indirectly urges a man to overcome the difficulties of life. He learns great lessons and becomes wiser as a person.

Exercise 6: Failures are the pillars of success

"It is not life that matters, it is the courage that you bring to it", writes Hugh Walpol in his famous novel 'Fortitude'. It is true that failures make man feel nervous and less confident but there is no life without courage. Without failures man becomes easy going. He gives up making efforts. In fact, failures are the stepping stones to success. One should not be daunted by failure. Browning says, "Not failure but low aim is crime". Mahatma Gandhi failed many times in his efforts to bring freedom to India but he persisted in his aim and at last he brought freedom to our motherland. Einstein was an utter failure in his early life, but he became the greatest scientist in the world. Thus, it is better to have tried and failed than never to have tried at all. Surely, failures are the pillars of success.

Exercise 7: United we stand, divided we fall

United we stand and divided we fall is one of the most popular truism, which has stood the test of time right from the beginning of the civilization. A stick can be easily broken even by a child but several sticks bound together cannot be broken even by a wrestler. It makes us realize that unity is strength. Modern progress is all due to the result of a united action of the world. A family, a society, and a country cannot make any progress if there is no unity among its members. If alone, one can be assaulted by a robber, but if one is in a group, none will dare touch him. A family is strong when it possesses both physical and moral strength. The unity of a nation depends not on the number of individuals but on their natural feeling of sincerity and loyalty towards their nation. History stands witness to the fact that families and nations have progressed by united actions. India was kept under foreign rule for years together mainly because we were not united. But as a united nation we overthrew the English rule in our land. Unity is, therefore, a powerful weapon with which all adversities can be challenged.

Exercise 8: Honesty is the best policy

All men desire peace, happiness and success in life. In an effort to discover how best man can conduct himself in life, it is pointed out that honesty is the best course of action. The type of honesty that is expected of men is very difficult to achieve and follow. One should not consider honesty in a narrow sense. It is not related to money matters alone or dealings in business. In its wider sense, honesty is found in every phase of life; in our thoughts, words, deeds, etc. Honesty breeds trust and confidence. One has to be true not only in his private life but also in his dealings with others. The structure of our society is so complicated that it is hard to follow the principle of absolute honesty in our daily lives. But if one becomes really honest he is certainly rewarded in the end. And it is sure that in long run everybody is bound to feel the value of honesty.

REVIEW QUESTIONS

Some Important topics for writing paragraphs:

1. Look before you leap
2. Virtue is its own reward
3. Work is worship
4. Charity begins at home
5. Rome was not built in a day
6. The power of press
7. Speech is silver, silence is gold
8. Knowledge is power
9. Time and tide wait for none
10. We live in deeds and not in years

Precis Writing

21 CHAPTER

INTRODUCTION

Right from the beginning of our educational career, we are trained to write the central idea of a poem or the summary of a passage. All these skills remain important throughout our life because summarization can be done only if there's a clear understanding. This is why great importance is given to précis writing in professional courses. A précis writer's aim should be to get to the given message. From examination point of view, précis writing is another type of question a student would be required to attempt.

DEFINITION

The word ***précis*** is a French word. It means ***'exact' or 'terse'.*** It is pronounced as PRA-SEE. There is no change in the spelling of its plural but it is pronounced as PRA-SEEZ. In English, this word is connected with the word 'Precise'. In fact 'precise' is an adverb. 'Be precise' means 'be brief'. So we may define 'précis' as a summary of a long passage reduced to about one-third of the original length without missing any of the essential points. It is a restatement of the main idea in shortened form.

The Chamber's 20th Century Dictionary and **The Oxford Dictionary** define a précis as "a precise or abridged statement".

According to **Collins,** to make a précis of given passage "is to extract its main points, and to express them as clearly and in as few words as possible. In fact, a précis is just a straightforward statement of the bare fact without any unnecessary trimmings."

Précis, as used in English language today, denote a clear, brief, accurate, well-connected abstract, summary or gist of a written or spoken matter. The objective of précis writing is to bring out faithfully the salient or main idea or theme.

ESSENTIALS OF PRÉCIS WRITING

1. Completeness
2. Compactness

3. Brevity
4. Clarity
5. Coherence
6. Logical sequence

1. Completeness

The précis of a given passage should be the faithful and brief representation of the ideas of the author in your own simple language. No material points should be omitted. The précis writer has to abridge what is already penned by the original writer. He can neither add nor exclude even a single idea from the given passage.

2. Compactness

The words and sentences should convey a sense of unity with each other.

3. Brevity

Brevity means economy of words. It is like the process of separating grain from chaff, retaining only the grain and throwing away the residue. In fact, brevity is the essence of a good précis. It can be achieved by avoiding repetition and by omitting ornamental phrases.

4. Clarity

The précis should be a clear and brief presentation of all the essential ideas and main points of the essential passages.

5. Coherence

All the sentences of the précis should be interconnected to each other in order to bring coherence in a paragraph.

6. Logical Sequence

The sentences and ideas flow one after the other in the précis. In this way the main theme of the paragraph should run through the sentences in order to impart a beautiful and coherent look to the exercise.

ABRIDGING SENTENCES

The following are some of the ways of abridging sentences. Mastery over the language and a good vocabulary are a great asset to students in such cases.

(a) Condensation of Ornamental Language

(i) **Original:**The vast field of criticism in which we are entering, innumerable readers have already put their sickles. Yet the harvest is so abundant the negligent search of a straggling gleaner may be rewarded with a sheaf. (Macaulay)

Précis: Although many critics have already commented on this subject, it is so immense that even a casual critic may find something new to say about it.

(ii) **Original:** The rain continued without intermission throughout the night and did not cease even for a moment until after the day had dawned.

Précis: The rain continued till dawn.

(b) Omission of Less Important Ideas

(i) **Original:** The King and his people, the victor as well as his victims, the rich and the poor, all are subject to death.

Précis: All are subject to death.

(ii) **Original:** We might further state that we would be glad to supply any of these machines on a trial basis.

Précis: We would be glad to supply any of these machines on trial.

(c) Abridgement of Phrases

- The word is no longer in use. — *The word is obsolete.*
- The two countries are in a state of antagonism to each other. — *The two countries are hostile to each other.*
- This is beside the point. — *This is irrelevant.*
- Do not put off till tomorrow what you can do till today — *Do not postpone things.*
- This man is given to the luxuries of the table. — *The man is an epicure.*

(d) Abridgement of Clauses

(i) **Noun Clause**

- That he could be so brave surprised everyone. — *His bravery surprised every one.*
- I do not know what the result has been. — *I do not know the result.*
- The victor showed no mercy to those whom he captured. — *The victor showed no mercy to his captives.*

(ii) Adjective Clause

• The man who is honest is respected.	*The honest man is respected.*
• The place was inhabited by people who could neither read nor write.	*The place was inhabited by illiterate people.*
• The hills we could see in the distance were covered with snow.	*The distant hills were covered with snow.*

(ii) Adverbial Clause

• A holiday was declared by the principal although he was reluctant to do so.	*A holiday was reluctantly declared by the principal.*
• She stood as if she were turned into stone.	*She stood petrified.*
• When they had investigated the matter they found that the loss was nominal.	*On investigation they found the loss to be nominal.*

REQUIREMENTS OF PRÉCIS WRITING

(Do's and don'ts of précis writing)

1. Supply a suitable title to the Précis by locating the key sentence in the passage.
2. Use your own language. Avoid copying from the original.
3. Don't disturb the sequence of ideas, arguments etc.
4. Avoid repetition and omit ornamental phrases.
5. Give maximum information within the required limit.
6. The précis should be ideally written in indirect speech and the third person.
7. Don't divide précis into paragraphs.
8. Don't change any facts.
9. Don't make any comments.
10. Don't try to write a patched Précis or a smaller version of the original.
11. Unless otherwise mentioned, the précis must not exceed one-third of the original passage.

SOLVED EXERCISES

Exercise-I

It is the fashion nowadays to bewail poverty as an evil and to pity the young man who is not born with a silver spoon in his mouth; but I heartily subscribe to president Garfield's doctrine that the richest heritage a young man can be born to is poverty. I make no idle prediction when I say that is the class from whom the good and the great will spring. It is not from the sons of millionaires or the nobles that the world "receives' its teachers, its inventors, its statesmen, its poets, or even its men of affairs. It is from the cottage of the poor that all these spring. We can scarcely read one among the few immortal names that were not "not born to die," or who have tendered exceptional service to our race, who had not the advantage of being cradled, nursed and reared in the stimulating school of poverty.

Main Points

1. *Poverty is not an evil.*
2. *Poverty is the richest heritage for man.*
3. *The truly great men in the world were born and trained in poor homes.*

Heading: **Poverty is a great blessing**

Précis: *It is wrong to call poverty a curse; it is, in fact, a great blessing. It is the priceless gift for a young man. In every field of life the greatest persons of the world were trained and disciplined by poverty.*

Exercise-2

When men began to live together in one place, rules had to be made about health. Almost all the elaborate rules regarding health and behaviour, which were laid down in the Old Testament had a strong basis at the time, although some of them are out of date now. We know so much more about the human body now and about how to keep our cities healthy that one would think we should have solved this problem of health long ago. But as civilization grows more difficulties seem to arise. We hear of new diseases now from every country on the globe, which had never been heard of years ago. The more artificial the world becomes the more difficult it is for the human body to adapt itself to the environment. The rushing motor cars not only kill and injure thousands but also make us more anxious. Machinery does the heavy work which kept our bodies fit and strong. The more dependent we grow on machines, the more the body's power for fighting disease is reduced. Also when human beings get bored they eat too much, drink alcohol and get discontented. Discontentment causes unhappiness. Unhappiness causes physical as well as mental illness.

Main points

1. *Rules for maintenance of good health existed in olden days also.*
2. *Modern life is artificial.*
3. *Machines have reduced man's power of resistance against diseases.*
4. *Boredom causes unhappiness and diseases.*

Heading: **Health in the Machine Age**

Précis: *Rules regarding health are as old as the society itself. Old rules become obsolete as time passes because, as civilization advances more and more difficulties arise. New diseases are cropping up every day because of changing life-styles. As machines perform the hard physical labour that kept the human body healthy, man's power to resist disease is reduced. Moreover, boredom makes man discontented and unhappy, and that causes diseases.*

Exercise-3

Learning is the knowledge of what is not generally known to others; and which we can only derive secondhand from books and other sources. The knowledge of what is before us, or about us; which appeals to our experience, passion and pursuits, to the bosoms and business of men, is not learning. Learning is the knowledge of what none but the learned know. He is the more learned man who knows the most of what is farthest from common life and actual observation, that is of the least practical utility, and least liable to be brought to the test of experience, and that, having been handed down through the greatest number of intermediate stages, is most full of uncertainties, difficulties and contradictions. It is seeing with the eyes of others, hearing with others' ears, and pinning our faith on their understanding.

The learned man prides himself in the knowledge of names and dates, not men or things. He thinks and cares nothing about his next door neighbour but he is deeply read in the tribes and castes of the Hindus and Calmus Tartars. He can hardly find his way into the next street, thought he is acquainted with the exact dimensions of Constantinople and Beijing. He does not know whether his oldest acquaintance is a knave or a fool but he can deliver a pompous lecture on all the principal characters in history. He cannot tell whether an object is black or white, round or square, and yet he is a professed master of the laws of optics and the rules of perspective. He knows as much of what he talks about as a blind man does of colours. He cannot give a satisfactory answer to the plainest question, nor is he ever in the right in any of his opinions on any matter that really comes before him and yet he boasts of himself as an infallible judge on all these points, of which it is impossible that he or any other living person should know anything but by conjecture. He is an expert in all the deeds and in most of the living languages; but he can neither speak his own fluently nor write it correctly.

Main points

1. *Learning is the knowledge of the obscure and the uncommon.*
2. *Learning is of no practical value.*
3. *A learned man is ignorant of the things around him.*
4. *He does not know what he talks about.*

Heading: The Ignorance of the Scholar

Précis: *The knowledge of everyday experience is not learning. Learning is the knowledge of what is known to none except the learned man. It is obscure, full of uncertainties and difficulties and is obtained second hand. The learned man takes pride in the knowledge of the remotest things, although he is perfectly ignorant of the things around him. He cannot read the character of his oldest friends, although he pronounces judgement on historical personalities. He does not know the next street although he has complete knowledge about the remotest cities of the world. He talks authoritatively on a subject of which he or any other person on earth knows nothing. In short, he does not know anything of what he talks.*

Exercise-4

A great many men and women, in spite of all our humanitarian and democratic prejudices, do not want to be cultured and are not interested in the higher life. For these people, existence on the lower animal level is perfectly satisfactory. Given food, drink and the company of their fellows, sexual pleasures and plenty of noisy distractions from without, they are happy. They enjoy physically, but hate mental exercise. They cannot bear to be alone or to think. Contemporary urban life, with its jazz bands, its Negroid dancing, its movies, theatres, football matches, newspapers and the likes, is ideal for them. They can live their entire lives without once making a serious mental effort (for the work which most of these people do is mainly mechanical and requires little or no thought), without once being out of sight or sound of some ready distraction.

The notion that one can derive pleasure form arduous intellectual occupation is, to such people, merely absurd. More leisure and more prosperity for them means more dancing, parties, movies, and other distractions. Most of the inhabitants of ancient Rome belonged to this type; so do probably most of the inhabitants of modern New York and London. And unless some system of eugenics is practiced in the interval, there is no reason to suppose that the inhabitants of the great cities in the year 5000 A.D. will be radically different.

Main Points

Criticism of the modern way of living: Eat, drink and be merry. Inner life, intellectual interest and thinking habits missing from the modern civilization.

Heading: Philosophy of Modern Life

Précis: *Most of us in modern times are satisfied with a mere animal existence. The guiding principle of the modern civilization seems to be: Eat, drink and be merry. People of today have a strong distaste for mental exertion and deeper thinking. With the superfluities and distractions of our modern way of living, life is devoid of any deeper interest, intellectual pursuits and profound thinking.*

Unless some eugenic measures are taken, the future generations are not likely to be very different from the people of today.

Exercise-5

The power of the film cannot be left in the hands of irresponsible people. The purposeless squandering of film resources for the gain of a few people is the curse of film production today. The same sense of responsibility should mark the production of a film as the production of a book by the major publishing houses. The name of the production should be publicized as the names of the author and publisher of a book. The public is learning to assess the quality of a film by the reputation of the producer and director involved in its production.

Main Points

1. *The control of films by profiteers.*
2. *Need of responsibility in film production.*
3. *Comparison with book production.*
4. *The status of film directors.*

Heading: ***Reforms in Films***

Précis: *The control of the film industry by profiteers has proved a disaster. The standards governing the publication of books should also apply to films. The directors and producers of good films deserve the status of good authors and publishers.*

Exercise-6

When Ishwar Chandra Vidyasagar was working as a professor in the Sanskrit College, Calcutta, his mother sent him word that he should see her a once in their native village in Midnapur. He immediately applied to the principal of the college for leave, but the principal would not grant his prayer. Ishwar Chandra, therefore, submitted his letter of resignation stating therein that he considered it a disgrace to continue in service to the distress of his mother's feelings. The college authorities were taken aback and had to climb down. Leave was granted. He set out at noon and walked till night to reach the banks of the Damodar. It was impossible to cross the rain-swollen Damodar at night. When he went to the riverside the following morning, he saw that the river had taken a terrible shape and the ferry boats had ceased to ply. He offered the boatmen a large reward, but they dared not make the attempt. So he jumped into the river and proceeded to swim across. The men standing on the bank were amazed and exclaimed in one accord that the Brahmin was bent upon committing suicide. But, protected by his mother's blessings, he fought his way through the mighty waves and reached the bank in perfect safety.

Main Points

1. *Ishwar Chandra Vidyasagar, professor in Sanskrit College; message from his mother.*
2. *Leave granted when he submitted his letter of resignation.*
3. *The Damodar swollen; boatmen refused to take him across; Ishwar Chandra Vidyasagar jumped into the river; reached in safety*

Heading: **Mother's Blessings**

Précis: *When Ishwar Chandra Vidyasagar was a professor in Sanskrit College, Calcutta, he received a message from his mother asking him to see her at once. The principal did not grant him leave until he submitted his resignation. On his way, he found the Damodar in flood. The boatmen refused to take him across the swollen river. Thereupon, he jumped into the river and protected by his mother's blessings, reached the other bank in safety.*

Exercise-7

The great advantage of rising early is the good start it gives us in our day's work. The early riser has done a large amount of hard work before the other men have got out of bed. During the early morning the mind is fresh, and there are few sounds or other distractions, so that work done at that time is generally well done. In many cases the early riser also finds time to take some exercise in the fresh morning air, and this exercise supplies him with a fund of energy that will last until the evening. By beginning so early, he knows that he has plenty of time to do thoroughly all the work he can be expected to do, and is not tempted to hurry over any part of it. He goes to bed early and takes a refreshing nap and after a sound night sleep rises early next morning in good health and spirits for the labours of a new day.

It is very plain that such a life as this is far more conducive to health than that of the man who shortens his waking hours by rising late, and so can afford, in the course of the day, little leisure for necessary rest. Anyone who lies in bed late, must, if he wishes to do a full day's work, go for exercise for the benefit of his health. But in spite of all his efforts he will probably not produce as good a result as the early riser, because he misses the best working hours of the day.

Main Points

1. *Early rising gives a good start to the day's work; mind is fresh; no disturbance; time to take exercise; thorough in work.*
2. *Disturbed sleep; working hours shortened by the habit of rising late; this habit is not good for health.*
3. *The late riser misses the best working hours; not as great a success as an early riser.*

Heading: **In Support of Early Rising**

Précis: *Early rising gives a good start in the day's work. In the early morning the mind is fresh and the atmosphere is calm. The early riser can also take exercise in the morning. He is always punctual and thorough in his work. He enjoys a peaceful sleep at night. The late riser, on the other hand, is causing harm to his health. The late riser misses the best working hours and so, inspite of his best effort is never as great success as an early riser.*

Exercise-8

"I should not like to think, my friends, that after all the years in which we have travelled together and shared common talks, that you are going to desert me. We have contributed much to the welfare of the poor. From the view of their general conditions of life, we have penetrated the fortress of evil and driven forth drink and despair wholly from their midst. This internal strife will surely cause us to fall as a house divided against itself."

N.B. *It should be noticed that in making the Précis of a speech the following points should be kept in mind.*

(i) *The introductory remarks, viz., He told his friends, Addressing his friends, he said, etc.*
(ii) *The use of past tense.*
(iii) *The use of the third person (for impersonal form).*

Main Points

This is rather a difficult passage, full of metaphorical expressions. The main ideas are:

(i) *Long cooperation.*
(ii) *Impossibility of desertion.*
(iii) *Contribution to moral and social welfare.*
(iv) *Dangers of disunity.*

Heading: **Appeal for Continued Cooperation**

Précis: *He told his friends that, after such a long association, desertion was impossible. Their contribution to the moral and social well-being of the poor was great and disunity would prove disastrous now.*

Exercise-9

You hear every day greater number of foolish people speaking about liberty, as if it were such an honourable thing. Far from being that, it is in the broadest sense, dishonourable and an attribute of the lower creatures. No human being, however great and powerful, was ever so free as a fish. There is always something that he must or must not do while the fish may do whatever it likes. All the kingdoms of the world put together are not half so large as the sea, and all the railroads and wheels that ever were or will be invented are not so easy to use as fins. You will find on fair thinking that it is his restraint which is honourable to man, not his liberty, and what is more, it is restraint, which is honourable even in the lower animals. A butterfly is more free than a bee; but you honour a bee more just because it is subject to certain laws, which befit it for orderly function in bee society. And throughout the world, of the two abstract things, liberty and restraint, restraint is always the more honourable.

It is true, indeed, that in these and all other matters, you never can reason finally for the justification for the goodness of both, liberty and restraint are equal when they are nobly chosen; but of the two, I repeat, it is restraint which characterizes the higher creatures and betters the lower creatures; and from the ministering of the archangel to the labour of the insect, from the poising of the planets to the gravitation of a grain of dust, the power and glory of all creatures and all matters consist in their obedience, not in their freedom. The sun has no liberty. Its liberty will come - with its corruption.

Heading: ***Liberty and restraint***

Précis: *Restraint is a greater virtue than liberty. Liberty is characteristic of the lower creatures, but man is not, like the fish, free to do whatever he likes. Even in lower creatures, restraint is considered more honourable than liberty. We honour the bee, which is subject to the laws of bee society, more than the butterfly, which is free to move. However, both liberty and restraint are good when nobly chosen. But restraint characterizes the higher creatures and raises the lower ones. All the objects in the universe obey certain laws. Even the sun and the dust of which our body is made, knows no freedom.*

Exercise-10

The value of a university for educational purposes lies not principally in its examination, not even wholly in its teaching, however admirable that teaching may be. It lies, and must lie, in the collision of minds between student and student. We learn at all times of life, but perhaps most when we are young and much from our contemporaries as from anybody else, and when we are young we learn from our contemporaries what no professor, however eminent can teach us. Therefore, it is that I admire those solitary students, who, under great difficulties come up to Edinburgh or some other university and without intercourse with their fellows, doggedly and perseveringly pursue their studies, very often under serious domestic pressures. I, therefore associate myself entirely with what Lord Rosebery said of athletics. "I do not think that the athletic movement has been overdone. I believe, on the contrary, that the intercourse between students which it has produced, organizations to which it has given birth, and the good fellowship which it has secured, are of infinite educational value".

Heading: **The Value of a University**

Précis: *The value of a university consists chiefly in the healthy mental intercourse between students. During our youth we learn from our contemporaries what no professor can teach. A student, however diligently he may pursue his studies, cannot reap the fullest advantage of his university life unless he comes in close contact with his fellow students. The athletic movement has served a great educational purpose in this respect. It has facilitated intercourse between the students and promoted a spirit of good fellowship among them.*

Exercise-11

When you come to a good book you must ask yourself, "Am I inclined to work as an Australian miner would? Are my pickaxes and shovels in good order, and I in good trim myself, my sleeves well up to the elbow and my breath good, and my temper?" And keeping the figure a little longer, even at the cost of tiresomeness, for it is a thoroughly useful one, the metal you are in search of being the author's mind or meaning his words are as the rock, which you have to crush and smelt in order to get at it. And your pickaxes are your own care, wit and learning; your smelting furnace is your own thoughtful soul. Do not hope to get at any good author's meaning without these tools and that fire: often you will need the sharpest, finest chiselling and potentiate fusing, before you can gather one grain of the metal.

And, therefore, first of all, I tell you, earnestly and authoritatively (I know I am right in this), you must get into the habit of looking intensely at words, and assuring yourself of their meaning, syllable by syllable, the function of signs, sound in functions of signs. That the study of books is called literature and that a man versed in it is called, by the consent of nations, a man of letters instead of a man of books, or of words, you may connect with that accidental nomenclature this real principle; that you might read all the books in the British Museum (if you could live long enough), and remain an utterly illiterate, uneducated person; but that if you read ten pages of a good book, letter by letter, that is to say with real accuracy, you are, for even in some measure, an educated person.

Heading: **The Importance of Careful Reading**

Précis: *To extract the utmost value of a book a man must work at it like a miner extracting metal from a rock. He must have his wit and learning as keen and his thoughtfulness should be as bright, as the miner has his pickaxes and smelting furnace. He must learn to study words intensively, letter by letter. A man might read all the books in the British Museum, and yet remain uneducated. But anyone* *who has read ten pages of a good book with real attention is in some measure educated.*

Exercise-12

The chains of slavery for centuries have been broken off by the brave sons of India, and the Independent Bharat is now moving on the path of progress at full speed.

Our country, which was once spiritually awakened, is not making scientific and material progress keeping in view its ancient cultural heritage. People of various castes and creeds live together in peace and harmony in this subcontinent. Inspite of differences of customs and manners, of food and clothes, and of languages, the cultural integrity of our country was never impaired. In order to maintain the cultural unity of this vast country, the provincial languages should come forward like sisters to worship their mother *'Bharti'*. The national task before us is so vast and urgent that we must all take it up with a far greater resoluteness and devotion than ever before. It brooks no delay. The mother invites us all to stretch out our untiring hands. Let us dedicate ourselves to this ideal, forgetting all our differences. What our country now needs are the muscles of iron and nerves of steel – a gigantic will, which nothing can resist, which can penetrate into mysteries and secrets of the universe and accomplish this uphill task in any fashion, even if it means going to the bottom of oceans and meeting death face to face.

Heading: ***India After Independence***

Précis: *India after her independence is moving fast on the path of scientific and material progress but not losing sight of her ancient cultural traditions. People of various castes, religions, customs, colours and languages live in this country bound by cultural unity. Now the time has come when all the people, forgetting all their differences whatsoever should rise up and join the difficult task of nation building. What our country needs now are the untiring labour and the irresistible will of the people to built up and develop the nation. The writer notes that in ancient times many persons were involved in one work. As a result, labour was wasted. Nowadays, things have changed and people have started dividing the work among themselves so as to do it far more quickly and easily. It is a happy sign.*

Exercise-13

Bearing His cross upon His shoulder, like the commonest and most wicked criminal, Jesus Christ, surrounded by the persecuting crowd went out of Jerusalem to a place called Golgotha in the Hebrew language. And having come to a hill called Mount Calvary, they hammered cruel nails through His hands and feet and nailed Him on the cross, between two other crosses, on each of which was nailed a common thief in agony. A writing in three languages; Hebrew, Greek and Latin proclaiming "Jesus of Nazareth, the King of the Jews" was hung over His head.

None was there to take pity on Him; but one disciple and four women. God bless those women for their true and tender hearts. They were the mother of Jesus, His mother's sister Mary the wife of Cleophas, and Mary Magdalene who had twice dried His feet upon her hair. The disciple was he whom Jesus loved-John. When Jesus saw them standing at foot of the cross, He said to His mother that John would be her son to comfort her when He was dead; and from that hour John was son to her, and loved her.

Heading: The Crucifixion of Jesus Christ

Précis: *Jesus Christ was nailed to a cross like a vile criminal at Golgotha. His persecutors hung a writing over His head, proclaiming Him the 'King of the Jews'. His persecutors were merciless to Him. None pitied Him except four women (including His mother, His mother's sister Mary the wife of Cleophas and Mary Magdalene). His beloved disciple John was also there. Jesus said to His mother that John would be her son from now. And so he was.*

Exercise-14

To be good is noble but to teach how to be good is nobler- and no trouble" said a well known writer. This may account for the great preponderance of preaching over practice. We do not mean the preaching which we get from the pulpit, but that which is given freely and without stint in buses, in the streets and even in the homes of our land. Where is the parent who does not discover himself telling his child not to do just what he himself does regularly? How many people are there who are certain that they know just how to make a fortune, and who tell others so? – and they have never made anything themselves, save financial mistakes. The man who never swam a stroke feels perfectly competent to tell another how to swim. The man who cannot find his way even to a modest competence knows just how to save the nation from all its economic ills.

It is not trouble to preach, but it is considerable trouble to carry out what we preach. It is so true that the honest preacher preaches to himself even more than to his hearers in every season. Only the man who is striving to climb the loftiest heights knows just how difficult is the way. And so the man who climbs as he preaches will preach earnestly, and effectively, because he is trying to answer his own prayers and work out his own salvation.

Heading: The Supremacy of Preaching over Practice

Précis: *To preach goodness is noble than to practise it. It is generally seen that those who fail in practice are best suited to the work of preaching. The man who knows how to make a fortune is the one who does nothing but make financial mistakes. The man who never swam knows how to instruct another in swimming. The man who cannot succeed even in a small competition knows just how to save* *the country from all its economic troubles. The truth is that only a man who is himself striving to reach a certain goal can most earnestly and effectively tell others the way to success.*

Exercise-15

Progress in life depends a good deal on crossing one threshold after another. Sometime ago a man watched his little nephew try to write his name. It was hard work, very hard work. The little boy had arrived at an effort threshold. Today, he writes his name with comparative ease. No new thresholds confront him. This is the way with all of us. As soon as we cross one threshold, as soon as we conquer one difficulty, a new difficulty appears, or should appear. Some people make the mistake of steering clear of thresholds. Anything that requires genuine thinking and use of energy is considered an impediment. They prefer to stay in a rut where thresholds are not met. Probably, they have been at their job for a number of years. Things are easy for them. They make no effort to seek out new obstacles to overcome. Real progress stops under such circumstances.

Some middle-aged and elderly people greatly enrich their lives by continuing to cross new thresholds. One man went into an entirely new business when he was past middle life and made success of it. De Morgen didn't start to write novels until he was past sixty. Psychologists have discovered that man can continue to learn throughout life. And it is undoubtedly better to try, and fail, than not to try at all. Then one can be placed in the category of the Swiss mountaineer of whom it was said, 'He died climbing.' When a new difficulty rises to obstruct your path, do not complain, accept the challenge. Be determined to cross this threshold as you have crossed numerous other thresholds in your past life. In the word of the poet, do not rest but strive to pass 'from dream to grander dream'.

Heading: ***Overcoming Difficulties***

Précis: *Progress in life depends upon our conquering new difficulties at every turn. There can be no real progress where people move in a rut and avoid new obstacles and everything that requires genuine thinking and use of energy. Some elderly people try to maintain their enthusiasm in life by continuing to overcome every new difficulty. We should never complain of the difficulties that obstruct our path but grapple with them hopefully and heroically.*

UNSOLVED EXERCISES

Exercise-16

It is customary to say that in this machine age there is less room than formerly for the craftsman's joy and skilled work. I am not at all sure that this is true. The skilled workman nowadays works, it is true, at quite different things from those that occupied the attention of the medieval guilds, but he is still very important and quite essential even in the machine economy. There are those who make scientific instruments and delicate machines, there are designers, there are aeroplane mechanics, chauffeurs, and hosts of others who have a trade in which skill can be developed to almost any extent. The agricultural labour and the peasant in comparatively primitive communities is not, so far as I have been able to observe, nearly as happy as a chauffeur or an engine driver. It is true that the work of the peasant who cultivates his own land is varied, he ploughs, he sows, he reaps. But he is at the mercy of the elements and is very conscious of this dependence whereas the man who works on a modern mechanism is conscious of his power and acquires the sense that man is the master, not the slave, of natural forces. It is true, of course, that work is very uninteresting for the large body of mere machine menders who repeat some mechanical operation over and over again with the minimum of variation, but the more uninteresting the work becomes, the more possible it is to get it performed by a machine. The ultimate goal of machine production is a system in which everything uninteresting is done by machine and human beings are reserved for the work involving variety and initiative.

Vocabulary

1. *Customary*	*Normal, usual, common*
2. *Formerly*	*Before this time*
3. *Medieval*	*Of middle ages*
4. *Primitive*	*Ancient*
5. *Initiative*	*Quality of taking early steps*

Main Points

1. *It is commonly but wrongly assumed that in the machine age the craftsman cannot feel elated.*
2. *Of course machines do quite some work, but they are by and large used for dreary type of work.*
3. *A person working on modern machine is less dependent upon the mercy of elements as compared for example to a peasant; as such he develops the sense of independence rather than dependence.*

Exercise-17

Under the present system of mass education by means of classes, too much stress is laid on teaching and too little on active learning. The child is not encouraged to discover things on his own, thus losing intellectual independence and all capacity to judge for himself. The over-taught child is the father of the newspaper reading, advertisement believing, propaganda swallowing, demagogued man, the man who makes modern democracy the force it is. Moreover, lessons in class leave him mainly unoccupied, and therefore bored. He has to be coerced into learning what does not interest him, and the information acquired mechanically and reluctantly by dint of brute repetition is rapidly forgotten. Quite naturally, the child being bored and unoccupied, is also mischievous. A strict external discipline becomes necessary unless there is to be chaos, and pandemonium. The child learns to obey, not to control himself. He loses moral as well as intellectual independence.

Such are the defects in the current system of mass education. Many others could be mentioned, but they are defects in detail and can be classified under one or other of the three main categories of defects - sacrifice of the individual to the system, psychologically unsound methods of teaching and irrational methods of imposing discipline. We need a new system of universal education of the same kind as that which has proved itself so successful in the training of detectives and infants, but modified so as to be suitable for other boys and girls. We need a system of individual education.

Letter Writing

22

CHAPTER

IMPORTANCE OF LETTER WRITING

A letter is like a conversation-'a piece of conversation by post.' In the modern times society has become much more extensive and complex. We daily meet with new acquaintances, form new friendships and new associations. There was a time when letter writing was considered an art, but now it has become a necessity. Of course, there exist other means of communication, like telephone, telex, telegraph etc. telephonic message is also widely used nowadays, but the message communicated through this media cannot be kept in memory for a long time. Besides, this media is quite expensive. A letter is the cheapest and the most common device for developing new contacts.

Letters facilitate maintenance of a constant touch with the outer world. Men, who have never met, nor are even likely to meet, can maintain close personal or business relations with one another. Easy and effective communication or information is possible through letters.

For a successful man, therefore, the cultivation of the art of letter writing is as necessary as the art of public speaking. It is only due to letter writing that a businessman can find markets very easily all over the world. A written letter can carry assurance of transactions, confirmation of dealings and is a reliable record for further references. To create the best relation, therefore, letters should be written in a clear and understanding way.

ESSENTIALS OF A GOOD LETTER

A letter is a piece of composition in which one has to observe certain long established conventions or formalities. A good letter is supposed to be marked with the following qualities:

1. Clarity

A good letter shows its idea directly and clearly. We should be clear about three points:

a. What is the objective of writing the letter?
b. What is to be communicated?
c. Which medium will be the most suitable for this purpose?

In order to achieve clarity, we should use short sentences. Short sentences communicate better because of mind limitations. Besides, we should use only one sentence to express one idea.

2. Simplicity

A letter must be simple and easy. Simple and short words are more effective than pompous and heavy words. According to Chesterfield, "Every paragraph of the letter should be so clear and unambiguous that the dullest fellow in the world will not be able to mistake it, nor be obliged to read it twice in order to understand."

3. Conciseness

A letter must be as simple and as brief as possible. Transmission of maximum information by using minimum words should be our aim in letter writing. In order to achieve conciseness we should include only relevant facts. Repetition should be avoided and there should be proper organization of the message. Vague words and roundabout ways of expression should be avoided.

4. Positive and Pleasant Approach

The charm of a letter is chiefly the charm of the writer's personality. In a letter, the reader accepts calmly and coolly, all the no, regrets and sorry, if expressed in a positive manner. An approach with a negative beginning irritates the reader. A positive approach, on the other hand, convinces the reader of the writer's helplessness. In fact a positive and pleasant approach says 'no' in a sugarcoated manner. As a rule, we must try to avoid negative words like, fear, mistake, unpleasant, unwelcome, disagree etc. We should use positive and pleasing words like please, thank you, welcome, appreciate, happy, agree etc.

5. Consideration for the reader

In our letters we must show consideration for the reader. The writer must take into consideration the nature, the post and the mental level of the receiver so that the reader can read it with ease.

6. Correctness

A good letter is always correctly written and is always in correct form. The letter must be free from mistakes, errors of punctuation, misspelling or grammatical incorrectness etc. The information must be accurate.

LETTER WRITING TIPS

Here are a few practical letter writing tips that you may find helpful when writing a letter:

1. Keep it short and to the point

Letters involving business (personal or corporate) should be concise, factual, and focused. Try to never exceed one page or you will run the risk of losing your reader. If necessary, call the recipient on the phone to clarify any fuzzy points and then use the letter just to summarize the overall situation.

2. Focus on the recipient's needs

While writing the letter, focus on the information requirements of your audience, the intended addressee. If you can imagine in your "mind's eye" the intended recipient seated across a desk while you are explaining the subject of the letter. What essential information does that person need to know through this communication? What will be their expectations when they open the letter? Have you addressed all of these?

3. Use simple and appropriate language

Your letter should use simple and straightforward language for clarity and precision. Use short sentences and don't let paragraphs exceed three or four sentences. As much as possible, use language and terminology familiar to the intended recipient. Do not use technical terms and acronyms without explaining them, unless you are certain that the addressee is familiar with them.

4. Re-read and revise it

Do a first draft of the letter, and then carefully review and revise it. Put yourself in the place of the addressee. Imagine yourself receiving the letter. How would you react to it? Would it answer all your questions? Does it deal with all of the key issues? Are the language and tone appropriate? Sometimes reading it out a loud to oneself can be helpful. When you actually "hear" the words it is easy to tell if it "sounds" right or not.

5. Check spelling and grammar

A letter is a direct reflection of the person sending it, and by extension, the organization that the person works for. When the final content of the letter is settled, make sure that you run it through a spell and grammar check. Sending a letter with obvious spelling and grammar mistakes looks sloppy and unprofessional.

CLASSIFICATIONS OF LETTERS

There are various kinds of letters. We may roughly divide letters into three classes:

- Informal/Personal letters
- Formal letters
- Business letters

A personal letter is a way of communicating between two people (sometimes more) who are usually well acquainted. The personal letters establish bonds of family or social relationship.

A letter of application by a job-seeker is a **formal letter,** addressed as it is to a relatively or a totally unacquainted stranger holding a certain position. Hence, the formal letter like the business letter, calls for a certain amount of formal communication. However, it cannot be grouped under business letters.

When a letter is written on behalf of an organization to another organization or individuals to transact a business it is called a **business letter**. It includes all kinds of letters that may be written while conducting business transactions.

Informal vs. Formal letters

A personal letter is **subjective** in nature. The objective of a personal letter is to establish a personal contact or to keep alive a bond of personal relationship. A personal letter is supposed to express personal feelings of the writer as it is written to a relative or a close friend. The style of such a letter is informal and the tone friendly and intimate. Formality has no place in personal letter. It should be written in an informal style.

A **business letter** is **objective** in nature. It may be written to an organization or a person whom the writer has never met, nor is even likely to meet. Since a business letter is written to achieve a definite purpose and often gives rise to legal obligations, we have to be more accurate, clear, correct, precise, courteous and reasonable in our approach.

Both letters, however, reflect politeness, simplicity and a sense of humour.

All types of letters have their respective rules or formalities. First we take up to discuss here what we call personal letters.

PERSONAL/INFORMAL LETTERS

A personal letter or an informal letter, as the name implies, is much less rigid in its format. It can either be printed or handwritten. The tone is informal. The address of the recipient is omitted. Traditionally the sender's address appears on the right hand corner and the date comes directly under the address.

Parts/Elements of an informal letter

1. Your Address

Traditionally, the sender's complete postal address appears at the top right hand corner of the letter. First, you should mention the name of the house, then the number of the house and then the name of the street on the first line and the city, state and pin code on the second line.

2. Date

Put the date on which the letter was written in the format Month Day Year i.e. March 20, 2007 or Day Month Year i.e. 20, August, 2007. Skip a line between the date and the salutation.

3. Salutation

The salutation in personal letters varies with the degree of affection or intimacy that exists between the writer and the addressee. Usually salutation starts out with Dear so and so or Hi so and so.

4. Body

The body is where you write the content of the letter. Simplicity, naturalness, unaffected language, these are some of the things to be looked for in a good personal or friendly letter. There should be absolute freedom from all condescension and you should talk to your friend or relative in a simple homely language. Avoid commonplace beginnings as "I was delighted to get your loving letter", or "I am quite well and hope you to be the same". Instead, you may acknowledge the receipt of your letter in this way, "It was so kind of you to write to me" or "Your letter has made me so happy" etc.

The paragraphs should be single spaced with a skipped line between each paragraph. Skip 2 lines between the end of the body and the closing.

5. The Complimentary Close

It lets the reader know that you are finished with your letter. Like the salutation, the closing of a letter varies with the degree of affection or intimacy that exists between the correspondents. A few expressions that are commonly used are; Yours sincerely, Sincerely yours, Yours truly, With best regards, Yours affectionately, Yours ever, With love and so on. Note that there is a comma after the end of the closing and only the first word in the closing is capitalized.

If you want to conclude your letter with a sentence it should always end with a full stop. For example, "I look forward to a reply from you."

6. Signature

Your signature will go in this section. It is usual to sign with one's first name only, assuming that the writer is on friendly terms with the person. Skip a line after your signature and the P.S.

7. Post Script (P.S.)

If you desire to add some important information which you have forgotten to mention earlier, you write a P.S. and the message after that.

A post script could be used in a personal communication, but it should not find a place in formal/business letters, as here it shows a casualness not accepted in formal writing.

FORMAL/BUSINESS LETTERS

A business letter should be properly planned and carefully drafted so that the purpose of writing it is adequately fulfilled. Even a two-line letter of enquiry is written with a specific purpose. If it is not drafted carefully, not only will the purpose of writing be defeated but it may also cause financial loss and embarrassment to the organization.

Apart from its primary purpose, a business letter always has the secondary purpose of building the goodwill of the organization which sends it. Carelessly written letters can never fulfill this purpose.

Parts/Elements of a Business Letter

Most business letters, regardless of their purpose, have the following basic parts;

1. Heading or letterhead
2. Date
3. Reference
4. Inside address
5. Attention line
6. Salutation
7. Subject and reference
8. Body or substance of the letter
9. Complimentary close
10. Signature
11. Enclosure

1. Heading or letterhead

Heading contains information relating to the name of the firm and its address. Most business organizations use printed letterhead for correspondence. It contains the name of organization, address, pin code, telephone / fax / telegraphical address/ e-mail, website address, symbols and trademarks etc.

The name of the firm and its address are usually given at the top centre or right side of the paper. If a firm prefers to put much of the information at the bottom of the letter head, we may call it **letterfoot**. But the firm's name should always be written at the top.

2. Date

Date serves the purpose of identification. It enables quick reference in future and helps in prompt action and orderly filing. The date consists of the month, the date of the month and the year. Normally it is written below the address (about 2 line spaces below the last line of letter head)

(ex. 9 October, 2006 (or) October 9, 2006 (or) 09.10.2006

While writing the date, the abbreviations for months and the years should be avoided. The names of the month and the year are always written in full. No suffix as 'st' 'nd' or 'th'(1st, 2nd or 16th) is added to the date.

3. Reference

The reference is printed below the date line. It is always written close to the left margin. The reference identifies both the department and its section from which the letter is being sent or the particular file in which the letter is to be found. Stating the reference helps quick and easy future references.

4. Inside Address

Inside address is typed on the top left hand side, about 2 line spaces below the date line. It contains the name and full address of the person or the organization to whom the letter is written. These details should not be abbreviated. It is bad business manners to do so. While addressing an individual, 'Ms.' can be used both for a married and an unmarried woman. While addressing a firm, **Messers** (messieurs, meaning gentlemen) is used before the name as the plural for Mr. Messers is used while addressing firms with titles that contain personal names, like Messers. Williams Ltd. (or) M/s. Robert & Co. 'Mmes' (Mesdames) is used as the plural for 'Mrs.' Punctuation marks are generally not used in the address. The inside address must be similar to the address on the envelope.

5. Attention Line

Attention line is used when the writer of a letter wishes to direct it to a particular person or official (either by designation or name) in an organization. It is written below the inside address but above the salutation and is underlined. For example,

Kind attention: Mr. G. K. Pandey, Director

6. Salutation

The salutation is the complimentary greeting with which the writer opens his letter. For ordinary business purposes, 'Dear Sir' is commonly used for addressing a person. It is the term of politeness, respect and affection.

7. Subject and Reference

Purpose of writing the subject is to enable the reader to know at a glance what the message is about. The subject tells us the main theme of the letter. It is written about one / two lines below the salutation, before starting the body of the letter. If it is a reply to an earlier business letter, its reference no. and date may also be mentioned in a separate line below the subject. These two must be separate and must stand out clearly to attract the attention of the reader.

8. Body

The main purpose of writing a letter is to convey a message. This is done through the body of the letter. It is better to divide the body of the letter in two or more paragraphs.

Para-1 (Opening paragraph)

The opening paragraph establishes the relation of this letter to any previous correspondences that have taken place in the past. The letter should open with the expression of pleasure, gratitude or acknowledgement. Therefore, it should reflect a positive approach and a friendly attitude and should arrest the interest of the reader. If the letter fails here, it will totally fail to achieve its purpose.

Para-2 (Main paragraph)

This paragraph contains the subject matter of the letter. It writes the main message that the writer wants to convey. The writer should make himself absolutely clear about what he wants to say.

Para-3 (Closing paragraph)

In the closing paragraph, the writer may assure of his sincerity of purpose, express his confidence in the reader and also write what exactly is needed. It must be natural and logical, final and complete.

The entire body of the letter should reflect a positive approach and a friendly attitude and it must contain a definite appeal for the purpose for which letter is written. Punctuations should be marked in their proper places.

9. Complimentary close

The complimentary close is merely a polite way of ending a letter. It is written in a separate line at the foot of the letter. Just as the salutation is the written equivalent of "Good morning", so the complimentary close is the written equivalent of "Good Bye". Salutation and complimentary close should correspond to each other. 'Yours sincerely' or 'Yours faithfully' are conventionally used as complimentary close.

10. Signature

The signature is the signed name of the writer. It is the writer's distinguishing mark. Generally all important correspondence is signed by the head of the business firm. The name and designation of the signatory is typed in parenthesis below the closing line, providing enough space for the signature.

11. Enclosure

If anything like cheque, draft or any document is to be attached to the letter, a mention should be made of these enclosures in the letter after the signature and at the left side margin. The short form of enclosure is Encl. or Enclos.

Further points

Postscript

(Latin: Post Scriptum or P.S.) After completing a letter, if the writer wants to add further information, he can do so by writing a note at the bottom. This is called postscript. From the viewpoint of a good business letter, it should preferably be avoided as it indicates that the letter is not planned properly.

C.C. or Carbon Copy Notation

Sometimes copies of the letter are sent to different persons. At the left hand side bottom of the letter, after writing C.C., the names and the addresses of these persons are written. The names of the persons should be arranged either in order of importance or alphabetically.

Nota bene (N.B.)

It means take notice. When some special points are to be added in order to catch the attention of the reader, the writer can do so by writing N.B., below the letter at the left hand side.

Per pro signature (signature per procuration)

When the firm delegates the authority of signing letters to an officer by executing a legal instrument called 'Power of Attorney' in his favour, the signature is called per pro (*pp*) signature. In all these cases he will be binding the company legally.

Identification Mark or Reference Initials

These marks are put in the left margin to identify the typist of the letter, one or two spaces below the signature. Usually, the initials of the officer who dictated the letter are placed first. After that the initials of the person who typed the letter are put. For example; JSK: NNB (JSK are the initials who has dictated the letter and NNB of the one who has typed it).

LAYOUT OF FORMAL AND INFORMAL LETTER

As computer literacy has gripped the world, according to the latest format of letter writing (formal or informal) every detail begins very close to the margin i.e., to the left.

A. Informal

24, Kavery Apartments
Sector- 6, Vaishali
Hyderabad

14th April, 20.....

Dear Dev

Body (para 1)

....

....

....

....

(para 2)

....

....

....

(para 3)

....

....

Yours affectionately
Neha

B. Formal

The Hindustan Watch Company

36, Munirka

Mumbai-1

29.1.20..........

Mr. Ashutosh Sinha
A.B.C. Co. Ltd.
24, South Patel Nagar
New Delhi-8

Dear Sir

Sub: ....

Body (para 1)

....
....
....
....

(para 2)

....
....
....

(para 3)

....
....

Yours faithfully

(Vimal Kumar)

Regional Sales Manager

Informal/Friendly Letters

EXAMPLES

1. Write a letter to your uncle who is living in America, describing the state of India at present.

XYZ
12/3, Avas Vihas Colony
Lucknow

26th Nov 20......

Dear Uncle

It gives me great pleasure to share with you that our country has been steadily growing in the right direction under the able leadership of our Prime Minister.

This government has a vision to propel the country into the 21st century and become a developed country by the year 2020. You would agree with me that unless the infrastructure and the power situation improves, it is difficult for a country to progress further. Recently, our country had an agreement at the highest level with America to get the support in civil nuclear energy and that would definitely set a pace to the transformation, as we all have been dreaming of.

The government has taken many projects for improving the infrastructure and it is believed that in the years to come, we will have similar highways, as are available in America or any other developed country.

India has become the preferred destination for investment by the Western and European countries. This is more so because of the democracy in India and also the availability of the skilled manpower at a much reasonable cost. With this, a lot of automobile companies have also entered India and there is a good competition going on among various manufacturers. The automobiles are now available at a reasonable price. But our roads are not capable of handling this traffic and every-day there is a scene of traffic jam and this increases air pollution too. The government is now seriously considering introducing Metro Rail Services in the National Capital Region and other metro cities. Let's hope that this becomes a reality soon.

Presently, the population of India has crossed the figure of 110 crore. The agricultural land is also shrinking fast due to urbanization. So what matters most is to see more avenues or a revolution in the farming sector so that we can improve the yield manifold. Otherwise, it would be difficult to feed the increasing population and this may lead to anarchy in the years to come.

When you come back to this country after a gap of 10 years, I am sure that you will hardly be able to recognize some of the towns and villages of this land. We all look forward to your long overdue visit in the coming month of December.

With warm regards

Yours Faithfully

XYZ

2. Write a letter to your uncle, thanking him for sending you a birthday present.

13.12.20………

XYZ
44, Karol Bagh
New Delhi

My Dear Uncle

It was a pleasant surprise when I opened the parcel, which the courier boy delivered at our home yesterday. I found a wrist watch inside the box sent to me by you as my birthday gift.

It was really very kind of you to have remembered my birthday and to have made it a delightful and exciting event for all of us by sending this token of your affection. Everybody in the family appreciated the gift and remembered you for your love and affection towards us.

For my own part, I do not know how I can adequately thank you for sending me the present and wishing me many happy returns on my birthday. I am indeed very grateful to you for this expression of love on the occasion of my birthday and wish you many long years of joy and prosperity.

Yours affectionately
XYZ

3. Write a letter to your elder brother, giving an account of an interesting debate recently held in your college.

XYZ
West Campus Hostel
National College of Pharmaceuticals
Nainital

12.1.20..........

My Dear Brother

Our college has revamped its old debating society and has now become as active as it was in your college days. The society recently organized interesting debates during the first semester of this year which attracted a large gathering of both students and outsiders. The subjects discussed were 'Co-education', 'Information Technology Revolution', 'Brian Drain' and 'Students and Politics'. In the debate on 'Students and Politics', which was held last week, about twenty-four speakers took part, that is twelve on either side.

Some speakers said that politics must, under no circumstances, be allowed to divert students from their studies, while the other group opined that it is necessary for students to actively participate in politics so that they may get practical training in life and turn out to be rational human beings. The speakers argued that the youths' participation in India's struggle for independence was undoubtedly significant for they possessed great energy and strength. That was the time when the whole country was ablaze with the fire of revolt. But now the conditions are changed. The politics of today does not mean to us a struggle with some foreign rule as it meant in the past but it is a science of planning for national welfare. The relation of students with politics has, therefore, to be reviewed in the light of modern conditions.

The debate on the whole reviewed youths' participation in the light of modern conditions. It was a very thought provoking debate. When it was over, both the debaters and the audience left the hall with a feeling of having participated in a very satisfactory performance. I shall probably write to you again about the work of our debating society when it has gone through another performance at the end of this month.

Yours affectionately
XYZ

4. Write a letter to your landlord, requesting him to carry out repairs in the house in which you live.

111, Model town
Ghaziabad

12.1.20.........

Dear Mr. Gupta

I am writing this to inform you that your house needs urgent repairs after the recent heavy rains, which have done some damage to its roofs and walls.

The roof of the kitchen had been leaking throughout the period of rains and it was a problem for us to keep the place dry for cooking purposes. On close inspection, I found minor holes at many places along the entire surface of the roof and it appears that rain water has been seeping through these holes for the last many months. Plaster from the ceiling and walls of the drawing room is constantly falling on the floor and spoiling the furniture. In fact, the whole house is in an awful state, and is causing us a lot of inconvenience.

Now that the rainy season is over, it is time to carry out repairs. I would request you to instruct your agent who collects rent from your tenants to undertake this repairing job in time so that your house does not suffer further damage as a result of neglect. I should also expect that you will be good enough to order a coat of varnish on the doors and windows to give them a better look.

Yours sincerely
XYZ

5. Write a letter to a friend inviting him to accompany you to a hill station.

12, Railway Road
Patiala
April 12, 20..........

My Dear Sudarshan

You must be looking forward to the approaching holidays with a mixed feeling of pleasure and expectations. I do not know how you have planned to spend them. Here at home there is always talk about our forthcoming visit to Nainital, where father has decided to take all of us this summer. He will be on leave from office during early next month and we have decided to go to this hill station on the 3rd or 4th of May and hope to stay there for about three weeks. Would it be convenient for you to join us and give us the pleasure of your company during our trip to Nainital?

When father proposed that we should spend the coming holidays at Nainital, I at once thought of inviting you, and when I mentioned to him that I intended to seek your company, he was very glad and said I must immediately write to you extending this invitation on behalf of both of us. Please let me know when you would be reaching this place to accompany us to Nainital. I hope you will not disappoint us by writing a no to this invitation. Nainital is a beautiful hill station. Your company will make it doubly charming.

Pay my best regards to your parents.

Yours lovingly
Ashish

6. Write a letter to your father, requesting him to increase your monthly allowance.

Law College Hostel
Chandigarh

12.1.20.........

My dear father

I am quite well and hope the same for you all at home. My hostel economy, over which I have been exercising a rigid control for all these months, now seems to be getting out of hands. As a result, I find myself unable to meet my boarding expenses. In addition, I need tuition for two months in the subject of mathematics. I am sure that this tuition will certainly upgrade my percentage. The tutor demands Rs. 300/- per month. I require some help books also.

Under these circumstances I would request you to increase my monthly allowance by at least five hundred rupees. I do not want to be much of a burden on you. I require this amount for three months only. It gives me pain to make this demand on your financial resources, which I know are not limitless. But taking into consideration my necessity I hope you will very kindly agree to this increase in my allowance. I can assure you that I shall not squander any part of it, as I am determined to restrict my wants to the bare minimum.

With best regards

Yours affectionately
XYZ

7. Write a letter congratulating your friend on his success in the UP Seat Entrance examination.

12, Railway Road
Patiala
April 12, 20....

Dear Shiv

Accept my heartiest congratulations on your brilliant success and getting 86th rank in the UPSE examination. I am overjoyed to know about your achievement. This is the result of your sincere labour and single-minded dedication. You have always been very studious and hard working. Hope you will get a good Government Engineering College of your choice.

We all friends are very proud of you. When are you inviting us to a feast to celebrate your success? My parents send their congratulations and good wishes to you.

Once again I congratulate you and wish you a bright and successful career.

Yours sincerely

Avinash

8. Your tenant who lives on the second floor has a habit of playing a musical instrument loudly at night, which disturbs you especially during the examination days. Complain to him politely about your getting disturbed and suggest the steps he could take to solve the problem.

Rahul Verma

123, Eros Apartments

Nawab Ganj

Kanpur

22.1.20.......

Dear Khosla Uncle,

We have great pleasure in having you as a tenant with us for the last 4 years or so. In fact, more than a tenant, you had been a part of our family. Further to this, it is nice to hear the melody of the musical instrument you play at night. I would also like to learn playing the instrument from you sometime during our summer vacations.

However, I would like to bring to your kind notice that my exams are scheduled to start from the 4th of February 20......... and nowadays I am busy preparing for the same. Since you play the musical instrument in the night, incidentally the time when I also study, it deviates my attention and am unable to concentrate on my studies.

It would be nice if you could kindly take the following precautions while playing the instrument;

- Reduce the volume of the instrument
- Shut the windows/doors so as to contain the noise from dissipating further
- Play the instrument when we do not study, may be from 6 p.m. to 7 p.m.

I shall appreciate your consideration to any of the above mentioned suggestions or as you feel appropriate so that I am not disturbed in my preparation for the exams.

Thanking you in anticipation

Yours faithfully

(Rahul Verma)

9. A friend, living abroad, has written to you asking for information about a particular Engineering College in your city, which he/she intends to join. Write a letter detailing the same and why you would consider it useful to your friend.

Rajni Verma
123, Ashiana Apartments
Nawab Ganj
Noida

08.1.20.....

Dear Shalu

I acknowledge the receipt of your letter dated 1.1.20..... It was really nice to hear from you after a long time.

You have shown your interest in joining the National Institute of Technology at Noida. Yesterday I had been to the Director of that institute and collected some of the information as desired by you.

The institute has the following branches: -

- Computer Science & Technology
- Information Technology
- Mechanical Engineering
- Electrical Engineering

The admission to this institute is through an entrance exam conducted by UPSEE. The exam is normally held in the last week of April every year. However, there are a few seats available in each branch reserved for NRIs like you.

The institute has a well maintained infrastructure and is self contained. It has a separate girls' hostel as well, which is well within the premises of the institute. Since we have been residing very close to this institute, you can have a choice of either staying with us or in the hostel.

In case you wish to apply for the admission, I would send you the prospectus and the application form, which will be on the counter for sale in the last week of January.

How are uncle and auntie? Please convey my regards to them.

Wishing you all the best and hoping you to be soon with us,

Yours truly

Rajni

10. You have been selected to participate in a cultural program in another country but the dates clash with your college's final examinations. However, you are still very keen to participate. Write a letter to your parents stating the pros and cons of the situation and asking them to advice.

Boys' Hostel
Ghaziabad

22.1.20.........

Dear Mummy and Papa

I have recently got an invitation from ABC Institute, USA to participate in their cultural program, which is scheduled to be held from 22.2.20.....to 25.2.20........... at Osaka, USA. All the expenses towards travelling like airfare, lodging and boarding shall be borne by the ABC Institute. We may have to bear only the incidental expenses, which may be about US $ 50 per day.

I need to seek your guidance, as I am not able to decide on my own. Since our exams are to start from 10th February onwards, Physics exam, which is the last, will take place on 23rd Feb. This is once in a lifetime opportunity to participate in such an international cultural program but at the same time, exams are also equally important.

I have analyzed the pros and cons of the situation and my analysis is that even if I take a risk of not appearing in the Physics exam, this can be taken care of at the time of supplementary exams, which will take place in the month of April. The only negative point is that I will not be clearing it in the routine way and the result will get delayed by 2 months. However, it will have no impact, as the next session will start only in the month of May.

With this letter to you, I would like to seek your kind advice for my next course of action as the last date for confirming the acceptance of the invitation to participate in the program is 30.1.20..........

May I kindly request you to give your guidance in this regard.

How's every body at home. Please convey my love to dear Sonu & Monu.

Yours sincerely,
Piyush

Formal/Business Letters

1. Write an application to the Principal for sick leave.

12.4.20........

The Principal
National College of Pharmacy
Kirti Nagar
New Delhi

Sir

With due respect I am to inform you that I have been suffering from high fever since last night. The doctor has advised me to take rest for four days. So I am unable to come to the college and attend classes.

I, therefore, request you to grant me leave for four days with effect from April 12, 20...to April 15, 20......

Thanking You

Yours obediently

Rakesh Agarwal
B.Pharm I-Sem
Vivekanand Boys Hostel
Room No. 27

2. Write a letter to the Director- Ministry of Environment & Forests to initiate necessary action to curb the noise pollution caused by loudspeakers during the day by shopkeepers.

16.12.20.......

Amit Khanna
44, Govind Apartments
Saket
New Delhi

Ministry of Environment & Forests
Paryavaran Bhawan
CGO Complex
Lodi Road
New Delhi

Dear Sir

Subject: Noise pollution caused due to loudspeakers

I, the resident of Govind Apartments, New Delhi, am concerned about the noise pollution caused due to loudspeakers, which are invariably played every day by the shopkeepers (mainly music shops). This affects me and the other students living in this locality. We are unable to concentrate on our studies due to the noise caused by them.

We understand that there is a provision in the law, issued by MOEF, that the noise level should not be more that 75 dB(A) (Decibel) in day time. However this law is not being adhered to by the shopkeepers and there is no enforcement of law by the concerned Pollution Control Board namely Uttar Pradesh Pollution Control Board, Lucknow.

We request that the Pollution Control Board enforce such laws, which have been laid down for the benefit of society at large.

This will help students like us to concentrate more on our studies.

Hoping to have a favourable response from you.

Yours faithfully

(Amit Khanna)

3. Write a letter to the president, Municipal Committee of your town, pointing out the inadequacy of the street lights in your locality

11.02.20.....

Rajendra Prasad
44, Adarsh Colony
Surat

The President
Municipal Committee
Surat

Dear Sir

Subject :Inadequate street light in our locality

I am a resident of Adarsh Colony and would like to draw your kind attention towards the locality of Adarsh Colony, in which most of the streets present a picture of complete darkness after sunset and it is sometimes difficult to pass through them without bumping against a cyclist or fellow pedestrian.

The main road passing through the central part of the locality is lighted only at a few points. The side streets running from this road are almost entirely unlit. It is not difficult to imagine how troublesome it is for the residents of this locality to move from one house to another or from one street to an adjoining one in dark nights these days.

Adarsh Nagar is a beautiful locality where all other amenities such as good roads, drainage system and water supply systems etc. have been adequately provided. However, the pathetic maintenance of the street lights project the image of this area as a deserted place.

I would, therefore, request you to please depute your supervisor / engineer for reviewing the present conditions for the lighting arrangement of the streets and initiate a long-term corrective action for maintenance of these facilities so that a common man is not deprived of these basic facilities any more.

Thanking you

Yours faithfully

(Rajendra Prasad)

4. Write a letter to the concerned authority, complaining about the irregularity of electricity supply in your locality.

20.9.20........

XYZ
23, Gandhi Nagar
Varanasi

The Executive Engineer
Uttar Pradesh Electricity Board
Vidyut Bhawan
Varanasi

Dear Sir

Sub: Irregular Electricity Supply in Gandhi Nagar, Varanasi

We, the residents of Gandhi Nagar, would like to bring to your kind notice the hardships we have been going through due to the irregularity in supply of electricity by your department.

Apart from a regular power cut in the morning from 4:30 a.m. to 7 a.m., the power goes off intermittently on many occasions during the day and evening time.

We are the students of B.Pharm and have to get up and study in the early hours of the morning. However, due to frequent power cuts, this has not been possible and it is ultimately affecting our performance in the class.

We would like to draw your kind attention that this power cut situation be kindly reviewed for changing the power cut timings from early hours to daytime so that the power is available in the morning and evening hours.

We shall be thankful for your immediate action in this regard.

Yours faithfully

(XYZ), (ABC), (OPQ)

5. Draft a letter to Hindustan Watch Company, Mumbai –1 asking for a copy of their latest catalogue. State that you propose to stock watches for sale. Ask for their best trade for supplying of watches and clocks.

A.B.C. Co. Ltd.
24, South Patel Nagar
New Delhi-8

15.4.20.....

The Hindustan Watch Company
40, Munirka
Mumbai-1

Dear Sir

Sub: Requisition for quotation and catalogue for watches and clocks

We take pleasure in introducing ourselves as one of the leading stockists of watches and clocks in Chandigarh. We deal with all the reputed brands in watches and clocks manufactured in India. Our sales turnover last year was Rs.30 lakhs.

In order to expand our business further, we would like to have an association with your company as a stockist and distributor of the clocks and watches manufactured by you for the entire South Delhi region.

We, therefore, request you to please send us your latest catalogue of clocks and watches along with the most competitive prices to us.
An early response will be appreciated.

Yours faithfully

(XYZ)
Proprietor

6. Draft a suitable reply in response to the request for quotation and product catalogue of clocks and watches requested by Mr. XVZ.

The Hindustan Watch Company
Munirka
Mumbai-1

29.4.20........

Mr. XYZ (Proprietor)
A.B.C. Co. Ltd.
24, South Patel Nagar
New Delhi-8

Dear Sir

Thank you for your letter xxxxx, dated 15.4.20..... and the interest shown in our products. We have carefully gone through the contents of your letter and appreciate your concern, desiring to become a stockist and distributor for the products manufactured by us.
We are enclosing herewith the latest product catalogue along with the quotation for your consideration. Kindly note that we offer a dealer margin of 15% over the maximum retail price (MRP). Apart from this, we also offer a bonus of 3% for meeting the sales target set mutually for each year.
Should you require any further clarification in this regard, please feel free to meet us or call our Sales Manager for any assistance.
Looking forward to a good business relationship with you,

Yours faithfully
(A B C)
Regional Sales Manager

7. As a Purchase Manager of an organization you had ordered 5 generator sets of 5 KVA each. When the consignment arrives, you find 2 generator sets do not confirm to the specifications you had approved. Draft a claim letter asking for reasonable adjustment.

10.8.20.......

ABC Co. Ltd.
44, New Patel Nagar
Ahmedabad

The Regional Manager
ABC Yamaha Limited
A-2, South Extension
New Delhi

Dear Sir

Sub: Generator sets supplied by you not confirming to the agreed specifications

This refers to our order no. HPP/ 01-02/811 towards the supply of 5 gensets of 5 KVA each.

We would like to inform you that we have received these gensets on 8.8.20....... and noted that 2 of the gensets received do not confirm to the specifications agreed upon by us mutually. You may kindly recall our discussion and the purchase order that all 5 gensets were required with an additional feature of self-start. However, out of the 5 gensets received, only three of them have this additional feature whereas the remaining two do not have this feature.

We would, therefore, request you to kindly depute your representative to our office for carrying out necessary modifications/replacement of these two sets.

We shall be grateful to you for your prompt action in this regard.

Yours faithfully

(XYZ)
Purchase Manager

8. Assume that 12 room heaters out of 50 have been received by your firm in damaged condition from Jupiter Electrical Appliance Co. Ltd., 26 Park Street, Kolkata. As a manager of your firm write a complaint letter to the supplier, Mr. Ravi Mohan, seeking replacement or adjustment for the goods. Invent necessary details.

ABC Co. Limited
28, MG Road, Kolkatta - 12

Ref: RKS/01/005

23.1.20.........

Jupiter Electrical Appliance Co. Ltd.
26, Park Street
Kolkatta - 8

Dear Sir

Sub: Receipt of room heaters in damaged condition
Ref: Our Purchase Order no. xxxxxxx dated 12.12.20.......

This refers to our purchase order as mentioned above for the supply of 50 room heaters.

We received the room heaters sent by your firm on 22.12.20......... as per the details mentioned above. However, we would like to bring to your notice that on opening the cartons, we observed that out of the 50 room heaters received, 12 room heaters were found in badly damaged condition.

These room heaters are beyond use and we request you to look into this matter and replace the damaged room heaters immediately.

Alternatively, you may like to adjust the amount equivalent to 12 room heaters against the supply of water cooler to us for which the purchase order will be released shortly by us.

Kindly confirm in either case and inform about your line of action immediately.

Yours faithfully

(XYZ)
Commercial Manager

9. As Sales Manager of Jupiter Co. Ltd., draft a letter offering replacement.

Jupiter Electrical Appliance Co. Ltd.
26, Park Street, Kolkata - 8

Ref: RM/01-125

28.1.20.......

ABC Co. Ltd.
28, MG Road
Kolkatta - 12

Attention : Mr. XYZ – Commercial Manager

Dear Sir

Sub: Replacement of damaged room heaters
Ref : Your letter RKS/01/005 dated 23.1.20......

This refers to your letter regarding the receipt of damaged room heaters against our supply made to you last week.

We have advised our Service Department to immediately contact your office and take necessary steps towards replacement of these 12 damaged room heaters. Apparently, the damage was caused due to the negligence of the transporter as at the time of dispatch all room heaters were ensured to be in good condition by our Quality Assurance Section. However, we shall further analyze the cause of the damage and initiate necessary corrective measures at our end to prevent such damages from reoccurring in future.

We sincerely regret the inconvenience caused to you.

Assuring you of our best services

Yours faithfully

(Ravi Mohan)
Regional Sales Manager

10. As a Business Manager, you have ordered for your firm a supply of tractor tyres. The letter was sent to the supplier two weeks ago, but you have received no reply as yet. Write a suitable and a polite letter to the supplier.

ABC Co. Ltd.
28, MG Road
Kolkata - 12

11.10.20..........

Regional Manager-Sales
Ceat Tyres Limited
18, Venkateshvarya Road
Chennai

Dear Sir

Subject: Non receipt of tyres against our purchase order no. AC/02/009

This refers to your quotation no. AB /Tyres/Ceat/022 dated 20.8.20........ for the supply of tyres of tractors.
We would like to inform you that we have sent you a draft of Rs. 250,000 on 25.8.20.......towards the supply of 50 tyres. As per the agreement, the tyres were to be received by us within a week's time.
Kindly note that we have neither received the tyres nor any communication from you in this regard.
We would request you to kindly acknowledge the receipt of our purchase order and the demand draft and inform us about the delivery schedule of tyres.
A quick response shall be highly appreciated.

Yours faithfully

(ABC)

Managing Director

11. Write a letter to the telephone department about the discrepancy in your telephone bill. Request them to adjust your telephone bill and send the revised bill. Invent necessary details.

XYZ
123, Shastri Nagar
New Delhi

23.01.20.........

The Assistant Engineer (Telephones)
Shastri Nagar Exchange
New Delhi

Dear Sir

Sub: Discrepancy in my telephone Bill
Ref: Telephone no. 2775894, Bill no. 234567, dated 15.01.20......

This refers to the telephone bill received for the period November~December, 20......... against my telephone connection as mentioned above.

I would like to inform you that in the said telephone bill, the amount of Rs. 3500/- has been charged towards five international calls made to the USA. It may kindly be noted that we do not have ISD facility in our telephone connection.

It appears that some mistake has occurred at your end at the time of billing, resulting in this discrepancy in my telephone bill.

I, therefore, request that:

- You may kindly get your records verified for these international calls made from my telephone.
- Based on the investigation, my bill be corrected and the revised bill sent to me immediately for further action.

I shall be thankful for your immediate response.

Yours faithfully

(XYZ)

12. Your club plans to organize a youth festival in the city. As the president of the club, write a letter to the Managing Director of Honda Motors Limited giving details and requesting him to sponsor it.

Century Club
19, Park Avenue
New Delhi –110004

12.10.20.......

The Managing Director
Honda Motors Limited
23,Vasant Vihar
New Delhi –110002

Dear Sir

Subject: Sponsoring of Youth Festival

We represent ourselves as the Century Club, which is organizing a "Youth Festival" for generating money for the benefit of financially weaker section of women in our society.

The Youth Festival would offer free display to the various products produced by these women and put them up for sale, which market has been witnessing during the last couple of years. The festival will be held from 25.10.20.....to 28.10.20....... at Pragati Maidan, New Delhi.

We take the opportunity to invite your esteemed organization to participate in this festival by way of sponsoring it.

We are sure that by participation, your organization will also be benefited as it is estimated that at least 100,000 persons will visit this festival every day.

For further details in this regard, you may call us as per your convenience but before 18.10.20……….

We would really appreciate your cooperation and an early response.

Yours faithfully

(XYZ)
President
Century Club

13. As the Secretary of an organization it is your duty to secure a speaker at a meeting. Write a letter to some person, real or imaginary, asking him to be a speaker on the importance of having environmental management system in the organization. Tell him that the organization will pay for the travelling expenses but not for the talk.

12.10.20……….

ABC limited
28, Kasturba Gandhi Marg
New Delhi - 110013

Kind Attention: Mr. xxxxx

Dear Sir

Sub: Request to deliver a speech on the need for introduction of Environmental Management System

This refers to our previous communication in this regard.

We are keen to implement the Environmental Management System in our organization and may seek your professional assistance at the time of its implementation. However, in order to make the management understand the importance of having this Environmental Management System and its benefits, which can be reaped after its implementation, we would like to invite you for delivering a speech at our factory situated at Kolkata.

Kindly note that no professional charges will be payable towards this speech. However, we will be pleased to reimburse your to and fro airfare.

A line of confirmation shall be highly appreciated and shall assist us in chalking out a suitable plan for the said speech.

Yours faithfully
(xyz)
Secretary

14. Assuming that you are the Managing Director of a company, draft a formal invitation to Mr. R. K. Dubey, Managing Director of ABC Limited for lunch on 20th January at Hotel Holiday Inn, New Delhi.

12.1.20…….

Mr. R. K. Dubey
Managing Director
ABC Limited
Dehradun

Dear Mr. Dubey

You will be pleased to know that our association - Indian Tyres Manufacturers Association, has now been registered and we have formally received all the necessary approvals from the concerned authorities.

In order to further discuss and chalk out the strategy for representation to the government for reduction of excise duty on tyres, it is desired that we meet at a common place along with other association members.

In this connection, we have fixed a meeting at 11 a.m. followed by lunch at Hotel Holiday Inn, New Delhi on 20th January, 20.......

Kindly make it convenient to attend and confirm.

Thanking you

Yours faithfully

C. L. Narang

(Managing Director)

15. Assuming that you are R. K. Dubey, draft two letters in reply to the above mentioned invitation:

- **Accepting the invitation**
- **Expressing your inability to accept it as you have another important engagement on the same date**

Accepting the invitation

18.1.20............

Mr. C. L. Narang

Managing Director

CBA Limited

New Delhi

Dear Mr. Narang

I am in receipt of your letter dated 12.1.20.......and noted the contents there in. The news of registration of our association is really encouraging.

As suggested, I shall be attending the meeting at Holiday Inn as per the plan for further discussion on the sensitive issue.

Thanking You

Yours faithfully

R. K. Dubey

(Managing Director)

Expressing your inability to accept it as you have another important engagement on the same date.

Dear Mr. Narang

I am in receipt of your letter dated 12.1.20.......... and am very much pleased with the news of registration of our association.

However, due to another important meeting already scheduled for the day, I will not be in a position to attend the meeting as planned.

Kindly send me the minutes of meeting after the said meeting is held.

Thanking You

Yours faithfully

R.K. Dubey

(Managing Director)

16. Draft an informal invitation to Shri M. K. Kashyap for dinner with you on January 26, 20..........

Ranjeet Goel

4, Old Traven Road

Calcutta

12.1.20.......

Dear Kashyap Ji

It had been a long time since we met and shared our sweet memories. With the passage of time and the responsibilities showered on us by our companies, it has really become a humdrum (monotonous) life outside the office.

I suggest that we should take some time off the office hours and sit together. In this connection, I have arranged a dinner for you and your family at my residence on 16.1.20.....

Kindly make it convenient to come over to my house for dinner with your family.

With best wishes

Yours truly

Ranjeet Goel

17. Write a letter to a travel agency requesting to book you by flight No. IC 456 from New Delhi to Mumbai on 17th February 20......

12/2/20.......

Century travels
18, Barakhamba Road
New Delhi

Subject: Air ticket booking
Attention: Ms. Karina

Dear Madam

You are requested to book an air ticket as per the following details in my name and ensure that the ticket is delivered to my office latest by day after tomorrow:

Date of Journey - 17.2.20........
Flight No. - I C 456
Sector - New Delhi – Mumbai

Please raise the bill directly in the name of my company and send along with the ticket for payment.

Thanking You

Yours faithfully

(Sanjeev Khosla)
Dy. Manager - Personnel

REVIEW QUESTIONS

Informal letters

1. Write a letter to your aunt describing your recent educational field trip.
2. Write a letter to your father narrating your experience at the camp organized by your college.
3. Write a letter to your sister explaining your role in the English play staged by your college in inter-college competition.
4. Write a letter to your friend making enquiries about the recent burglary at his residence.
5. Write a letter to your brother asking him to tell you about his debut at the cricket match.
6. Write a letter to your mother enquiring about her health and requesting her not to strain herself while recovering from jaundice.
7. Write a letter to your pen friend in Canada, describing a typical Indian marriage.
8. Write a letter to your pen friend, who is living abroad, introducing yourself and drawing his attention to the common interests you share.
9. Write a letter to your father giving your first impression of your college.

Business/Formal Letters

1. Write a letter to your local newspaper complaining about the noise pollution in your town.

2. Write a letter to the editor of a local newspaper complaining about the cattle menace in your locality.
3. Write a letter to the health officer of your city to arrange for a stricter supervision over adulterated provisions.
4. Write a letter to a bookseller ordering books worth Rs. 1000/-.
5. Write a letter to the principal of your college requesting him to issue a character certificate.
6. Write a letter to the editor of a local newspaper describing the sports day of your college.
7. Write a letter to a dealer ordering a TV set for your house.
8. Write a letter to a hotel manager at a hill station inquiring about accommodation in the hotel for your forthcoming visit.
9. Write a letter to your bank manager complaining about the unprofessional attitude of his bank staff.
10. Draft a suitable reply to a customer who has complained that the quality of goods supplied to him was not upto the mark. Invent the necessary details yourself.
11. You have noticed that a local bus service has become inefficient in recent weeks. Buses are infrequent and sometimes a number of them are going to the same place at the same time. Write a letter complaining to the General Manager, State Roadways Transport Services, Ghaziabad about the inadequate services and to initiate necessary corrective measures.
12. You had sent a parcel to your friend who lives in Mumbai. However, the parcel and its contents were found damaged at the time of receipt of the parcel. Write a letter to the Postmaster complaining about the damaged parcel and claiming the value of the same.

23 CHAPTER

Essay Writing

WHAT IS AN ESSAY

The word '**essay**' derives from the French infinitive *essayer*, 'to try' or 'to attempt'. An essay is a short piece of writing that discusses, describes and analyzes one topic. It can discuss a subject directly or indirectly, seriously or humorously. It can describe personal opinions, or just report information. An essay can be written from any perspective, but essays are most commonly written in the first person (*I*), or third person (subjects that can be substituted with the 'he', 'she', 'it', or 'they' pronouns).

IMPORTANCE OF ESSAY WRITING

Essay writing is the most important branch of composition. In the process of essay writing, the student has to gather up ideas associated with the topic, analyze them, reject the irrelevant ideas and choose the relevant ones. This process acts as a health tonic to the powers of the mind of the student. His intelligence grows keener, reason sharper and imagination livelier. Emphasizing the necessity of writing, Bacon says that writing 'makes a man exact', which means that it gives clearness of the mind and consistency to thoughts. The importance of essay writing, therefore, chiefly consists in testing the students' ability to present their thoughts in an organized way and their intellectual capability.

HOW TO COLLECT THE MATERIAL FOR WRITING AN ESSAY

The first and commonest difficulty felt by every beginner in essay writing is the lack of material. The students can collect the material by following these three methods:

1. Reading

"Those who do not read can have nothing to think and little to say," writes Dr. Johnson. Students, who want to write good essays, should cultivate the habit of reading books of all kinds; stories, novels, history, politics, biography, science etc.

In this respect, students are advised to keep a regular notebook on their person in which they can take down notes in order to get the best out of what they study.

2. Observation

All knowledge does not come from books. We may learn a lot from the life around us. We also learn by personal observation; what we see and hear and observe ourselves. Writing descriptions of familiar objects and daily occurrences; the types of people we meet, buildings, street scene, natural scenery, and the habits of animals and birds etc. helps a lot.

3. Thinking

The most significant source of ideas that a student should count upon for writing essay is his own mind. He should think for himself what he has read in books and observed in life. He should use his own reason to see whether what he gets is right or wrong, he should compare and contrast the various ideas gathered on a particular subject and exercise his own power of discrimination and judgement.

So every student who aspires to be a proficient essayist should read much, write more and think most. This is the only way in which he can keep himself in possession with ready material for any topic to write on. A student is also required to arrange his ideas and material into a systematic and logical order before attempting to give them the form of an essay. This process is called the outline of the essay.

THE STRUCTURE OF THE ESSAY: The five-paragraph essay

An essay can have many purposes, but it will have the same basic format. Many students' first exposure to the genre is the five paragraph essay. The format requires an essay to have **five paragraphs**, **one introductory paragraph, three body paragraphs**, each of which presents an idea to support the topic together with supporting evidence and development and **one concluding paragraph** which restates the thesis and summarizes the supporting points. The use of this format is controversial. However, it teaches students how to organize their thoughts clearly in writing.

1. The introduction

The introduction is the first paragraph in your essay, and it is of the greatest importance.

- **Capture the reader's interest**

It's a good idea to start your essay with a really interesting statement, in order to grab the reader's interest. Avoid starting out with a boring line like, *"In this essay I will explain...."*

- **Introduce the topic**

The next few sentences should explain your first statement.

- **Make a claim or express your opinion in a key sentence.**

Your key sentence should provide your specific assertion and convey clearly your point of view.

2. Body

The body of the essay will include three paragraphs, each limited to one main idea that supports your topic.

- Do not deal with several ideas at one place. Treat each idea separately. Your essay must be an organic whole consisting of paragraphs and each paragraph must be a unit in itself, i.e., it must contain only one idea.
- The middle of your essay should aim at sustaining the interest and satisfying curiosity of the reader. For this purpose, two methods are suggested. One is to dwell upon what are called the pros and cons of the subject. The second method of handling of the essay is to look at the given subject from different angles of vision; social, political, economic and philosophical.
- Many pages will not bring you more marks. You should state your idea, then back it up with two or three sentences of evidence or examples. Strike out unnecessary repetitions and redundant expressions.

3. Conclusion

The final paragraph will summarize your main points.

- It should point out your main points, but should not repeat specific examples.
- Never insert a new idea into the conclusion of your essay.
- In giving your opinion at the end of the essay, avoid the use of the first personal pronoun 'I' as 'I think', 'It seems to me'. Such expressions should be changed into 'It is thought', It seems'.
- It is also not very fitting to end your essay by such expression as 'In conclusion we may....', 'To sum up, therefore....', etc.

TYPES OF ESSAYS

According to various forms and purposes of composition, essays may be classified as under:

1. Descriptive Essays

The aim of descriptive essay is to provide a vivid picture of a person, location, object, event or debate. It explains the "what, why, how, when, and where" of a topic and enables the reader to imagine the item described. For example, a descriptive essay about a tree would explain what it's made of, why it grows, when it grows, and so on.

2. Narrative Essays

The aim of narrative essay is to describe some event or series of events. The focus of the essay is often to identify more clearly the point of view of the narrator. Narrative essay may deal with historical stories of legends, biographies, an accident or a natural disaster, a journey, a story etc.

3. Compare and Contrast Essays

The aim of compare and contrast essay is to develop the relationship between two or more things. Generally the goal is to show that superficial differences or similarities are inadequate, and that closer examination reveals their unobvious, yet significant relations or differences.

4. Persuasive Essays

A persuasive essay tries to persuade the reader to accept an idea or agree with an opinion. The writer's purpose is to convince the reader that his or her point of view is a reasonable one. The persuasive essay should be written in a style that grabs and holds the reader's attention and the writer's opinion should be backed up by strong supportive details.

5. Argumentative Essays

Argumentative essays are most often used to address controversial issues over which there is some evident disagreement. An argument is a position combined with its supporting reasons. Argumentative essay, thus, sets out a main claim and then provides reasons for thinking that the claim is true.

6. Reflective Essay

A reflection is a thought on some subject or an idea arising in the mind. So a reflective essay consists of reflections or thoughts on some topic, which is generally of an abstract nature, for example, habits, virtues (like truthfulness, patriotism) or socio-political and domestic topics. In treating such themes, one should try to reason and support one's statements with facts and arguments.

7. Evaluation Essay

Evaluation essay describes a thing or event and explains its importance, value, and/or relevance.

STYLE IN WRITING

Style is the most important part of writing. It is the manner of expression that endears the writer to the reader.

- **Acquisition of a vast vocabulary**

To be able to express oneself with ease and grace, one must have a vast vocabulary.

- **Simplicity**

Write in a simple, concise, clear, direct and natural style. Affectation in writing is as bad as affectation in manners in speech. Use of obsolete words, poetic or high flown expressions, foreign words and phrases and colloquial terms is best avoided.

- **Brevity**

Observe economy in the use of language and try to convey the maximum sense in minimum words.

- **Check your writing**

Nothing can substitute revision of one's work. By reviewing what one has done, one can improve weak points that otherwise would be missed. Reread your paper. Does it make logical sense? Due regard should be paid to spelling, punctuation and grammatical correctness.

THE CINEMA-ITS ADVANTAGES AND DISADVANTAGES

Thomas Alwa Edison's invention of 'kinetoscope' which showed silent films has occupied in recent years a position of deep influence in the society. Cinema has reached hundreds of millions of people every day, feeding them with ideas, moving their emotions and moulding their thoughts. It has laid its grip on the imagination of every class of people; upper, middle and lower. Its influence has penetrated every aspect of our daily life.

ADVANTAGES

- **An Aid to Education**

The cinema has a great educative value. The cinema, as a teacher and reformer, instructs and guides people. There are many educational films. Scientific films are assets to lectures, as with their help knotty topics are lucidly explained in an attractive manner. Subjects like history, geography, botany, chemistry and other branches of learning are no longer boring subjects, which one reads in schools and forgets. Rather they have become more interesting by the exhibition of documentary films on the various topics. The two world wars, the rise and fall of the Moghul empires, India's struggle for freedom, the great tragedy of migration, the stories and preaching of great epics, weather forecast, and so on all come alive to us today. Films depicting the growth of a plant or a flower or an animal in adverse weather conditions have proved useful in the teaching of botany, zoology and natural history. Now we are more aware of the happenings in the world than our forefathers were. Apart from reading about the global happenings we actually see them on the screen. This medium elevates our thoughts and promotes a healthy spirit of international understanding and cooperation. Besides, the incidents and stories on human physiology and psychology enacted by actors come to life and prove more instructive. Naturally the impact of the actions seen on the screen remains vivid in our minds.

Even cartoon films also educate children while entertaining them. As the films progress, children watching them are introduced to the world of animals and stories.

- **A Reformer**

Films made on social issues expose the evils and weaknesses of our present day structure of society. They exhibit widely such social evils as untouchability, caste system, dowry system, divorce, poverty, drunkenness, prostitution and widowhood. These films act as reformers and encourage rapid social advancement. In addition, as a universal teacher and reformer, cinema influences both the educated class and the ignorant masses equally.

- **No Time and Space Limitation**

The barriers of time and space are also covered by this medium. H.G. Wells, in his novel *The Time Machine*, published in 1895, envisaged a wonderful machine which made travel between various time zones possible, so that people could travel in their past, present and future. The novel established Wells' reputation as a writer of extraordinary power and imagination. In Peter F. Hamilton's novella, *A Second Chance at Eden,* a scientist develops a method to create artificial telepathy, or 'affinity' in the year 2058. The repercussions on society are tremendous; the workers in the habitat Eden, where affinity is first used, participate in communal telepathy, letting others feel their emotion, crime plummets and a harmony sets in. Children born with the affinity gene spliced in show completely balanced personalities as they open their minds to each other. One person says "This is Eden, only one step down from paradise." Today's cinema is absolutely capable of doing the same. It is capable of depicting the total life span of not only an insect but also that of a man.

- **As an Art**

Cinema has a great artistic potential. Now the films are being treated as an ultra modern fine art. Although it is linked with other arts like music, dance and drama, cinema has its own separate and unique artistic individuality.

- **Means of Entertainment and Recreation**

Cinema is the most popular means of public entertainment and source of recreation today. Generally, films are made on social themes. After a day's hard work, it helps people in chasing away all their boredom and relaxing their minds and bodies. By watching cinema representing their own life in a refined and subtle manner, they drown all their fatigues, worries and tensions in romantic fantasy, even though it sometimes appears farfetched.

- **Eradication of Illiteracy**

The world's recent stress on eradication of illiteracy and adult education has received a fillip through this medium. Films shown in television could serve this purpose and have been able to spread the word around.

DISADVANTAGES

As we know, all films, like literature, do not have good themes, there are many which present negative aspects of the society. The negative traits could include glamour, sex, violence, drugs and black marketing.

- **Lure of Money and Glamour**

The affluence and glamour shown in films misleads and allures society, especially the young boys and girls. The lavish life-styles depicted, lead to a craving in them to get rich quick and the villains who flout the laws of the country become ideals for our misguided youth. Many of them end up by totally ruining their future and career.

- **Sex and Violence**

Nowadays the number of adult films is increasing. Popular cinema, even after censoring, is packed with sex and violence. The vulgarity in the scenes, songs and dances misguide the young generation. The eveteasing incidents that occur so often are due to this influence.

- **Underworld Activities**

Further, the underworld activities such as smuggling, robberies, drugs, murders etc. depicted on the screen also have a bad influence on the young minds of the society. When they see their favourite character doing everything that is against the law, they also develop the urge to imitate such behaviour in real life.

- **Wastage of Time and Money**

The majority of viewers belong to the poor/middle class and students. They waste a lot of time and money in watching a movie again and again. Too much of cinema going is fraught with danger to eyesight, health, money and time. Students, addicted to cinema, often miss classes in school/college to watch films. They not only waste their parents' hard earned money, but also the time they could spend purposefully in the pursuit of academic work.

- **Conclusion**

Since all people are not of the same caliber and differ in their levels of intelligence, the influence of cinema on different people is also different. It would differ according to their own background, mental make-up and psychological temperament. On the whole, cinema is a very powerful medium for imparting education and recreation, propaganda and publicity. Its influence on individuals, irrespective of age, group and gender is deep and capable of altering their attitude. Cinema, therefore, needs stricter control through censorship. At an International Film Festival Nehru had observed that, "the films must not be allowed to degrade one's artistic and aesthetic sense and the values for which one must stand."

HOBBIES/MY HOBBY

A hobby is any interesting subject or pursuit which we take up for our amusement in our leisure hours. Cultivating a hobby is one of the best ways of keeping the mind busy in a creative way. It all adds to one's mental growth.

- **Hobby - Its Meaning**

One of the toys that little boys play with is the 'hobby-horse'. This is a long stick fitted with a wooden horse's head, painted to look real. The child puts this between his legs, and prances about, pretending to be riding a horse. From this word 'hobby-horse' we get the word 'hobby', which means 'an amusement', and we speak of a man 'riding' his hobby.

- **Different Kinds of Hobbies**

It is a good thing to have a hobby of some sort. Hardly is there a person who does not have a hobby of his own. Not only among the educated and cultured people, hobby finds its place in the society of uneducated people also. There are many hobbies that one can take up and is sure to learn something new and interesting. What is a business to a person may be a hobby to another. There are many different kinds of hobbies. Most common of them are reading, listening to or playing music, stamp collecting, painting, gardening and so on.

- **My Hobby - Reading**

My hobby is reading. I am a passionate lover of books and get pleasure in reading them. Books have a great importance in life. As Bacon says, reading makes a man complete. Books give us knowledge. Besides, good books can be a constant company and a source of pleasure. Apart from the books which are prescribed for academic studies, I read other books, newspapers and periodicals. I cultivated this hobby when I was a student of class VI. Since then I have been nurturing it and gaining knowledge. I am sure it will prove immensely beneficial to my career in the long run. In literature I have read Milton's 'Paradise Lost', Spenser's 'Fairy Queen', Marlow's 'Dr. Faustus', Hazlit's and Addison & Steel's 'Collection of Essays' etc. Among the romantic poets I like to read Shelly. The more I read his poems like 'Ode to the West Wind', the more I feel inspired by his revolutionary ideal.

Besides, I have read Wordsworth's and Keat's poems also. Among the Indian writers, I have a great fascination for Rabindra Nath Tagore. Besides books on literature, I also read books by contemporary authors and those related to personality development. There are some books which have created an undying impression on my mind. Some of them are Mahatma Gandhi's 'My Experiments With Truth', APJ Abdul Kalam's 'The Wings of Fire' and 'Ignited Minds', Stephen Covey's 'Seven Habits', Shiv Khera's 'You can Win', and Paulo Coelheo's 'The Alchemist' etc. Besides, I read magazines like, 'Competition Success Review', 'India Today', 'Reader's Digest', 'Business Management', etc.

- **Conclusion**

Thus, my hobby has a creative and instructive effect on me. Moreover, it is easy on the pocket to. I do not have to spend a lot over it. I have taken life membership of Sahitya Academy and British Council Library. Both the libraries are quite rich and have a good collection of books. I just go to these libraries and read books and magazines. I love being in the libraries and feel an indescribable joy and peace within myself.

NEWSPAPERS - THEIR GOOD AND EVIL EFFECTS

As the word 'NEWS' stands for North, East, West and South, the newspaper is a swift vehicle for the conveyance of news from all the four directions of the world. It keeps us in touch with the events of the world.

GOOD EFFECTS OF NEWSPAPERS

- **The Educative Value**

The educative value of newspaper is immense. The articles which appear in the pages of newspaper cover all those aspects of life which confront us daily. A newspaper covers almost every sphere of human activity. These articles covering a variety subjects; scientific, educational, cultural, literary, commercial, etc. add to our knowledge and broaden our outlook. It is rightly said that 'the careful reader of a few good newspapers can learn more in a year than most scholars do in great libraries.'

- **Promotes International Understanding**

The newspapers perform a noble service of bringing man nearer unto man by carrying the account of objects, individuals and experience of one country to the other. Today, owing to the widespread circulation of newspapers the world looks like a huge universal box in which people of the earth think, feel and live in close affinity. In the words of Lord Oxford, "The pen is mightier than the sword....A journalist can shatter the bonds of narrow-minded nationalism and unite the world into one and the same chain of brotherhood."

- **Mouthpiece of the People**

The newspapers not only publish news but express opinions of the people also. They mould and mend public opinion. Through them the public expresses its ideas and sentiments, grievances and emotions and expect necessary action from those at the helm of things.

- **An Instrument of Democracy**

As the basis of democracy is public opinion, all government and political parties try to popularize themselves through the press. They criticize each other and also give their judgements on important matters. And again, newspapers help the common man to form his views about politics, economics and the social aspects of life.

- **Commercial Significance**

Newspapers, as an instrument of publicity and propaganda, have a great commercial significance. They regularly publish reports of international markets in gold, silver, stocks and shares etc. As an advertising agent, the newspapers create a link between demand and supply by bringing together the buyer and seller. The tradesmen, with anything to sell, use the newspapers freely to let the public know what goods they have for selling. The columns like, employment news, matrimonial, situations vacant help masses in that direction. Besides, the propaganda value of newspaper is really great. A popular newspaper can dethrone leaders and change governments overnight.

BAD EFFECTS OF NEWSPAPERS

Like every other institution, the system of newspaper also has some peculiar evils and shortcomings of its own. Newspapers are practical and short lived. They are read today and thrown tomorrow. Deliberate perversion of facts, prejudice of caste and religion, and malicious propaganda are the other evils that go to defeat the noble aim of newspapers. In our own country, different newspapers are used by different political parties for the purpose of propaganda. Such papers create a spirit of revenge, bitterness and misunderstanding among the people. Sometimes rich people take newspapers in their hands and use them as means to attain personal profit. Often in their bid for cheap popularity, newspaper editors insert in their columns domestic scandals, divorce cases, coloured stories of crimes, social abuses, obscene jokes and pictures, imaginary love affairs and other sensational issues. These things corrupt the young and degrade the moral tone of society.

- **Conclusion**

In spite of all the havoc that the press has created newspaper is one of the potential factors in the development of human civilization. The newspaper, in modern times, has come to exercise a tremendous influence on the public as well as private life of man. It is a universal teacher, instructor and guide holding up the torch of knowledge in the midst of darkness. It is a trenchant and impartial critic of public administration, of law and justice. As a social reformer the newspaper patiently reforms the abuses of society. It is the epitome of democracy and freedom. As an advocate of universal liberty, equality and fraternity, the newspaper destroys all the barriers which separate man from man and nation from nation. When the newspaper has attained so much power and importance, its responsibilities also increase. Journalists and editors should work with a spirit of intellectual honesty. Regard for truth and service to man should be the guiding principles of their conduct. They should never hesitate in portraying what is true and beneficial for mankind.

THE USE AND ABUSE OF ADVERTISING

Advertising is an effective marketing tool aiding the cycle of production, employment, income and consumption. There is hardly any place where one does not find advertising of some kind. It may be a roadside hoarding in a remote area, or a rough illustration on the side of a mud building or a huge colourful advertisement on a traffic signal or on television. All types of advertisements nurture only one aim behind them; to attract the public to buy a product of one particular company as opposed to the products of another. In this way advertising and consumerism have begun to influence even human relations on an everyday basis.

KINDS OF ADVERTISEMENTS

Advertising is mainly of four kinds; informative, innovative, persuasive and competitive. Informative advertising educates the consumers and makes them aware of the goods and services that are available. Innovative advertising is the necessary result of technological innovation and its benefits to society. Persuasive advertising is an appeal to the prospective buyer to decide in favour of a particular product. Competitive advertising enables consumers to evaluate the utility of a product or service.

USES OF ADVERTISING

- **Effective marketing tools**

There is no denying the fact that advertising has penetrated every aspect of human existence. In everyday life we find that advertising aims at selling goods and services, exploring new avenues and markets and, finally, reaching out to those people and places that have remained untouched by its ever expanding shadows and shades. Consistent with the growth of science and technology, advertising has become increasingly sophisticated. The use of newspaper, magazines, radio, television, and internet etc. has brought knowledge of the world and demand for all kinds of goods and services to the farthest corners of the world.

- **Handling Social Issues**

In addition to commercial advertising, there is social advertising, which is aimed at the welfare and well being of the people. Advertising finds a crucial place in this new approach of solving social issues. Advertising sells not only goods but ideas as well. Ideas like national integration and communal harmony have been spread through advertising. For example, the green revolution could not have come about in India without the help of radio and TV advertising. This type of advertising is not for a specific class but the masses who can be educated about socially relevant issues like health, family, welfare, literacy etc.

ABUSES OF ADVERTISING

Undoubtedly, in today's context carrying out campaigns through social communication is of paramount importance. The society, economy, politics and media exposure are bringing about changes which are so radical and dynamic that they are creating dissonance and upheavals.

- **Psychological Impact on the Consumer**

Advertising, though a close companion of market economy, has brought some menaces to modern life. Advertising through the mass media, like newspapers, magazines, radio and television cost a huge sum, leading to increase in prices of goods and services. Besides, in the name of educating the consumer about his rights to choose the right product, the mass media continuously instigates the consumer that material things and sensual pleasures are what life is about and the happiness lies in luxury items like automatic appliances and colourful automobiles. Sometimes, it creates unnecessary demand for goods and services. When this instant gratification does not get translated into reality, the world seems to fall apart.

- **Negative Impact on Culture**

Advertising also has a negative impact on the culture, literature, language of the people across geographical boundaries. The young generation is easily lured into giving up society's time honoured values and having a craving for unnecessary items without caring for consequences.

- **The Question of Ethics**

Many advertisements are just misleading the people through false propaganda. How many manufacturers are really honest while advertising their products? The bewilderment that advertising causes sometimes can cost heavily on one's pocket or even on one's life.

- **Conclusion**

Advertising not only influences the buyer's perception but also his response to social problems. It has its negative effects but the positive side far outstrips the negative side.

TERRORISM - A GLOBAL THREAT

- **Terrorism is an Evil**

Evil lurks all around us. It takes the form of political torture, genocide, terrorism, and assassination. It also exists within the private sphere, in the form of domestic violence, child abuse and sexual abuse. Our popular culture is saturated with unimaginable evil and violence; with psychopaths, sociopaths, and serial killers. The menace of terrorism has been increasing tremendously over the years. Several countries, including the world's mightiest power, are affected by the scourge of terrorism which has taken many forms; bomb explosions, assassinations and sometimes indiscriminate killings, blackmail, threats of murder if the demanded ransom is not paid and hijacking.

- **Definition of Terrorism**

Terrorism in the Webster's New American Dictionary is defined as "the systematic use of intense fear as a means of coercion." Terrorism, by definition, is the use of violence, or the threat of violence, to create a climate of fear in a given population. In this day and age, the term terrorism includes the use of terrorism as a means of revenge and also as a means of suppression. Terrorist violence targets ethnic or religious groups, governments, political parties, corporations, and media enterprises. The popular image of terrorism is of extremist groups trying to rebel or promote their ideologies by blowing up airplanes, buses, government buildings, or taking hostages.

Organizations that engage in acts of terror are almost always small in size and limited in resources compared to the populations and institutions they terrorize. Through publicity and fear generated by their violence, they seek to expand their influence and power to affect political change on local, national or international level.

- **Terrorism in the National Sphere**

Since the mid-1980s, India's share of terrorism related incidents and civilian casualties has been on the rise. Assam, Jammu and Kashmir, Hyderabad and North-East, all are in the grip of this powerful monster. Nowadays, terrorist organizations seem to have perfected their modus operandi. Serial, high-intensity blasts in crowded places of metropolitan cities get them the best results; maximum damage and the loudest message. Both national and international terrorist outfits believe in the cult of the gun and the bomb. Such incidents require strategizing, meticulous planning, extensive logistic support and trusted execution.

- **Terrorism in the International and National Arena**

The incidents of international terrorism that come to mind foremost include the September 11 attack on the twin towers, the PLO hijacking Israeli airplanes or Osama Ben Laden bombing the American embassies in Africa (Kenya and Tanzania). Palestine-Israel, Lebanon and Gaza strip, Afghanistan, Kosovo in Albanis, Sri

Lanka, etc. the roots of terrorism are deeply rooted. In fact the whole world is facing terrorism. What can motivate someone to strap bombs on their bodies and blow themselves and others to make a statement?

- **The Fund and Support**

Only large and well organized outfits with considerable means, expertise and support can carry out such deeds. The funds which feed the terrorists come from various sources-foreign supporters and collaborators, drug money, the yields of bank robberies, and stray looting of persons carrying bags containing cash etc. Terrorists recruit young people in their ranks. It has been noticed that most of the terrorists are misguided youths. Idealistic fervour, apparently, inspires them to join the rank.

- **Ways to Prevent Terrorism**

Terrorism is an element of modern society that cannot be escaped. Acts of terrorism occur during both, times of war and times of peace. Some are to prove a point, others to show defiance. Terrorism can never be completely eliminated because the human race will always find a reason for there to be violence. No culture is perfect. However, we can take steps to prevent such seemingly senseless attacks. The current situation requires a well defined, comprehensive, multidimensional policy and action plan to deal with terrorism. Governments and their citizens must be better equipped to fight terrorism. We need tougher anti-terrorism laws. At the same time, adequate care should be taken to prevent the abuse of such laws. The people's cooperation is also vital. We must ensure that the perpetrators of terrorist acts are punished promptly. Governments must be one up on terrorist outfits and know the plans before they are put into action. Legal punishment to terrorists, their active or logistic supporters, and corrupt officials who enable smuggling of arms and explosives into India, needs to be made more severe. Successful terrorists always find a way to stay one step ahead of the authorities. This has to stop. If a certain group claims responsibility for an act of terrorism, no matter what the motive may be, that group must be attacked with all possible resources. The G7 (the world's most powerful countries) signed a declaration in 1996, which clearly states; "We reaffirm our absolute condemnation of terrorism in all its forms and manifestations, regardless of its perpetrators or motives. Terrorism is a heinous crime, and there must be no excuse or exception in bringing its perpetrators to justice.

SCIENCE AND TECHNOLOGY: A BLESSING OR CURSE

The tremendous advancement made by science and technology in different spheres of human life has completely changed the face of the earth. If our ancestors could see the marvels of our time, they would be greatly bewildered and amazed. They would probably agree that there was no age in the past which was so good and at the same time so bad as ours.

SCIENCE: A BLESSING

If you look at it one way, science and technology are essentially a means of developing ways in which we can change our environment to suit our needs. These needs often include the need for food, the need for heat, the need for entertainment and so on. As science progresses further, we discover improved methods of satisfying these needs, such as by developing farming, irrigation, fertilization, mechanization and computerization.

Science has always been seen as a quest for knowledge that quenches man's thirst for the ultimate truth. In the Arabian Nights we read the story of the wonderful lamp of Alladin, which obeyed the commands of its owner and erected in one single night a beautiful palace with every possible luxury. Nowadays modern science is much like Alladin who **controls and commands the forces of nature**. These very forces of nature, which will otherwise destroy us, have become our friends. They carry us on land, sea and through the air at a terrific speed, convey in the twinkling of eye our messages to our friends miles away from us and do other things more miraculous than are related to have been done by the spirits of the Arabian Nights.

The **discovery of steam power and electricity** has changed the face of the world. There are enormous industries with gigantic machines belching out large scale produce. **In the field of medicine**, antibiotics like penicillin and streptomycin, most complicated surgical operations like heart transplantation, X-ray, ultrasound and electric shock etc. have done wonders. It is true that science has given eyes to the blind, ears to the deaf and speech to the dumb. Apart from these, with the help of computing, power quality of life has soared. Take **entertainment** for example. At first we could only amuse ourselves with 'physical' objects such as balls and sports, then we developed radios, televisions, computer games and virtual reality. Automobiles, televisions, vacuum cleaners, microwave oven, hi-fis, telephones all have **added comfort and luxuries to our lives.** In recent years, there has been a new and relatively unpredicted trend – the rapid increase in international communication via the Internet. Computing and communication technology have advanced to the point that we can converse with anyone else across the world.

SCIENCE: A CURSE

However, our needs are not always so benign. More refined technologies brought huge improvements in the quality of life, but so often we see science as a way of creating ever more deadly weapons to ensure our survival. C.E.M. Joad has rightly said that "science has given us powers fit for the gods, yet we use them like small children." With its stress on the experimental and rational modes of enquiry, science has made our outlook towards life more practical and logical.

Machines were made to be man's slaves yet he has grown so dependent on them that they are in a fair way to become his masters. Prosperous cottage industries have been replaced by huge mills and factories. As a result instead of thriving villages, cities of smoke have come up. **Machines have snatched away from us the calm of mind and peace of our environment**. No doubt, science has **developed wealth and material prosperity** of man but wealth is not the be all and end all of human life. Our material achievements, highly refined means of recreation and articles of luxuries have fallen heavily on us. We have begun worshipping material success and are caught in the entangling apparatus of money and machinery. Greedy for tangible gains, we have become violent, restless, thoughtless and undisciplined.

Sometimes our most pressing need is the need to survive against aggressors. All other needs are subordinate to survival; after all, what use is having a highly developed culture when you have no means of defending yourself against the country next door who has just developed gunpowder? In fact, we even map out our history according to **new arms developments**, the turning points of history are entwined with the invention of the catapult, the cannon, gunpowder, submarines, fighters and bombers, V2 rockets, nuclear bombs and most recently space-based and airborne laser strategic defence.

Earlier, conflict only concerned a few dozen or hundred people with swords or spears, or a few thousand people with rifles. In the Nuclear Age, tens of millions of people have died in violent wars. Long range bombers, intercontinental ballistic missiles, neutron bombs and cruise missiles are all designed to destroy others. Terrorists can purchase biological weapons that could wipe out millions of people and entire cities in one go.

- **Conclusion**

Throughout history, science and technology have proved to be a see saw of sorts, with its ups and downs, benefits and disadvantages, all increasing with time. Today, the quality of life in first world countries is excellent; life expectancy is high, general affluence is high, entertainment is readily available. But we also live with the terrible, ever present knowledge that one skirmish, one conflict, one *mistake*, could destroy the delicate balance of the see saw and our weapons are such that, if used, they could render the Earth uninhabitable. Anyhow, it is not science but its misuse on the part of man that has wrought so much of havoc. It is true and we cannot deny that with the ultimate amalgamation of the different strands of science, and the convergence of technology and humans, science has the opportunity to improve our lives forever.

STUDENT UNREST

All over the world, whether it is Japan, America, India, Indonesia or Pakistan, students' unrest or students' indiscipline is becoming an everyday phenomenon. From a difficult question paper to the issue of fee structure, the students raise a hue and cry over any and every issue. We find them taking part in demonstrations, slogan shouting, and even destruction of public property such as buses and the school or college furniture. Even invigilators, teachers and principals are manhandled by the students. What does it show? Plain lack of discipline or mere venting of frustration adopting some unconventional mean? Whatever the case may be, there is no doubt that the phenomenon has assumed alarming proportions. We have to go deep into the cause and apply whatever correctives may appear to be feasible and effective.

- **A Rootless Generation**

In this age of Science and Information Technology, information and knowledge have become the driving forces for growth and development. New discoveries every day are making man conscious of his hidden powers. He has become more logical, not prepared to accept anything without questioning. With that, the moral development of a child is neglected in the schools and colleges. Established values and ethics of the society have lost their appeal and the students are lacking in the basic values of life. The result is a rootless generation, cut off from the past, and facing an uncertain future. The students, being the members of this rootless generation, have lost all direction and are not willing to listen to anybody.

- **Large and Unmanageable Classes**

One of the factors responsible for student unrest is the large and unmanageable classes that the teachers have to handle. The students are huddled together in a classroom, and it looks as if the teacher is addressing a meeting. The tutor-taught relationship, which should be an inspiring association of minds, comes down to the commercial level. The result is that students get neither proper attention nor guidance. They take advantage of this fact to play mischief in class. It is, therefore, necessary to reduce the number of students in a class, so that the tendency towards mischief may be checked and every student gets the equal opportunity to receive guidance from the teacher.

- **Crises of Character**

Another cause of indiscipline among students is that we are passing through a 'crises of character'. This is because there is no emphasis on character formation. There is a discrepancy everywhere between principles and practices which the students of all ages are noticing day in and day out. In the classrooms they are taught the virtues of purity in public life, but in practical life they observe fraud and corruption everywhere. Consequently, they feel confused and really do not know what is expected of them.

- **Sense of Frustration**

One of the important causes of student unrest is a sense of frustration among the students of today. Uncertain about their future they are just drifting aimlessly through all the years of college life. They do not know what is in store for them at the end of their academic career. The educational system is to be blamed for this state of affairs. Education should be job oriented, so that the student should know beforehand the niche in which he will find himself at the end of his educational career. This will give him a sense of purpose and direction.

- **Exploitation by Politicians**

Another reason for student unrest is their exploitation by politicians. The unscrupulous politicians do not hesitate to make use of the students to agitate against grievances, with which they are not directly concerned. The educators should see that politics must, under no circumstances, be allowed to divert students from their studies. These politicians do not infiltrate into the campus and use the students for their own ends.

- **Careless Attitude of Parents**

Lack of interest on the part of parents is another factor which contributes to the breeding indiscipline in young minds. Life is becoming so complicated and busy every day that there is almost no home life left. Most of the parents are so busy in their business or social circle that they have little time for their children. Thus, careless and indifferent homes produce undisciplined children.

- **Conclusion**

The students of today are the hope of tomorrow. They must be provided with a healthy outlet for their bottled up energy; otherwise they will find expression in unhealthy activities. It is for the parents, teachers and politicians to realize their responsibility towards the young generation and guide it properly. Besides, there should be reorientation of education to make it more purposeful. Sufficient avenues should be opened up by way of self-employment. Once the causes of student unrest are known, it is not difficult to device remedial measures. Mahatma Gandhi said, "For the students there should be no party politics. There should be no Socialist, Communist, Congress or other groups among students. They should be all students first and last, determined to gather as much knowledge as possible, and that for the sake of the service of the people, not for the sake of getting jobs."

IMPACT OF COMPUTERS ON SOCIETY

In the modern day computers are our main source of knowledge. The mechanization was basically responsible for the first industrial revolution. The second industrial revolution is the automation and computerization. The mechanization helped man to amplify his physical power manifold, while computerization has multiplied his intellectual capacity more than a thousand times. There is hardly any human activity which is not affected computers in some way or the other. Be it industrial management and production, health, education, agriculture, defence, crime detection, communication or travel. The result of this is that even a home environment begins to take on a mechanized look. Naturally, the social and economic implications of computerization are too evident for any realist to see.

Almost everything one knows is run or made by computers. Cars and jets are designed on computers, traffic signals are run by computers, most medical equipment uses computers and space exploration was started with computers. Most of the jobs today require the use of computers. These 'mechanical brains' have made a huge impact on our society. Even nonprofessionals make use of computers, and reinforcing this is the fact that people now are able to make use of computers in their homes for entertainment as well as communication. It would be hard if we didn't have the computer around. Let's visualize a world without computers. People in the medical field wouldn't have had found a lot of cures to diseases, since most cures are found with the help of computers. Movies like Jurassic Park, Toy Story, A Bug's Life, Godzilla and most others would never have been made without computers because they used computer graphics and animation in them. Pharmacies would have a hard time keeping track with what medications to give to patients. Counting votes would be impossible without computers and most importantly, space exploration wouldn't be possible without them. It's a pretty tough life without computers. Some may not agree and say, "Well, we don't need computers to live on." This doesn't hold true anymore. Computers help in curing diseases, make entertainment a lot better, keep track of important records, etc. Without computers, the very fabric of life would not be the same.

Advantages

Computers changed the world immensely. It helped man step forward into the future. Thanks to computers, space exploration came true, new designs of vehicles and other transportation were made, entertainment became more advanced, medical science made more cures for diseases, etc. The computers impacted our lives in many ways. We may not notice it but they did make life a lot easier. Without computers, the world would be a harder place to live in. Thanks to them, everyday life is easier for us. Some people may disagree but most wouldn't. Some people say that computers are taking away man's power. That may be true but computers did make the impossible possible.

Computers and Communication

Communication is as vital as labour and capital for modern industrial growth. Transmission of information is called communication. Instant communication is so vital for an industrial establishment having branches in different parts of the world. Continuous assessment of the performance of various branches from a central station helps the management to make economic, marketing and business decisions at the right time. Computer communication, through its Local Area Network (LAN), Wide Area Network (WAN) and Integrated Services Digital Network (ISDN) can connect urban cities, and villages. Different countries are brought together through computer network and geostationary satellites. The communication speed has crossed 16 million bits per second (mbps). In a modern industrial scenario where patience is not considered a virtue, this much speed of data transmission is most essential. Computerised communication doesn't involve the use of Morse Codes or short hand, but complete files in readable form. Pictures and drawings also can be transmitted as such. Digital telephone systems, satellites, car phones, teleconferences, voice mail boxes and electronic mail systems are the end products of computerised communication systems. We now have mobile offices. These facilities are of great help not only for industrial growth but also for day to day administration.

Entertainment

Another area that computers impacted tremendously is **the entertainment**. Most people like science fiction or action movies, especially the ones with the neat looking effects. Well, those graphics are made by computers only. Most of the movies today use computer graphics to make things more realistic but not real. Computer graphics are used on spaceships, aliens, monsters, and all special effects without which almost no movie gets made these days. Godzilla was created by computer animation, texturing, and graphics to make him more realistic then the older version in which they used a man in a costume to play godzilla. This wasn't the only movie made with computers. There are even movies completely made by computers like Jurassic Park, Toy Story and A Bug's Life.

It is not only movies that use computer animations and graphics. Games on the latest game consoles like the PC, Playstation and Nintendo 64 used computers to make the coolest games ever. That's how computers have impacted today's entertainment.

Education

Education is an instrument of change for any society. With the introduction of computers, education assumes new dimensions and values. A new language and a new grammar befitting a computer culture has become operational. In the past, more importance had been given to subjects like history, literature, and culture. These subjects are very essential and expose students to factors like the origin, growth and survival of humanity. Nevertheless, the employers who engage people for manning business, industry, construction and marketing expect something more than just the knowledge in human history and culture. The educational system should adopt itself to the changing needs. Mental weakness is more dangerous than physical disability.

Fortunately, our educational system is ready to accept changes arising due to the deep penetration of computers in daily life.

In hi-tech era audiovisual aids, video tape, closed circuit TV and satellite transmissions are widely used for dissemination of ideas and information. In the distant education system, the computer network has wide application, which is more economical and effective than any other means.

Health

Computer technology has also helped healthcare through its contributions. In the medical field, the use of computers has come as a boon. In a computerised medicare system, chances of human error are minimized or completely eliminated. Pathological tests, scanning and continuous monitoring of body conditions of a patient being operated on, all are done through computer. The storage of a patient's data in computer makes future diagnosis easier. The disease data are made available for research and analysis. Using computers, the best medicine available for a particular disease and its availability can be ascertained. If hospitals are connected through LAN and WAN, communication between hospitals can be made easier and for emergency, the best source can be tapped and precious lives can be saved. Through such a medicare system, a healthy population emerges. They live longer and happier.

Business

In addition to entertainment, education and healthcare being greatly facilitated through computers and the internet, it must be remembered that business communications is also enhanced. Businesses use computers for keeping track of accounts, money, or items that they need greatly and use. Besides, all business presentations, which are vital for any business organization, are prepared using computers.

Other Fields

Other areas that computers impacted are energy conservation, machine and process control, space exploration, automobile designing and research and development. There are other fields like defence, crime detection, weather forecast, geological and oceanographic investigations, which have direct impact on social and economic functions of society. Using Super Computers and INSAT we are in a position to forecast Weather correctly, which is of great use for farmers. Natural calamities can be predicted and remedial measures can be taken to minimize damage.

Mineral and oil deposits underground and under deep sea bed can be detected through satellite photos using laser beams.

Disadvantages

However, there are also **problems** that come along with computers. The problems that one faces with internet transactions by and large have everything to do with the interference that one receives from files such as internet cookies and hacking software, and these are the kinds of things that can damage the confidence with which consumers, retailers, etc. conduct day to day business using computer systems. However, the world still remains enchanted with the way that business transactions are conducted through computer technology.

Conclusion

Computers today have changed the very fabric of life. Many technical products today, ranging from cars to kitchen implements contain computer chips. Businesses and entertainment uses them to make profits, education uses them to help educate students better, the medical field too uses computers in many different ways. In areas such as banking, warehouse and goods distribution management, and communication, computers have become indispensable. Without the help of computers, none of this would be possible. The world would be a dull and primitive place.

MEDIA & ENTERTAINMENT

The Indian media and entertainment sector is poised to enter a golden era. The industry is one of the largest markets in the world seeing strong growth. The corporatization of the film industry, a booming television sector, a fast growing radio sector, a growing market for print products, and similar other technological changes are propelling growth. India is ready to embrace and grow along with the changes the industry is undergoing globally.

Cinema

The Indian film industry is among the largest in the world, producing 1041 films annually. **Bollywood,** the Hindi film industry, commanding a 40 per cent share in the Indian film market, is gaining a global audience. Regional films too are making an impact. A number of factors are bringing about the change. For one, new technologies like DVDs and the internet are ensuring that viewership is not confined to specific areas. The country has over five million home video and DVD subscribers and current penetration levels are expected to grow 31 percent, according to an analytical report.

A spurt in the number of **multiplexes** in the country has changed the entire complexion of Indian films, their budgets, the way they are made and the audiences they are made for.

The corporatization of the film industry has also enabled it to discover new revenue streams. Showcasing international films dubbed in local Indian languages has helped the dubbing industry grow at 25-30 per cent over the last five years and international films are now reaching out to wider audiences. This is having a ripple effect, driving growth in film merchandising and music sales. Merchandising for "Spiderman 2" which was dubbed in Hindi collected over US$ 2 million in India in its first week, the highest ever for a Hollywood film!

Animation and Special Effects businesses are also waiting to grow in India. According to the National Association of Software and Services Companies (NASSCOM), the animation industry is growing at 25 per cent and is expected to reach US$ 869 million by 2010, thanks largely to India's creative skills, cost advantage, a growing domestic market and the growing maturity of animation studios. A first indication of times to come is Sony Pictures Imageworks' US$ 5 million investment in Frameflow India, the Chennai, based animation and special effects company for back office work.

Television

The television industry in India is currently in its prime. It has over 350 channels and is today the third largest television market in the world. It reaches over 119 million television households, which is almost the same size as the entire US market, but covers only about 60 per cent of the total households in the country. Of these, about 50 million receive cable television services. The low penetration promises a huge untapped potential for growth in this industry.

Advertising spending on Indian television has been growing at 21 per cent a year. In fact, television's growth and influence in India is so immense that it actually rivals the country's film industry. But the two segments now work together to reach India's surroundings in niche ways.

Music

The Indian music industry in the past was completely dominated by film music, which was an integral part of Indian films and music rights brought in as much as 15 per cent of a film's earnings. That has changed now, and music videos and non-film albums are driving growth. The music sector is pegged to grow at 4 per cent over the next five years.

India has now emerged as one of the world's largest markets for **mobile music**. India sells almost as much digital music as it does CDs and cassettes. According to the Céllular Operators' Association of India, the size of the mobile music industry in 2006 was about US$ 115 million (including ring tones and is going to be around US$ 170 million by the end of 2007. Growing at a scorching pace of 50 per cent, this segment is expected to exceed the sales of physical music; compact discs and cassettes. India has over 140 million mobile phone consumers and over 6 million new subscriptions are added each month, which means that one in five Indians will own a phone by the end of 2007. Clearly, mobile entertainment promises to be a new avenue for growth.

Radio

Radio is the main source of news and entertainment for most of India, reaching out to 99 per cent of the population. While All India Radio, the public service broadcaster, hogs the top tier in coverage, private FM has become the second tier and recently, the government has opened up the third tier, community radio, thus providing the sector a further impetus to grow.

The sector has been seeing strong growth and 2007 is expected to be the year of the radio. According to industry estimates, India will have 600 stations (250 All India Radio and 350 private) in 100 odd cities this year.

Government Initiatives

The Union Cabinet has cleared the community radio policy allowing nonprofit organizations with a three-year track record to set up and run stations.

Marking the first time that **the state government** enters the entertainment industry, the Kerala Venture Capital Fund has acquired 40 per cent equity in the production house Symphony Entertainment Private Ltd.

The government allows 20 per cent FDI in FM radio and recommended shifting to revenue sharing regime from the current licence fee structure.

The government changed its media policy in 2002 and relaxed foreign ownership restrictions in the newspaper category. Today, 26 per cent foreign equity holding in news-related print media is allowed, though editorial management must remain Indian.

The Road Ahead

The liberalization of the media sector has played a key role in encouraging investments in this sector. Higher investments will open up new opportunities and will propel growth in the sector. Subsequent to the policies being put in place, eighteen media companies will float public issues in 2007. Global Broadcast News (CNN-IBN) and Cinemax India have recently gone public. Others in the pipeline are Sony SET, DQ Entertainment, Indian Express Newspapers, Brahma Interactive, Broadcast Initiatives, Raj Television Network, SRS Entertainment and 12 others which are awaiting SEBI approval.

REVIEW QUESTIONS

Some important topics for writing essays:

- Unemployment
- Environmental Threats
- Cultural Pollution
- Good Manners
- The Film I Liked Most
- Value of Games
- My Ambition in Life
- My First Day in the College
- Visit to an Exhibition
- A Railway Journey

- Dowry System in India
- National Integration
- Science and Human Happiness
- Students and Politics
- Importance of Leisure
- Hostel Life
- Friendship
- Relevance of English Language
- Modern Entertainment
- Education for Women
- The Policy of Economic Liberalization
- Importance of Technical Education
- Information Technology Revolution

Unit III

Paralanguage

- Various Aspects of the Voice
- Stress/Accent
- Eye Contact for Small and Large Groups

Paralanguage: Aspects of the Voice

24 CHAPTER

SPEAKING STYLES

Human speech is a very dynamic phenomenon with nearly endless forms of variations. The ways in which we express ourselves vary from one situation to another, depending on the context and speaker's intentions. A speaker might vary his or her speaking style depending on the listener and the situation, using different expressions, pronunciations and tone of voice. The manner of pronunciation is quite strict when a more formal speaking style is used; the talker makes an effort to be easily understood by modifying the articulation to make speech slower and acoustically more distinctive. These are also the characteristics of clear speech.

PARALINGUISTICS & PARALANGUAGE

Paralinguistics is the systematic study of how a speaker verbalizes. While verbal communication consists of the content of words, paralanguage comprises the way/manner in which the speaker speaks. Is the content of your message contradicted by the attitude with which you are communicating it? Researchers have found that the tone, pitch, quality of voice, and rate of speaking convey emotions that can be accurately judged regardless of the content of the message. As 'para' means 'like', 'paralanguage' literally means 'like language'. The important thing to gain from this is that the voice is important, not just as the conveyor of the message, but as a complement to the message. As a communicator you should be sensitive to the influence of tone, pitch, and quality of your voice for effective interpretation of your message by the receiver.

VOICE

Inspite of significant strides made by technology, the voice continues to remain the primary tool of communication. The human voice conveys the meaning or message. Thus, the voice heightens the importance of the most difficult element of speech delivery—effective articulation and voice modulation. The clearer the voice, the more effectively it will convey the meaning.

The voice tells us so much about the speaker's sex, background, education, training, attitude, and temperament. Any voice which is used for communication has to be first worked on at a physical level to unleash its full natural potential. This stage of voice training aims to create an optimal & healthy voice for broadcasting, singing, acting and speaking.

Speakers differ from each other in terms of voice quality (which is the main reason for our being able to recognize individuals' voices even over the telephone), but they also introduce quite a lot of variation into their voices for particular purposes. A considerable amount of research in this field has been carried out in recent years, and we have a better understanding of the meaning of such terms as creaky, breathy voice and harshness.

In order to make our message effective, we need to give our attention to the following points:

a. Pitch Variation/ Tone

The pitch of the human voice is continuously variable, and is necessary to make speech effective. Pitch refers to the varying intensity of the voice, i.e. it refers to what the listener hears as high or low tonal properties, to rising and falling voice patterns. Those who speak in monotones fail to keep the listener's attention.

Tone is the phonological correlate of pitch. Tone, i.e. pitch variation, can serve different purposes across languages.

- **Pitch variation affects the meaning of a word**. This means that one sequence of sounds can have different meanings depending on the tone pattern with which it is produced, i.e. whether it is produced at a continuous high level, a rising or a falling level.
- In a language such as English, **pitch variation can be used to express the intention of the speaker**. Your tone of voice and behaviour may show that you are nervous even though you want to appear calm. Similarly, they may show that you are confused even though you want to appear confident. Tone variations in your voice and your corresponding boy language may suggest such attitudes as sincerity, trust, respect, hope, or admiration. On the other hand, slight chages in these clues may reveal such attitudes as suspicion, mistrust, dislike or resentment. All of these signals are part of the total context of the message. The listener must consider these signals, as well as the words and sentences themselves, in order to interpret what you are saying.

b. Speaking Speed

We speak at different speeds on different occasions and while conveying different parts of a message. Speed of speech is measured by the number of spoken words per minute. Speech is more interesting to the listener when the speed is varied.

If the speaker's average speed is too slow, the listener becomes bored and impatient. On the other hand, if the average speed is too fast, the listener does not have enough time to understand the message and once again he will lose interest.

As a general rule, we should present the easy parts of a message speedily and the difficult and complicated parts of the information should be conveyed slowly. Easy information, if conveyed at a slower pace, becomes irritating as it is likely to be understood easily. On the other hand, the difficult or highly technical part of the information, if conveyed rapidly, will become difficult to understand. It has also been observed that in a state of anxiety or urgency we tend to speak fast. When we are relaxed we speak at a comfortable speed.

c. Pause

The speed of speaking is also accompanied by pause. We should not go on speaking without pausing. A pause can be highly effective in emphasizing the upcoming subject and in gaining the listener's attention. However, the pauses should be at the right moments. The incorrect use of pauses or the frequent arbitrary pauses spoil the speech and can create problems. It is, therefore, necessary for a speaker to carefully monitor his pauses with regard to where and when to give a pause in his speech.

During a conversation pauses are often inserted with sounds or utterances like, 'ah', 'oh', 'uh', 'um', 'you know', 'actually', 'ok' etc. These pauses are called 'non-fluencies'. A careful use of these non-fluencies can add to the fluency of the speaker and give him time to relax. But too frequent use of these non-fluencies may irritate the listener.

d. Voice Modulation or Waviness

We should speak loud enough for all the audience to hear. As a general rule, the loudness of our voice should be adjusted according to the size of our audience. The larger the audience the louder our voice should be. In fact we become more convincing by adjusting our volume from loud to soft.

Good speakers do three things with their voices to maintain audience interest:

- **Be enthusiastic:** This will communicate your interest and excitement for your topic and help generate audience interest too.
- **Exaggerate voice modulation:** Modulation in conversational speaking is difficult to detect when you are speaking in front of an audience. Exaggerate inflection when you are making points or demonstrating some kind of emotion.
- **Do not speak in a monotone:** Monotone does not necessarily mean speaking in a low, droning voice. Some speakers speak in a loud monotone. You must modulate your speaking at whatever volume you are speaking at, whether loud, medium, or soft.

e. Accent Neutralization

Accent neutralization or accent modification involves a systematic training process focused on modifying speech patterns. It includes a professional speech evaluation followed by working on clarity of speech sounds, pronunciation, intonation and rhythm of speech. Speaking with a noticeable accent may undermine your communication skills both professionally and socially. People may not understand what you are saying and you may have to repeat yourself. Your listeners may pay more attention to your accent than to what you are saying. Accent neutralization is also a requirement for certain professions like news anchoring on a national network or call center work.

Accent neutralization helps those, who are proficient with the English language, and speak with a neutral, globally understood English accent.

STRESS/ACCENT

Stress is the use of muscular energy while articulating words. When a word or a syllable in word is produced louder, more lengthy, with higher pitch or with more quality, it will be perceived as stressed. For the speaker, stressing a word means using more force and making it seem stronger than other words in the same speech, for the listener it means more loudness.

a. Word Stress

The situation of strong stresses in words is called word-stress. In each word, at least one syllable must be stressed, i.e. must be more prominent than other syllables. Take 3 words, for example, photograph, photographer and photographic. Do they sound the same when spoken? No. Because ONE syllable in each word is STRESSED (stronger than the others).

- PHOtograph
- phoTOgrapher
- photoGRAPHic

This happens in ALL words with 2 or more syllables: TEACHer, JaPAN, CHINa, aBOVE, converSAtion, INteresting, imPORtant, deMAND, etCETera among others.

The syllables that are not stressed are 'weak' or 'small' or 'quiet'. Native speakers of English listen for the STRESSED syllables, not the weak syllables. People tend to judge speakers based on their ability to pronounce words correctly and clearly. If you use word stress in your speech, you will instantly and automatically improve your pronunciation and comprehension.

Generally speaking, there is no easy formula determining which syllable of polysyllabic English words bears the main stress. Therefore the learner is advised to learn the stress of each word individually. Every good dictionary indicates the location of word accent; it is necessary to refer to the dictionary to find out the accentual pattern.

b. Sentence Stress

The manner of giving appropriate degrees of stress to words in sentences is called sentence – stress. With sentence stress, some words in a sentence are STRESSED (loud) and other words are weak (quiet). The stressing of words in sentences varies according to the degree of emphasis one wishes to give to particular words. There are nearly always some words in a sentence, which are of greater importance than others. The more important words are generally nouns, adjectives, demonstrative pronouns, adverbs and principal verbs. The native speaker of English generally stresses these words in a sentence. Among the unstressed words, we have articles, prepositions, helping verbs and the personal pronouns. In the following sentence, for example, do we say every word with the same stress or force? No. The important words in this sentence are WANT and GO.

'We WANT to GO.'

In fact all words are important which give the hearer a new piece of information. For example: (We make the important words BIG and the unimportant words small.)

- We WANT to GO.
- We WANT to GO to WORK.
- We DON'T WANT to GO to WORK.
- We DON'T WANT to GO to WORK at NIGHT.

Importance of Stress

Word stress is an essential part of the word shape. Stress may change the meaning of the speech. Placing of stress on the right syllable is very important in English. Every word has a certain characteristic accentual pattern. No one can learn the pronunciation of an English word without learning its stress. Therefore, it should be very carefully marked either on a word or a sentence. Putting stress on right places is essential for

(i) Intelligibility
(ii) Understanding
(iii) Comprehension
(iv) Checking of wrong parts of speech

Most Indian speakers of English put stress on the wrong syllables. Consequently, their pronunciation becomes unintelligible to the native speaker of English.

Accents in Compound words

By compound words we mean words, which are made up of two words. Most compound words (with or without a hyphen) have the main accent on the first element. For example;

GOLDsmith	TEA-party	ANYthing
SCHOOLMaster	PREfix	DAYtime
HAIRbrush	CHURCHyard	BACKbone

There are a few compound words, which have the stress on the second element. They are mostly compound with '-ever' or '-self' for example;

WhenEVER	YourSELF	ThemSELVES
HowEVER	HerSELF	OurSELVES

Stress Shift

Stress changes its place in different meanings. Words with the same stem do not keep the primary stress on the same syllable. It may vary from syllable to syllable. Stress shift is quite normal in derivatives. (**Derivative** is a word that has been developed or produced from another word. For example, 'happiness' is a derivative of 'happy').

For example:

- aCademy
- acaDemic
- acadeMician
- Politics
- politiCal
- poliTician
- inFerior
- inferiOrity

Stress changes according to function

Stressing syllables or parts of spoken words also changes the meaning. The accentual pattern depends on whether the word is used as a noun, an adjective or a verb. If the word is used as a noun or adjective the stress falls on the first syllable. And if the word is a verb, the stress comes on the second syllable. For example:

Noun / Adjective	Verb
• CONduct	• conDUCT
• DIgest	• diGEST
• OBject	• obJECT
• REcord	• ReCORD
• PREsent	• preSENT
• INcrease	• inCREASE
• SUBject	• SubJECT
• PROgress	• proGRESS

This way of looking at language takes us into the area of phonetics that is the 'Science of Speech Sounds'. Though it is not of immediate concern to us, but every educated speaker knows how important it is in conversation to put stress on the word or part of the concerned word.

EYE CONTACT FOR SMALL AND LARGE GROUPS

Universally it is believed that the eyes and the face are the most expressive parts of our body. Of all the ways in which we communicate with people, eye contact is most powerful. When we look at somebody's face we focus primarily on his eyes and try to understand what he means. The eyes, along with the eyebrows, eye lids and the size of pupils convey our innermost feelings. In his book, "Eye to Eye: How People Interact" Dr. Peter Marsh says, how we look at other people, meet their glaze and look away can make all the difference between an effective encounter and one that leads to embarrassment or even rejection. Whether it is a loving gaze, hostile stare, nervous glance or a refusal to look altogether, the duration of the contact reveals our interest in the other party and the situation. To look at a person and maintain an eye contact invites a person to continue an interaction whereas to turn away and break the contact can indicate loss of attention and discontinues an interaction.

It is perceived that if the speaker maintains eye contact with the listener, he is more confident than the one who does not. Furthermore, an eye contact provides feedback on how well the communication system is functioning.

Eye contact is an important way to build the emotional bond and likeability. The longer the eye contact between two people, the greater the intimacy that develops. Others rarely interrupt two people engaged in a conversation if they have consistent eye contact. Eye contact also plays a significant role in the persuasion process.

There are subtle silent rules to eye contact and they vary from culture to culture. **In social situations,** one should make short frequent glances. Making eye contact for too long a duration can be seen as threatening. Failing to look at others causes suspicion, as honesty and the ability to look someone in the eyes are very closely related. **In normal conversation**, eye contact acts as the regulator of turn taking. To start a communication with someone, we need to first establish eye contact. If that person looks back, 'permission' has been granted to begin speaking. **In a group presentation,** it is important to maintain eye contact with the audience. The listener should also look more at the speaker in order to show his responsiveness and interest. **Too much of eye contact** is considered to be aggressive and dominant while **too little** is seen as a sign of nervousness, being shifty, submissive or inattentive. Therefore, one is able to establish effective eye contact to support or emphasize the spoken word as most people can't keep eye contact when they are bending the truth.

Maintaining eye contact when talking (or listening) to someone gives an impression that you/they are confident and honest. **Making little eye contact** can say that the other person doesn't like you, is nervous or shy, or perhaps believes that he is higher in status and thinks that eye contact isn't necessary. **Refusing to make eye contact** shows arrogance and contempt as if the other person is insignificant. Therefore, most people can't keep eye contact when they are bending the truth.

REVIEW QUESTIONS

1. What do you understand by paralanguage? Describe its basic elements.
2. Do you think that pitch variation is necessary to make speech effective? Describe in detail.
3. What is the significance of pauses in public speaking?
4. Write a note on the importance of stress in oral communication.
5. Write short notes on the following:
   a) Speed variation in speech
   b) Eye contact for small and large groups
   c) Accent neutralization
   d) Voice modulation

Unit IV

Non-verbal Communication and Presentation Techniques

- Non-verbal Communication
- Presentation Techniques
- Role-Play
- Debate

Non-verbal Communication

25

CHAPTER

WHAT IS NONVERBAL COMMUNICATION

Communication is the transfer of information from one person to another. Most of us spend about 75 percent of our waking hours communicating our knowledge, thoughts, and ideas to others. The social anthropologist Edward T. Hall claims 60 percent of all our communication is nonverbal. If verbal communication deals with words, sentences and spoken expressions, nonverbal communication constitutes body movements, gestures, expressions etc.

Nonverbal communication can be defined as communication that takes place without the use of words. Research suggests that nonverbal communication is more powerful than what people say.

Scientific analysis in the field of NLP (Neuro-Linguistic Programming) research has discovered that we perceive in three ways:

- 55 %- visually (body language)
- 38%-vocally (tone of voice)
- 7%-verbally (spoken words)

DEFINITION OF NONVERBAL COMMUNICATION

Tortoriello, Blott, and DeWine: ".... the exchange of messages primarily through non-linguistic means, including kinesics (body language), facial expressions and eye contact, tactile communication, space and territory, environment, paralanguage (vocal but non-linguistic cues), and the use of silence and time."

COMPONENTS OF NONVERBAL COMMUNICATION

The main components of the system are:

- **Kinesics (body language)** Body motions such as shrugs, foot tapping, drumming fingers, eye movements such as winking, facial expressions, and gestures
- **Proxemics (proximity)** Use of space to signal privacy or attraction
- **Haptics** Touch

- **Oculesics** Eye contact
- **Chronemics** Use of time, waiting, pausing
- **Olfactics** Smell
- **Vocalics** Tone of voice, timbre, volume, speed
- **Sound symbols** Grunting, mmm, er, ah, uh-huh, mumbling
- **Silence** Pausing, waiting, secrecy
- **Posture** Position of the body, stance
- **Adornment** Clothing, jewellery, hairstyle
- **Locomotion** Walking, running, staggering, limping

IMPORTANCE OF NONVERBAL COMMUNICATION

Nonverbal communication tells us something about the relationship between people.

Just as language uses sets of symbols to convey meaning, our body, consciously as well as unconsciously, carries massages, attitudes, moods, warmth, indifference, feelings and so on. We have, however, to infer these meanings from body language-the face, eyes, gestures, postures and physical appearance, each of which has its own functions. In this connection it is important to point out that all bodily movements, postures, gestures etc. are guided by our thought processes, emotions and feelings.

According to **Paul Ekman,** "We talk with our vocal cords, but we communicate with our facial expressions, our tone of voice, our whole body."

Understanding nonverbal communication has immense practical use. On the grounds that, 'It's not what you say, it's the way you say it', Nonverbal communication has been a focus of attention for some time for below stated reasons:

- The refinement of presentation skills
- Confidence building, creativity
- Skill development
- Can repeat the message the person is making verbally
- Can contradict a message the individual is trying to convey
- Can substitute a verbal message.

KINESICS OR BODY LANGUAGE

Body language plays a key role in communication and an awareness of it and how it can vary from culture to culture, can be particularly important in helping students develop their ability to understand it in a real environment. Regarding the importance of body language, management consultant **Nancy Austin** says, "When people don't know whether to believe what they are hearing or what they are seeing, they go with the body language-it tells the truth. You can play fast and loose with words, but it is much more difficult to do that with gestures."

Body language is used especially to express feelings. For instance if we do not like someone, it is often difficult to say that directly to the person. However we can make it clear either intentionally or unintentionally through body language. It is difficult to lie or cover up our feelings through body language. Very often, body language is unintentional and involuntary. People may give their true feelings away by not being aware of their body language. Research has shown that most people pay more attention to, and believe more readily, their impression of how a person acts through body language than what is said through words. As a consequence, we tend to doubt, or put a question mark behind the spoken words if they do not correspond with the language of the body.

The features of body language

Body language is made up of a whole range of features many of which we combine together without ever thinking about what it is we are doing or what we are expressing.

The features of body language are

- Facial expression
- Eye contact
- Gesture
- Posture

FACIAL EXPRESSION

Facial expression is one of the most obvious and flexible forms of communication. Facial expressions usually communicate emotions and can easily convey mood, attitude, understanding, confusion and a whole range of other things. A smile, frown, raised eyebrow, corners of lips, the cheeks, yawn, and sneer all convey information. In fact every facial muscle is an instrument of communication. There are eight basic facial expressions generally associated with happiness, surprise, fear, anger, sadness, bewilderment, astonishment and contentment, which are universally found in all cultures. We can easily mark all the signals sent through these parts of the face by others and observe our own expressions by looking at ourselves in a mirror.

For example, smiling is a powerful sign that transmits:

- Happiness
- Friendliness
- Warmth
- Liking
- Affiliation

Thus, the expressions tell the attitudes of the communicator. Researchers have discovered that facial expressions continually change during interaction and are monitored constantly by the recipient. It follows, then, that we can change our behaviour by changing the inner nature.

However, certain facial areas reveal our emotional state better than others. For example, the eyes tend to reveal happiness or sadness, and even surprise. The lower face also can reveal happiness or surprise; the smile, for example, can communicate friendliness and cooperation. The lower face, brows, and forehead can reveal anger.

EYE CONTACT

Eye contact is a direct and powerful form of nonverbal communication. When we look at somebody's face we focus primarily on his eyes and try to understand what he means. Thus, looking at people and meeting their eyes are the first step towards striking up friendship and making positive impressions.

The eyes, along with the eyebrows, eyelids and the size of pupils convey our innermost feelings. According to **Austin,** "Eye contact is the most remembered element in forming an impression of someone. You must acquire the ability to sustain direct eye contact if you want to be taken seriously."

- Eye contact with audiences conveys candor and openness.
- People who make eye contact open the flow of communication and convey interest, concern, warmth and credibility.
- It elicits a feeling of trust.
- Eyes rolled upward are associated with fatigue.
- Failing to make eye contact in many cultures is associated with being dishonest or having something to hide.
- Eye contact also plays an important role in turn taking during conversation. Among a group of people, a speaker will often make eye contact with the person he or she wants a response from.
- Someone who wants to enter or interject a conversation will catch the eye of the person speaking to indicate that he/she wants to interrupt, and likewise someone who no longer wants to listen will avoid eye contact.
- People who know each other well can communicate mutual understanding with a single look.
- Eye contact is also a way of communicating attraction.

GESTURES

Gestures- the physical movements of head, arms, legs, hands, and torso -all play a very important role in conveying meaning without using words. Different finger, thumb or hand gestures can convey a range of meanings in different cultures, from insults to approval or even attraction. Shaking hands, touching, holding, embracing, pushing, or patting on the back all convey messages. They reflect an element of intimacy or a feeling of (or lack of) attraction. For example,

- Pounding fist on a table shows anger.
- A forefinger held high above the head shows number one.
- A forefinger and a thumb touching to form a circle stands for O.K.
- Handshaking and bowing are greeting gestures.
- Smiling can often cover a gamut of emotions: happiness, anger, confusion, apologies, or sadness.
- Displaying an open mouth (such as yawning or a wide-open laugh) is considered rude.
- Arms spread apart convey the meaning of wide.
- Holding a head high is a sign of honour, self-respect, confidence, and integrity.
- A head bent low (depending upon the situation) would show modesty and politeness.
- Nodding the head sideways or back and forth conveys the intended meaning more eloquently than words.
- Handshake conveys crucial messages about power, status and concern for the person we meet.

It is important to note that gestures are not used individually but in relation to another person, and acquire meaning at particular times.

'Open' and 'Closed' Gestures

Our gestures often tell something about us that we are not able or willing to communicate verbally. "Open" gestures show that a person is ready and willing to communicate, "closed" are present when there may be something standing in the way of honest, complete communication.

List of 'open' and 'closed' gestures

Open Gesture	*Closed Gesture*
open hands	hand covering mouth
palms up	making fists
unbuttoning jacket	peering over top of glasses
spontaneous eye contact	glancing at exit
smile	frown
leaning forward	leaning back
relaxed	rigid
hands away from face	looking at floor
standing straight	moving away
feet apart	legs crossed, shaking foot
shoulders squared	fidgeting
uncrossed legs	locked ankles
welcoming handshake	folded arms
touching	cold shoulder
patting	open palm tapping
rubbing palms together	hand wringing

affirmative head nods	head lowered
eye contact	lack of eye contact
calm use of facial movements	staring or eyes closed
body positioned towards another	rocking
seating arrangement with no barriers	stalling for time (light pipe, clean glasses, etc.)

POSTURE

A person communicates numerous messages by the way he walks, talks, stands and sits. Leaning forward or backward, standing or sitting erect, slouching or bending sideways-all these postures make an immediate impression on the person's mind.

Posture can communicate a number of things.

- Posture can convey a whole range of attitudes, from interest or the lack of it, to degrees of respect or subordination.
- Speakers often use posture to punctuate what they are saying, shifting forward in their seat or leaning towards their interlocutor to punctuate an important point, or slumping back to indicate that they have finished making a point.
- Standing erect, but not rigid, and leaning slightly forward communicates that the person is approachable, receptive and friendly.
- In order to look confident and in charge one should sit squarely in a chair, feet on the floor and shoulders straight.

Thus, in our day-to-day communication we should carefully notice details about the way we speak, gesticulate and move. Graceful movements and confident posture improves the atmosphere and makes the other people interested in us.

APPEARANCE

Physical appearance, which includes clothing, hair, cosmetics, jewellery etc., is very meaningfully related to our body language (face, eyes, gestures, and postures etc.)

It is generally said that 'first impression is the last impression' and 'a man is generally recognized by his dress and address.' By address means the way a person speaks to others. No doubt the speaker's gestures, facial features, posture and such would be perceived in relation to his/her attire. A dress may be formal or informal, but it should fit the situation. A person's dress speaks a lot about his attitude to life, to work, to his colleagues and his own feelings.

It is not just the dress or clothes that are important for any occasion but also shoes, hairstyle, perfume etc. that convey meaning in nonverbal form.

ADVANTAGES OF BODY LANGUAGE

Body language forms a very important part of our day to day communication. It expresses our inner feelings, our conflicts and our attitudes. Often a warm handshake or a hug conveys intimacy much more than words. Similarly loss of eye contact, yawning or slumping in the chair can express boredom or loss of interest.

1. Body language is the most easily visible aspect of communication. It helps the receiver of the message in decoding the message.
2. Body language complements verbal communication. Specially in fact-to-face communication, no message can be completely sent across without the accompaniment of facial expressions and gestures. It helps in establishing rapport.
3. Body language adds intensity to the process of communication. In the absence of any gestures, change of posture, and proper eye contact any face-to-face communication will look ineffective.
4. Body language goes a long way to improve the overall atmosphere and looks of the organization.

LIMITATIONS OF BODY LANGUAGE

1. Words, spoken or written, can be taken seriously, but body language cannot always be taken seriously.
2. People belonging to different cultural backgrounds send out different body signals. They are, therefore, liable to be misinterpreted.
3. Body language requires extra care in getting the right message. It becomes ineffective if the listener is ineffective.
4. Use of body language is not very effective in large gatherings.
5. Body language is effective in face-to-face situation among two people or a small number but it is ineffective in a large gathering.

NONVERBAL TIPS FOR IMPROVED COMMUNICATION

- Make yourself comfortable with the other person. Avoid being too close or too far away physically. (Within two feet is a comfortable range.)
- Be relaxed and attentive. To gain acceptance lean slightly towards the other person. Avoid slouching or sitting rigidly.
- Maintain frequent eye contact. Avoid staring, glaring, or looking away.
- Give nonverbal communication while the other is talking, such as a simple nod of approval.
- Keep gestures smooth and unobtrusive. Don't let them compete for attention with your words. Avoid letting your gestures reveal emotional frustration.
- Your rate of speech should be average or a bit slower. Avoid sounding impatient or hesitant. Control the tone of your voice. Avoid sounding cold and harsh.
- Maintain a clearly audible voice—neither too loud nor too soft.
- Your feet and legs should be unobtrusive. Avoid using them as a barrier.

- Smile when appropriate; look pleasant and genuine.
- Stay alert through long conversations. Closing eyes and yawning usually blocks communication.

Even without the utterance of words, the language of the body speaks volumes. Everything about you, be it outward or subtle, communicates something to somebody else. The words you use, your facial expressions, what you do with your hands, your tone of voice, and your level of eye contact will determine whether people accept or reject you and your message.

Maple says, "Nonverbal messages come from deep inside you, from your sense of self-esteem. To improve your body language, you have to start from inside and work out. If you are comfortable with yourself, it shows. People who know who they are have a relaxed way of talking and moving. They always come across well."

PROXEMICS OR SPACE LANGUAGE

Nonverbal communication involves not only body language but also the space around us, time and our physical environment. How we use space and what we do in certain spaces we create tell much about us. Thus, each of us has a space language. This space language is crafted by our culture.

Just as 'kinesics' is the study of body language, 'proxemics' is the study of how we communicate with the space around us.

Since 'proximity' means 'nearness', proxemics has come to be regarded as 'personal space language'. The spatial dimension or distance between us and other people tells us something important about our relations and the nature of our communication with them. According to **Edward T. Hall**, placing ourselves in the centre we can present the space around us in the form of the following concentric circles:

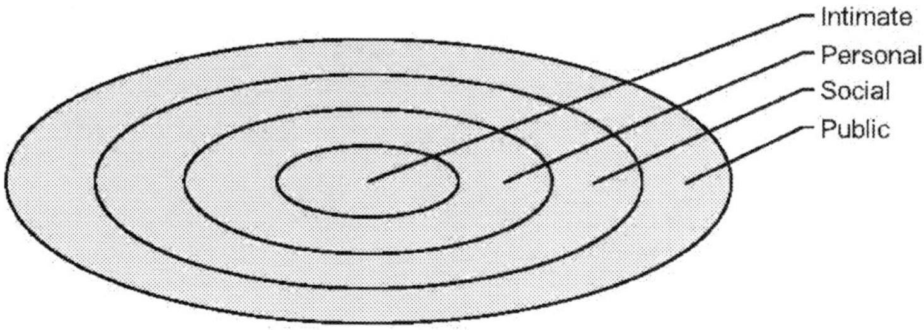

Fig.

1. **Intimate:** Physical touch or contact to 18 inches
2. **Personal:** 18 inches to 4 feet
3. **Social:** 4 to 12 feet
4. **Public:** 12 feet or as far as we can see and hear. (Range of seeing and hearing)

In each of these spaces, our communication behaviours differ and convey different meanings. We change the volume and the tone of our voice when someone is 18 inches from us and when he is 12 feet away. For example, consider the volume of your voice when someone is 18 inches from you. Do you shout? whisper? Now contrast the tone of your voice when someone is 12 feet away. Unquestionably, there is a difference, just because of the distance involved.

Communication through 'physical touch' is nonverbal. Used properly, it can create a more direct message than dozens of words; used improperly it can build barriers and cause mistrust. Touch can create a positive perception in the person being touched. Touch carries with it favourable interpretations of immediacy, affection, similarity, relaxation, and informality.

Our 'personal space' is usually reserved for our close friends, colleagues, and visitors. 'Social space' is best used for formal or official purpose. 'Public space' is exclusively meant for formal meetings/announcements.

Space is both 'fixed' and 'semi-fixed'. In fixed space we consider permanent features like walls, room size, the building, its total capacity, places, corners etc. In semi-fixed space the physical features are changeable or likely to be arranged. For example, the same furniture can be rearranged for an interview, a group discussion or for an oral presentation.

The way group of people use the space determines their respective places. People who begin conversation and those seated at the front are usually considered leaders of the group. A group of people seated around a table means communication in the form of a conference.

Time

Time is a very important factor in all communication. Just as there is a body and space language, there is also a time language. That is, how we give meaning to time communicates to others. It includes how you manage your daily schedule. Do you arrive early for most appointments? Do you prioritize telephone calls. Do you prepare agendas for meetings? How you respond to time communicates to others and others' use of time communicates to you. In terms of nonverbal communication, time orientation becomes part of the message we send to and receive from another.

Surroundings

Our surroundings, including colours, layout and design, occupy an important place in nonverbal communication. Every aspect of our surroundings has a symbolic significance in communication. For example; every body is impressed by a tastefully furnished office. It conveys the mood, personality, vision etc. of an organization. Artists and interior decorators believe that different colours project different meanings.

REVIEW QUESTIONS

1. What do you mean by 'kinesics' or body language? Discuss the various types of nonverbal communication.
2. Define communication. Discuss the significance of nonverbal communication.
3. What do you mean by the saying, "the face is the index of the heart"?
4. Write a detailed note on eye contact.
5. How can we make effective use of body language?
6. It is correct to say, 'Silence speaks louder than words." Justify your answer.
7. Discuss the advantages and limitations of body language.
8. Write short notes on:

    a. Gestures
    b. Appearance
    c. Use of space and time in nonverbal communication
    d. Techniques of making nonverbal communication effective
    e. Facial expressions

Presentation Techniques

26

CHAPTER

INTRODUCTION

The ability to plan, organize and present ideas and information effectively is an asset in any profession. Presentation skills are very useful for business, sales, training, public speaking and self-development. The reason, perhaps, is that the purpose of a presentation is more precisely and more correctly defined. Presentation is used mainly when a person wants to deliver a message, an idea or information to an audience (of any size).

There may be many occasions for a presentation, such as launching a new product, starting a training course, presenting a new business plan, making a sales proposal or making a contribution to a conference etc. According to the occasions, presentation format and media and purpose vary a lot-oral, multimedia, powerpoint presentations, short impromptu presentations, long planned presentations; but every successful presentation follows some principles.

Definition: Presentation is a formal face-to-face communication in which there is generally one individual facing a group. It is an audio or visual way of communication with an aim to deliver a message to the audience. Every presentation has to be made to mark an occasion.

In order to make a successful presentation one has to take the following steps:

1. **Preparing for Presentation**

   Preparing for presentation is the key to how successful it will be. It means that the person proposing to make a presentation must structure his presentation from the beginning to the end. He should keep in mind the following points:

   - Why are you presenting and what is the purpose? Is it going to be a presentation for a seminar or a conference or for launching a new product?
   - If possible, the location of the presentation should be visited before the event. Much depends on the size of the room, public address equipment, audiovisual equipment etc.
   - Is there sufficient time for the presentation and discussion thereafter?

- What has been happening till the time the presentation is going to take place?

2. **Audience Analysis**

   An audience is not just a gathering of individuals at one place. It has a collective personality of its own. Analyze your audience and target your presentation to their knowledge and understanding. Besides, we must also see:

   - The size of the audience that is likely to influence how formal or informal the presentation is going to be.
   - The age, sex, educational background, experience, nationality of audience etc. have a great relevance to the presentation.
   - It is also important to know whether one is going to make a presentation before an all male, all female, or a mixed audience.
   - Audience analysis should continue during the presentation. Their body language immediately gives us the feedback as we speak and illustrate. Their facial expressions, smiles, stares, lip movement etc. give us ample idea of their reactions, and guide us through our speech.

3. **Planning the Content**

   The most important step towards making a presentation is to plan it out in writing in detail, showing exactly what you propose to say in the beginning, the middle, and the end.

   - **Beginning**

   a. Introductory remarks.
   b. Statement of the objective, giving reasons for making this presentation.
   c. Draw the main points of the presentation.

   - **Middle**

   a. Go through your points logically and sequentially.
   b. Illustrate the points with examples.
   c. Put a time limit on each of the points. Certain points may need more time than others.
   d. Summarize as you go along.

   - **End**

   a. Give a summary of the whole.
   b. Emphasize the main points made in the beginning or in the middle.
   c. Give a conclusion.
   d. End your presentation with something that the audience will remember. Even if it is something simple like a visual or a closing statement.

- **Questions**

a. Plan for questions and don't be taken by surprise.
b. Ask for them if none are forthcoming.
c. If you don't understand a question, ask for clarification.

4. Types of Presentations

Having planned out the presentation, one has to decide upon the method of presentation. There are three types of presentations, which are generally used.

(i) Reading the paper

In this method the speaker writes out his entire speech and reads it out before the audience. Advantage of this method is that accuracy is best maintained in it. Sometimes the reader sinks into dull monotones, misses punctuation marks and fumbles for words.

(ii) Memorized Presentation

In this method the speaker writes and memorizes the entire speech. But sometimes the speaker may forget some important point, and it spoils the entire effect of the presentation. That is why most speakers memorize key parts and use notes to help them during the presentation.

(iii) Extemporaneous Presentation

Extemporaneous method is the most effective method. In this method the speaker carefully plans his speech and then he speaks as if he is getting the idea on the spur of the moment.

5. Rehearsal of Presentation

Rehearsal is a necessary part of presentation.

- Practice is important so that the speaker can gain self-confidence.
- Repeated rehearsals help the speaker in overcoming nervousness. He can make any changes, if necessary and perfect his performance.
- Only a rehearsal can ensure coordination of efforts. It gives the speaker a clear idea of where, when and how to use visual aids to support his presentation.
- Rehearsal helps in keeping an eye on the time. Time management is important if you have a time limit.

6. Use of Visual Aids

Use of visual aids makes a presentation more effective. In order to make a presentation effective, there is a large range of visual aids in use like charts, chalk boards, film slides, transparencies, diagrams, maps, pictures etc. The presenters can use these devices according to the purpose of the message.

Guiding Principles for the Use of Visual Aids

- Visual aids are used to emphasize the main points of the presentation.
- Whatever the visual aid used in the presentation, make sure that they are visible to the whole audience.
- Visual aids should add to the impact of your presentation. They must be fitted well into the presentation.
- Whatever you use, whether it's OHP, flipchart or computer presentation, keep it simple and clear.
- Proper emphasis must be laid on the visual aid. The speaker must point to it with bodily action and with words.
- The speaker must look at the audience more than at the visual aid.
- Avoid turning your back on the audience when writing on the visual aids. If this isn't possible, be sure that you don't continue speaking when doing so.
- If the speaker is using a software package like Powerpoint, which is specifically designed to produce presentation material, bullet points are most effective.
- Keep the bullet point size large on slides. Use 18-24 point size, with up to 32 point for titles.
- Keep graphs large and simple.
- Use colour to differentiate elements.
- Label graphics, graphs and maps clearly.
- A slide should carry only essential information.

7. **Presenting**

- Be prepared: don't forget pens even if you are using visuals, or anything else that you have prepared for use in your presentation. Keep your visuals in order to save time.
- Speak clearly. If you have a quiet voice, use a microphone. There's little point in being a brilliant speaker if no one can hear you.
- Vary the tone of your voice and the pace you speak at, though better slower than too fast.
- Be careful of the 'ums', 'you knows' etc.
- What people often remember are the mental pictures. If you have suitable anecdotes, do use them.
- Make eye contact with your audience, not the floor, the ceiling or the OHP.
- Use pauses. It gives you time to think and the audience time to reflect.
- Be natural up there.
- There may be information/diagrams/charts on the visual that you don't want the audience to see until later. If so, cover that part with a piece of paper and remove when appropriate. This will stop the audience from reading ahead while you are talking about the current part.

8. Don't forget the audience

Everyone in your audience deserves to feel included. Always make sure that you are including the audience in your speech. Scan the room if and when you can. Be aware that your eyes tell the story as much as your voice. Even if you're far away from the last row of the audience, the people there deserve to feel that you are trying to reach them. Looking their way is one of the ways to achieve that.

9. Body language:

Body language accounts for over 90% of a conversation. Usually when we communicate with or see people, we only respond to what is being said, heard or generally seen. When we don't know someone, we observe their body language to get first impressions of them. Our body language gives others an impression of ourselves or shows our emotions.

- **Posture**

Standing tall and upright as much as possible is the natural alignment of your head and body without the use of tension. Everyone has a different posture. This may be slumping your shoulders forward or hanging your head.

Your posture may show how you will approach a situation. For example, if you stand with your shoulders hanging, arms folded, and leaning on one side, it will look as if you aren't ready for or interested in the task at hand. Should you stand with strong shoulders, head up, arms out by the side and closed fists, you will look as if you are ready for anything, no matter how much the stress involved.

- **Facial Expression**

We use facial expressions to get our points across in the right context. For example, a simple smile can make others feel more at ease while a frown will make you appear as aggressive or unsure of something.

- **Eye Contact**

Of all the ways by which we communicate with people, eye contact is the most powerful.

In his book, "Eye To Eye: How People Interact", Dr. Peter Marsh says, "Honesty and the ability to look someone in the eye are very closely related." When someone talks to you, do they look directly at you or look away? Looking at people and meeting their eyes are the first steps toward striking up friendships and making positive impressions.

In presentation, the best advice is to make short frequent glances. Maintaining eye contact when presenting gives an impression that you are confident and honest. The goal is always to use your eyes in a relaxed way so that you never make others feel uncomfortable. Make eye contact with different people for about 2-3 seconds as if you are talking to them personally. This will keep them all involved.

- **The Space Around You**

Those who stand always look more powerful to those people who are sitting down. This is because they are taking up more space. So if you feel comfortable standing, use it to look as though you have a higher status then those around you.

When you move around, the more space you take up can make others seem influenced by your presence.

If you are sitting, you can still give an image of power. If standing isn't appropriate, use more space by stretching your legs out or by having your arms at the side of the chair.

Finally, everyone gets nervous when doing a presentation, so you're not alone. Don't let this get to you and do whatever you feel necessary to make you more at ease. This, again, can be done by involving the audience.

Practice Questions

Q.1 Write a note on presentation techniques.

Q.2 Why is it necessary to have an idea of the location of the presentation?

Q.3 How will you overcome nervousness if you are asked to make a presentation?

Q.4 Write a detailed note on the use of visual aids in presentation?

Q.5 Write short notes on the following:

a. Factors affecting presentation skills
b. Audience analysis
c. Types of presentations
d. Rehearsal of presentation

Role-Play 27

CHAPTER

WHAT IS ROLE PLAY

Role play is a face-to-face communication in which participants are required to act out the role of an individual in a particular situation or circumstance. As skill in oral communication demands that one should play one's role as a speaker with confidence and competence, likewise, an individual's skill in role-play consists in his ability to get the maximum knowledge in the minimum time with more concentration and understanding.

In this exercise, participants are made to act out real life situations in a protected environment. Their behaviours, speech and feelings during the play form the basis for self-appraisal. They can also learn a gesture, an attitude or a style of presentation from the roles played with professional skill and recorded by some famous dramatists.

DEFINITION OF ROLE PLAY

Larsen-Freeman: Role plays, whether structured or unstructured, are important in the communicative approach because they give learners an opportunity to practice communicating in different social contexts and in different social roles.

Ladousse: Role play uses different communicative techniques and develops fluency in the language, promotes interaction in the classroom and increases motivation.

SIGNIFICANCE OF ROLE PLAY

A role play is a highly flexible learning activity which has a wide scope for variation and imagination. Students have the opportunity to try out new behaviours in a safe environment, which helps them develop long term motivation. In addition to encouraging genuine communication, active involvement, and a positive attitude, the simulated "real life" problems help students develop their critical thinking and problem solving skills.

In fact, role playing is a useful technique for thinking about difficult situations before they occur. This technique allows a person to change his perception by getting him to role play a different person and see how he would approach the problem. Different people use different bits of information and knowledge to approach the same problem and it is extremely helpful to view a task from different angles. Role playing is an excellent exercise for

- Sparking brainstorming sessions
- Helping group problem solving
- Increasing communication skills
- Encouraging participation
- Developing team work and cooperation
- Analyzing problems from different perspectives
- Implementing brainstorming methodology in simulations of real cases
- Experimenting with different solutions to a problem
- Solving problems creatively in groups
- Getting an opportunity for action learning
- Exercising creative techniques in a risk-free environment
- Developing personality of a person by facing challenges

Role playing happens when a group of people act out roles in a particular scenario. The scenario is usually based on a problem that needs a solution, a situation that needs to be examined more closely, or a case or issue that demands a different perspective.

HOW TO USE THE ROLE PLAY TECHNIQUE

Role playing happens when a group of people act out roles in a particular scenario. Normally the only items required for a role play are a script, or an idea and one or more participants. The situations acted out by the participants are usually related to real life situations appropriate to their work place. After the role players have been identified, they act out the parts as they would normally or perhaps try new behaviours shown to them during training.

Role plays are normally followed by group discussion. After the scenario has been played out, the role players, the rest of the group and the trainer carry out a critique of the role play. They identify good or bad points, include suggestions for others' behaviours and suggest other possibilities. And by repeating the scenarios, participants can understand how different approaches might work, so that an ideal approach can be identified.

Types of Situations

Role playing is when a group of people act out roles for a particular scenario. There are several types of situations which can be role played, linked to practical tasks which participants need to perform.

a. One to one

This means situations where the participant has to deal with other person in a conversation, interview or discussion. 'One to one' role plays are best done in small groups.

b. Group role play

In this situation a group of people assume different occupations and then interact with each other in new ways. A whole group of people may also assume the same occupation.

c. Team role play

Team role play is similar, except that two or more teams actively participate. The participants are asked to get into groups of five and choose a leader in each group. All the information is given to the leaders who assign individual roles to each group member.

How it works

There are three stages to a standard role play session:

(1) The set up
(2) The play
(3) The follow up/discussion

(1) Setting Up the Play

In the set up stage, the facilitator sets the stage. This means describing the scenario and assigning roles to participants.

(2) The Play Stage

The second, or play stage of the session is when the trainee participants act out their roles and the play is carried out.

(3) The follow up/discussion

It is important for all the trainee participants to discuss what happened. At the end of role playing, the participants are asked to discuss the role play, their strategies, their solutions, relevance to real world situations, and alternative solutions. This is important for role play based learning as it helps to reinforce the aim and purpose of the activity. Apart from that, participants are asked to jot down their feelings, comments, thoughts and perceptions about their learning experience related to the role play. Such an exercise is useful for self-reflection and self-observation.

Role playing requires students to

- Take on a role (imagine they are someone else)
- Imagine a situation (pretend they are in another time and place)

- Improvise in their choice and language
- Develop an acquaintance with the subject

Some students find their new persona liberating, others find pretending to be embarrassing. It is a good way for them to try out their knowledge and improve fluency in a classroom situation. However, reading a set dialogue is not role play. Many role plays are based on cards or situations described by the trainer.

Problems and solutions

A number of problems arise in organizing role plays in the class. These include:

- Timing, especially not leaving enough time for analysis afterwards
- Overacting and non-real behaviour by participants
- Non-participation by some course members
- Participants get too personally involved, not being able to drop their roles after the session

Some guidelines for solutions to these problems are:

- Provide clear but brief background notes and tasks for the role play.
- Ensure good briefing before the role play, so that everyone understands the situation, and what is expected of them.
- Include information in the background facts to 'hold back' participants from extreme positions
- Setting clear time limits in advance
- Appointing observers with a clear brief to observe, note and report to the class
- The educator should avoid interrupting unless essential. Pass notes if necessary

Thus, role play based on real situations often works best. Role playing is an effective method of increasing awareness, enhancing participant analysis of field situations, and familiarizing participants with the roles, aims, perspectives and positions of people whom they will meet in the field. It encourages innovative thinking and creativity, and behavioural skills in a relatively non threatening setting, and can create the motivation and involvement necessary for learning to occur.

REVIEW EXERCISES

1. What is role play? Explain general rules for role playing.
2. Write a note on the types of situations which can be role played.
3. What is the importance of role play? How can you make a role play activity more effective?
4. What types of problems occur in conducting role play? How can they be solved? Discuss.

5. Write short notes on:
   (a) Three stages to a standard role-play session
   (b) Follow up session
6. Conduct a role play on the following situations:
   - You have just arrived home an hour later than your parents allow. Your father/mother is waiting for you at the door.
   - You are a passenger in a taxi.

Debate

CHAPTER 28

What is a Debate?

A debate is an analytical, logical and factual analysis of the topic with opposite perspectives. Everything has two perceptions to it. A debate is an amalgamation of opposite flow of thoughts to reach a perfect conclusion. A healthy debate facilitates an opportunity to put forward the speaker's perception, his views, his opinions and his facts.

Four types of debate:

1. **Parliamentary Debate:** This is the type of debate that goes on in colleges and universities.
2. **Lincoln-Douglas Debate:** (also called Value Debate) In LD debate two contestants will debate topics centered around moral issues.
3. **Cross Examination Debate**: (also called Policy Debate or Team Debate). In this type of debate two teams (two students each), one representing the affirmative position and one representing the negative position, will debate topics of public or government policy.
4. **Academic Debate:** (also called Creation/Evolution Debate). This type of debate is purely academic in nature.

We shall limit ourselves here to discussing formal contest debating in educational institutions.

Why Debate?

A debate is a verbally oriented test. It is the most commonly organized activity to improve the speaking skill of students. Since students are not so comfortable while speaking on a public forum, they are encouraged to participate in these arguments before an audience. This gives them confidence and effectiveness.

General Rules for Debate

Speakers are given a topic, which is mostly a controversial subject. Some of the speakers speak in favour of the topic; some of them speak against it. When the debate is arranged, the speaking time is divided equally between the teams. All the speakers with their solid arguments and examples in support of their line of thought try to convince the audience. They express their ideas as forcefully as they can to win approbation. Sometimes speech is followed by a questioning period.

Speakers have so many devices to make **the beginning of the speech** gripping. For example, they can begin with an anecdote, a shocking statistical figure, a joke, a challenging question, a mock submission to what they intend to disprove, and so on. They may also begin with a quotation in prose or in poetry. **The main body of the speech** maybe in the form of numbered list of arguments; or it may be an analysis of the subject taking into account both the aspects of it but asserting the superiority of the one favoured by the speaker's viewpoint. **The conclusion of the speech** is as important as the beginning. It must heighten the effect to the right degree. It should be forceful, sweeping the opposite viewpoints away. If the introduction of the speech was a provocation, the conclusion should precipitate all the ideas stirred into a solid outcome. **The style** should be interesting throughout. Contemplate the topic by viewing it from all angles. Nothing should be irrelevant or superfluous because the time is limited. The attention of the audience has to be retained by introducing questions and examples etc.

Tips for Effective Communication in Debate

- Collect as much matter as possible to comprehend the subject.
- Walk to the podium with confidence. Let your face express your self-confidence, concentration, and friendliness.
- Stand erect, but neither like a frozen statue nor making awkward movements; like shifting your weight from one foot to the other too frequently.
- Respect and listen to other debaters. This helps you to invalidate the arguments of your opponent in your speech.
- Presentation is more important than subject-matter. Arrange your ideas in the most persuasive order. Let your speech be neither incomplete nor too long and monotonous.
- Modulate the voice. Let your tone and pitch vary. Use emphasis and pauses.
- Time constraint should be kept in mind.
- Never forget the audience for whom you speak. They must understand what you speak.

Evaluation of Debate

The most universally acceptable criterion of debate judging is the following:

- **The team doing the better debating is the winner**

Conceivably, more than one process might be employed to determine which team does the better debating. Probably the most universally acceptable criterion would be this:

Rule 1. The team doing what the proposition requires is the winner. Debate topics are worded so that one team must succeed and one team must fail in meeting the requirements of the proposition. The successful team, having done the better debating, is declared the winner.

Rule 2. The judge must remain strictly neutral and impartial with regard to the subject matter for debate. He cannot aid one team or the other by injecting his own personal opinions into the decision.

Rule 3. Arguments or evidence which occur to the judge, but which are not employed in the debate, have no place in the decision. However, if the judge happens to possess some significant facts not employed in the debate, he should mention them after his decision, as a suggestion for future use.

Rule 4. The judge has no right to consider an argument weak unless the opposing team shows that it is, or unless the team making the argument fails to support it with adequate evidence or reasoning.

Rule 5. The judge must not accept ideas which are not backed by reasonable proof. Unsupported assertions and purely emotional appeals must not be considered. The use of emotion is legitimate in driving home a point but the point must also be supported by evidence or logic if it is to be considered.

Rule 6. Impartiality applies to the judgement of the debate techniques. The entire decision must be based on what the teams accomplish, not on what the judge personally believes a good debate case on that subject to be.

Violations of Rules

Rules of debate exist to define the procedure and the playing field. They are similar to rules of football. In that violation means a penalty of some sort but not necessarily loss of the game. Of course, in a tight situation the penalty could, in either game, mean the difference between victory and defeat.

REVIEW QUESTIONS

1. What do you mean by debate? Why is this way of communication so popular in today's world?
2. Explain the general rules for debate.
3. Write a note on the different types of debate.
4. What is the importance of debate? How can you make a debate activity more effective?
5. What are the criteria of judgement in a debate?
6. Conduct a debate on the following topics:
    - Should students be allowed to take part in politics?
    - Uses and abuses of mobile phones in a student's life.
    - Should India follow the western civilization or continue to follow its own?
    - Brain drain will affect the development of the society.
    - Reservation poses a threat to national unity and integration.
    - The aim of cinema is entertainment not education.

Unit V

Application of Behavioural Science

- Personality Types
- Decision Making
- Motivation
- Attitude
- Thinking

Personality type

29

CHAPTER

INTRODUCTION

The word "personality" is derived from the Latin word 'persona', meaning 'to speak through'. Originally, it denoted the masks worn by theatrical players in ancient Greek dramas, gradually the term included the actors' role as well. The initial conception of personality was a superficial social image that an individual adopt in playing life roles. Personality has also been viewed as the individual's most striking characteristics which make him unique.

Definitions of Personality

Personality refers to the overall impression that an individual makes on others. It is the sum total of characteristics that are stable and do not change either over a period of time or from situation to situation.

George Kelly: "Personality is the individual's unique way of making sense out of life experiences."

Floyd L. Ruch: "Personality can be described as how a person affects others, how he understands and views himself, and his pattern of inner and outer measurable traits."

Gordon Allport: Personality is "an internal something that guides and directs all human activities."

Characteristics of personality

1. Personality is an abstraction based on inferences derived from behavioural observation.
2. It is only though the study of personality that the special properties that distinguish one person from another can be made clear.
3. Personality includes genetic and biological tendencies, social experience and changing environmental circumstances.

Factors affecting personality

Personality refers to the process of change in relation to psychological growth and development of a person. It is important to know the factors which provide change or development of a personality.

There are two broad categories of characters which influence the formation and development of personality. These are:

- Biological factors
- Environmental factors

Factors affecting personality

Biological factors	*Environmental factors*
• Heredity • Brain • Physical Features	• Culture • Family • Social • Situational

1. **Biological factors**

   Every individual gets his physical appearance, sex, temperament and mental characters from his parents.

   a. **Heredity:** Genes and hormones determine physique and our physique shapes our personality. (Physique: eye colour, hair colour, skin colour, height, attractiveness, and nervous system etc.)

   b. **Brain:** An individual's personality develops on the structure of the brain.

   c. **Physical Features:** The external features of a person represent his personality but in a narrow sense. External features influence others to some extent.

   Our personality is formed on the basis of how others react to our appearance and intelligence. For example; a short person who is usually laughed at develops a defence mechanism which is reflected in his personality. Similarly, intelligence or lack of it creates a certain impression on other people. Also certain body functions affect the behaviour tendencies. For example, underactive thyroid gland makes a person tired, sluggish and unable to concentrate.

2. **Environmental factors**

   Environment factors include the culture in which a person is brought up, the norms among our family, friends, and social groups and other influences that we experience.

   a. **Culture:** Culture is the sum total of learned behaviour traits which are manifested and shared by the members of the society. It is a unique system of perceptions, beliefs, values, norms, patterns of behaviour of individuals in a society.

Culture establishes the norms, attitudes and values that are passed along from one generation to the next. Individuals born into a particular culture are exposed to the existing values, beliefs and norms of that culture concerning an acceptable form of behaviour. A person and his culture are so interwoven with each other that it is difficult to distinguish the individual from his cultural context.

However, individuals within the same culture can differ in their behaviour and personality formats. This is due to the existence of subcultures within the culture.

b. **Family:** In family an individual identifies himself with some member of his family like the father or mother. The identification can be viewed through the similarity of behaviour, desire or motives. It starts from the mother-child relation and later on envelops other family members too.

c. **Social:** In social groups a person acquires the wide range of behavioural patterns which are customary to the social group he belongs to. Friends, peers at work, associates, groups to which an individual belongs, all influence a person's behaviour. Norms and laws of the society in which the individual exists also have a great affect in the development of a person's personality.

   Socioeconomic level of the family, family size, birth order, race, religion, parents' educational level, geographic location etc. play an important role in personality development. For example;

- A person brought up in a poor family and a person brought up in a rich family.
- Only child of the family and a child with four brothers and sisters.
- First-born child is more responsible and rational.

d. **Situation:** A person acts differently in different situations. Events and experiences that a person goes through determine a person's personality. If the situation is favourable he will behave in a different manner than in unfavourable situations.

All these factors are interrelated and interdependent. According to **Ron Indlow and Fergus Panton**, "Personality is determined by both the influences of one's inherited genes and his social and physical environment and experience."

Types of theories of Personality

1. **Sigmund Freud's Psychoanalytic theory of personality**

   According to Freud, the mind has two portions:

   I. **Conscious mind**: a small portion giving conscious experience.

II. **Subconscious mind:** larger portion having impulses, passions and primitive instincts which affect our behaviour.

He divided personality into three parts: Id(require pleasure in imagination), Ego(wants reality) and Super ego(goes for perfection).

- **Id:** The id consists of everything psychological that is inherent and present at the time of birth. Id represents a storehouse of instincts-all wishes and desires-that subconsciously direct and determine our behaviour. Id is largely childish, irrational, never satisfied, demanding and destructive to others. But id is the foundation upon which all other parts of personality are erected.
- **Ego:** The ego represents the rational component of personality and is governed by the reality principle. Ego is rational. It keeps a psychological balance between id's impulsive demand and superego's restrictive guidance.
- **Super Ego:** The super ego represents the moral branch of personality. As a child grows and absorbs parental and cultural attitudes and values, he develops a super ego. The primary concern of super ego is to determine whether the action proposed by 'ego' is right or wrong, so that the individual acts in accordance with the values and standards of the society.

Freud believed that all the three produce integrated behaviour. Conflict between the Id impulses are controlled by Ego and Super Ego which form the motivating source of personality.

2. Type theory

a. **Sheldon's physiognomy Theory:** William Sheldon identifies some relationship between the physique types of individuals and their personality temperaments. He identifies three body types:

- **Endomorph:** He is a short fat man. The person is social, relaxed and good tempered. He seeks comfort, loves fine food, eats too much, is jovial, affectionate and liked by all persons.
- **Mesomorph:** He is basically strong, athletic and tough. He is fond of muscular activity; he tends to be hard hearted, highly aggressive and self-assertive.
- **Ectomorph:** He is tall, thin and poorly developed physically. Though physically weak, he is brilliant. He is absent-minded, shy and likes loneliness.

b. **Carl Jung's Extrovert-Introvert Theory**

According to Carl Jung, personality is divided into two categories-extrovert and introvert.

- **Extrovert** is optimistic, outgoing, gregarious, and sociable. He is basically objective, a reality-oriented individual who is much more a doer than a thinker. He expresses his ideas openly and takes interest in other people and events.

  An extrovert is competent for the interaction work like sales, publicity and personal development.

- **Introvert** is shy and inward-directed. He is less sociable and avoids social contacts. He is withdrawn and absorbed in his inner life. He will be guided by his own ideas and philosophy. He is rigid and less flexible and subjective.

  An introvert is competent for the work which requires thought and analytical skill.

c. **Type 'A' and type 'B' personalities:** most of the people lie between the above two extremes and can be evaluated by Type 'A' or type 'B' personalities.

  - **Type 'A' Personality:** Hard working, impatient, aggressive, competitive, and highly achievement oriented. They are productive and workaholics.
  - **Type 'B' Personality:** Easy going, social, not time bound, not competitive. They are better with work involving judgement and accuracy.

3. **Trait theory:** A personality trait can be defined as "an enduring attribute of a person that appears constantly in a variety of situations." According to trait theory:

   - Traits distinguish one personality from another.
   - Individuals can be described in terms of construction of traits such as affiliation, achievement, anxiety, aggression and dependency.
   - The differences in personality between two individuals are assumed to be the result of differences in the traits that each person has.

4. **Social learning theory:** Social learning theory is based on the sum total of all (knowledge, attitudes, values, skills, personality traits etc.) that a person has learned. According to it:

   - Personality development is more a result of social variables than biological drives.
   - Motives can be traced to know conscious needs and wants rather than unconscious desires.
   - There are two methods of learning; direct experience and observing others.

REVIEW QUESTIONS

1. Define personality. What are its major determinants?
2. Describe the various theories of personality.
3. Describe the various factors which affect personality development of an individual.
4. Name the important personality types.
5. Describe the Freudian stages of personality development.
6. Write short note on:
   (1) Personality traits
   (2) Personality types
   (3) Social learning theory

Decision Making

30

CHAPTER

DEFINITION AND ELEMENTS OF DECISION MAKING

We use our decision making skills to solve problems by selecting one course of action from several possible alternatives. According to R. A. Killian, "a decision in its simplest form is a selection of an alternative."

Definition

"Decision making is a conscious and human process which involves both individual and social phenomenon based upon factual and value premises. It concludes with a choice of one behavioural activity from among one or more alternatives with the intention of moving towards some desired state of affairs."

Elements

- A decision represents an action chosen from a number of possible alternatives.
- It is a human process which is taken by a conscious mind which involves knowledge, desire, feeling and temperament.
- Decision is taken regarding rules, policies and changes etc.
- The decision can affect both long and short term plans.
- It is always result-oriented.
- It is complex and variable.
- **Three aspects of human behaviour** are involved in decision making:
  a. **Cognition –** Activities of the mind associated with knowledge.
  b. **Conation –** The action of the mind implied by such words as willingness, desire, and aversion.
  c. **Affectation –**The aspect of mind associated with emotion, feeling, mood and temperament.

KINDS OF DECISIONS

Decisions fall into two categories:

1. Strategic decisions
2. Tactical decisions

1. Strategic decisions

- Strategic decision is a major choice of actions having long-term effect.
- It affects major action plan in an organization.
- It is generally taken when the problem is complex.
- It directly contributes in achieving the organizational objectives.
- It is only taken by high level managers.

2. Tactical decisions

- Tactical decision relates to day-to-day working of an organization.
- It is made in the context of well-set policies and procedures.
- It has only short-term effect.
- The decision is mostly repetitive, for example, purchase of raw materials, assigning duties to employees, etc.
- It is mostly taken by lower level managers.

DECISION MAKING PROCESS

Decision making process is a dynamic concept rather them static. Every decision, therefore, is the outcome of a dynamic process which is influenced by multiple forces.

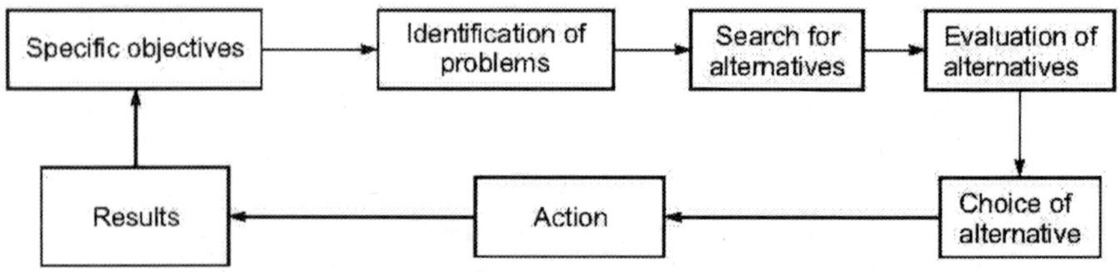

Fig. Decision making process.

1. **Specific objective:** Every action of human being is goal directed. This is true for decision making also which is an action. The starting point in any analysis of decision making involves the determination of whether a decision needs to be made. Objective setting provides a framework for the decision and provides clue in identifying the problem and its possible solution.
2. **Problem Identification:** Decision making occurs as a reaction to problem. Identification of problem is the real beginning of decision making process. **A problem is the gap between present and desired state of**

affairs on the subject matter of decision. It is just like the diagnosis of patient by the doctor. When a doctor makes a diagnosis he has a fairly clear concept of what a healthy person is. However, one person's problem is another person's satisfactory state of affairs; therefore a problem cannot be labelled as a problem (like a disease.)

A problem can be identified by its diagnosis and analysis.

- **Diagnosis**: Diagnosing the real problem implies knowing the gap between what is and what ought to be.
- **Analysis**: Diagnosis of the problem gives the understanding of what should be done in terms of decision making. The analysis of the problem requires finding out who would make decision, what information would be needed, and from whom the information is available.

3. **Search for alternatives:** A problem can be solved in several ways, therefore, the decision maker must try to find out the various alternatives available in order to get the most satisfactory result of decision.

   A decision maker can use several sources for identifying alternatives; his own past experience, practices followed by others and using creative techniques (new ideas).
4. **Evaluation of Alternatives:** After evaluating all the alternatives available, the decision maker selects the one that will meet the choice criteria.
5. **Choice of alternative:** The evaluation of various alternatives presents a clear picture as to how each one of them contributes to the objectives under question. A comparison is made among the various alternatives and the best one is chosen. In choosing an alternative, the decision maker can go thorough three approaches; experience, experimentation, and research and analysis.
   - (i) **Experience:** Past experiences are helpful if the decision maker has solved similar problem earlier.
   - (ii) **Experimentation:** It is generally used in scientific inquiry.
   - (iii) **Research and Analysis:** Used when major decisions are involved.
6. **Action:** Once the alternative is selected, it is put into action. The decision should be implemented at appropriate time and in proper way to make the action more effective.
7. **Results:** When the decision is put into action it brings certain results. Results provide indications whether decision making and its implementation is proper. The feedback may also help in reviewing the decision. The decisions should be modified according to the changes in the circumstances.

EFFECTIVE DECISION

The decision making process goes through the various stages and the basic objectives of all these stages are to solve problem through the decision. The solution of the problem depends on how effectively the decision is made and implemented. Thus, an affective decision is one which is action – oriented, goal-directed, and provides efficiency in implementation.

1. **Action-Oriented:** Decisions are action-oriented and are directed towards relevant and controllable aspects of the environment. Decisions are totally pragmatic in nature and their value is dependent on the success of the actions that follow. (**Pragmatic**: solving problem in a practical way).
2. **Goal-Directed:** Organizations are goal-directed units and, therefore, decision-making should be goal directed to enable the organization to meet its objectives.
3. **Efficiency in implementation:** Decision making should take into account all the possible factors; not only in terms of external context but also in internal context so that a decision can be implemented properly.

STEPS TO EFFECTIVE DECISION MAKING SKILLS

Any decision can be made effective if decision making process is followed properly. The attempt should be to make a realistic decision rather than attempt at an ideal decision.

(1) **Categorical Interpretation:** Problem should be defined properly. The criteria and alternatives can be ranked and weighed to reflect their importance.

(2) **Application of limiting factor:** The decision maker should be aware of all the possible consequences of each alternative.

(3) **Adequate Information:** (Problem clarity) It is very important to have accurate and adequate information about the situation for decision making, otherwise the quality of the decision will suffer.

(4) **Considering others' views:** While making decision, others' views should also be considered adequately.

(5) **No time or cost constraints:** For getting full information.

(6) **Maximum pay off:** The national decision maker will choose the alternative that gives the highest perceived value.

IMPROVING CREATIVITY IN DECISION MAKING

Creativity and critical thinking is essential for making effective and unique decisions. Creativity is the ability to combine ideas in a unique way or to make unusual associations between ideas. Creativity allows the decision maker to fully understand the problem, including seeing problems that others can't see. Creativity also helps the decision maker identify all viable alternatives. Creative thinking is important to bring about normal and unique ideas. Critical thinking is necessary to criticize and test these ideas so that they are feasible and beneficial.

Creativity needs freedom from constraints and especially from time pressures. Creative people are motivated and they do their best within free and supportive environments.

Five factors that block an employee's creativity

1. Expected evaluation: How the work is going to be evaluated.
2. Surveillance: Being watched while one is working.
3. External motivators: Emphasizing external rewards.
4. Competition: Facing a win-lose situation with other people.
5. Constrained choice: Being given limits on how one can do one's work.

Suggestions for stimulating creativity

1. Experiencing and improving skills through special training, education or talent development.
2. Using creative relevant thinking skills such as brain storming, or metaphor techniques.
3. Motivation indicating an inner drive or impulse to meet the challenge.

THREE ETHICAL DECISION CRITERIA

1. **Utilitarianism:** Decisions are made so as to provide the greatest goal for the greatest number. Utilitarianism dominates through decision making. Utilitarianism promotes efficiency and productivity.
2. **Rights:** Rights in decision making means respecting and protecting the basic rights for individuals.
3. **Justice:** Fair and impartial.

GROUP DECISION MAKING

Group decision making is the most important activity of an organization.

Advantages of group decision making:

1. A group is equipped with more complete information. An individual cannot have the same volume of information and knowledge.
2. Group decision making has the advantage of diversity of views. An individual will look at any issue from his own point of view.
3. It has new creative ideas and solutions to problem.
4. It increases the acceptability of a solution.
5. It is democratic in character.
6. It has the advantage of expert opinion given by some well informed member.
7. It will look after everybody's interest.
8. It strengthens employer-employee relationship.

Disadvantages of group decision making:

1. Group decisions are time consuming.
2. In group decisions, it is difficult to fix responsibility.
3. Group decisions are often dominated by a handful of members.
4. In group decisions, irrelevant discussions defeat the purpose of the group.

DISTINCTION BETWEEN INDIVIDUAL AND GROUP DECISIONS

Decisions are made either individually or by a group. Mostly it is a combination of both.

Individual decision	Group decision
1. Less time is required	Time consuming process.
2. The quality decision is not always taken.	Usually quality decision is taken.
3. It is a competitive decision.	It is a supportive decision.
4. It has no value when it comes under government policy.	It is valued when it is taken by the management itself.
5. The decision is taken by the individual, hence no problem.	The decision is taken by a group which is hindered due to different opinions.

SOME COMMON ERRORS IN DECISION MAKING

The quality of the decision can make the difference between success and failure. Not all decisions are made fast and correct. There are some common errors that should be avoided in making decision:

1. **Indecisiveness:** Decision making is a very heavy responsibility. The fear of its outcome makes some people timid about making a decision. They take a long time in making a decision and this may result in the loss of a good opportunity. The persons must be confident as well as quick in deciding.
2. **Postponing the decision until the last moment:** This drawback results in decision making under pressure of time and gives poor quality of decisions.
3. **Failure to isolate the root cause of the problem**: The success of the decision depends upon the correct definition of the problem. It is a common practice to cure the symptoms, rather than the causes. It is necessary to separate the symptoms from the causes.
4. **Failure to assess the reliability of informational sources:** Very often we take it for granted that the other person's opinion is very reliable and trustworthy and we do not check for the accuracy of such information for ourselves. It is decision maker's moral duty to analytically judge the accuracy and reliability of the information that is provided to him.

5. **The method for analyzing the information may not be effective:** Since most decisions have to be based upon a lot of information, many factors must be dependable. Therefore, a model must be built which incorporates and handles many variables in order to help the decision maker. Also, it is necessary to define the objectives and criteria as early in the decision making as possible. It is necessary to be bold in implementing the decision and following it through.

REVIEW QUESTIONS

1. What do you understand by decision making? Describe the basic elements of decision making.
2. Discuss various steps in decision making.
3. Discuss decision making process briefly.
4. Discuss the kinds of decisions in an organization.
5. Describe the essential characteristics of a good decision. How a decision can be made effective?
6. What are the factors that influence decision making?
7. Distinguish between individual and group decisions?
8. Write short notes on:
   - **a.** Common errors in decision making
   - **b.** Group decision making
   - **c.** Improving creativity in decision making
   - **d.** Styles of decision making

Motivation

31 CHAPTER

WHAT IS MOTIVATION

Some "why" questions: Why do you go to class every day? Why do students study for hours to pass examinations? Why do professors teach students, and why do they test students? Why did you pick out those shoes or those pants to wear today? Each of these questions has an answer...there is some **motive** for engaging in those behaviours. Nearly all the conscious behaviour of human beings is motivated. The internal needs and drives lead to tensions, which in turn result into actions. The need for food results in hunger and hence a person is motivated to eat.

This motivating mechanism can be called many things—a habit, a belief, a desire, an instinct, a need, an interest, a compulsion, or a drive. No matter what its label, it is to inspire people to work, individually or in groups in ways such as to produce best results. Indeed, the motivation comes from the verb "to move." It is the will to act. It is the willingness to exert high levels of effort towards organizational goals, conditioned by the efforts and ability to satisfy some individual need.

We may define a **motive (or motivation) as a need, want, interest, or desire that drives someone (or an organism) in a certain direction.**

Psychologically we may define the field of motivation as the study of **goal-directed behaviour.** People differ by nature, not only in their ability to perform a specific task but also in their will to do so. **Stronger 'will' reflects stronger motivation to achieve a goal.** People with less ability but stronger will are able to perform better than people with superior ability and lack of will. **This 'will' to do is known as motivation.**

DEFINITIONS OF MOTIVATION

William G. Scott: Motivation means a process of stimulating people to action to accomplish desired goals.

Mac Farland: Motivation refers to the way in which urges, drives, desires, aspirations, strivings, needs, etc. explain the behaviour of human beings.

Viteles: Motivation represents a dissatisfied need which creates a state of tension or disequilibrium causing the individual to move in a goal directed pattern towards restoring a state of equilibrium by satisfying the need.

MOTIVATION PROCESS

The basic motivation process can be depicted as follows:

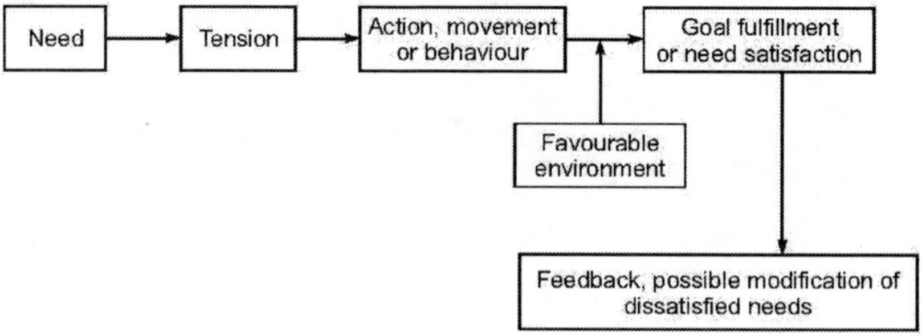

Fig.

The needs and desires affect or change a person's behaviour which becomes goal-oriented. Thus, need is the base for motivation which is a kind of mental feeling in an individual that he needs 'something'. This 'lack of something' creates tension in the mind of the individual. Motivated person tries to overcome this tension by engaging himself in a behaviour or activity through which he satisfies his needs. Satisfaction of one need leads to feeling of another need. The greater the tension, the more activity will be needed to bring about relief and hence higher the motivation.

If the need is not satisfied because of some reasons, the person may feel **frustration,** which can be defined as the accumulation of tension due to non-fulfillment of needs.

CHARACTERISTICS/NATURE OF MOTIVATION

Following are the characteristics of motivation:

1. **Urges or Desires:** Motivation requires some urges or desires which can be fundamental or for ego-satisfaction.
2. **Effort:** The amount of effort put into the activity identifies the strength of the person's work related behaviour. Hard work usually reflects high motivation.
3. **A continuous process:** Motivation is a permanent part of a human being. Motivation is continuously goal-directed. Once a goal is achieved, a higher goal is selected and efforts are exercised towards this higher goal.
4. **Internal feeling**: As needs are feelings in the mind of a person that he lacks certain things, motivation is also an internal feeling. It is a psychological phenomenon which generates within an individual.

5. **Time management:** All possible efforts have to be made to achieve a target within a framework of time.
6. **Direction:** All business is goal-oriented. Direction determines the quality of the anticipated output.
7. **Totality:** Person in totality, not in part, is motivated.
8. **Effectiveness:** Motivation increases the efficiency and effectiveness of the individual or organization.

TYPES OF MOTIVATION

(1) Achievement Motivation

It is the drive to pursue and attain goals. An individual with achievement motivation wishes to achieve objectives and advance up on the ladder of success. Here, accomplishment is important for its own shake and not for the rewards that accompany it. It is similar to 'Kaizen' approach of Japanese Management.

(2) Affiliation Motivation

It is a drive to relate to people on a social basis. Persons with affiliation motivation perform work better when they are complimented for their favourable attitudes and cooperation.

(3) Competence Motivation

It is the drive to be good at something, allowing the individual to perform high quality work. Competence motivated people seek job mastery, take pride in developing and using their problem solving skills and strive to be creative when confronted with obstacles. They learn from their experience.

(4) Power Motivation

It is the drive to influence people and change situations. Power motivated people wish to create an impact on their organization and are willing to take risks to do so.

(5) Attitude Motivation

Attitude motivation is how people think and feel. It is their self-confidence, their belief in themselves, their attitude to life. It is how they feel about the future and how they react to the past.

(6) Incentive Motivation

It is where a person or a team reaps a reward from an activity. It is "You do this and you get that", attitude. It is the types of awards and prizes that drive people to work a little harder.

(7) Fear Motivation

Fear motivation coerces a person to act against will. It is instantaneous and gets the job done quickly. It is helpful in the short run.

DIFFERENCE BETWEEN MOTIVATION, SATISFACTION, INSPIRATION AND MANIPULATION

MOTIVATION refers to the drive and efforts to satisfy a want or goal, whereas SATISFACTION refers to the contentment experienced when a want is satisfied. In contrast, INSPIRATION is bringing about a change in the thinking pattern. On the other hand, MANIPULATION is getting the things done from others in a predetermined manner.

THEORIES OF MOTIVATION

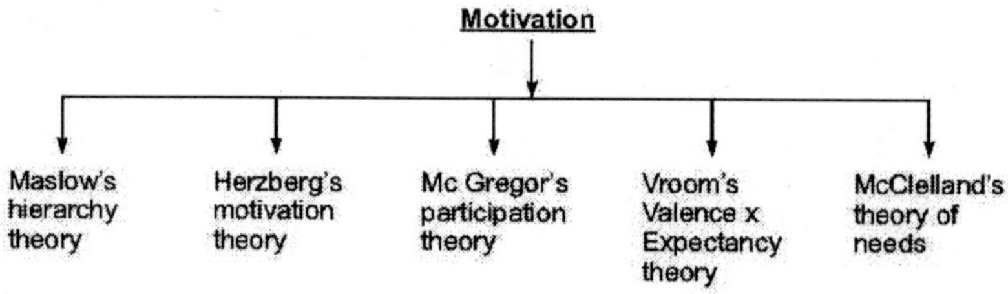

Fig.

1. Maslow's hierarchy of needs: (Theory of human motivation)

One of the most widely mentioned theories of motivation is the hierarchy of needs theory put forth by psychologist Abraham Maslow. Maslow saw human needs in the form of a hierarchy, ascending from the lowest to the highest, and he concluded that when one set of needs is satisfied, this kind of need ceases to be a motivator.

We may define the Need Hierarchy as - **a systematic arrangement of needs according to priority, which assumes that basic needs must be met before less basic needs are aroused.**

As per his theory these needs are:

(1) Physiological needs- These are the most basic and important needs for sustaining the human life. Food, water, warmth, shelter, sleep, medicine and education are the basic physiological needs which fall in the primary list of need satisfaction. Maslow was of an opinion that until these needs were satisfied to a degree to maintain life, no other motivating factors can work.

(2) Safety and Security needs - These needs refer more to the long term survival than day-to-day needs. These are the needs to be free of the fear of losing a job, property, food or shelter. It also includes protection against any emotional harm.

(3) Social needs (Belongingness and Love): Since people are social beings, they need to belong and be accepted by others. After obtaining a safe environment to live and establishing some long term plans, people try to satisfy their need for affection, acceptance and friendship from family members, friends, and lovers.

(4) **Esteem needs-** Once people begin to satisfy their need to belong, they become concerned with esteem, both by themselves and by others. This kind of need produces such satisfaction as power, prestige, status and self-confidence. It includes both internal esteem factors like self-respect, autonomy and achievements and external esteem factors such as states, recognition and attention.

(5) **Cognitive needs -** Needs at this level are based on acquiring knowledge and understanding of the world, people, behaviour, etc. (If you are in college to learn (not simply to get a degree) then you are attempting to fulfill your cognitive needs.)

(6) **Aesthetic needs -** Aesthetic needs include beauty and order in life.

(7) **Self-Actualization -** Maslow regards this as the highest need in his hierarchy. In fact, according to Maslow, very few people actually reach this level. Self-actualization is the need to fulfill one's own potential. It is the drive to become what one is capable of becoming, it includes growth, achieving one's potential and self-fulfillment. It is to maximize one's potential and to accomplish something.

Thus, people's work performance depends upon their ability to do their assigned work as well as the 'will' to do so.

Because Maslow believed that all needs vary in strength, he arranged them in a pyramidal form to indicate which have more strength. The most basic needs (like shelter and food) are vital to daily survival, and are at the bottom, while needs that are less important to staying alive are higher on the pyramid.

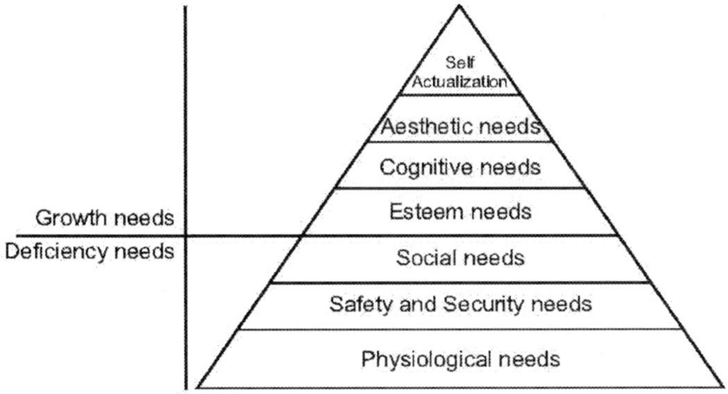

Maslow's Pyramidical from of needs

Fig.

Needs have a certain priority. As the more basic needs are satisfied, an individual seeks to satisfy the higher needs. If his basic needs are not met, efforts to satisfy the higher needs should be postponed.

2. Frederick Herzberg's motivation-hygiene theory

Frederick Herzberg developed a theory based on this observation, naming it the 'Hygiene Theory'. His theory is also known as two-factor theory or hygiene theory. He stated that there are certain satisfiers and dissatisfiers for employees at work. **Intrinsic factors** are related to job satisfaction, while **extrinsic factors** are associated with dissatisfaction. He devised his theory on the question, "What do people want from their jobs?" He asked people to describe in detail, such situations when they felt exceptionally good or exceptionally bad. From the responses that he received, he concluded that opposite of satisfaction is not dissatisfaction. Removing dissatisfying characteristics from a job does not necessarily make the job satisfying. He states that the presence of certain factors in the organization is natural and the presence of the same does not lead to motivation. However, their non-presence leads to demotivation. In a similar manner there are certain factors, the absence of which causes no dissatisfaction, but their presence has a motivational impact.

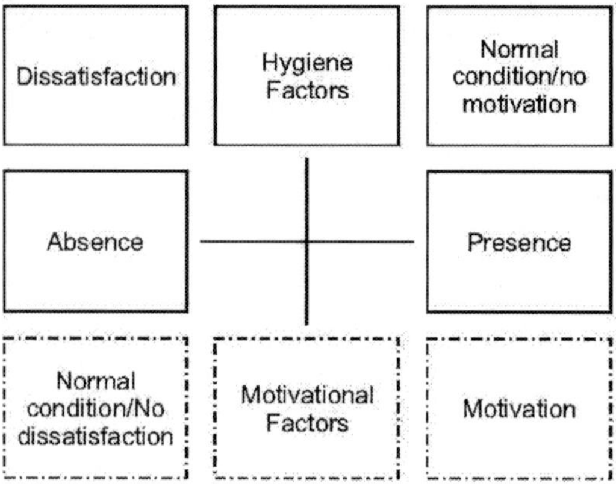

Fig.

Extrinsic Motivation: This type of motivation includes those external factors which are financial in nature. It is based on the assumption that the behaviour which results in positive rewards tends to be repeated. It includes company policy, higher pay, retirement plans, working conditions, peer relationship, security, profit sharing scheme, paid vacation, health and medical insurance etc.

Examples of Hygiene factors are :

Security, status, relationship with subordinates, personal life, salary, work conditions, relationship with supervisor and company policy and administration.

- **Intrinsic Motivation:** This type of motivation includes those factors which are related to feelings of achievement and accomplishment of the individual. These factors are known as **job motivation factors**.

Examples of Motivational factors are :

Growth prospects, job advancement, responsibility, challenges, recognition and achievements.

3. Mc Gregor's Participation Theory: (Theory X and Theory Y)

McGregor, in his book "The Human side of Enterprise" states that people inside the organization can be managed in two ways. The first is basically negative, which falls under the category X and the other is basically positive, which falls under the category Y. After viewing the way in which the manager dealt with employees, McGregor concluded that a manager's view of the nature of human beings is based on a certain grouping of assumptions and that he or she tends to mould his or her behaviour towards subordinates according to these assumptions.

Theory X (negative theory):

Under the assumptions of theory X :

- People inherently dislike and whenever possible, will attempt to avoid work.
- Because people dislike work, they have to be forced, persuaded or threatened with punishment to achieve goals.
- They must be ordered or controlled to do work to achieve objectives.
- They prefer to be directed.
- They are lazy and avoid responsibility.
- They have lack self-motivation and ambition.
- They are self-centered.
- They are indifferent to organizational needs.
- By nature they dislike any change.

Negative Motivation: This motivation is based upon the use of force, power, fear and threat. The fear of punishment or unfavourable consequences affects the behavioural changes. Examples are fear of failure in the examination, job insecurity.

Theory Y (positive theory):

Under the assumptions of theory Y :

- People have great potential for work.
- Physical and mental effort at work is as natural as rest and play.
- They view work as being as natural as play and rest.
- They will exercise self-direction and control towards achieving objectives they are committed to.
- They learn to accept and seek responsibility.
- They want rewards, recognition and appreciation.
- They try to become leaders rather than being lead.
- No thrashing of any kind is required.

Positive Motivation: Positive motivation involves proper recognition of employee's efforts and appreciation of employee's contribution towards the organizational goal achievement. Such motivations improve the standards of performance, lead to good team spirit and pride, a sense of co-operation and a feeling of belongingness and happiness.

4. Vroom's Valence x Expectancy theory

The most widely accepted explanation of motivation has been propounded by Victor Vroom. His theory is commonly known as expectancy theory. The theory argues that the strength of a tendency to act in a specific way depends on the strength of an expectation that the act will be followed by a given outcome and on the attractiveness of that outcome to the individual. To make this simple, expectancy theory says that an employee can be motivated to perform better when there is a belief that the better performance will lead to good performance appraisal and that this shall result into realization of personal goal in form of some reward. Therefore, an employee is :

Motivation = Valence x Expectancy.

The theory focuses on three things :

- Efforts and performance relationship
- Performance and reward relationship
- Rewards and personal goal relationship

This leads us to a conclusion that :

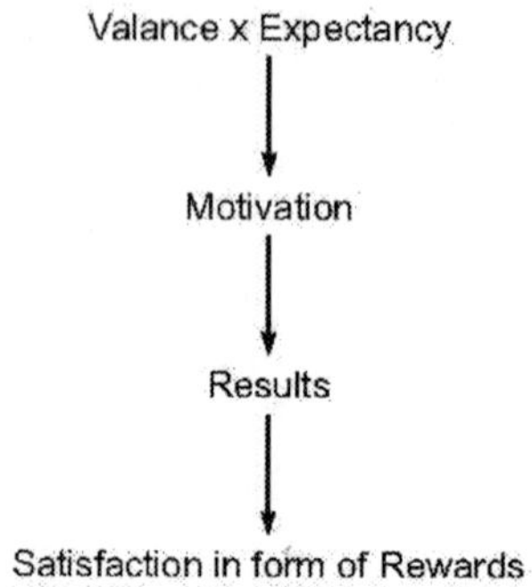

Fig.

5. McClelland's Theory of Needs

David McClelland has developed a theory on three types of motivating needs:

1. Need for Power
2. Need for Affiliation
3. Need for Achievement

Basically, people with high need for power are inclined towards influence and control. They like to be at the centre and are good orators. They are demanding in nature, forceful in manners and ambitious in life. They can be motivated to perform if they are given key positions or power positions.

In the second category are the people who are social in nature. They try to affiliate themselves with individuals and groups. They are driven by love and faith. They like to build a friendly environment around themselves. Social recognition and affiliation with others provides them motivation.

People in the third area are driven by the challenge of success and the fear of failure. Their need for achievement is moderate and they set for themselves moderately difficult tasks. They are analytical in nature and take calculated risks. Such people are motivated to perform when they see at least some chances of success.

McClelland observed that with the advancement in hierarchy the need for power and achievement increased rather than affiliation. He also observed that people who were at the top later ceased to be motivated by this drive.

IMPORTANCE OF MOTIVATION: Motivation is one of the most important factors determining organizational efficiency. Thus, motivation is important as:

1. Motivation generates will to do the work.
2. Motivated employees put higher performance (80-90%) as compared to other employees (20-30 %)
3. Motivated people stay in the organization and their absenteeism is quite low.
4. All organizational facilities will go waste in the lack of motivated people to utilize these facilities effectively.
5. Organizations are created in the society. Because of the changes in the society, changes in technology, value system etc., organization has to incorporate those changes. Motivated people accept, introduce & implement those changes.

According to **Collins Cobuild Dictionary**, "If you are motivated to do something, you are caused to feel determined to achieve something and willing to work in order to succeed."

The performance level of human beings is determined by two factors: level of ability to do a certain work and level of motivation. These two factors are multiplied not added. These can be summarized as follows;

Performance = ability X motivation

REVIEW QUESTIONS

1. Define motivation. Discuss its importance.
2. Discuss the process of motivation.
3. Describe Maslow's need hierarchy theory of motivation.
4. What do you understand by positive and negative motivation?
5. Write a note on the types of motivation.
6. Write short notes on:
   a. Importance of motivation
   b. Achievement motivation
   c. Characteristics of motivation
   d. Difference between extrinsic and intrinsic motivation
   e. McClelland's Theory of Needs

Attitude 32

CHAPTER

WHAT IS ATTITUDE

Human behaviour is a complex phenomenon. It is a system, by which a human being senses external events and influences, interprets them, responds to them in an appropriate manner and learns from the result of these responses. People's attitudes and values have significant impact on their behaviour, both within the organizational context and other social context.

- Attitudes are simply expressions of how much we like or dislike various things.
- Attitudes express our evaluations or judgements concerning objects, people or events. The statements may be favourable or unfavourable.
- Our attitudes are based on information. They reflect how one feels, thinks, perceives and acts about something.
- As we constantly acquire new information, our attitudes are always open to revision. For example, if we say 'we like this job', we are expressing our attitude about work.

DEFINITIONS OF ATTITUDE

Munn: Attitudes are learned predispositions towards aspects of our environment. They being positively or negatively directed towards certain people, services or institutions.

Reitz: Attitude is the persistent tendency to feel and behave in a favourable or unfavourable way towards some object, person or ideas.

Schermerhorm: Attitude is a predisposition to respond in a positive or negative way to someone or something in one's environment.

M. L. Blum and T. S. Naylor: By attitude we mean the beliefs, feelings and action tendencies of an individual or group of individuals towards objects, ideas and people. Quite often people and objects or ideas become associated in the minds of individuals and as a result attitudes become multidimensional and complex.

CHARACTERISTICS OF ATTITUDE

1. Attitudes affect the behaviour of an individual. They are expressed by terms such as liking-disliking, pro-anti, favouring-not favouring, and positive-negative.
2. Attitudes are acquired through learning over a period of time. The process of learning starts right from childhood and continues throughout the life of a person.
3. Attitudes are invisible as they constitute a psychological phenomenon which cannot be observed by the behaviour of an individual.
4. Attitudes are pervasive. Every individual has some kind of attitude towards the objects in his environment.

THREE COMPONENTS OF ATTITUDE

Attitudes have three basic elements:

1. **Cognitive components:** The thought, opinion or belief segment of an attitude. For example, "The belief that discrimination is wrong", is a value statement. It is a cognitive component.
2. **Affective component:** The emotional or feeling segment of an attitude. It is reflected in the statement, "I don't like John."
3. **Behavioural component:** An intention to behave in a certain way towards someone or something.

By measuring and integrating these three elements, a person's attitude towards a given situation can be established. However, expressions one makes publicly to others are not always the same as the expressions one makes privately to oneself.

SOURCES OF ATTITUDES

The formation of attitude can be classified into two main sources:

1. Direct experience
2. Social process

1. Direct experience

- Attitude formation takes place with the direct experience of an object or person.
- Attitudes are based on one's previous experience.
- Attitudes, formed on direct experience, are stronger and are not easy to change.
- These are present in our cognitive process.

2. Social process

- The attitudes are learned.

- Generally individuals learn things from the environment in which they interact.
- Attitudes, like values, are acquired from parents, teachers and friends. In our early years, we begin modeling our attitudes after those we admire or respect. We observe the way family and friends behave, and we shape our attitudes and behaviour to align with theirs.
- People imitate the attitudes of popular persons or those persons whom they admire and respect.
- In contrast to values, our attitudes are less stable. Advertisements, for example, attempt to change our attitudes towards a certain product or service.
- In an organization, attitudes are important because they affect job behaviour.
- Culture also affects in forming certain attitudes.
- Religious organizations also form certain attitudes.

TYPES OF ATTITUDES

In general, a person may have a **positive attitude,** which is a good outlook towards life, or **negative attitude** which means continuous complaining about the problems in life.

1. Positive attitude:

- Positive attitude is the foundation of success.
- A person who thinks positive for exchange of views and learning, finds opportunities in every difficulty.
- Decent behaviour and good temperament.
- Positive and wishful thinking.
- Loves company and social life.
- Sees what is good in others.
- Known for love, compassion, optimism, and self esteem.
- Respects the sentiments and religion of others.

2. Negative attitude:

- An employee's negative attitude about work may be reflected by sub-standard output of work.
- Recessive absenteeism.
- Excessive complaining about work environment.
- Disobedience to rules or authority.

These attitudes can be changed either by simple persuasion or by training and coaching. The following ways of changing can be used:

a. Proper information
b. Low level of fear

c. Persuasion of peers and friends
d. By cooperation
e. Guidance and proper counselling
f. Association towards some groups

THE PROCESS OF INFLUENCE OF ATTITUDE ON BEHAVIOUR

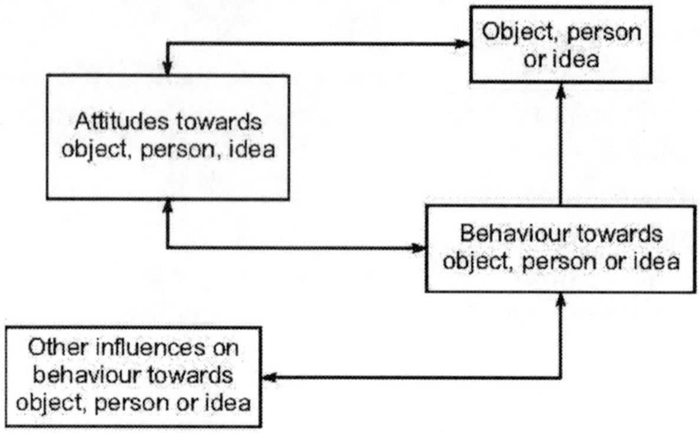

Fig.

Attitudes alone do not influence behaviour but these act with other factors such as personality, perception, motivation etc.

FUNCTIONS OF ATTITUDES IN INFLUENCING THE BEHAVIOUR

1. **Instrumental:** Attitudes serve as a means to reach a desired goal.
2. **Ego-defensive:** Attitudes protect the person from facing threats in the external world. They also make the person aware of his own unacceptable impulses.
3. **Value Orientation:** Attitudes express a person's values or enhance his self-identity.
4. **Knowledge:** The knowledge function of attitudes is based on a person's need to maintain a stable, organized and meaningful structure of the world. Attitudes provide a standard against which a person evaluates aspects of the world.

These functions of attitudes affect the individual's way of interpreting the information coming to him.

Value and Attitude

Attitudes are not the same as values, but the two are interrelated. Both have significant impact on people's behaviour. Values represent basic convictions that a specific mode of conduct is personally or socially preferable. They generally identify a person's moral structure on which the concept of good or bad and right or wrong is based. Some of the values are freedom, self–respect, honesty, obedience, equality.

- Values generally influence attitude and behaviour.
- Attitudes are specific and related to distinct objects, people or ideas. Values are more general and not related to any object or situation.
- Values are beliefs on which attitudes depend and we decide how we should behave.
- Values contain statements of good or bad associated with the attitudes which people hold.

REVIEW QUESTIONS

1. Define attitude. What are the characteristics of attitude?
2. Discuss the formation of attitudes.
3. What are the differences between value and attitude?
4. Discuss the influence of attitude on behaviour.
5. Can attitudes be changed? Discuss.
6. Write short notes:
   a. Positive attitude
   b. Negative attitude
   c. Importance of positive attitude

Thinking 33

CHAPTER

THINKING

During most of our working hours, and even when we are asleep and dreaming, we are thinking. It is hard not to think.

What do we do when we think? Loosely speaking, we mentally or cognitively process information. Thus, **thinking consists of the cognitive rearrangement or manipulation of both, information from the environment and the symbols stored in long-term memory.**

(A symbol represents some event or item in the world) Thinking can also be considered a process that meditates, or goes between stimuli (motive) and responses. **Images** and **language** symbols are used in much of our thinking.

Artistic Thinking: Some thinking is highly private and may use symbols with very personal meanings. Dreams are an example of artistic thinking.

Directed Thinking: Thinking that is aimed at solving problems or creating something new is called Directed Thinking. It is the type of thought we value so much in the great human thinkers.

Both thinking and language go through regular stages of development as a child grows.

THE THINKING PROCESS

The symbols that we use in thinking are often words and language, and therefore thinking and language are closely related. A language has many symbols and gives us rules for using them. The availability of language symbols makes human thinking more sophisticated. Although language is a powerful tool in human thought, as when "we talk to ourselves" internally, images are another important type of symbol used in thinking.

Images and Thinking

People vary remarkably in how much they use images in their thinking. When we use images to think, they are not usually complete "pictures in the head". They are usually incomplete. In general, the images are abstractions of certain features from previous experience. The incomplete abstract images seem to be constructed from elements stored in long-term memory.

For example, an elephant might be imagined as the size of a mouse, or a mouse imagined as the size of an elephant. Variations of this kind in the sizes of images indicate that images are constructions.

Language and Thinking

For many people much of the time, a good deal of thinking involves the use of word symbols and the rules of grammar to join the words into phrases and sentences. The words, their meanings and the rules for joining them together are stored in our semantic long-term memories. This knowledge about language is called **linguistic competence.**

When we think with language, we draw on this store of information to use language as 'a tool of thought'. Psychologically, thinking is actually a kind of inner speech. According to this idea, people make small movements of the vocal apparatus when they think and carry on their thinking by talking to themselves.

CONCEPTS

Concepts are important language symbols used in thinking. A concept is a symbolic construction that represents some common and general feature of many objects or events. Examples are man, woman, red, angle, anger, etc. The human ability to form concepts enables us to classify things into categories. With a concept of 'red', for example, we can sort objects into red and not red. The features we select define the concept and form the basis for making classifications. When the classification has been made we tend to behave toward and think about members of the class in similar way. Thus, as concepts are ways of classifying the diverse elements in the world around us, they are convenient tools to use in thinking about the world and in solving problems.

Basic and natural concepts

These basic and natural concepts are easily acquired and appear in thinking very early in life and to some degree reflect the way the brain processes and sorts information. For example, natural concept is the division of the colours of the spectrum into the categories red, green and blue. Basic categories, such as 'chair', true', and 'fruit' are other examples of natural concepts.

Acquired concepts

Many of our concepts are acquired more slowly and with more effort. These concepts are acquired by discrimination, learning and by seeing examples of a concept in different contexts.

Definition

A third way of acquiring new concept is by definition. Many of the concepts acquired in the later stages of a person's education are learned in this way. Definition, then, helps us acquire concepts by describing them in terms of other words or concepts with which we are already familiar.

PROBLEM SOLVING

What is a problem? In general, it is a difference between one situation and another situation we wish to produce-our goal. The thinking that we do in problem solving is directed towards this goal and motivated by the need to reduce discrepancy between one state of affairs and another. In trying to reach this goal, we use information available to us from long-term memory and from our 'here and now' perception of the problem situation before us. We process this information according to rules that tell us what we can and cannot do.

Rules in problem solving

Many of the rules in solving problems concern the changes that are permissible in going from one situation to another. Two major types of such rules are algorithm and heuristics.

Algorithm

An algorithm is a set of rules, which, if followed correctly, will guarantee a solution to a problem. (Example: Mathematical problems)

Heuristics

Heuristics are strategies, usually based on our past experience with problems, that are likely to lead to a solution but do not guarantee success. One common strategy or heuristic is to break the problem down into small subproblems, each a little closer to the end goal.

DECISION MAKING

Decision making is a kind of problem solving in which we are presented with several alternatives, among which we must choose.

CREATIVE THINKING

In creative thinking, something new is sought. The creative thinker, whether an artist, writer, or scientist, tries to create something "new".

Insight Learning: Persistent effort usually leads to insight, which is the actual solution. Some new ideas seem to come suddenly after little progress has been made over a long period of time; this sudden occurrence of new ideas is called insight.

Creative thinking is said to proceed in four stages; preparation, incubation, evaluation and revision.

Preparation: The thinker formulates the problem and collects the facts and material required for the new solution. Preparation in the form of education, training and research is an essential foundation on which to build creativity.

Incubation: If the creative thinker finds that the problem cannot be solved after a lot of concentrated efforts, he turns away from it. Incubation is a time for thought and reflection. The conscious mind usually looks for familiar channels which are known and thus not new or creative. But the subconscious mind, free from the constraints of the conscious mind, is able to look at the issue from new angles or put information together into new combinations.

Evaluation: The apparent solution is tested to see if it satisfactorily solves the problem. Frequently the insight turns out to be dissatisfactory and the thinker is back at the beginning of the creative process. In other cases the insight is satisfactory but needs some modification or the solution of minor problems to be a really good new idea.

Revision: It gives us a general picture of the steps frequently involved in the solution of problems by most talented and creative people. Another approach to the study of creative thinking is to see how it differs from the more routine kinds of thinking we do.

NATURE OF CREATIVE THINKING

Convergent Thinking: It is concerned with a particular end result. The thinker gathers information relevant to the problem and then proceeds, by using problem solving rules to work out the right solution.

Divergent Thinking: It includes a variety of thoughts about a problem. It includes artistic thinking and some convergent thinking.

Artistic thinking: Some thinking is highly private and may use symbols with very personal meanings. Dreams are an example of artistic thinking.

CHARACTERISTICS OF CREATIVE THINKERS

- Creative people are usually intelligent and often have a special talent.
- They are generally motivated to solve the problems that interest them.
- They prefer complexity.
- They are more self-assertive and dominant.
- They are more independent in their judgement.

EFFECTIVE THINKING

While positive thinking allows one's mind to accept new ideas and creative thoughts, effective thinking involves directing one's thoughts towards specific goals. Daydreaming, relaxation, and free association allow the mind to come up with new or unusual ideas or idea fragments.

Without a specific goal in mind, random thoughts and ideas may not be particularly useful. **Gerald Kushel**, the author of **Effective Thinking for Uncommon Success** says that to be an effective thinker, you need to have goals and a commitment to those goals. He outlines four steps towards effective thinking:

1. **Take Notice**. Take stock of where you are or what you are doing. Is it moving you toward your goal?
2. **Pause**. Take a break when you get off-track.
3. **Identify Effective Thoughts**. When a thought enters your head, identify it as effective or defective, positive or negative.
4. **Choose**. We can choose our thoughts. It's the underlying premise of positive thinking. It's true of effective thinking and creative thinking as well. Choose to focus on those thoughts that bring you closer to your goals.

Thus, effective thinking means clearly defining what creative challenge a person needs to meet. It is involved not only in arriving at a decision but also in carrying it out. Effective thinking would involve exploration of the subject, the generation of alternative views, listening to the views of others, considering the context and purpose of the thinking - and then designing a way forward.

CHARACTERISTICS OF EFFECTIVE THINKERS

There are general habits and intentions which effective thinkers are supposed to have. These include:

- Considering all factors
- Generating alternatives
- Listening to others
- Defining the objective

THINKING SITUATIONS

1. **Plan and action:**
    - Getting things done.
    - Making something happen.
    - Thinking is involved not only in arriving at a decision but also in carrying it out.
    - Planning is usually an essential part of getting something done.

2. **Decision and evaluation:**
   - Judging the value of an option, Is this worth doing?
   - Making decisions and making choices.
   - Why decision making can be so difficult.
3. **Problem-solving and design:**
   - Finding solutions to problems, and designing solutions to problems.
   - In a sense any design task is also a problem solving task because there is something to be achieved and no obvious way of achieving it
4. **Coping and organizing:**
   - Coping with confusion and mess.
   - Creating order out of chaos.
   - Organizing different elements so that the whole works.
5. **Negotiation and conflict:**
   - Two party situations. Each side trying to get what it wants.
   - This extends from win/win or mutual benefit negotiation to argument and conflict.
6. **Communication and persuasion:**
   - The transfer of information.
   - The transfer of perceptions.
   - Getting other people to see what you want them to see.
   - Clarity of communication.
   - Opening up perceptions in persuasion.
7. **Exploration and discussion:**
   - Making a map of the situation.
   - Getting as much information as possible.
   - Investigation, hypothesis and hypothesis testing.
   - Explanation: what is going on?
   - Discussion with the purpose of exploring a situation: different information and different views.
8. **Opportunity and initiative:**
   - Thinking is reactive: we are forced to think about something.
   - In this situation we look at initiatives, we set out to think about something because we want to.
   - Looking for opportunities.

REVIEW QUESTIONS

1. What is thinking? Explain the thinking process.
2. What is a problem? Explain the rules of problem solving.
3. What is creative thinking? Explain the stages in creative thinking
4. Define concepts. Explain various types of concepts.
5. Write a note on the development of effective thinking.
6. Write short notes on:
   a. Characteristics of a creative thinker
   b. Effective thinking
   c. Thinking situations

Appendices

- Appendix A - Punctuation and Capitalisation
- Appendix B - Idiomatic Expressions with Prepositions
- Appendix C - Distinction Between Similar Expressions
- Appendix D - Common Errors
- Appendix E - Previous Years Question Papers

Punctuation and Capitalisation

A

APPENDIX

Punctuation marks are signals to the readers. In speaking, we can pause, stop, or change our tone of voice. In writing, we use the following marks of punctuation to emphasize and clarify what we mean.

RULES OF PUNCTUATION

Punctuation is a tool of written communication; it helps to understand the divisions in the sentences. If punctuation marks are not used, the writer will not be able to impart a clear message to the reader. Wrong punctuation marks lead to misunderstanding and confusion. The rules of punctuation should be carefully followed. These rules are briefly explained below:

Marks of Punctuation

Period	.
Question Mark	?
Exclamation Mark	!
Comma	,
Semicolon	;
Colon	:
Hyphen Dash	-
Quotation Marks	" "
Parentheses	( )
Brackets	[ ]
Apostrophe	'
Ellipses	....

Period

Period Used

- At the end of declarative and imperative sentences
- At the end of indirect questions

- At the end of requests phrased as questions
- After abbreviations

Question Mark

Question Mark is used

- At the end of a direct question
- At the end of each item included in a series of questions
- At the end of a short direct question that follows a statement

Exclamation Mark

The exclamation mark is used to express strong feelings or an urgent command. It is used

- After a word
- A phrase
- Or a sentence

Comma

A comma is used

- For introducing a short quotation
- For separating the co-ordinate clauses of a compound sentence
- For separating a subordinate clause that precedes the main clause
- For separating a long introductory phrase
- For separating parenthetical terms
- For separating a series of words or word groups in a sentence
- For separating the terms of direct address
- For writing figures in thousands
- For indicating omitted words in a sentence
- For separating the day of month from the year

Semicolon

The semicolon is a stronger pause than a comma

The semicolon is used

- For separating coordinate clauses of a compound sentence when the co-ordinating conjunction is omitted
- For separating clauses that are punctuated by commas

Colon

The colon is used

- For indicating explanation or enumeration of a word, phrase or sentence

- For introducing a direct, formal and long quotation
- For separating hours, minutes and sometimes seconds

Hyphen and Dash

Hyphen is used

- After these prefixes: pro, anti, ex, self, vice
- Between two adjectives
- Between compound numbers written in words

Dash is used

- For separating explanatory clauses and changes in expression
- For emphasizing an appositive

Quotation Marks are used

- For enclosing an unusual word or phrase with special trade meaning
- For enclosing direct quotations

Parentheses

Parentheses are used

- For supplementary explanations
- For enclosing enumeration

Brackets

- The brackets are used for enclosing added material in the direct quotations

Apostrophe is used

- For showing the plurals of figures, words and abbreviations
- For indicating omission of letters in words
- In the Genitive Case of Nouns

Ellipses

- An ellipses is used for indicating omission of words from quoted material

THE USE OF CAPITALIZATION

Here are the general rules of capitalization.

1. **Capitalise Proper Names, Place Names, and words used as names.**
   - I thought Kristy would be at Vicky's party.
   - Chicago is known as The Windy City.

2. **Capitalise the first word of a sentence.**
    - The sand on the beach was white.
3. **Capitalise Dates and Historical Events**

    Capitalise the names of the days of the week, months, holidays, and historical events and periods. Do not capitalise the names of seasons.
    - Mother's Day is always the 3rd Sunday in the month of May.
    - Canada's Confederation was obtained in 1867.
    - Daylight Savings Time begins in the fall.
4. **Capitalise the Points of the Compass**

    When the points of a compass are used to designate specific geographic regions, capitalise them; do not capitalise them when they are used to indicate direction. Also capitalise words derived from points of the compass when they are used to designate people.
    - Have you ever gone out West?
    - The Northerners often go shopping down South.
    - We are experiencing strong westerly winds.
5. **Capitalise Artistic and Literary Works**

    Capitalise all "important" words in titles of books, magazines, newspapers, articles, reports, movies, programs, songs, plays, and so on. Also Capitalise the first word, last word, and a word following a colon or dash.
    - The Great Works of Edgar Allen
    - The Good, the Bad and the Ugly
    - Fireman Saves Cat Caught in Tree
6. **Capitalise Religious Titles and Supreme Beings**

    Capitalise religious titles such as holy days, names of saints and denominations, and references to supreme beings. Do not capitalise words derived from religious works.
    - The Bible
    - God
    - Saint Paul
    - biblical
    - saintly
7. **Always Capitalise the Pronoun 'I'.**
    - I love to stay up late, but I hate to get up in the morning.
8. **Capitalise Races, Nationalities, and Languages**
    - The Chinese district of New York is known as China town.
    - You must always speak English in class.

9. Direct Quotations

Capitalise the first word of a direct quotation that is a complete sentence.

- Cheryl asked, "Did you like Africa?"

10. Of Sentences That Follow Colons

Capitalise the first word of a sentence that follows a colon.

- He gave me these directions: Turn right at the stop sign and continue straight for two kilometres.

11. Of Questions Within Sentences

Capitalise the first word of a question within a sentence.

- The biggest problem seems to be, 'When will the work be completed?'

Underlining and Italics

Underlining and italics are not really punctuation, but they are significant textual effects used conventionally in a variety of situations. Before computerized word-processing was widely available, writers would underline certain terms in hand-written or manually typed pages, and the underlining would be replaced by italics in the published version. Since word processing today allows many options for font faces and textual effects, it is generally recommended that you choose either underlining or italics and use it consistently throughout a given document as needed. Whichever you choose, italics or underlining should be used:

i. To indicate titles of complete or major works such as magazines, books, newspapers, academic journals, films, television programmes, long poems, plays of three or more acts
ii. Foreign words that are not commonly used in English
iii. Words used as words themselves
iv. Words or phrases that you wish to emphasize

Idiomatic Expressions with Prepositions

B

APPENDIX

Below is a list of the "Idiomatic Use of Prepositions." It is impossible to list all of the prepositional combinations, but several of the most troublesome are given below. When in doubt about the appropriate preposition for a particular word or expression, consult a dictionary.

- **a need for:** All babies have a need for constant attention. (A need *for*, not a need *of*)
- **abide by:** I promise to abide by your decision.
- **abstain from:** If you do not know anything about the candidates, abstain from voting.
- **accord with:** The two rival companies finally reached accord with each other.
- **according to:** According to my grammar teacher, *whom* is never a subject.
- **accuse of:** Tim has been accused of stealing watermelons.
- **accustomed to:** I am not accustomed to this kind of weather.
- **acquiesce in:** I did not acquiesce in the unjustified suppression of evidence.
- **acquitted of:** The accused man was finally acquitted of the crime.
- **adapted for:** This program is especially adapted for television. (prepared for)
- **adapted to:** I have not adapted to this climate. (become accustomed to)
- **adhere to:** You must adhere to the contract you signed.
- **admit of:** This document admits of conflicting interpretations. (to give the possibility of something)
- **admit to:** He admitted to his part in the robbery. (to confess or tell the truth about)
- **adverse to:** The decision of the court is adverse to our interests.
- **agree on/upon:** The committee members could not agree on a course of action. (to decide on; to have the same opinion about)
- **agree to:** We will agree to your proposal if you will postpone action. (to promise to follow something)
- **agree with:** In all matters of importance, I promise to agree with you. (to have the same opinion about)

- **aim to prove:** I aim to prove that your accusation is unjust.
- **alarmed at:** Beach residents are alarmed at the news of the hurricane's approach.
- **amazed at *or* by:** I am amazed at your audacity.
- **amendment to:** The first amendment to the Constitution guarantees the freedom of the press.
- **annoyed at:** The clerk was very annoyed at the customer's condescending tone. (not annoyed *with*)
- **answerable to:** You are answerable to your supervisor.
- **apologize for:** You should apologize for starting the erroneous rumour. (Apologize *for* doing something)
- **apologize to:** He apologized to me for that rude remark. (Apologize *to* a person)
- **as far as:** As far as that goes, I've never seen him before in my life.
- **angry about:** I was angry about the missing jewels. (angry *about*, not angry *at*, a fact or situation)
- **angry with:** I get the impression that you are angry with me. (angry *with* a person)
- **aspire to:** He is a quiet man who does not aspire to distinction.
- **as regards:** As regards the subject of capital punishment, I am against it.
- **assent to:** Please remember that I did not assent to your proposal.
- **attend to:** We must stop talking and attend to the business at hand.
- **avail oneself of:** One should avail oneself of every opportunity to learn something new.
- **blames him for it:** As a witness to the accident, I cannot blame him for it.
- **can't help feeling:** I can't help feeling guilty about not going last night. (NOT can't help but)
- **capable of:** I wonder if Jim is capable of rational thinking.
- **censorship of:** Does he believe in the censorship of books?
- **charge with:** The police are going to charge him with assault.
- **coincide with:** Mark Twain's death coincided with the appearance of Halley's comet.
- **collide with:** Drive carefully or you might collide with another car.
- **compare to:** use compare *to* for similarities.
- **compare with:** use compare *with* to show differences or similarities.
- **compatible with:** His actions are not compatible with our standards of conduct.
- **comply with:** I shall make every effort to comply with your request.
- **concern about:** I am concerned about your poor eating habits. (to give attention or worry to)

- **concern with:** I am rather concerned with the publication of this book. (to busy oneself; to take interest or part in something)
- **conclude from:** He concluded from her expression that his mother was not happy.
- **concur with:** I concur with you in your estimate of the damage.
- **confer with . . . about:** The supervisor conferred with the committee about the proposal.
- **confide in:** Please feel free to confide in me when you have a problem.
- **confide (something) to:** He did not confide his problem to me.
- **conform to:** The new building must conform to the specifications of the building code.
- **consist of:** His diet consisted of potato chips, pretzels and soda.
- **consistent with:** My actions were consistent with your recommendations.
- **convince (someone) of:** It is often difficult to convince him of anything.
- **critical of:** She is very critical of my efforts.
- **deficient in:** The food is good, but it is deficient in vitamins.
- **deprive of:** Because of poor grades, Sue will be deprived of all privileges.
- **derived from:** Resin is derived from the pine tree.
- **die of or from:** Many people die from heart attacks, but many others die of old age.
- **differ with:** He differs with me on every issue.
- **different from:** Every person is different from every other person.
- **disappointed in:** I was disappointed in the performance of our glee club.
- **disapprove of:** I disapprove of your choice of words.
- **dissent from:** Frequently one court Justice will dissent from the majority opinion.
- **dissuade from:** I will certainly try to dissuade you from doing something foolish.
- **divest of:** The governor has decided to divest the sheriff of all responsibility.
- **doubt that:** I doubt that he even noticed our absence.
- **eager to:** He was eager to start the trip.
- **engrossed in:** The little boy was engrossed in the monster movie.
- **enter into:** We entered into a lengthy political discussion.
- **emphasis on:** Try to put emphasis on the positive points.
- **familiar to:** Your face is not familiar to me. (familiar *to* someone)
- **familiar with:** I am familiar with the campaign issues. (familiar *with* something)
- **find fault with:** Lately you seem to find fault with everything I do.
- **free from:** They are never entirely free from doubt and fear.

- **graduated from:** Every one of the ten children graduated from college.
- **identical with:** Try to find a costume identical with mine.
- **ignorant of:** He was arrested because he was ignorant of the law.
- **impervious to:** He is impervious to subtle reminders.
- **importance of:** Don't you understand the importance of being on time?
- **impressed with:** She was not impressed with his efforts to get her attention.
- **in accordance with:** In accordance with your request, I have the book with me.
- **in need of:** He is in need of transportation.
- **in proportion to:** Price increases in proportion to demand.
- **in search of:** The immigrants who came to America in the nineteenth century were in search of a better way of life.
- **inconsistent with:** His latest business deal was inconsistent with his usual code of ethics.
- **independent of:** They decided to proceed, independent of outside help.
- **indifferent to:** Some people seem indifferent to heat, cold, and pain.
- **infer from:** I infer from your remark that you have never been here before.
- **infected with:** Mr Jones is infected with AIDS.
- **inferior to:** This new car is inferior to last year's model.
- **in search of:** John spent many heartbreaking years in search of success.
- **insist on:** Newspaper editors should insist on accuracy in reporting.
- **interfere with:** Police promised not to interfere with the demonstration.
- **interfere in:** You should not interfere in your neighbor's affairs.
- **jealous of:** That man is jealous of every man who speaks to his wife.
- **kind of:** I have never liked that kind of jelly. (*kind of = type of*)
- **long for:** Every man longs for some type of recognition in life.
- **married to:** He is married to a millionaire.
- **necessity for:** The necessity for action is clearly understated.
- **object to:** I do not object to your going with us.
- **obliged to (+ verb):** He felt obliged to say something nice to her.
- **oblivious of:** She was oblivious of everything around her.
- **overcome by:** She was overcome by his statement. (overcome *by* a fact)
- **overcome with:** She was overcome with joy when her grandchild was born. (overcome *with* an emotion)
- **part with:** I cannot bear to part with any of my books.
- **partial to:** You seem to be partial to the color blue.
- **participate in:** Freshmen are not permitted to participate in some activities.

- **persevere in:** He was tired, but he continued to persevere in his effort to win.
- **persist in:** If you persist in bothering your sister, she may kick you.
- **pertain to:** Your comment does not pertain to the subject we are discussing.
- **pleased with:** I am pleased with your suggestion.
- **preferable to:** Even a simple game is preferable to inactivity.
- **prevail on:** Perhaps you can prevail on your father to take your friend to the race.
- **prevent someone from:** Try to prevent them from leaving today.
- **prior to:** Prior to leaving for the beach, Cindy gathered her towel and sunscreen. (*prior to* = *before*)
- **provide for:** Be sure to provide for all possible emergencies.
- **provide someone with:** He did not provide me with enough money for the trip.
- **reason with . . . on:** Try to reason with your mother on the issue. (reason *with* someone *on* an issue)
- **refrain from:** Everyone should refrain from repeating malicious gossip.
- **regardless of:** Regardless of your desire to have your test score immediately, your score will not be ready till tomorrow.
- **rejoice at:** The whole country rejoiced at the news of the prince's marriage.
- **required of:** An oath of allegiance is required of all members.
- **replace with:** We will need to replace these curtains with blinds.
- **responsible to . . . for:** I am responsible to your mother for your safety. (responsible *to* someone *for* something)
- **result in:** Tardiness may result in suspension. (a cause *results in* an effect)
- **result from:** Obesity may result from overeating and lack of exercise. (an effect *results from* a cause)
- **rich in:** This country is rich in many natural resources.
- **short of:** Just before payday, we are all a little short of cash.
- **secede from:** I hope that no state will ever secede from the Union again.
- **similar to:** Your taste in clothes is similar to mine.
- **speak to . . . about:** I must speak to you about your grades. (speak *to* someone *about* something)
- **substitute for:** This class may substitute for your thesis.
- **succeed in:** The prisoner did not succeed in his attempt to escape. (not succeed *at*)
- **superior to:** A pipe organ is superior to an electronic organ.
- **surprised at:** I am surprised at your sudden interest in chemistry. (not surprised *with*)

Distinction Between Similar Expressions

C

APPENDIX

1. (a) **Go to sea** (become a sailor)
   (b) **Go to the sea** (go on a voyage)
2. (a) **Go to school** (attend school for lessons)
   (b) **Go to the school** (for any other purpose)
3 (a) **Go to market** (for making purchases)
   (b) **Go to the market** (for any other purpose)
4 (a) **Go to bed** (go to sleep)
   (b) **Go to the bed** (go to the place where bed is)
5 (a) **Go to play** (for the purpose of taking part in the game)
   (b) **Go to a or the play** (go to the theatre for seeing the acting)
6 (a) **Work in hand** (work in which engaged)
   (b) **Work on hand** (work not yet done)
7 (a) **At no time** (never)
   (b) **In no time** (very soon)
8 (a) **In an hour** (Just after an hour)
   (b) **Within an hour** (before the hour is over)
9 (a) **In the North** (North but inside; e.g., Kashmir is in the North of India)
   (b) **To the North** (North but outside; e.g., Kabul is to the North of India)
10 (a) **Work hard** (diligently)
   (b) **Work hardly** (scarcely)
11 (a) **Little hope of success** (no hope)
   (b) **A little hope of success** (some hope at least)
12 (a) **Few persons** (none)
   (b) **A few persons** (some at least)
13 (a) **Shot the bird** (killed)
   (b) **Shot at the bird** (aimed to kill the bird)
14 (a) **To search a man** (to examine his body and clothes)
   (b) **To search for a man** (to find out a man)
15 (a) **Believe a man** (believe his statement)
   (b) **Believe in a man** (have faith in his honesty)

16 (a) **Meet a man** (knowingly)
(b) **Meet with a man** (by chance)
17 (a) **Wait for a man** (expect him)
(b) **Wait upon a man** (serve him)
18 (a) **A black horse and cow** (a black horse and a black cow)
(b) **A black horse and a cow** (a black horse and a cow which is not black)
19 (a) **A neighbour to one** (living near one)
(b) **Neighbour to one** (kind to one)
20 (a) **Kalidas** (Kalidas himself)
(b) **A Kalidas** (a poet like Kalidas)
21 (a) **Suffer from a headache** (suffer from an occasional attack of headache)
(b) **Suffer from headache** (suffer from a disease, namely headache)
22 (a) **The poet and scholar** (one person)
(b) **The poet and the scholar** (two persons)
23 (a) **Picture of Ram** (picture of Ram)
(b) **Picture of Ram's** (picture of which Ram is owner)
24 (a) **English** (English language)
(b) **The English** (the English people)
25 (a) **Set the book on fire** (burn the book)
(b) **Set the book on the fire** (place the book on the fire)
26 (a) **Think little** (to have a poor opinion)
(b) **Little Think** (think scarcely)
27 (a) **Come late** (come after fixed time)
(b) **Come lately** (come recently)
28 (a) **Go home direct** (go home without stopping anywhere)
(b) **Go home directly** (go home at once)
29 (a) **Has come** (coming is finished)
(b) **Is come** (in the state of having come)
30 (a) **Is to go** (decided to go)
(b) **Has to go** (under obligation to go)
31 (a) **Who is he?** (What is the name of the person?)
(b) **What is he?** (What is the occupation of the person?)
(c) **Which is he?** (Which is he among a group of persons?)
32 (a) **The greatest poet** (the greatest poet of the male and female poets)
(b) **The greatest poetess** (the greatest poet of all the female poets)
33 (a) **The eldest son** (the first born son)
(b) **The oldest son** (the oldest of living sons)
34 (a) **Well** (in good health)
(b) **Well off** (quite rich)

35 (a) **A garden flower** (a flower which grows only in gardens)
(b) **A flower garden** (a garden of flowers)
36 (a) **Dead in sin** (great sinner)
(b) **Dead to sin** (free from sin)
37 (a) **Go before Monday** (go up to Sunday)
(b) **Go by Monday** (go upto Monday)
38 (a) **Live at Aligarh** (live in the city of Aligarh)
(b) **Live in Aligarh** (live in the district of Aligarh)
39 (a) **Eat the fruit** (eat the whole of the fruit)
(b) **Eat of the fruit** (eat a part of the fruit)
40 (a) **Live on grass** (feed on grass)
(b) **Live in grass** (live inside the grass)
41 (a) **Deal the cards** (distribute the cards)
(b) **Deal in cards** (sell cards)
42 (a) **Take heart** (acquire courage)
(b) **Take to heart** (to be deeply affected)
43 (a) **Enquire of one** (ask one something)
(b) **Enquire for one** (desire to know one's whereabouts)
44 (a) **Stop at Agra** (for some time while going to another place)
(b) **Stop in Agra** (live in Agra temporarily)
45 (a) **Want of one** (expect from one)
(b) **Want with one** (to have business with one)
46 (a) **At fault** (puzzled)
(b) **In fault** (to blame)
47 (a) **Lose one's only son** (to lose the only son whom one had)
(b) **Lose one's son only** (to lose one's son and none else)
48 (a) **Look sick** (appear to be sick just now)
(b) **Look sickly** (appear to be unhealthy)
49 (a) **I have done the work** (I myself have done the work)
(b) **I have the work done** (I have got the work done by somebody else)
50 (a) **I can do it** (I can do it without the help of anybody)
(b) **I alone can do it** (I and nobody else can do it)
51 (a) **Was to come** (decided to come)
(b) **Had to come** (obliged to come)
52 (a) **Arrive home safe** (to be safe when arriving home)
(b) **Arrive home safely** (to have no difficulty on the way)
53 (a) **As you are poor** (because you are poor)
(b) **Poor as you are** (although you are poor, yet ....)
54 (a) **Seem to be poor** (appear to be poor)
(b) **Seem to have been poor** (appear to have been poor before)

55 (a) **Shall die** (destined to die)
(b) **Will die** (determined to die)

56 (a) **Be honest** (it implies determination)
(b) **May be honest** (it implies a mere wish)

57 (a) **A most interesting play** (interesting in a high degree)
(b) **The most interesting play** (no other is more interesting)

58 (a) **May I do this work** (I want to do this work but I seek your permission to do it)
(b) **Shall I do this work** (I want to know if you wish me to do this work)

59 (a) **The jury was** (the members of the jury taken as a whole)
(b) **The jury were** (the members of the jury taken individually)

60 (a) **I would help you if I would** (I would help you if I had the power to help you. I had the will to help you but not the power)
(b) **I could help you if I would** (I could help you if I had a will to help you. I had the power to help you but not the will or intention)

61 (a) **A member of society** (one of the human beings who constitute society)
(b) **A member of a society** (a member of a particular association)

62 (a) **You love me more than he** (you love me more than he loves me)
(b) **You love me more than him** (you love me more than you love him)

63 (a) **Find easy** (find no difficulty in understanding)
(b) **Find easily** (find with no difficulty)

64 (a) **Complain to the man** (bring a complaint against the man)
(b) **Complain of the man** (bring a complaint against the man before somebody)

65 (a) **Proceed to the work** (begin the work)
(b) **Proceed with the work** (resume the work, which had been postponed for a time)

66 (a) **See one go** (see one leave the place)
(b) **See one going** (see one when one was on the way)

67 (a) **He teaches English as well as writes it** (he teaches English and also writes it)
(b) **He teaches English as well as he writes it** (he teaches and writes English with equal proficiency)

68 (a) **Tell me briefly** (tell me in few words)
(b) **Tell me shortly** (tell me in a short time)

69 (a) **Are you going?** (the speaker wants to know whether you are going)
(b) **Are you coming?** (it implies that the speaker is also going)

70 (a) **Get drunk** (to become drunk)
(b) **Get drink** (to bring wine)

71 (a) **To have regard for** (to have respect for)
(b) **To be regardful of** (to be careful about)
72 (a) **Called me** (shouted my name and asked me to come)
(b) **Called on me** (visited me at my house)
73 (a) **Begin this book** (commence to read this book)
(b) **Begin with this book** (begin this book before beginning any other)
74 (a) **Close the bargain** (finish the bargain)
(b) **Close with the bargain** (accept the bargain)
75 (a) **Dispense the books** (distribute the books)
(b) **Dispense with the books** (do away with the books)
76 (a) **Grasp the chain** (hold the chain tightly)
(b) **Grasp at the chain** (attempt to catch the chain)
77 (a) **Guard this man** (protect this man)
(b) **Guard against this man** (take every precaution against this man)
78 (a) **Inquire the matter** (ask what the matter is)
(b) **Inquire into the matter** (investigate the matter by careful examination)
79 (a) **Repair the house** (put the house in good order)
(b) **Repair to the house** (go to the house)
80 (a) **Work the machine** (manage the machine)
(b) **Work at the machine** (be engaged with the machine)
81 (a) **Attend the meeting** (to be present in the meeting)
(b) **Attend to the meeting** (to pay attention to the business of the meeting)
82 (a) **Come soon** (refers to the time taken in coming. It means to come in as short a time as possible)
(b) **Come quickly** (refers to the manner of coming. It means to come on at as rapid a pace as possible)
83 (a) **To have business** (to have a particular affair which demands attention and settlement)
(b) **To have a business** (to have some occupation as a merchant or a shopkeeper)
84 (a) **To have enough food** (to have sufficient food)
(b) **To have enough of food** (to have overeaten oneself)
85 (a) **Nothing like a battle** (nothing resembling a battle, meaning that the struggle is a trivial affair)
(b) **Nothing like the battle** (meaning that no such battle has occurred before, in other words, the struggle is the most serious)

Common Errors

D

APPENDIX

COMMON ERRORS IN THE USE OF ARTICLES

1. I have good knowledge of the French.
2. The iron is a kind of material.
3. I like using knife and fork while eating.
4. Thousand people were there.
5. Sometimes the life is hard.
6. She's little Hitler.
7. I'd like coffee, please.
8. There were three questions. First two were relatively easy but third one was tough.
9. Don't forget to invite Guptas.
10. I wanted it but I did not have money.
11. We started late in afternoon.
12. Going for the morning walk is an useful habit.
13. More she thought about it, more depressed she became.
14. There is Mr. Green to see you.
15. There was little milk in the bottle. She gave it to the baby when it started weeping.
16. He leads very busy life so he goes everywhere by a car.
17. He uses the mock-heroic style to depict a violence.
18. One should be true to one's promises in order to earn name in the life.
19. "Music is Science but singing is an art", said the music teacher.
20. The seed of all the modern amenities lies in the Science.
21. We should spend good part of the day in outdoor activities and games.
22. He should mix his authority with little of courtesy and common sense.
23. It is a pity that the son of millionaire should indulge in stealing.
24. He is a heir to the throne.
25. He is a Duke of York.
26. I have to make an humble proposal.
27. He has been appointed as the Vice-Chancellor.
28. You will find this topic in the V chapter.

29. You will find this topic in fifth chapter.
30. I read Times of India.
31. I have never seen a house where I spent my childhood.
32. Brahmaputra is one of the longest rivers, which originates in Himalayas.
33. He found himself in a trouble when he saw no rickshaw outside the station.
34. He said that he did not feel any need to discuss the episode in the detail.
35. In the conclusion it may be asserted that the poet preaches some moral lesson.
36. Mr. Sinha is a very wise and an intelligent officer.
37. The man is the only creature that is endowed with the power of speech.
38. I saw an one eyed man.
39. The Parliament has passed this bill.
40. He is in the trouble.
41. Beauty of Kashmir is remarkable.
42. Kalidas is regarded as Shakespeare of India.
43. Draw the curtain to shut out sun.
44. Oranges are sold by dozens.
45. She is always in news.
46. The historians love to study old books.
47. The society should look after the old.
48. A honorary secretary is one who is not paid for his services.
49. Himalayas are spread all along the north of India.
50. The audience attentively listened to the scholarly and the interesting speech of the president.
51. They are the brother and the sister.
52. A man is mortal.
53. She got headache.
54. The children like sweets.
55. His mother is M.Sc.
56. It was an unique experience.
57. There is an university in this city.
58. He was condemned to the hell.
59. What sort of fellow is he?
60. Of tea and coffee I prefer latter.
61. Richard is senior than Paul by four years.
62. Ganges is the holiest of all the other rivers.

CORRECTIONS

1. I have **a** good knowledge **of French.**
2. **Iron** is a kind of material.
3. I like using **a** knife and fork while eating.

4. **A** thousand people were there.
5. **Sometimes life** is hard.
6. She's **a** little Hitler.
7. I'd like **a** coffee, please.
8. There were three questions. **The** first two were relatively easy but **the** third one was tough.
9. Don't forget to invite **the** Guptas.
10. I wanted it but I did not have **the** money.
11. We started late in **the** afternoon.
12. Going for **a** morning walk is **a** useful habit.
13. **The** more she thought about it, **the** more depressed she became.
14. There is **a** Mr. Green to see you.
15. There was **a** little milk in the bottle. She gave it to the baby when it started weeping.
16. He leads **a** very busy life so he goes everywhere **by car**.
17. He uses the mock-heroic style to depict violence.
18. One should be true to one's promises in order to earn name in life.
19. "Music is **a** Science but singing is an art", said the music teacher.
20. The seed of all the modern amenities lies in Science.
21. We should spend **a** good part of the day in outdoor activities and games. (suggests the sense of one)
22. He should mix his authority with **a** little of courtesy and common sense.
23. It is a pity that the son of **a** millionaire should indulge in stealing.
24. He is **an** heir to the throne.
25. He is Duke of York.
26. I have to make **a** humble proposal.
27. He has been appointed as Vice-Chancellor.
28. You will find this topic in V chapter.
29. You will find this topic in **the** fifth chapter.
30. I read **The** Times of India.
31. I have never seen **the** house where I spent my childhood.
32. **The** Brahmaputra is one of the longest rivers, which originates in Himalayas.
33. He found himself in trouble when he saw no rickshaw outside the station.
34. He said that he did not feel any need to discuss the episode in detail.
35. In conclusion it may be asserted that the poet preaches some moral lesson.
36. Mr. Sinha is a very wise and intelligent officer.
37. Man is the only creature that is endowed with the power of speech.
38. I saw **a** one eyed man.
39. Parliament has passed this bill.
40. He is in trouble.
41. **The** beauty of Kashmir is remarkable.

42. Kalidas is regarded as **the** Shakespeare of India.
43. Draw the curtain to shut out **the** sun.
44. Oranges are sold by **the** dozens.
45. She is always in **the** news.
46. Historians love to study old books.
47. Society should look after the old. .(no article is used before collective noun)
48. **An** honorary secretary is one who is not paid for his services.
49. **The** Himalayas are spread all along the North of India.
50. Audience attentively listened to the scholarly and interesting speech of the president.
51. They are brother and sister.
52. Man is mortal.
53. She got a headache.
54. Children like sweets.
55. His mother is **an** M.Sc.
56. It was **a** unique experience.
57. There is **a** university in this city.
58. He was condemned to hell.
59. What sort of **a** fellow is he?
60. Of tea and coffee I prefer **the** latter.
61. Richard is senior **to** Paul by four years.
62. **The** Ganges is the holiest of all the rivers.

COMMON ERRORS IN THE USE OF NOUNS

1. I spent the holidays with my family members.
2. There is no more place in this compartment.
3. What are you writing in your copy.
4. I am reading a new poetry.
5. There was a joker at the circus.
6. We did not have a good play of football.
7. We saw a theatre.
8. He does not like taking part in a drama.
9. He is a short-statured gentleman.
10. There are two females sitting in the compartment.
11. He was wearing a new dress.
12. The almirah contains books, papers and others.
13. He did not put his signs on this paper.
14. He is my cousin brother.
15. He had a great number of money.
16. There is a tree in the front side of our college.

17. I could not take a bath in the sea.
18. The gentry of the town was invited to the feast.
19. I like fruits and vegetables.
20. You must continue your study.
21. Summer vacations are near.
22. Politics are a dirty game.
23. My mean is limited.
24. He purchased a land.
25. His wage is low.
26. We have already had our meal.
27. The earthquake did many damages.
28. There was a letter on the ground of this room.
29. I was in the centre of the room.
30. Please grant me one day leave.
31. We use woods as fuel.
32. The house's walls are damaged.
33. She reached the age of two scores and one.
34. Five B.A. and two M.A. applied for the job.
35. My scissor is blunt.
36. He needs a spectacles.
37. His hair are white.
38. I want two breads.
39. He gave me many informations.
40. He has five grey hair.
41. Her appearance is just like her mother.
42. My thank is due to him.
43. Your's faithfully.

Correct

1. I spent the holidays with my **family** (or I spent the holidays with **members of my family**).
2. There is no more **room** in this compartment.
3. What are you writing in your **notebook**.
4. I am reading a new **poem**.
5. There was a **clown** at the circus.
6. We did not have a good **game** of football.
7. We saw a **play**.
8. He does not like acting in a **play**.
9. He is a short-statured **man**.
10. There are two **women** sitting in the compartment.
11. He was wearing a new **suit**.

12. The almirah contains books, papers and **such things.**
13. He did not put his **signature** on this paper.
14. He is my **cousin.**
15. He had a **good amount** of money.
16. There is a tree **in front of** our college.
17. I could not **have a bath** in the sea.
18. The gentry of the town **were** invited to the feast.
19. I like **fruit and vegetables.**
20. You must continue your **studies.**
21. Summer **vacation is** near.
22. Politics **is** a dirty game.
23. My **means are** limited.
24. He purchased a **plot of land.**
25. His **wages are** low.
26. We have already had our **meals.**
27. The earthquake did **much damage.**
28. There was a letter **on the floor** of this room.
29. I was in the **middle** of the room.
30. Please grant me **one day's leave.**
31. We use **wood** as fuel.
32. **The walls of the house** are damaged.
33. She reached the age of **two score** and one.
34. **Five B.A.s and two M.A.s** applied for the job.
35. My **scissors** *are* blunt.
36. He needs a **pair of spectacles.**
37. His hair **is** white.
38. I want **two loaves (or two pieces) of bread.**
39. He gave me **much** information.
40. He has **five grey hairs.**
41. Her appearance is just like her **mother's.**
42. My **thanks are** due to him.
43. **Yours** faithfully.

COMMON ERRORS IN THE USE OF PRONOUNS

Incorrect

1. I, You and he have done the work.
2. I will send him to your's.
3. I feel myself ill today.
4. Those who attended yesterday should get yourselves marked present.

5. I beg to take your leave.
6. His very sight annoyed me.
7. He is the best speaker who could be found in the college.
8. Each of these men read books.
9. We all could not reach there in time.
10. Here is my letter, please read.
11. He enjoyed during the summer vacation.
12. None of us have done work.
13. Any of these two boys can come.
14. The boy is my cousin who stood first in the mile race.
15. Neither Ram nor Sohan are responsible for this mistake.
16. It is me.
17. Nobody was there but I.
18. The committee was divided in its opinion.
19. This is the chair whose leg was broken today.
20. This is the table whose price is very cheap.
21. He went there and enjoyed.
22. If I were him, I would not go there.
23. None of us have met him.
24. Sohan and Mohan love one another.
25. You are abler than him.
26. I was glad at my mother coming.
27. Is it me you wish to see?
28. Our game is cricket, there is tennis.
29. Each of the girls had their prizes.
30. He is one of those who performs his obligation.
31. It is not I who is to blame.
32. You are better than him.
33. One should obey his elders.
34. We should enjoy.
35. Why did you absent yesterday?
36. Everyone should mind their own business.
37. Who are you searching for?
38. I like such books which are well printed.
39. What is it which pains her?
40. Your handwriting is like Mohan.
41. Your clothes are cheaper than Sheela.
42. I hate you meeting him again and again.
43. Everyone is known by the company which he has.

Correct

1. **You, he and I** have done the work.
2. I will send him to **your house**.
3. I **feel ill** today.
4. Those who attended yesterday should **get themselves** marked present.
5. I beg to take **leave of you**.
6. **The very sight of him** annoyed me.
7. He is the best speaker **that** could be found in the college.
8. Each of these men **reads** books.
9. **None of us could** reach there in time.
10. Here is my letter, **please read it**.
11. He **enjoyed himself** during the summer vacation.
12. None of us **has** done work.
13. **Either of these two** boys can come.
14. The **boy, who** stood first in the mile race, is my cousin.
15. Neither Ram nor Sohan **is** responsible for this mistake.
16. It is **I**.
17. Nobody was there but **me**.
18. The committee **were** divided in their opinion.
19. This is the chair **the leg of which** was broken today.
20. This is the table **the price of which** is very cheap.
21. He went there and **enjoyed himself**.
22. If I were **he**, I would not go there.
23. None of us **has** met him.
24. Sohan and Mohan love **each other**.
25. You are abler than **he** (is).
26. I was glad at my **mother's coming**.
27. Is it **I** you wish to see?
28. Our game is cricket, **theirs** is tennis.
29. Each of the girls had **her** prize.
30. He is one of those who **perform their obligations**.
31. It is not I who **am** to blame.
32. You are better than **he**.
33. One should obey **one's** elders.
34. We should enjoy **ourselves**.
35. Why did you absent **yourself** yesterday?
36. Everyone should mind **his** own business.
37. **Whom** are you searching for?
38. I like such books **as** are well printed.
39. What is it **that** pains her?

40. Your handwriting is like **that of** Mohan.
41. Your clothes are cheaper than **those of** Sheela.
42. I hate **your** meeting him again and again.
43. Everyone is known by the company **he has**.

COMMON ERRORS IN THE USE OF ADJECTIVES

Incorrect

1. Mohan is wiser than all students.
2. His work is superior than his brothers.
3. Neither of these five persons came to see me.
4. Either of you eight can take up this work.
5. He gets only passing marks in all subjects.
6. Today I feel somewhat uneasy.
7. Ram is my older brother.
8. This tree is the eldest one here.
9. There were no less than fifteen girls there.
10. The first two boys will get the prize.
11. Both of them have not come.
12. Kalidas is greater than any other poets in the world.
13. Open your book at ten page.
14. Among the two he is cleverer.
15. He is more handsome than the others.
16. I intend spending my future life/remaining life in Dehradun.
17. I am hopeless to get through the examination.
18. Your loving friend.
19. He obtained nearly cent percent marks.
20. The gold is yellow.
21. Each and every person wore a Gandhi cap.
22. He is a coward/miser man.
23. Mohan got few marks in the examination.
24. I can offer you few rupees that are in my pocket.
25. This is the latter edition published on Mulk Raj Anand.
26. Mohan's statement is more right than Sohan's.
27. All the class left the room.
28. Mohan has little money that he wishes to spend.
29. Rich should help poors.
30. I have no rupee.
31. Sita is cleverest of all other girls.
32. He is richer than wise.

33. He is the richest and honest man.
34. It is much hot today.
35. She sat nearest to me.
36. He was present on both days.
37. I will not buy some book.
38. He has no other friends except Sunil.
39. No poet is as great as Tagore.
40. She is studying in class seventh.
41. The great Napoleon attacked Western Europe.
42. Great are always humble.
43. He is junior of me.
44. This dress is inferior with that.
45. This truth is more universal.
46. Kolkata is further than Allahabad from here.
47. Your name is the latest in this category.
48. In the epidemic many a men perished.
49. I possess few books, only four or five.
50. There is little milk in the cup, which is sufficient for tea.
51. Each one of the three girls stayed behind.
52. She is wiser of you.
53. He is taller than the two brothers.

Correct

1. Mohan is wiser than all **other** students.
2. His work is **superior to** his brothers'.
3. **None** of these five persons came to see me.
4. **Any** of you eight can take up this work.
5. He gets only **pass** marks in all subjects.
6. Today I feel somewhat **unwell.**

NOTE: 'Uneasy' denotes restlessness of the mental state.

7. Ram is my **elder** brother.
8. This tree is the **oldest** one here.
9. There were no **fewer** than fifteen girls there.

NOTE: 'Less' denotes degree, quantity; 'Fewer' denotes number.

10. The **two first** boys will get the prize.
11. **Neither of them has** come.
12. Kalidas is greater than any other **poet** in the world.
13. Open your book at **page ten**.
14. He is the **more clever of the two.**

15. He is the **most** handsome **of all**.
16. I intend spending **the rest of my life** in Dehradun.
17. I have **no hope of getting** through the examination.
18. **Yours loving** friend.
19. He obtained nearly **full** marks.
20. **Gold** is yellow.
21. **Each person/Everybody** wore a Gandhi cap.
22. He is a **cowardly/miserly** man. /He is a **miser**.
23. Mohan got **a few** marks in the examination.
24. I can offer you **a few** rupees that are in my pocket.
25. This is the **later** edition published on Mulk Raj Anand.
26. Mohan's statement is more **correct** than Sohan's.
27. **The whole** class left the room.
28. Mohan has **a** little money that he wishes to spend.
29. Rich should help **the poor**.
30. I have no **money**.
31. Sita is **the cleverest** of **all** girls.
32. He is **more rich** than wise.
33. He is the richest and **most** honest man.
34. It is **very** hot today.
35. She sat **next** to me.
36. He was present on **both the** days.
37. I will not buy **any** book.
38. He has no other **friend than** Sunil.
39. **No other** poet is as great as Tagore.
40. She is studying in **the seventh class**.
41. **Napoleon The Great** attacked Western Europe.
42. **The great** are always humble.
43. He is junior **to** me.
44. This dress is inferior **to** that.
45. This truth is **universal**.
46. Kolkata is **farther** than Allahabad from here.
47. Your name is the **last** in this category.
48. In the epidemic many a **man** perished.
49. I possess **a** few books, only four or five.
50. There is **a** little milk in the cup, which is sufficient for tea.
51. **Every** one of the three girls stayed behind.
52. She is wiser **than** you.
53. He is taller **of the two brothers**.

COMMON ERRORS IN THE USE OF VERBS

Incorrect

1. He was failed.
2. He tells that he is going to school.
3. Will you please see my answer paper.
4. I advised him but he would not hear me.
5. I hope you will fail in the examination.
6. I requested him for a loan but he denied.
7. Keep these books on the table.
8. I always put my books in the almirah.
9. I could not avail of his offer.
10. What is the data in this case?
11. Try as we will, we would not succeed.
12. Mohan as well as you are to blame.
13. Either you or he have taken my money.
14. Neither Sohan nor his brothers is going.
15. This subject is hard to be learnt.
16. He shouts at me while talking as if I am deaf.
17. You speak as if you don't know the facts.
18. We preferred dying rather than surrendering.
19. They seemed to have been more careful about their studies in those days.
20. Dare he to do it?
21. I have committed myself to help him with money.
22. He made me to do this work.
23. I regard it a fun.
24. Those who might have seen the place know how beautiful it is.
25. I thought that you may have read this note.
26. I would advise you buy the same medicine as I have.
27. He is one of the noblest men that I ever knew.
28. He no sooner went in than the girl began to speak ill of him.
29. There are many a student who do not know even this.
30. Either he or I is to blame.
31. He as well as I is guilty.
32. He abstained from going out in sun lest he may get the sun stroke.
33. He asked had we written our exercise.
34. Ram said can he read this book.
35. Krishan asked to Mohan why your father is angry.
36. He does not care for my advice.
37. I do not care for you.

38. He does not care for his books.
39. I met a man who was my friend some time ago.
40. He had been studying in the college since a long time.
41. I went out for walking yesterday.
42. If I did this, I shall be fined.
43. When I shall go to Delhi I shall see the Janpath.
44. If I would have done this, I would have done wrong.
45. I have left rowing.
46. I left playing when my friend arrived there.
47. I should take your leave.
48. After some time he knew what he had done.
49. He should not cut jokes in the presence of others.
50. He knows to teach you.
51. He cut his pencil.
52. I asked my servant to bring water.
53. I like to play chess.
54. He is troubling me unnecessarily.
55. My foot is paining.
56. My head is paining.
57. I have received a hurt on my arm.
58. Mohan gave a speech on the prize distribution day.
59. Krishan made a lecture.
60. He has learnt how to sit on a cycle.
61. He could not get down from his cycle.
62. Will you take out your shoes.
63. I have ordered for a cup of tea.
64. I have disposed my cycle.
65. They respected me when I arrived there.
66. He struck a blow on my face.
67. I lived with him for a day.
68. I hope he must come.
69. Will you open the light.
70. Please shut the light.
71. I availed of the opportunity.
72. Don't absent from the classroom.
73. He need not to go there.
74. He cannot dare to see me.
75. I would rather die than to see him.
76. I had better take to leave of you.
77. Entering the room, the clock struck five.
78. This book is not worth to buy.

79. The poet and scholar are dead.
80. Law and order have to be maintained.
81. The Ministry is divided in the language issue.
82. The committee have issued its report.
83. Sheela as well as her sister were present.
84. The building with all its furniture were sold.
85. Ram as well as Shyam have gone there.
86. Either I or you is at fault.
87. Either you or your brother have broken my glass.
88. Either he or I is guilty.
89. I have never and will never go there.
90. Everyone of them have a book.
91. Each of the four boys have gone there.
92. Neither he went there nor I did.
93. If I was you, I should not do it.
94. I wish I was there.
95. The train stayed here for five minutes.
96. I have worked here for the last ten years.
97. It is up to him to go or to stay.
98. I cannot but like her.
99. His grandfather died since last Monday.
100. Latter on he knew his mistake.
101. He was my teacher five years ago.
102. The enemy has flown away.
103. You need not to worry.
104. He had better to give up his studies.
105. I hope to have met you.
106. Playing hockey, my leg was broken.
107. I prevented him to go there.
108. I forbade him from smoking.
109. He succeeded to win the election.
110. Sitting in my room, the radio could be heard.
111. Being very cold, I kept indoors.
112. I did not know him about him coming.
113. You may depend on me coming in time.
114. I insisted on him going there.

Correct

1. He **failed.**
2. He **says** that he is going to school.
3. Will you please **look at** my answer paper.

4. I advised him but he would not **listen to** me.
5. I **fear** you will fail in the examination.
6. I requested him for a loan but he **refused.**
7. **Place/put** these books on the table.
8. I always **keep** my books in the almirah.
9. I could not **avail myself** of his offer.
10. What **are** the data in this case?
11. Try as we **may**, we would not succeed.
12. Mohan as well as you **is** to blame.
13. Either you or he **has** taken my money.
14. Neither Sohan nor his brothers **are** going.
15. This subject is hard **to learn.**
16. He shouts at me while talking as if I **were** deaf.
17. You speak as if you **did not** know the facts.
18. We preferred dying rather than **surrender.**
19. They **seem** to have been more careful about their studies in those days.
20. Dare **he do** it?
21. I have committed myself to **helping** him with money.
22. He made me **do** this work.
23. I regard it **as** fun.
24. Those who **may** have seen the place know how beautiful it is.
25. I thought that you **might** have read this note.
26. I would advise you **to buy** the same medicine as I have **bought**.
27. He is one of the noblest men that I **have ever known.**
28. **No sooner had he gone** in than the girl began to speak ill of them.
29. There **is** many a student who **does** not know even this.
30. Either he or I **am** to blame.
31. He as well as I **am** guilty.
32. He abstained from going out in the sun lest he **should** get the sun stroke.
33. He asked **if we had** (or **whether we had**) **written** our exercise.
34. Ram **asked if he could** read that book.
35. Krishan asked Mohan why **his** father **was** angry.
36. He **pays no heed** to my advice.
37. I do not care **for what you do.**
38. He does not **take care** of his books.
39. I met a man who **had been** my friend some time ago.
40. He had been studying in the college **for** a long time.
41. I went out for **a walk** yesterday.
42. If I **do** this, I shall be fined.
43. When I **go** to Delhi I shall see the Janpath.
44. If I **had** done this, I **should** have done wrong.

45. I have **given up** rowing.
46. I **stopped** playing when my friend arrived there.
47. I should take **leave of you.**
48. After sometime he **realized** what he had done.
49. He should not **make** jokes in the presence of others.
50. He knows **how to** teach you.
51. He **mended** (or **sharpened**) his pencil.
52. I **told** my servant to bring me water.
53. I **should like** to play chess. **Or** I **want** to play chess.
54. He is **giving me trouble/ treating me badly/ bullying me** unnecessarily.
55. My foot is **hurting**. **Or I have a pain in** my foot.
56. My head is **aching.**
57. I **have hurt** my arm.
58. Mohan **delivered** a speech on the prize distribution day.
59. Krishan **gave** a lecture.
60. He has learnt how to **ride** a cycle.
61. He could not get **off** from his cycle.
62. Will you take **off** (or **remove**) your shoes.
63. I have **ordered a cup** of tea.
64. I have **disposed of** my cycle.
65. They **showed me respect** (or **treated me with respect**) when I arrived there.
66. He **struck me** in the face or **hit me** in the face.
67. I **stayed** with him for a day.
68. I hope he **will** come or I am sure he will come or he must come.
69. Will you **turn** the light **on.**
70. Please **turn off** the light.
71. I **availed myself** of the opportunity.
72. Don't **absent yourself from** the classroom.
73. He **need not go** there.
74. He **dare not** see me.
75. I **would rather die than** see him.
76. I **had better take** leave of you.
77. Entering the room, **I heard** the clock strike five.
78. This book is not **worth buying.**
79. The **poet and scholar is dead**. (or The **poet and the scholar are dead.**)
80. **Law and order has** to be maintained.
81. The **Ministry are** divided on the language issue.
82. The committee **has** issued its report.
83. Sheela as well as her sister **was** present.

84. The building with all its furniture **was** sold.
85. **Ram as well as Shyam has** gone there.
86. Either I or you **are** at fault.
87. Either you or your brother **has** broken my glass.
88. Either he or I **am** guilty.
89. I have never **gone** and will never go there.
90. Everyone of them **has** a book.
91. Each of the four boys **has** gone there.
92. Neither **did he go** there nor **did I**.
93. If **I were** you, I should not do it.
94. I wish **I were** there.
95. The train **stopped** here for five minutes.
96. I **have been working** here for the last ten years.
97. It is up to him **to go or stay**.
98. I cannot **help liking** her.
99. His grandfather **has been dead since** last Monday.
100. Later on **he realized** his mistake.
101. He **had been** my teacher five years ago.
102. The enemy has **fled** away.
103. You need **not worry**.
104. He had **better give up** his studies.
105. I hope to **meet** you.
106. Playing hockey, **I broke my leg**.
107. I prevented him **from going** there.
108. I forbade him **to smoke**.
109. He succeeded **in winning** the election.
110. Sitting in my room, **I could hear the radio**.
111. **It being** very cold, I kept indoors.
112. I did not know about **his coming**.
113. You may depend on **my coming** in time.
114. I insisted on **his going** there.

COMMON ERRORS IN THE USE OF ADVERBS

Incorrect

1. On seeing his wife he was very pleased.
2. It is much hot today.
3. I was very annoyed at his attitude.
4. This mango is very bad to be eaten.
5. All the water flowed out of the bucket by and by.

6. You should go directly to your father.
7. He must do this work whether he will or not.
8. It is much harmful than useful.
9. He was too happy to meet me.
10. Such language sounds harshly.
11. I am going to the college everyday since six years.
12. Most likely I shall come to see you tomorrow.
13. The boy was named as Mohan.
14. He did his sum wrongly.
15. The whole country feels deeply the loss of its leader.
16. It is no one else but me.
17. The table is very heavy.
18. The sugar is too sweet.
19. The weather is too cold.
20. I was much pleased to see you.
21. Call him anything else than a fool.
22. He goes there frequently.
23. Does he play well? Of course, he does.
24. Firstly you should be regular, and secondly, hard-working.
25. He fluently spoke.
26. I explained briefly my idea.
27. He cannot even write correct Hindi.
28. He knows to disgrace others.
29. I am very pleased to see you.
30. I did it presently.
31. Your statement is somewhat true.
32. She is so weak in English.
33. I tell you in brief I....
34. The train reaches Delhi soon.
35. Yesterday in the night, he came to see me.
36. I liked it on the whole.
37. Of course Krishan is the most handsome boy in our family.
38. I care a bit for you.

Correct

1. On seeing his wife he was **much pleased**.
2. It is a **very hot** today.

3. I was **much annoyed** at his attitude.
4. This mango is **too bad** to be eaten.
5. All the water flowed out of the bucket **little by little**.
6. You should go **direct** to your father.
7. He must do this work whether he will or **no**.
8. It is **more harmful** than useful.
9. He was **very happy** to meet me.
10. Such language sounds **harsh**.
11. I am going to the college everyday **for** the last six years.
12. Most **probably** I shall come to see you tomorrow.
13. The boy was **named** Mohan.
14. He did his sum **wrong**.
15. The **whole of country** feels deeply the loss of its leader.
16. It is **none** else **than** I. Or it is **not other** than I.
17. The table is **too** heavy.
18. The sugar is **very** sweet.
19. The weather is **very** cold.
20. I was **very** pleased to se you.
21. Call him anything else **but** a fool.
22. He **frequently** goes there.
23. Does he play well? **Certainly**, he does.
24. **First** you should be regular and **secondly**, hard-working.
25. He **spoke fluently**.
26. I **briefly explained** my idea or I explained my idea briefly.
27. He cannot **write even** correct Hindi.
28. He knows **how** to disgrace others.
29. I am very **much** pleased to see you.
30. I did it **just now**.
31. Your statement is **partially** true.
32. She is **very weak** in English.
33. I tell you **in short** I....
34. The train reaches Delhi **quickly**.
35. Yesterday **evening** he came to see me.
36. I **liked the whole** of it.
37. Krishan is **certainly** the most handsome boy in our family.
38. I care a **little** for you.

COMMON ERRORS IN THE USE OF PREPOSITIONS

Incorrect

1. Send this letter on this address.
2. Do not interfere in my work.
3. I object your remarks.
4. He is blind in one eye.
5. You must attend your work.
6. I am angry with your rudeness.
7. He is angry at me.
8. I do not desire for a change.
9. I am suffering with fever.
10. He is afraid from the dog.
11. This is different to that.
12. I was satisfied by his work.
13. Ram married with Sita.
14. The president called for a meeting.
15. I signed on the agreement.
16. I arrived to this conclusion.
17. I met him in the way.
18. I am sorry at his loss.
19. Do not knock the door.
20. He was charged of theft.
21. He was accused with theft.
22. He invited me at tea.
23. Do not find fault in my work.
24. He deprived me from my pen.
25. I congratulate you for your success.
26. What is the time in your watch.
27. He is jealous with me.
28. Translate this passage in English.
29. I am accustomed with cold weather.
30. He is in the committee.
31. I have no pen to write.
32. He has resigned from the post.
33. I arrived in the place at exact time.
34. He wastes much money in trifles.
35. He set the house to fire.
36. He does not devote much time for studies.
37. There is another side of this question.

38. Just listen me for a while.
39. I do not approve for your conduct.
40. He does not pray God.
41. I have no interest for music.
42. He has no taste in painting.
43. He is tired from life.
44. He was late for an hour.
45. He is absorbed with his work.
46. He climbed on the tree.
47. I told the whole thing on his face.
48. He is ashamed from his rudeness.
49. I have something to ask from you.
50. I am indifferent about politics.
51. Place the lamp upon the table.
52. He gave me an opportunity for reading his letter.
53. He is capable for doing hard work.
54. He washed his hands in water.
55. His name precedes before mine.
56. The jar is full with water.
57. I want to get rid from him.
58. We must guard ourselves from bad habits.
59. I searched my dog.
60. I waited my father.
61. A deputation waited for the Prime Minister.
62. His leg is operated.
63. He disposed off the complaint.
64. There is no use of acting this.
65. He was convicted on the charge of murder.
66. He will be cured from fever.
67. I tried to save him but of no purpose.
68. She burst with tears.
69. He died from cholera.
70. She is quick in speech.
71. He met an accident.
72. He failed from four marks.
73. He introduced me with his friends.
74. I aspire for the new post.
75. Do not quarrel on a trifle.
76. I shall explain them this report.
77. My brother did not reply me.

78. I walked to that place by foot.
79. She rides on a car.
80. We saluted to him.
81. He set on a tree.
82. You must pay for your bills.
83. She was overwhelmed by grief.
84. I have no sympathy for him.
85. The police will inquire about the real cause of trouble.
86. How is he related with you?
87. She repented for her mistake.
88. I subscribed this magazine.
89. I have no prejudice for you.
90. He does not fear from God.
91. I was late in the meeting.
92. They came back in a few days.
93. They are called with different names.
94. He boasts about his wealth.
95. I took the business into hand.
96. He complained of me to his brother.
97. Our examination begins from Monday.
98. He did not accede my request.
99. He did not comply to my request.
100. He came here on my invitation.
101. I caught him from the arm.
102. I regret at the delay.
103. He rejoiced on his success.
104. He did not agree with my proposal.
105. He did not agree to me.
106. He aims to be a teacher.
107. He takes pride of his wealth.
108. Anil is popular among his friends.
109. The teacher sits on his desk.
110. I was surprised by her failure.
111. He is trembling by cold.
112. I divided the cake in four parts.
113. Here is the book that you asked.
114. I expect a letter from my friend after a week.
115. The sun will rise before an hour.
116. This is the girl I was speaking.
117. He slept upto 4 O'clock.

118. I walked till the end of the street.
119. The cat is sitting upon a table.
120. The cat sprang on the table.
121. I do not have any influence upon him.
122. She jumped in the river.
123. There is a saying in the Hindus.
124. He has been acquitted from the charge.
125. Accompanied with his father he went to Simla.
126. I beat the dog by a stick.
127. The ceiling fan is on my head.
128. I passed near the railway station.
129. He attacked on Rama with a knife.
130. Please credit this sum in my name, or in my account.
131. Mohan prevented her to come here.
132. There is another side of the question.
133. Please divide these mangoes between these six boys.
134. I am confident to win this match.
135. My attempt to mend him was in vain.
136. He died with hunger.
137. He threw a blanket on himself.
138. He arrived to this conclusion.
139. He asked many questions to me.
140. We lack in good students in our college.
141. He wrote me a letter.
142. I shall explain him my fault.
143. There is no harm to do this work.
144. Please write this answer with ink.
145. I shall inform my father about this.
146. The cinema is on the back side of my house.
147. I met with your father yesterday.
148. This work was done during 1920-1922.
149. I will return within an hour.
150. Try to finish this work in an hour.
151. The pen is lying besides the inkpot.
152. Beside this, I have to do other work also.
153. He is kind upon me.
154. He deals with sugar.
155. I regret at the delay.
156. He has been operated from cancer.
157. He walked with a speed of five miles per hour.

158. This cloth will wear off soon.
159. I have no sympathy for him.
160. She is quick in speech.
161. Open your book on page 65.
162. I do not believe him.
163. I cannot agree to you with this proposal.

Correct

1. Send this letter **to** this address.
2. Do not interfere **with** my work.
3. I object **to** your remarks.
4. He is blind **of** one eye.
5. You must attend **to** your work.
6. I am angry **at** your rudeness.
7. He is angry **with** me.
8. I do not **desire a** change.
9. I am suffering **from** fever.
10. He is afraid **of** the dog.
11. This is different **from** that.
12. I was satisfied **with** his work.
13. Ram **married** Sita.
14. The president **called** a meeting.
15. I signed **the** agreement.
16. I arrived **at** this conclusion.
17. I met him **on** the way.
18. I am sorry **for** his loss.
19. Do not knock **at** the door.
20. He was charged **with** theft.
21. He was accused **of** theft.
22. He invited me **to** tea.
23. Do not find fault **with** my work.
24. He deprived me **of** my pen.
25. I congratulate you **on** your success.
26. What is the time **by** your watch.
27. He is jealous **of** me.
28. Translate this passage **into** English.
29. I am accustomed **to** cold weather.
30. He is **on** the committee.
31. I have no pen to **write with**.
32. He has resigned **the** post.

33. I arrived at the place **in time**.
34. He wastes much money **on** trifles.
35. He set the house **on** fire.
36. He does not devote much time **to** studies.
37. There is another side **to** this question.
38. Just listen **to** me for a while.
39. I do not approve **of** your conduct.
40. He does not pray **to** God.
41. I have no interest **in** music.
42. He has no taste **for** painting.
43. He is tired **of** life.
44. He was late **by** an hour.
45. He is absorbed **in** his work.
46. He climbed **up** (or **climbed**) the tree.
47. I told the whole thing **to** his face.
48. He is ashamed **of** his rudeness.
49. I have something **to** ask you.
50. I am indifferent **to** politics.
51. Place the lamp **on** the table.
52. He gave me an opportunity **of** reading his letter.
53. He is capable **of** doing hard work.
54. He washed his hands **with** water.
55. His name **precedes mine**.
56. The jar is full **of** water, or is **filled with** water.
57. I want to get rid **of** him.
58. We must guard ourselves **against** bad habits.
59. I searched **for** my dog.
60. I waited **for** my father.
61. A deputation waited **on** the Prime Minister.
62. His leg is operated **upon**.
63. He disposed **of** the complaint.
64. There is no use **in** acting this.
65. He was convicted **of** the charge of murder.
66. He will be cured **of** fever.
67. I tried to save him but **to** no purpose.
68. She burst **into** tears.
69. He died **of** cholera.
70. She is quick **of** speech.
71. He **met with** an accident.
72. He failed **by** four marks.

73. He introduced me **to** his friends.
74. I aspire **to the** new post.
75. Do not quarrel **over** a trifle.
76. I shall explain **to** them this report.
77. My brother did not reply **to** me.
78. I walked to that place **on** foot.
79. She rides **in** a car.
80. We **saluted** him.
81. He sat **in** a tree.
82. You must **pay your** bills.
83. She was overwhelmed **with** grief.
84. I have no sympathy **with** him.
85. The police will inquire **into** the real cause of trouble.
86. How is he related **to** you?
87. She repented **of** her mistake.
88. I subscribed **to** this magazine.
89. I have no prejudice **against** you.
90. He does not fear God.
91. I was late **for** the meeting.
92. They came back **after** a few days.
93. They are **called by** different names.
94. He boasts **of** his wealth.
95. I took the business **in** hand.
96. He complained **against** me to his brother.
97. Our examination begins **on** Monday.
98. He did not accede **to** my request.
99. He did not comply **with** my request.
100. He came here **at** my invitation.
101. I caught him **by** the arm.
102. I regret **the** delay.
103. He rejoiced **at** his success.
104. He did not **agree to** my proposal.
105. He did not agree **with** me.
106. He aims **at becoming** a teacher.
107. He takes pride **in** his wealth.
108. Anil is popular **with** his friends.
109. The teacher sits **at** his desk.
110. I was surprised **at** her failure.
111. He is trembling **with** cold.
112. I divided the cake **into** four parts.

113. Here is the book you **asked for**.
114. I expected a letter from my friend in a week.
NOTE: 'After' is used with a period of past and not with a period of future.
115. The sun will rise **within** an hour.
116. This is the girl I was **speaking of**.
117. He slept **till** 4 o'clock.
118. I walked **to the** end of the street.
119. The cat is sitting **on** a table.
120. The cat sprang **upon** the table.
121. I do not have any influence **over** him.
122. She jumped **into** the river.
123. There is a saying **among** the Hindus.
124. He has been acquitted **of** the charge.
125. Accompanied **by his** father he went to Simla.
126. I beat the dog **with** a stick.
127. The ceiling fan is **over** my head.
128. I passed **by** the railway station.
129. He attacked Rama with a knife.
130. Please credit this sum **to** my name, or to my account.
131. Mohan prevented her **from** coming here.
132. There is another side **to** the question.
133. Please divide these mangoes **among** these six boys.
134. I am confident **of winning** this match.
135. My attempt to mend him was **vain**.
136. He died **of** hunger.
137. He threw a blanket **over** himself.
138. He arrived **at** this conclusion.
139. He asked many questions **from** me.
140. We **lack** good students in our college.
141. He wrote a letter **to** me.
142. I shall explain **my fault to him**.
143. There is no harm **in doing** this work.
144. Please write this answer **in** ink.
145. I shall inform my father **of** this.
146. The cinema is **behind** my house, or **at the back of** my house.
147. I met your father yesterday.
148. This work was done **between** 1920-1922.
149. I will return **in** an hour.
150. Try to finish this work **within** an hour.
151. The pen is lying **beside** the inkpot.

152. **Besides** this, I have to do other work also.
153. He is kind **to** me.
154. He deals **in** sugar.
155. I regret **the** delay.
156. He has been operated **upon** for cancer.
157. He walked **at** a speed of five miles per hour.
158. This cloth will **wear out** soon.
159. I have no sympathy **with** him.
160. She is quick **of** speech.
161. Open your book **at** page 65.
162. I do not believe **in** him.
163. I do not agree **with** you (on this point), or to this proposal.

COMMON ERRORS IN THE USE OF CONJUNCTIONS

Incorrect

1. He has no other claim except his wealth.
2. As he has fever, so he cannot go with you.
3. Both Mohan and his Brother were not there.
4. Both Avinash as well as Subhash were present there.
5. Lions are both found in Asia and Africa.
6. He is very noble, but helps the poor.
7. College life is charming and school life is dull.
8. He is not only handsome but sensible also.
9. He dresses like his brother.
10. He does not speak before he is compelled.
11. Neither did I go nor he went.
12. Neither did I read nor I wrote.
13. I doubt that he will come.
14. His hat is equally beautiful as that of mine.
15. When you insult me I must go away.
16. I hope Sham will recover.
17. Now you have come, you relieve me.
18. He is not hardworking or intelligent.
19. We shall try and find them.
20. Not only he is a poet but an artist.
21. This is the reason I do not help you.
22. He had scarcely reached the station than the train started.
23. Though he worked hard but he failed.
24. No sooner we reached there when it began to rain.

25. Surinder will be appointed as a head clerk.
26. He weeps as if he is poor.
27. You act as though you are sad.
28. Either the action was just or unjust.
29. He or she is at fault.
30. Did you go to his hostel or house.
31. He was chosen to be a captain.
32. I have never written nor spoken to him.
33. She did not break it nor lose it.
34. Do not go out until they come back.
35. I have got nothing to say.
36. This is the same pen which he gave me.
37. Wait while I come, I won't be long.
38. He must wait for me until it rains.
39. Tell me when are you coming here?
40. No sooner he left the place, it began to rain.
41. Supposing if you fail, what will you do.
42. Unless you do not work hard, you cannot pass.
43. Not only did he abuse me, but beat me also.

Correct

1. He has no other claim **than** his wealth.

NOTE: After the adjective 'other' use 'than'. Don't use 'from', 'except', 'but'.

2. **As** he has fever, he cannot go with you.
3. **Neither** Mohan **nor** his brother was there.
4. **Both** Avinash and Subhash were present there.
5. Lions are **found both** in Asia and Africa.
6. He is very noble **and** helps the poor.
7. College life is charming **but** school life is dull.
8. He is **not only** handsome **but also** sensible.
9. He dresses **as his** brother.
10. He does not speak **unless** he is compelled.
11. Neither did I go **nor did he**.
12. Neither did I read **nor did I write**.
13. I doubt **whether** he will come.
14. His hat is **as** beautiful as that of mine.
15. **Since** you insult me I must go away.
16. I hope **that** Sham will recover.
17. Now **that** you have come, you relieve me.

18. He is **neither** hardworking **nor** intelligent.
19. We shall try **to** find them.
20. **Not only** is he a poet **but** an artist also.
21. This is the reason **why** I do not help you.
22. He had scarcely reached the station **when** the train started.
23. Though he worked hard **yet** he failed.
24. No sooner did we reach there **than** it began to rain.
25. Surinder will be appointed a head clerk.
26. He weeps as if he **were** poor.
27. You act as though you **were** sad.
28. The action was **either** just or unjust.
29. **Either** he or she is at fault.
30. Did you go to his hostel or **to** his house.
31. He was chosen a captain.
32. I have never written **or** spoken to him.
33. She did not break it **or** lose it.
34. Do not go out till they come back.
35. I have nothing to say.
36. This is the same pen **as** he gave me.
37. Wait **till I** come, I won't be long.
38. He must wait for me **while** it rains.
39. Tell me when **you are** coming here.
40. No sooner did he leave the place **than** it began to rain.
41. **Supposing** (or **if**) you fail, what will you do.
42. **Unless** you work hard, you cannot pass.
43. He **not only** abused me **but also** beat me.

Question Papers

E

APPENDIX

B. Pharm.

FIRST SEMESTER EXAMINATION, 2004-2005

PROFESSIONAL COMMUNICATION—I

Time : 3 Hours *Total Marks : 80*

Note : *(i) Attempt **ALL** questions.*
(ii) All questions carry equal marks.

1. Answer the following : **16**

(a) Write a letter to your uncle on his 70th birthday.

OR

Write a letter to your friend about your favourite game.

(b) Write an essay on any one of the following:

(i) Your Hobby
(ii) A Railway Journey
(iii) Good Manners

2. Answer the following :— **8**

(a) Write the summary of the passage of about 1/3 original length.

Up the River Hudson in North America are the Catskill Mountains. In a certain village at the foot these mountains, there lived long ago a man named Rip Van Winkle. He was a simple and good-natured person, a very kind neighbour and a great favourite among all the good wives of the village. Whenever there was a squabble in the family of Rip, the women in the village always took his part and laid all the blame on Dame Van Winkle.

The children of the village too would shout with joy, whenever they saw him. He helped at their sports, made playthings for them, taught them to fly kites and shoot marbles and told them long stories of ghosts, witches and Indians.

Rip had no love for labour, if it would bring him profit. He would sit for a whole day on a wet rock and fish without a murmur, even though he did not catch a single fish. He would carry a light gun on his shoulder for hours together and shoot only a few squirrels or wild pigeons.

He would never refuse to assist a neighbour even in roughest toil. The women of the village often employed him to run their errands and to do little jobs for them. In a word, Rip was ready to attend to anybody's business but his own. He was, however, one of those men who take the world easy. He would eat coarse bread or fine, whichever could be got with least thought or trouble. And he would rather starve on a penny than work for a pound.

If left to himself, Rip would have whistled away life in perfect contentment. But his wife always kept drumming in his ears about his idleness, his carelessness and the ruins he was bringing on his family. Rip and but one way of replaying to all her lectures-he shook his head, cast up his eyes and said nothing. He had one good friend at home and that was his dog Wolf which was as idle as the master.

(b) (i) Change the following from direct into indirect speech : **2+2**

(I) He shouted, "Let me go"

(II) He said, "I lived many years in China"

(ii) Change the following from Active to Passive Voice : **2+2**

(I) Sita loves Savitri.

(II) Mr. Krishnaji teaches us Grammer.

3. (a) Fill in the blanks with suitable preposition : **(8)**

(i) The river flows __________ the bridge.

(ii) The work was done __________ haste.

(iii) He died __________ his country.

(iv) Do not cry __________ split mile.

(b) Complete the following sentences by filling 'a', 'an' or the as may be suitable **(8)**

(i) Varanasi is __________ holy city.

(ii) __________ sun rises in the east.

(iii) Here is __________ elephant

(iv) __________ French defeated the Germans.

4. Answer *any two* of the following :— **(8×2=16)**

(a) Define communication. Discuss the significance of non-verbal communication.

(b) What is the importance of debates.

(c) Write a note on presentation techniques.

5. Write notes on *any four* of the following : — **(4×4=16)**

(a) Importance of positive attitude

(b) Personality types

(c) Achievement motivation

(d) Factors influencing decision making

(e) Creating thinking

B. Pharm.

FIRST SEMESTER EXAMINATION, 2005-2006

PROFESSIONAL COMMUNICATION—I

Time : 3 Hours *Total Marks : 80*

Note : *(i) Attempt **ALL** questions.*
(ii) All questions carry equal marks.
(iii) Be precise in your answer.

1. (a) Write a letter to your friend about teacher's day celebrations in your college. **(8)**

OR

Write a letter to your Principal asking for leave due to illness.

(b) Write an essay on any one of the following : **(8)**

(i) Visit to an exhibition

(ii) My first day in the college

(iii) Terrorism—A Global Threat

2. (a) Write the summary of the given passage, in about 1/3 the original length **(8)**

The great advantage of early rising is the good start it gives us in our day's work. The early riser has done a large amount of hard work before other men have go out of bed. In the early morning the mid is fresh, and there are few sounds or other distractions, so that work done at that time is generally well done. In many cases the early riser also finds time to take some exercise in the fresh morning air, and this exercise supplied him with a fund of energy that will last until the evening. By beginning so early, he knows that he has plenty of time to do thoroughly all the work he can be expected to do, and is not tempted to hurry over any part of it. All his work being finished in good time, he has a long interval of rest in the evening before the timely hour when he goes to bed. He gets to sleep several hours before midnight, at the time when sleep is most refreshing and after a sound night's rest, rises early next morning in good health and spirits for the labours of a new day.

It is very plain that such a life as this is far more conducive to health than that of the man who shortens his waking hours by rising late, and so can afford in the course of the day little leisure for necessary rest. Any one who lies in bed late, must, if he wishes to doe a full day's work, go on working to a correspondingly late hour, and deny himself the hour or two of evening exercise that he ought to take for the benefit of his health. But in spite of all his efforts, he will probably produce as good results as the early riser, because he misses the best working hours of the day.

It may be objected to this that some find the perfect quiet of midnight by far the best time for working. This is no doubt true in certain cases. Several great thinkers have found by experience that their intellect is clearest, and they can write best, when they burn the midnight oil. But even in such cases the practice of working late at night cannot be commanded. Few men, if any, can exert the full power of their intellect at the time when nature prescribes sleep, without ruining their health thereby; and of course the injury done to the health must in the long run have a bad effect on the quality of the work done.

(b) Change the following from direct to indirect speech : **(4)**

(i) He said to me, "What are you doing".

(ii) "Sit down, Boys" said the teacher.

(c) Change the following from active to passive voice : **(4)**

(i) His teacher praised him

(ii) Some boys were helping the wounded men

3. (a) Fill in the blanks with suitable preposition : **(5)**

(i) __________ rice they had curry.

(ii) I am fond __________ music.

(iii) It is ten o'clock __________ my watch.

(iv) Do not cry __________ split milk.

(v) I must start __________ dawn to reach in time.

(b) Complete the sentences with 'A', 'An' or 'The'. **(4)**

(i) Copper is __________ useful metal.

(ii) She is __________ untidy girl.

(iii) He is __________ better poet than novelist.

(iv) Aladin had __________ wonderful lamp.

(c) Complete the sentences using the correct word : **(2+2+3)**

(i) The earth __________ around the sun. (move, moves, moved)

(ii) He __________ a mill in this town. (have, has, is having)

(iii) He thanked me for what I __________ (have done, had done, have been doing)

4. Attempt *any two* : **(8×2=16)**

(a) Factors affecting presentation skills.

(b) Criteria of judgement in a debate.

(c) Techniques of making communication effective.

5. Write notes on any four : **(4×4=16)**

(a) Styles of decision making

(b) Factors influencing change of attitude

(c) Types fo motivation

(d) Development of effective thinking

(e) Personality of traits

B. Pharm.

FIRST SEMESTER EXAMINATION, 2006-2007

PROFESSIONAL COMMUNICATION—I

Time : 3 Hours *Total Marks : 80*

Note : *(i) Attempt **ALL** questions.*
(ii) All questions carry equal marks.
(iii) Be precise in your answer.

1. (a) Correct *any five* of the following sentences : **(8)**

(i) He gave me many good advice.
(ii) The news are wrong.
(iii) One of my sister is a doctor.
(iv) Each of them followed their plan.
(v) I, you and he deserves the award.
(vi) He achieved nearly cent percent marks.
(vii) He left for Delhi by 10.30 o' clock train.

(b) Transform the following sentences into passive voice. (*any five*)

(i) We bake the bread here.
(ii) A Belgian called Etienne Lenoir made the first motor car.
(iii) Someone took my purse.
(iv) One should check the details.
(v) People use this footpath all the time.
(vi) The soap opera 'Round the Corner' will end next year.
(vii) The quiz champion has lost his memory.

2. (a) Rewrite the following dialogue in continuous narrative in reported speech. **(8)**

"May I ask the name of this building ?" said the President kindly.

"It is called the department of justice" said the man bitterly. "I suppose because it is built up on the ruins of a fraud-the freed-man's bank."

"You speak bitterly my friend. Have you a complaint against it ?" said the President, encouragingly.

"I have sat here five and twenty years waiting to know whether the government would protect me from thieves that stole my land. I am poor; my antagonist are rich. I can get no opinion. The case never comes up."

(b) Write a letter of complaint (invent the necessary details yourself). **(8)**

OR

Write a letter to the editor of any newspaper inviting the attention of public to any civic cause.

3. (a) Make a precis of the following passage : **(8)**

India's secularism, her protection of weaker sections of society and minorities, the system of single citizenship, independent judiciary, independence of media-press, radio and television and, above all, the emotional tie to distinguish our culture and national character are the sine quanon of national unity and integrity. Our unity is found in our mental set up, style of living and thinking. Externally there is a great deal of diversity in caste, sect, religion, language, food, clothing and climate but internally we are united. Variety is the spice of life therein lies the beauty and glory of India.

(b) Write a short essay on any of the following topics. **(8)**

(i) Relevance of English language.

(ii) The policy of Economic Liberalization.

(iii) Cultural pollution.

(iv) Importance of Technical Education.

4. Attempt *any two* parts of the following : **(8×2=16)**

(a) Importance of body language.

(b) Write a note on debates and their relevance.

(c) Significance of non-verbal communication.

5. Write notes on *any four* of the following : **(4×4=16)**

(a) Effective thinking

(b) Positive attitude

(c) Steps in decision making

(d) Maslow's hierarchy of needs

(e) Define Personality. Name the important personality types.

B. Pharm.

(SEM. I) EXAMINATION, 2007-2008

PROFESSIONAL COMMUNICATION

Time : 3 Hours *Total Marks : 80*

1. (a) Write an application to the Manager (HR) of any Pharmaceutical company for the post of scientist. **8**

OR

Write a letter to a friend telling him the hazards of water pollution.

(b) Write an essay on any one of the following: **8**

(i) Policy of Economic Liberalization

(ii) National Unity and Integrity

(iii) Democracy in India.

2. (a) Write the precis of the following passage in about 1/3 of the original length:

The cinema is also an instructive as well as recreative wing of media. The developmental films make people aware of the programmes of the country. Patriotic and civic virtues are inculcated among people by constructive films.

The cinema is also criticized for the same vices as those of television. But these harms are also not irreparable. Besides, cinema has become the chief source of entertainment in the urban society. Hence cinema too occupies a significant place in refining the taste of people and in educating the society.

(b) (i) Change the following from direct into indirect speech : **2+2**

(1) I said "I am going".

(2) I spoke to him "shut up".

(ii) Change the following from Active to Passive Voice : **2+2**

(a) Sonal recorded her voice.

(b) Who shouted at her?

(a) Fill in the blanks with suitable words : **2+2+2+2**

(i) I will come back ___________ a day.

(ii) I have been staying at Surat ___________ two years.

(iii) I write ___________ blue ink.

(iv) She is ___________ brightest student in the class.

(b) Correct the following sentences :

(i) Neither of the experts were paid for.

(ii) I have ordered for the coffee.

(iii) I hope he will fail.

(iv) Please tell in brief.

4. Answer *any* **two** : **(8×2=16)**

(a) "For a successful communication verbal and non-verbal communication should go along." Comment.

(b) Write a script in 150 words for presentation in any business meet. (Invent the necessary details yourself)

(c) What do you mean by a Role Play? Do you think it is really possible.

5. Comment on any **four** of the following : **(4×4=16)**

(a) "Positive thinking as the tool for improving relationships and management of groups."

(b) "Attitude is always towards something."

(c) "Personality is an organised, consistent pattern of perception of the "I", around which the individual interacts and has experiences."

(d) "Decision making is choosing between alternatives."

(e) Herzberg's two factor theory of motivation.

Index